This book presents a mathematical programming approach to the analysis of production frontiers and efficiency measurement. The authors construct a variety of production frontiers, and by measuring distances to them are able to develop a model of efficient producer behavior and a taxonomy of possible types of departure from efficiency in various environments. Linear programming is used as an analytical and computational technique in order to accomplish this. The approach developed is then applied to modeling producer behavior. By focusing on the empirical relevance of production frontiers and distances to them, and applying linear programming techniques to artificial data to illustrate the type of information they can generate, this book provides a unique study in applied production analysis. It will be of interest to scholars and students of economics and operations research, and analysts in business and government.

T0339954

Production Frontiers

Production Frontiers

ROLF FÄRE

SHAWNA GROSSKOPF

C.A. KNOX LOVELL

CAMBRIDGE
UNIVERSITY PRESS

CAMBRIDGE UNIVERSITY PRESS
Cambridge, New York, Melbourne, Madrid, Cape Town, Singapore, São Paulo

Cambridge University Press
The Edinburgh Building, Cambridge CB2 8RU, UK

Published in the United States of America by Cambridge University Press, New York

www.cambridge.org
Information on this title: www.cambridge.org/9780521420334

First published 1994
This digitally printed version 2008

A catalogue record for this publication is available from the British Library

Library of Congress Cataloguing in Publication data
Färe, Rolf, 1942–
Production frontiers/Rolf Färe, Shawna Grosskopf, C.A. Knox Lovell
p. cm.
Includes bibliographical references.
ISBN 0 521 42033 4 (hard)
1. Production (Economic theory)   2. Efficiency, Industrial.
I. Grosskopf, Shawna.   II. Lovell, C.A. Knox.   III. Title.
HB241.F336   1994
338.5–dc20   92-34098   CIP

ISBN 978-0-521-42033-4 hardback
ISBN 978-0-521-07206-9 paperback

To
Carolina, Claire, Ian, Lisa, Jack and Glo

CONTENTS

FIGURES

TABLES

PREFACE

In recent years there has occurred a rapid increase in the volume of published research devoted to the analysis of efficiency in production. A small amount of this research has explored the theoretical foundations of efficiency measurement, but the vast majority of it has been empirical. The empirical research has investigated the nature and magnitude of, and occasionally the influences on, productive efficiency in a wide variety of industries, across a multitude of countries, and over a span of time stretching from Domesday England c. 1086 to the present. Some of the empirical research has been of primarily academic interest, some of it has had considerable public policy relevance, and some of it has been directed to managerial decision making. The research is interdisciplinary, having spread from economics to operations research and to the fields of management science, public administration, and a host of others. It seems to be having an impact in each of these fields.

Our primary motive for writing this book is to provide, in a single source, the theoretical foundations for the measurement of productive efficiency. Most of these foundations have appeared before, over a period of time and in a variety of sources, and we think it worthwhile to bring them together in one accessible source. Our second objective is to develop and illustrate an analytical technique that simultaneously characterizes the structure of efficient production technology – the production frontier of the title of this book – and measures efficiency relative to the frontiers. The technique we use is linear programming, which provides measures of efficiency relative to the nonparametric production frontier it creates in the process of solving the appropriate optimization problems. The illustrations we provide in most chapters are intended to encourage readers to become practitioners.

We recognize that the linear programming techniques we use are not the only techniques available for empirical efficiency analysis. Although it seems to us that the majority of the empirical analysis in management science uses nonparametric linear programming techniques, it also appears that most empirical analysis in economics uses parametric econometric techniques. We have chosen not to discuss econometric techniques in this book, because to have done so would have made a thin present-day book a fat future book. Nonetheless, in the concluding section of each chapter we provide references to the empirical literature, much of which is econometric.

We have written this book over a period of several years, in a variety of interesting locations. Aside from Carbondale and Chapel Hill, we have done a lot of writing in Adelaide, Barcelona, and Louvain-la-Neuve. We are particularly grateful to the Department of Economics at the University of Adelaide, and to CORE at Université Catholique de Louvain, for their generosity and hospitality. We have also benefited from careful reading and critical comments on earlier drafts of the manuscript by John Cubbin, Thom Mitchell, Henry Tulkens, Philippe Vanden Eeckaut, and readers for the Press.

We are grateful to Mariann Baratta for her professional handling of the typescript.

1

Introduction

1.0 The Objectives of this Study

We have four goals we wish to accomplish in this study. The first two are interlinked, and involve the development of a model of efficient producer behavior, and the simultaneous development of a taxonomy of possible types of departure from efficiency, in a variety of environments. These two goals are accomplished by constructing a variety of production frontiers, and measuring distance to the frontiers. The third goal is the development of an analytical and computational technique for examining the first two. The technique we use, linear programming, is one of several available techniques, but is the one we prefer. The fourth goal is a demonstration of the wide applicability of the approach we take to modeling producer behavior. We meet this fourth goal in a number of ways, but primarily by adopting an attitude throughout the study that this is a study in applied production analysis. We focus on the empirical relevance of producer frontiers and distance to them. We apply the linear programming techniques to artificial data to illustrate the type of information they can generate. And we frequently suggest problems to which these ideas can be applied.

Conventional microeconomic theory is based on the assumption of optimizing behavior. Thus it is assumed that producers optimize from a technical or engineering perspective by not wasting resources. Loosely speaking, this means that producers operate somewhere on the boundary, rather than on the interior, of their production possibility sets. Producers are also assumed to optimize from an economic perspective by solving some allocation problem that involves prices. Thus cost minimizing producers are assumed to allocate resources efficiently so as to operate on rather than above their minimum cost frontiers, and similarly for producers seeking other economic objectives. However for a variety of reasons not all producers succeed in solving both types of optimization problem in all circumstances. For this reason it is important to have a way of analyzing the degree to which producers fail to optimize and the extent of the departures from technical and economic efficiency. Ideally this analysis is integrated with the analysis of the structure of efficient behavior, and developed simultaneously with it, so that we have a model of efficient producer behavior and of departure from efficient behavior. The first two goals of this study are achieved through the development of such an integrated analysis.

There exist more than one way to meet the first two goals of our study. The approach we adopt is to formulate a model of efficient production and economic behavior using linear programming techniques. The fact that they are "tightly bounding" or "closely enveloping" techniques makes them ideally suited to the type of economic problem under consideration. Their bounding property enables them to serve well the goal of representing frontiers, and their tightness property provides a yardstick against which to measure efficiency.

The linear programming methodology is used to achieve the third goal of this study. The final goal is reached in part by actually formulating and then solving linear programs for various production problems, and in part by suggesting a variety of other problems for which these techniques have been used or would be suitable.

Interest in the general topic of production frontiers and the measurement of efficiency relative to these frontiers has grown greatly in the last decade. We shall develop the history of thought on the subject as we go, but it is not too much of an oversimplification to say that the few technical studies that were published prior to the mid-1970s were characterized primarily by the dust they gathered. Since then, however, interest has blossomed. It is now possible to find published "efficiency" studies in virtually every country and about virtually every conceivable market or nonmarket production activity. Interest has spread to policy issues of great import.

1.1 The Motivation for this Study

The basic motivation for writing a book on production frontiers and efficiency is an empirical one. Theoretical production analysis has always focused on production activity as an optimization process. The basic tools have been the (maximum) production frontier, the (minimum) cost frontier, the (maximum) profit frontier, and so on. For practically as long, empirical production analysis has focused on central tendency, or "average" or "most likely" relationships constructed by intersecting data with a function rather than surrounding data with a frontier. This dichotomy between theoretical frontiers and empirical functions has long bothered us, and we have not been alone. There have emerged from time to time attempts to reconcile the two phenomena by developing quantitative techniques for surrounding rather than intersecting data. We view this study as an effort to build an empirically oriented approach to the envelopment of production data that integrates the construction of production frontiers with the measurement and interpretation of efficiency relative to the constructed frontiers.

In addition to the pursuit of a logically consistent approach to the empirical development of producer theory, we are motivated to model production frontiers and producer efficiency by other considerations. Among the more persuasive to us are the following.

(a) The structure of economic frontiers is of inherent interest. It is important to know whether, for example, technologically efficient production is characterized by economies of scale or scope, and whether cost efficient production is characterized by subadditivity.

(b) The structure of economic frontiers can be different from the structure of economic functions constructed from the same data. Best practice is not just better than average practice, it may also be structurally different. It is important to know whether, and if so in what ways, the structure of efficient production differs from the structure of average production. Best practice may be better than average practice precisely because it exploits available substitution possibilities or scale opportunities that average practice does not. Public policy based on the structure of best practice frontiers may be very different from policy based on the structure of average practice functions.

(c) The distance between production frontiers and observed producers is of obvious policy interest. It is important to know how inefficient observed production is on average, and at what cost. It is also important to know what types of producers are most and least efficient, and what type of inefficiency is most prevalent. The distance between best practice and average practice was the focus of Salter's influential work; citing previous work of others, Salter (1966; 95-99) found the ratio of best practice to mean practice labor productivity to range from just over one to just under two in a variety of industries. Similar findings have been reported by Klotz, Madoo, and Hansen (1980), and Albriktsen and Førsund (1990). Although one may quarrel with the use of labor productivity as a performance measure, the point is that a wide gulf between best practice and average practice is not unusual.

Think of motivations (a)-(c) in the context of producers operating in conventional market environments pursuing conventional economic objectives. They apply with equal force to other producers, those operating in regulated or otherwise restricted market environments and those pursuing objectives other than the usual goal of profit maximization. Although the theory of such types of producers is well developed, it has not been integrated with any approach to measuring their efficiency. Thus a further motivation is to develop a framework for analyzing both phenomena.

(d)   It is useful to have a model of producers pursuing conventional objectives under constraint that generates constrained frontiers and constrained efficiency measures. The reason is simple: it is important not to falsely attribute the effects of the constraint to a failure to solve the optimization problem. An example is provided by budget-constrained (as well as resource-constrained, the typical assumption) profit maximization. Another example is provided by profit maximization under regulatory constraint that restricts input usage (e.g., rate of return regulation or affirmative action programs) or output supply (e.g., local content protection requirements or command economy assortment and delivery requirements).

(e)   It is useful to have a model of producers pursuing unconventional objectives that not only characterizes unconventional frontiers but at the same time measures performance relative to such frontiers. The reason is that it is important not to confuse successful pursuit of an unconventional objective with failure to achieve a misspecified conventional objective. An example is the labor-managed Illyrian firm; another is the profit-constrained revenue-maximizing firm. The list of possibilities is long.

The five motives just cited refer to an interest in characterizing efficient production technology, and measuring efficiency relative to that technology, under a variety of producer objectives and environmental constraints. Another motive relates to the techniques we apply to the problem. We employ the tools of mathematical programming throughout the study, and we use these same tools in our empirical work. By using linear programming techniques to develop our analysis of frontiers and efficiency we are extending an approach initiated many years ago by von Neumann (1938 [1945]), and many others. The linear programming approach to production analysis has a rich, if relatively brief, intellectual history, and we are following in distinguished footsteps. Although production analysis is dominated by the parametric approach of Hicks (1946), Samuelson (1947), and others, linear programming remains a useful way of modeling production activity. By using linear programming techniques in empirical work, we find ourselves in the minority once again, at least among economists we know, although the minority is distinguished. This reveals further motivation for our study.

(f)   It is useful to expose the profession, the bulk of a generation of which has grown up on a diet rich in calculus and richer still in least squares, to linear programming techniques. At a theoretical or modeling level, they are ideally suited to the task of constructing frontiers and measuring distances to calculated frontiers. At an empirical level they free investigators from having to impose unwanted structure on economic relationships of interest. At both levels they shift the emphasis of the investigation from a most likely relationship reflecting central tendency to a less likely relationship that focuses on extremal tendency.

Finally we have an interdisciplinary motive for conducting this study. Economics is not the only discipline interested in frontiers and efficiency. We are not alone. If interest on the part of economists in frontiers can be said to have been rekindled in the 1970s when the work of Debreu (1951), Koopmans (1951, 1957), and Farrell (1957) was rediscovered, then our rekindled interest is approximately the same age as the interest of the operations research–management science discipline in the same subject. A large and valuable body of work has emerged in the OR/MS field, and the two bodies of work have until recently developed mostly independently. The OR/MS approach has its own orientation, and relies heavily on linear programming techniques. These techniques and the way they are applied deserve a wide audience, which we hope to stimulate.

(g)   The OR/MS discipline has developed an approach (informatively dubbed "data envelopment analysis," or DEA) to the construction of production frontiers and efficiency measurement that deserves wider exposure among economists. It employs linear programming techniques, and it is similar in structure to a part of the framework we propose.

In light of the similarities between the economics and the OR/MS interests in efficiency measurement and its empirical applicability, it seems useful to quote at length from Lewin and Minton (1986), who seek to define a research agenda for determining organizational effectiveness. In their opinion (p. 529),

"... it would be desirable to have a theory-based mathematics for calculating the relative effectiveness of an organization (over time or in comparison to other referent organizations) which is:

1   capable of analytically identifying relatively most effective organizations in comparison to relatively least effective organizations;

2   capable of deriving a single summary measure of relative effectiveness of organizations in terms of their utilization of resources and their environmental factors to produce desired outcomes;

3   able to handle noncommensurate, conflicting multiple outcome measures, multiple resource factors and multiple environmental factors outside the control of the organization being evaluated; and not be dependent on a set of *a priori* weights or prices for the resources utilized, environmental factors or outcome measures;

4   able to handle qualitative factors such as participant satisfaction, extent of information processing available, degree of competition, etc.;

5   able to provide insights as to factors which contribute to relative effectiveness ratings; and

6   able to maintain equity in the evaluation."

These desiderata closely parallel our own objectives.

1.2   The Strands of Thought Drawn Together in this Study

Within the general area of production economics, we draw on three bodies of literature in developing our analysis of frontiers and efficiency. The first is the body of work concerned with the measurement of efficiency in production. We stress that our interest is in measurement rather than causation, not because we think that a search for the causes of the pattern of efficiency is unimportant but (i) because uncovering the pattern comes first, and (ii) because our comparative advantage lies with measurement rather than hypothesizing about causal factors. This means that we shall have little to say about property rights, and principals and agents, and incentive mechanisms, and competition versus monopoly, and private versus public provision, and so on. The second body of work we draw on in our analysis is the approach to production analysis developed by Shephard (1953, 1970, 1974). We find Shephard's approach valuable for a number of reasons to be detailed below, but one outstanding virtue of his approach is that it is based on distance functions. This is particularly useful because distance functions are intimately related to (radial) efficiency measures, and also because the use of distance functions makes it clear that multiple outputs are no harder to deal with than multiple inputs. The third body of work we draw on in our analysis is the linear programming activity analysis approach to the theory of production. Our model of physical (production) and value (cost or profit or other) frontiers is general, however, and can be analyzed using other techniques. There is nothing in the underlying theory that requires a linear programming formulation. We use it simply because it provides an elegant formulation of production economics and, at the same time, it provides a computationally feasible method of calculation, both of the appropriate frontier and of the distance to it. We now briefly consider these three strands of thought in turn.

1.2.1   The Measurement of Efficiency in Production Economics

The matter of productive efficiency has been of interest since Adam Smith's pin factory and before. However a rigorous analytical approach to the measurement of efficiency in production can be said to have originated with the work of Koopmans and Debreu. Koopmans (1951; 60) provided a definition of what we refer to as technical efficiency: an input–output vector is technically efficient if, and only if, increasing any output or decreasing any input is possible only by decreasing some other output or increasing some other input. Lest readers worry about whether Koopmans' definition implies the existence of (or our ability to determine) an absolute frontier, Farrell (1957; 255) and much later Charnes and Cooper (1985; 72) remind us of the empirical necessity of treating Koopmans' definition of technical efficiency as a *relative* notion, relative to best observed practice in the reference set or comparison group.

This provides a way of differentiating efficient from inefficient production states, but it offers no guidance concerning either the degree of inefficiency of an inefficient vector or the identification of an efficient vector or combination of efficient vectors with which to compare an inefficient vector. This issue was addressed by Debreu (1951), who offered the first measure of productive efficiency with his "coefficient of resource utilization." Debreu's measure is a radial measure of technical efficiency. Radial measures are nice because they focus on the maximum feasible *equiproportionate* reduction in all variable inputs, or the maximum feasible *equiproportionate* expansion of all outputs, in contrast to the more popular but less desirable maximization of output per unit of labor. Radial measures are also nice because they are independent of unit of measurement. However radial measures have a drawback: achievement of the maximum feasible input contraction or output expansion suggests technical efficiency, even though there may remain slack in outputs or inputs. That is, an input–output vector labeled efficient on the basis of Debreu's radial measure may be technically inefficient on the basis of Koopmans' definition because it may lie on the boundary of the production possibilities set but not on the efficient subset of the boundary. The trick is to derive an operationally useful efficiency measure that calls a vector efficient if and only if it satisfies the Koopmans definition. Various ways of dealing with this problem are introduced in Chapter 3 and used throughout the book.

Farrell (1957) extended the work initiated by Koopmans and Debreu by noting that production efficiency has a second component reflecting the ability of producers to select the "right" technically efficient input–output vector in light of prevailing input and output prices. This led Farrell to define overall productive efficiency as the product of technical and allocative, or price, efficiency. Implicit in the notion of allocative efficiency is a specific behavioral assumption about the goal of the producer; Farrell considered cost minimization in competitive input markets, although other behavioral assumptions can be considered. We do so throughout the book.

Although the natural focus of most economists is on markets and their prices and thus on allocative rather than technical efficiency, and although Farrell introduced the notion of allocative efficiency and its measurement, he expressed a concern about our ability to measure prices accurately enough to make good use of allocative efficiency measurement, and hence of overall economic efficiency measurement. This concern expressed by Farrell (1957; 261) has greatly influenced the OR/MS work on efficiency measurement; see Charnes and Cooper (1985; 94), who cite Farrell's concern as one of several motivations for the typical OR/MS emphasis on the measurement of technical efficiency. Notwithstanding the concerns of Farrell and many OR/MS practitioners, however, we show throughout the book that the linear programming techniques are quite capable of solving all sorts of price-dependent efficiency problems. If there is a problem, it lies with the availability and reliability of price data, not with the analytical and empirical technique we use to measure economic efficiency.

It should also be noted that the decomposition process initiated by Farrell has been taken further. Technical efficiency has been decomposed into the product of measures of scale efficiency, input congestion and "pure" technical efficiency by Färe, Grosskopf, and Lovell (1983). Efficiency measurement can be oriented toward the output side of the producer's operations, in which case revenue efficiency can be measured and decomposed into the product of (output price) allocative efficiency and technical efficiency, and the latter can be further decomposed into the product of scale efficiency, output congestion, and "pure" technical efficiency. Efficiency measurement can be oriented toward inputs and outputs together, in which case profit efficiency can be measured and decomposed, although the decomposition is not so straightforward as in the cases of cost efficiency and revenue efficiency. Several other types of efficiency, corresponding to different objectives or to the presence of different constraints, have been proposed, and some are considered in the chapters to follow. The practical advantage of being able to decompose efficiency, however defined and measured, lies in the resulting ability to quantify the magnitudes, and hence the relative importance, of the components. Knowing the magnitude and cost of inefficiency is useful, but so too is knowing where it is most problematic, e.g., internal to the production unit or in certain input markets or in certain output markets.

1.2.2 Shephard's Direct and Indirect Dual Approaches to Analyzing Production Technology and Producer Behavior

The second strand of thought we draw upon in this study relates to Shephard's (1970, 1974) models of technology and his (1953, 1970, 1974) distance functions. The models of technology include direct, indirect, and price space formulations, which we use in Chapters 3-4, 5-6 and 7, respectively. Although Shephard introduced each of these models of technology, he provided piecewise linear formulations for only the direct input and output correspondences (1970; 283-92, 1974; 5-13).

In contrast to the traditional scalar-valued production function, direct input and output correspondences readily admit multiple outputs and multiple inputs. They are thus well suited to characterize all kinds of technologies without having to resort to possibly unwarranted output aggregation prior to analysis.

Our indirect models of production, while based on Shephard's work, differ from his formulation in one respect. Shephard defined the indirect output correspondence in terms of the cost function (1974; 16), and he defined the indirect input correspondence in terms of the revenue function (1974; 24). Our formulations, which are equivalent to those of Shephard, are based on Shephard and Färe (1980), and they are defined on the direct correspondences with the addition of the appropriate value constraint. This formulation serves to clarify the notion of an indirect production correspondence, and it is particularly useful in the specification of linear programming models of indirect efficiency measurement.

Our two price space formulations of technology are based on Shephard's "cost structure correspondence" (1970; 232) and his "revenue correspondence" (1970; 234), and they are mappings from output space into subsets of cost-deflated input prices and from input space into subsets of revenue-deflated output prices, respectively. These two price space formulations lead naturally to the construction of two families of dual price efficiency measures.

The original distance function introduced by Shephard (1953; 5) is in our terminology a direct input distance function defined on the direct input correspondence. This distance function treats (multiple) outputs as given and contracts input vectors as much as possible consistent with technological feasibility of the contracted input vector. Among its several useful properties, the most important for our purposes is the fact that the reciprocal of the direct input distance function has been proposed by Debreu (1951) as a coefficient of resource utilization, and by

Farrell (1957) as a measure of technical efficiency. The theoretical and practical significance of this property can hardly be overstated, for it allows the direct input distance function to serve two important roles simultaneously. It provides a complete characterization of the structure of multi-input, multi-output efficient production technology, and it provides a reciprocal measure of the distance from each producer to that efficient technology.

While the principal role played by the direct input distance function is to gauge technical efficiency, it can also be used to construct input quantity indexes (Törnqvist (1936), Malmquist (1953)) and productivity indexes (Caves, Christensen, and Diewert (1982b)), a role we exploit in Chapter 9.

Similar remarks apply to the direct output distance function introduced by Shephard (1970) and the two indirect distance functions of Shephard (1974). Each can be used to characterize the structure of efficient production technology in the multiproduct case, to measure efficiency relative to that technology, and to construct output quantity indexes (Bergson (1961), Moorsteen (1961)) and productivity indexes (Caves, Christensen, and Diewert (1982b)), and to construct indirect productivity indexes (Färe, Grosskopf, and Lovell (1992)).

1.2.3   The Linear Programming Approach to Modeling Production Technology and Producer Behavior

Mathematical programming methods, in particular linear programming models, provide an elegant way of simultaneously constructing frontier technology from data and calculating the distance to that frontier for individual observations or activities. The frontier technology is formed as linear combinations of observed extremal activities (these being considered Salter's "best practice" activities), yielding a frontier consisting of facets. This technology can be shown to satisfy very general axioms of production theory and although it is not everywhere differentiable, as the number of activities increases the piecewise linear technology converges to the smooth neoclassical case.

Most of the formal linear programming theory appeared after World War II, although interest in linear inequalities was evident before that time. Dantzig (1963) is the person most closely associated with linear programming, largely because he (in conjunction with von Neumann) contributed the basic computational algorithm (the simplex method) used to solve these problems. Charnes and Cooper (1961) made considerable contributions to both theory and application in the early development of linear programming, and popularized its application in DEA beginning in the late 1970s.

The use of programming models to construct or represent technology was employed by von Neumann in his activity analysis and growth models. These general programming models also proved extremely useful in the theory of games. Another person associated with linear programming and activity analysis is Leontief (1941, 1953), who developed a special case of activity analysis which has come to be known as input–output analysis. Whereas Leontief's work was directed toward constructing a workable model of general equilibrium, our work here is more closely related to the microeconomic production programming models developed by Shephard (1953, 1970, 1974), Koopmans (1951, 1957), and Afriat (1972). In these models observed activities, such as the inputs and outputs of some production unit, serve as coefficients of activity or intensity variables forming a series of linear inequalities, yielding a piecewise linear frontier technology. Afriat (1972) showed how to relax the restriction that technology satisfy constant returns to scale, and Shephard (1974) provided a means of relaxing the assumption that technology satisfy strong disposability of inputs and outputs. The model used in this study, as well as the models derived by Koopmans and Shephard, all impose convexity on the reference technology. Models which maintain free disposability but relax convexity were introduced by Afriat (1972) and Dugger (1974), and continued by Deprins, Simar, and Tulkens (1984).

By tightly enveloping data points with linear segments, the programming approach reveals the structure of frontier technology without imposing a specific functional form on either technology or deviations from it. Moreover, the programming framework not only lends itself in a natural way to the construction of frontier technology, but it also provides an elegant and simple means of computing the distance to that frontier – as a maximum feasible radial contraction or expansion of an observed activity. This means of measuring the distance to the frontier yields an interpretation of performance or efficiency as maximal/minimal proportionate feasible changes in an activity, given technology. This interpretation is consistent with Farrell's (1957) efficiency measures, and with Debreu's (1951) coefficient of resource utilization. However neither Debreu nor Farrell actually formulated the efficiency measurement problem as a linear programming problem. Farrell and Fieldhouse (1962) foresaw the role of linear programming, but its development occurred later, with the work of Boles (1966), Bressler (1966), Seitz (1966), and Sitorus

(1966) for the piecewise linear case, and Timmer (1971) for the piecewise log-linear case.

Both piecewise linear and piecewise log-linear formulations are nonparametric. Aigner and Chu (1968) were perhaps the first to specify a parametric (Cobb–Douglas) frontier and use linear and quadratic programming methods to construct the frontier and measure efficiency relative to it. This parametric programming approach has been adopted by Førsund and Hjalmarsson (1987).

The resistance among economists to the adoption of linear programming techniques to analyze economic performance is due in large part to the fact that no account is taken of error, other than that arising due to failure to meet the behavioral goal, i.e., the resulting frontier is nonstochastic. This implies that the resulting efficiency scores may be contaminated by noise or measurement error (Schmidt (1985-86)). Another frequently raised concern is that the measures may be sensitive to outliers (evidence to the contrary is provided by Thompson et al. (1990) and Burgess and Wilson (1993)). These concerns are well founded, although most alternative computational techniques (such as stochastic parametric frontier approaches, and parametric deterministic approaches) share the outlier problem, and are subject to specification error problems. Three promising directions of research in this area are the use of resampling techniques (Boland (1990), N'Gbo (1991), and Simar (1992)), the application of semi-parametric methods (Härdle (1990) and Pinkse (1990)), and the application of chance-constrained programming techniques (Desai and Schinnar (1987) and Land, Lovell, and Thore (1988)).

Although the shortcomings of programming approaches to frontier analysis are fairly well known among economists, the benefits are less well appreciated. The aforementioned flexibility achieved by avoiding parametric specification of technology and the distribution of (in)efficiency is one such benefit. This approach lends itself more readily to decomposition into components of technical and price-related deviations from efficient performance than do regression-based approaches. Modeling restricted technologies or nontraditional behavioral goals is also very simple, as we demonstrate throughout the book, particularly in Chapter 10. Finally, the rich results possible using programming methods, which include slack variables and shadow prices, have not been fully appreciated or exploited. These are also developed at various points in the book.

1.3   The Relationship of Our Work to the Literature on Nonparametric Testing of Regularity Conditions and Behavioral Objectives

Linear programming approaches to efficiency measurement have proliferated in the OR/MS literature, largely due to the influence of Charnes and Cooper. In the economics literature on production frontiers, linear programming techniques are penetrating much more slowly, for reasons just mentioned. However heavy reliance is placed on linear programming techniques in a closely related research area that we wish to bring to the reader's attention. We refer to this literature, somewhat loosely, as the development of nonparametric tests of regularity conditions and behavioral objectives in production analysis.

Following his earlier work on the construction of utility functions (Afriat (1967)), which in turn was strongly influenced by Samuelson's (1948) revealed preference analysis, Afriat (1972) developed a sequence of tests of consistency of a body of production data with increasingly more restrictive regularity hypotheses on production technology. These tests, and similar tests of the same and other hypotheses proposed by Hanoch and Rothschild (1972), are all given linear programming formulations. Hanoch and Rothschild proposed conducting such tests on data prior to estimation using restrictive parametric functional forms. Diewert and Parkan (1983) suggested the use of such tests for the same general purpose, as a screening device. However they also suggested that this battery of tests might be used to construct frontiers and measure efficiency of data relative to the constructed frontiers. If a data set is not consistent with a linear programming test of a hypothesis (which may be either technological or behavioral or both), then for each observation an index of the severity of inconsistency is constructed and interpreted as an index of efficiency relative to that hypothesis.

Varian (1985, 1990) and Banker and Maindiratta (1988) have followed up on the Diewert and Parkan effort to make something of the information contained in the inconsistency of a data set with a regularity condition. Varian seeks to soften the "all-or-nothing" nature of the tests – either data pass a test or they do not – by developing a framework for allowing "small" failures to be attributed to measurement error in the data rather than to failure of the hypothesis under investigation. In so doing Varian has taken a step in the direction of introducing a stochastic element into the nonparametric linear programming approach to frontier analysis. Banker and Maindiratta take the inconsistency notion in a different direction, by using linear programming techniques to construct the tightest possible upper and lower bounds for production technology consistent with a hypothesis.

Each of these studies uses nonparametric linear programming models to test the consistency of a body of data, or a subset of a body of data, with a structural (e.g., constant returns to scale) or parametric (e.g., Cobb–Douglas) or behavioral (e.g., cost minimization) hypothesis. They were originally proposed as screening devices to check for data accuracy and "outliers," and also to provide guidance in the selection of parametric functional forms to use in econometric estimation and analysis. However as Diewert and Parkan pointed out, and as others have shown, these procedures can also be used to construct frontiers and measure efficiency. The overlap between this literature and the efficiency-measurement literature is substantial, and it offers a way of bringing closer together the nonparametric, nonstochastic linear programming approach and the parametric, stochastic regression-based approach to frontier analysis.

1.4   An Outline of this Study

The book can be read cover-to-cover to get a broad exposure to our approach to production frontiers. However it is also designed to allow the reader to focus more narrowly on specific topics of interest, by reading Chapter 2 in conjunction with various subsets of additional chapters. To guide further exploration, each chapter closes with a list of references to the literature.

Chapter 2 provides the foundation for all that follows, for it exposes the reader to various representations of production technology relative to which efficiency is calculated. In Section 2.1 we present various production correspondences, input and output, direct and indirect, and the graph of the technology. We also introduce cost and revenue functions. Each of these representations, and others as well, provides a way of characterizing *efficient* production technology, or a *production frontier*. In Sections 2.2 and 2.3 we explore two important features of the structure of efficient technology: returns to size (in terms of both scale and diversification) and disposability (both input and output). The significance of these two features lies in the fact that the presence of either type of size economy, or the absence of free disposability, represents observable sources of potentially remediable inefficiency. In Section 2.4 we introduce the piecewise technology we use throughout the book. Such a technology can be used to represent each of the production correspondences introduced in Section 2.1, and can be modified to accommodate any type of returns to size and any type of disposability. It can also be constructed using linear (sometimes nonlinear) programming techniques. In Section 2.5 we generate an artificial data set that is consistent with a parametric CET-CD technology. The data set consists of 20 observations on quantities and prices of two inputs and two outputs. This data set is then used to construct piecewise technologies, and to measure efficiency relative to the constructed technologies, throughout the book. This serves to show the reader how the theoretical notions developed in Chapters 3-10 are translated by means of mathematical programming techniques into empirical information concerning the structure of various production frontiers and the efficiency of each production unit relative to the frontiers.

1.4.1   Direct Efficiency Measurement: Chapters 2, 3, 4

Direct representations of production technology are provided in Chapter 2. Efficiency measures that seek cost-saving input contraction consistent with continued production of given outputs are developed in Chapter 3. Efficiency measures that seek revenue-raising output expansion consistent with continued employment of given inputs are developed in Chapter 4. Both of these families of efficiency measures can be decomposed into price-independent technical and price-dependent allocative components. Both technical components can be broken down into separate measures of scale efficiency, congestion, and "pure" technical efficiency. Both of these families of efficiency measures are based on a radial technical efficiency component that requires equiproportionate adjustment of all inputs or all outputs. Since these radial measures can leave unwanted slack in adjusted vectors, in Sections 3.3 and 4.3 we introduce nonradial technical efficiency measures that leave no slack. These nonradial measures generate a different decomposition of overall efficiency into its technical and allocative components. In Sections 3.4 and 4.4 we consider the measurement of scale efficiency when only cost and output, or revenue and input, data are available. Input-based measures and output-based measures are compared in Section 4.5. In Sections 3.5 and 4.6 we use the artificial data generated in Section 2.5 to illustrate the measurement and decomposition of direct input-based and direct output-based productive efficiency.

1.4.2 Indirect Efficiency Measurement: Chapters 2, 5, 6

Indirect representations of production technology are provided in Chapter 2. Whereas direct efficiency measures are either output-constrained (Chapter 3) or resource-constrained (Chapter 3) indirect efficiency measures allow somewhat more flexibility by allowing production units to be either revenue-constrained (Chapter 5) or cost-constrained (Chapter 6). Efficiency measures that seek cost-saving input contraction consistent with continued generation of given revenue at fixed output prices are developed in Chapter 5. Efficiency measures that seek revenue-enhancing output expansion consistent with a given budget and fixed input prices are developed in Chapter 6. Both sets of efficiency measures can be decomposed into technical and allocative components, and both technical efficiency measures can be further decomposed into scale, congestion, and purely technical components. In Sections 5.3 and 6.3 the two overall indirect efficiency measures are used to construct indexes of benefit effectiveness and expense effectiveness. These indexes can be thought of as modified benefit–cost ratios, the modification taking the form of replacing "actual" with "indirect efficient" values of either cost or benefit. This approach has the virtue of converting conventional benefit–cost ratios to potential benefit–cost ratios with either type of indirect inefficiency eliminated. Direct and indirect measures are compared in Section 5.4. Sections 5.5 and 6.4 use artificial data to illustrate the calculation and interpretation of the indirect efficiency measures.

1.4.3 Input-Based Efficiency Measurement: Chapters 2, 3, 5

Input-based efficiency measures can be either direct or revenue-indirect. A comparison of the two types of input-based efficiency measures provides an indication of the value of having the flexibility of being revenue-constrained rather than output-constrained.

1.4.4 Output-Based Efficiency Measurement: Chapters 2, 4, 6

Output-based efficiency measures can also be either direct, resource-constrained, or cost-indirect, budget-constrained. A comparison of the two shows the cost of being resource-constrained instead of being budget-constrained.

1.4.5   The Measurement of Price Efficiency: Chapters 2, 7

In Chapters 3-6 efficiency measurement takes place in an environment
in which input and/or output prices are given and input and/or output
quantities are variable. In Chapter 7 we examine an environment in
which the roles of prices and quantities are reversed, with prices being
the choice variables that are adjusted to achieve efficiency. One interpretation of this novel environment is that this is an accounting model,
or a planning model, in which the goal of the analysis is the identification of an efficient price vector. In Section 7.1 we seek cost-deflated
input prices which allow the production of target outputs, and in Section 7.2 we seek revenue-deflated output prices which are feasible with
given inputs. Each of these measures can be decomposed into technical and allocative components. A numerical example of price efficiency
calculation is provided in Section 7.3.

1.4.6   Graph Efficiency Measurement: Chapters 2, 8

In Chapters 3-7 efficiency is measured radially in a variety of con-
texts. In Chapter 8 efficiency is measured hyperbolically. In Chapter
3 (direct) cost efficiency is input based, relying on radial contraction of
inputs. In Chapter 4 (direct) revenue efficiency is output based, using
radial expansion of outputs. In Chapter 8 we introduce profit efficiency,
in which both inputs and outputs can be adjusted. The analog to the
radial efficiency measures of Chapters 3 and 4 is a hyperbolic efficiency
measure, which seeks the maximum equiproportionate input reduction
and output expansion consistent with production feasibility as given by
the graph of the technology. Although the relationship between overall
graph efficiency and the profit function is not so straightforward as the
relationships between cost efficiency and the cost function or between
revenue efficiency and the revenue function, it is nonetheless possible to
define overall graph efficiency and to decompose it into allocative and
three types of technical components. This is accomplished in Sections
8.1 and 8.2. In Section 8.3 we consider in some detail the special problem
of graph efficiency measurement when not all outputs are freely disposable. A particularly important application of this special case occurs
when a subvector of outputs is undesirable (e.g., pollutants) and cannot
be freely disposed due to environmental protection restrictions. A comparison of efficiency scores with and without free output disposability
imposed generates information concerning the cost to the production

unit of complying with the environmental restrictions; thus the degree of non-free disposability is associated with the stringency of the environmental constraint. Finally, in Section 8.4 the artificial data are used to illustrate the calculation of hyperbolic graph efficiency measures.

1.4.7 Efficiency Measurement and Productivity Measurement: Chapters 2, 9

If linear programming techniques can be used to construct piecewise linear technologies and to measure efficiency relative to the calculated technologies, then it stands to reason that the same techniques can be used to measure changes in technology, i.e., productivity change. The use of distance functions in the construction of productivity indexes was advocated by Malmquist (1953), and later by Bergson (1961) and Moorsteen (1961). In Chapter 9 we exploit the fact that distance functions are reciprocals of radial efficiency measures to explore the relationship between efficiency measurement and productivity measurement. In Sections 9.1 and 9.2 we introduce direct input-based and output-based productivity indexes, extending previous exploration by Caves, Christensen, and Diewert (1982b). In Sections 9.3 and 9.4 we introduce indirect input-based and output-based productivity indexes. All four indexes can be decomposed into technical change and efficiency change, and efficiency change can be further decomposed into changes in scale efficiency, changes in congestion, and changes in "pure" technical efficiency.

1.4.8 Miscellany: Chapters 2, 10

In Chapter 10 we take up a number of topics that represent potentially useful extensions of the efficiency measurement ideas developed in Chapters 3-9. In Section 10.1 we consider the problem of subvector efficiency measurement, one obvious application of which is to efficiency measurement in the short run, in which not all inputs are variable. The framework is more general, however, and allows for fixity of any set of inputs and/or outputs for whatever institutional reason is relevant, including the imposition of regulatory constraints or the presence of binding long-term contracts with input suppliers or output purchasers. We introduce direct and indirect subvector efficiency measures, and we provide linear programming models to calculate both types of measure. A comparison of these subvector efficiency measures with analogous measures in Chapters 3-6 can shed light on the cost of the subvector fixity constraint. In Section 10.2 we consider the problem of cost-constrained or revenue-constrained profit maximization. This material extends the graph efficiency measurement problem considered in Chapter 8 by appending to that problem an expenditure constraint or a revenue constraint. Thus this material can also be thought of as an extension of the revenue-indirect and cost-indirect efficiency measurement models of Chapters 5 and 6. Comparing the efficiency measures obtained here and in Chapter 8 provides a measure of the profit loss associated with the cost or revenue constraint. In Section 10.3 we develop a measure of the productive capacity of a unit and its rate of capacity utilization. These measures result from the solution of linear programming problems in which a subvector of variable inputs is unrestricted and its complementary subvector of capacity-defining inputs is bounded. In Section 10.4 we consider the problem of measuring gains from product diversification. Our notion of diversification is more general, and more useful, than the restrictive but currently popular notions of economies of scope or super-additivity of technology. It is more general because it does not require specialized and diversified production units to have the same technology or face the same input price vector. Our measure of the gains from diversification is based on a comparison of technical efficiency measures relative to separate and combined technologies, although we also develop a price-dependent measure of the gains from diversification.

1.5   References to the Literature

The maximization postulate on which we rely so heavily, but which we consistently relax, is perhaps most forcefully stated by Samuelson (1947; esp. Ch. 3). Alternative approaches which in our view go too far in the opposite direction include the "easy life" hypothesis of Hicks (1935; 8), the "satisficing" hypothesis of Simon (1955), the behavioral approach associated with Cyert and March (1963), and Leibenstein's (1966, 1976, 1987) and Stigler's (1976), X-efficiency paradigm. Our own position is much closer to Samuelson's, in that we assume purposeful, goal-directed behavior, but we enrich our behavioral models by allowing for failure in the optimization process.

Interesting essays on the value of efficiency measurement in public economics are provided by Barrow and Wagstaff (1989), Pestieau and Tulkens (1991), and Tulkens (1991).

The approach we take to the characterization of production technology and the measurement of efficiency relative to that technology is nonparametric and nonstochastic. The principal alternative approach is parametric and stochastic, and involves fitting regression equations. An excellent exposition of the latter approach is provided by Schmidt (1985-86). The two approaches, and variations on each theme, are developed and applied in a number of collections, including Aigner and Schmidt (1980), Dogramaci and Färe (1988), Lewin and Lovell (1990), Charnes, Cooper, Lewin, and Seiford (forthcoming), Sueyoshi (1991), and Fried, Lovell, and Schmidt (1993).

Generally thoughtful commentary on the nonparametric nonstochastic approach, in its DEA guise, is provided by Nunamaker (1985), Silkmans (1986), and Epstein and Henderson (1989).

Between the two extreme paradigms lie two others: a parametric nonstochastic approach, and a nonparametric stochastic approach. The former approach is well developed, and involves constructing parametric frontiers using mathematical programming techniques, an idea due to Aigner and Chu (1968) and used by many others, including Førsund and Jansen (1977) and Førsund and Hjalmarsson (1979a, 1979b). Schmidt (1976) has shown that under certain conditions this approach is equivalent to using maximum likelihood regression techniques to estimate a so-called "full frontier" relationship having only a one-sided disturbance term that captures inefficiency. The nonparametric stochastic approach is in its infancy, and involves "softening" the nonstochastic frontier while maintaining its nonparametric structure. The approach generally makes use of chance-constrained programming techniques developed for other purposes by Charnes, Cooper, and Symonds (1958), and has been advocated by Desai and Schinnar (1987), Land, Lovell, and Thore (1988, 1990), and Petersen and Olesen (1989). See also Seaver and Triantis (1989).

The two extreme approaches – the nonparametric nonstochastic approach and the parametric stochastic approach – have been combined in a two-step procedure by Thiry and Tulkens (1992). In the first step the nonparametric nonstochastic approach is used to isolate the efficient producers, to "filter" the data. In the second step the parametric stochastic approach is applied to the production technology. This two-step technique has been applied to an investigation of the cost efficiency of Belgian municipalities by Vanden Eeckaut, Tulkens, and Jamar (1993).

A few studies have compared the performances of various approaches to frontier construction and efficiency measurement. Artificial data have been employed by Bowlin, Charnes, Cooper, and Sherman (1985), Banker, Charnes, Cooper, and Maindiratta (1988), and Gong and Sickles (1992). Artificial data are useful for learning about alternative models, since the truth is known, but they teach nothing about the real world. Real data are useful for learning about the real world, but have the disadvantage that the truth is not known. Real data have been employed by van den Broeck, Førsund, Hjalmarsson, and Meeusen (1980) (Swedish dairy plants), Banker, Conrad, and Strauss (1986) (hospitals), Grosskopf, Hayes, and Yaisawarng (1989) (grain farms), Ferrier and Lovell (1990) (banks), Lovell and Wood (1992) (Soviet cotton refining), Burgat and Jeanrenaud (1990) (Swiss refuse collection), Simar (1992) (European national railways), and Førsund and Hernaes (1990) (Norwegian ferry transport).

The radial technical efficiency measures developed by Debreu (1951) and Farrell (1957), see also Ahlheim (1988), have been adopted by virtually every writer since, in both stochastic and nonstochastic environments and for both parametric and nonparametric technologies. Exceptions to the radial rule include Färe (1975), Färe and Lovell (1978), parts of Kopp (1981), Zieschang (1984), Petersen (1988), Deller and Nelson (1989, 1991), and very few others. This curiosity about nonradial efficiency measures has, however, created a cottage industry, not concerned with nonradial measures *per se*, but with the set of properties an efficiency measure should satisfy. Färe and Lovell (1978) suggested three independent properties: monotonicity, homogeneity, and indication (the measure is equal to one if and only if the input–output bundle is efficient). Since then Bol (1986, 1988), Russell (1985, 1988, 1990) and others have weakened some properties and added others, including commensurability (the measure is independent of units of measurement) and continuity. Perhaps not surprisingly, no measure satisfies all desirable properties. The latest word as of this writing on which measures satisfy which subsets of properties is Russell (1990).

The problem of nonparametric testing of regularity conditions and behavioral objectives originated in the work of Afriat (1967, 1972). The part of this work dealing with producers includes Hanoch and Rothschild (1972), Diewert and Parkan (1983), Varian (1984, 1985, 1990), Chavas and Cox (1988, 1990), Ray (1991), and Ray and Bhadra (1991). There is also a parallel line of research dealing with consumption economics.

Salter's (1966) work on best practice, average practice and efficient industrial structure has been continued by many, most notably Johansen (1972), Sato (1975), Summa (1986), and Førsund and Hjalmarsson (1987).

The potential sensitivity of policy prescriptions to differences in frontier technology and interior activity was noted by Lovell and Sickles (1988), in the context of an *ex post* analysis by Charnes, Cooper and Sueyoshi (1988) and Evans and Heckman (1988) of the breakup of the Bell System in the U.S. Additional policy-oriented applications of efficiency analysis, particularly to the efficiency and equity of labor markets, have been noted by Lovell (1991); see also Porter and Scully (1987).

2

Production Technology

2.0 Introduction

In this chapter we expose the reader to the production models relative to which efficiency will be evaluated. We include models whose map sets are in quantity space and models whose map sets are in price space. More specifically, the first group of models is divided into those which involve input quantities and output quantities, such as the graph of the technology and the input and output correspondences. The first group of models also includes those which are value constrained. In the value constrained group we include the cost indirect output correspondence and the revenue indirect input correspondence. Examples of models with map sets in price space include the dual input and dual output correspondences. All these models are introduced in Section 2.1.

To avoid an overwhelming number of technicalities, little or no discussion is devoted to the particular properties different models possess. However, in the piecewise linear formulation of these models developed in Section 2.4, the properties relevant for efficiency measurement are derived.

In Section 2.2 we introduce two sets of notions that model variation in the size of operation of a production unit. First we define returns to scale with respect to each of the seven models introduced above, and then we define the notion of returns to diversification. Thus in Section 2.2 both scaling and addition in production are discussed.

Disposability – both weak and strong – is discussed in Section 2.3. In particular, since some outputs may be "bads" and some inputs may cause congestion, we need both concepts. If, for example, outputs are strongly (also termed freely) disposable, then any output can be discarded without resource use or cost. However, if some outputs are "bads" it is logical to impose costly disposability, thus weak but not strong disposability should be imposed on outputs. Strong disposability of inputs excludes "backward bending" isoquants and thus cannot model noneconomic regions which arise because of congestion. Hence if congestion is the topic of inquiry, weak but not strong (free) disposability should be imposed on inputs.

In addition to disposability, we model three efficiency notions for inputs and outputs. The three notions are the isoquant, the weak efficient subset, and the efficient subset. These sets are ordered by inclusion and the isoquant contains the weak efficient subset which contains the efficient subset.

The basic piecewise linear versions of our production models are formulated in section 2.4. These models are shown to satisfy properties like closedness and boundedness, needed for efficiency measurement. Moreover, variations with respect to returns to scale and disposability are also introduced. We conclude the section with an example of a piecewise model that is nonlinear and parametric.

Throughout the manuscript, we provide computational examples that illustrate the construction and representations of technology and the corresponding measures of efficiency. Section 2.5 shows how the required data are constructed.

2.1 Representation of Technology

A production technology transforming inputs $x = (x_1, x_2, \cdots, x_N) \in \Re_+^N = \{x : x \in \Re_+^N, x \geqq 0\}$ into outputs $u = (u_1, u_2, \cdots, u_M) \in \Re_+^M$ can be represented by the output correspondence P, the input correspondence L, or the graph of the technology GR. The *Output Correspondence*

$$P : \Re_+^N \longrightarrow 2^{\Re_+^M} \qquad (2.1.1)$$

maps inputs $x \in \Re_+^N$ into subsets $P(x) \subseteq \Re_+^M$ of outputs. The set $P(x)$ is called the *Output Set*, and it denotes the collection of all output vectors $u \in \Re_+^M$ that are obtainable from the input vector $x \in \Re_+^N$. The output set is illustrated in Figure 2.1. The *Input Correspondence*

$$L : \Re_+^M \longrightarrow 2^{\Re_+^N} \qquad (2.1.2)$$

maps outputs $u \in \Re_+^M$ into subsets $L(u) \subseteq \Re_+^N$ of inputs. The *Input*

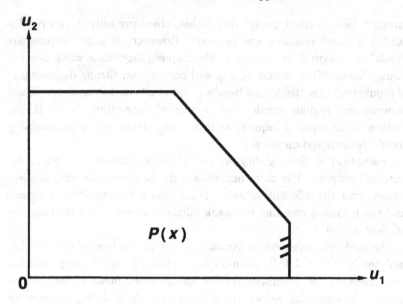

Fig. 2.1. *The Output Set*

Set $L(u)$ denotes the collection of all input vectors $x \in \Re_+^N$ that yield at least output vector $u \in \Re_+^M$. The input set is illustrated in Figure 2.2. The input and output correspondences can be obtained from one another by means of the relationships

$$L(u) = \{x : u \in P(x)\} \tag{2.1.3}$$

and

$$P(x) = \{u : x \in L(u)\}. \tag{2.1.4}$$

An input–output vector is feasible if $x \in L(u)$ or equivalently if $u \in P(x)$. The *Graph* of the technology is the collection of all feasible input–output vectors, i.e.,

$$GR = \{(x,u) \in \Re_+^{N+M} : u \in P(x), x \in \Re_+^N\} \tag{2.1.5}$$
$$= \{(x,u) \in \Re_+^{N+M} : x \in L(u), u \in \Re_+^M\}.$$

The graph is derived from either the input correspondence or the output correspondence. Conversely, the input and output correspondences are derived from the graph as

$$P(x) = \{u : (x,u) \in GR\} \tag{2.1.6}$$

and

$$L(u) = \{x : (x,u) \in GR\} \tag{2.1.7}$$

respectively.

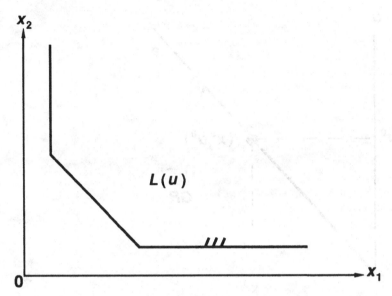

Fig. 2.2. *The Input Set*

The relationship between the input set, the output set and the graph is shown in Figure 2.3. The graph of the technology is the area bounded by the x-axis and the line $(0a)$. The output set is $P(x^\circ) = [0, u^\circ]$ and the input set is $L(u^\circ) = [x^\circ, +\infty)$. The relationship among P, L and GR is summarized in

(2.1.8)   **Proposition**: $u \in P(x) \iff x \in L(u) \iff (x, u) \in GR.$

Although the input set, the output set and the graph model the same production technology, they highlight different aspects of the technology. The input set models input substitution, and the output set models output substitution. The graph models both input substitution and output substitution, in addition to modeling input–output transformation.

The input set, the output set, and the graph have one feature in common. They provide representations of technology in terms of input quantities and output quantities. No prices are involved, and no behavioral assumption is required. If information on input prices and output prices is available, and if behavioral assumptions are made, it is possible to develop a number of price-dependent characterizations of technology.

Suppose that in addition to the output sets $P(x)$, output prices $r = (r_1, r_2, \cdots, r_M) \in \Re_+^M$ are known. If $P(x)$ is a nonempty compact set,

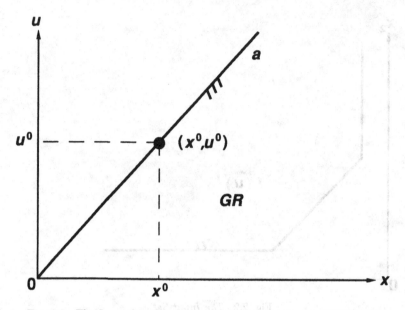

Fig. 2.3. *The Input Set, The Output Set, and The Graph of Production Technology*

the *Revenue Function*

$$R(x, r) = \max_{u}\{ru : u \in P(x)\} \tag{2.1.9}$$

$$= \max_{u}\{\sum_{m=1}^{M} r_m u_m : (u_1, u_2, \cdots, u_M) \in P(x)\}$$

provides an output price-dependent characterization of technology. It shows the maximum revenue that can be generated at output prices r from input vector x, and we note that it is homogeneous of degree $+1$ in output prices. The revenue maximization problem is illustrated in Figure 2.4.   Two outputs are produced by inputs according to the output set $P(x)$. Two revenue levels are indicated in the figure. The maximum feasible revenue is achieved at u^*. If the revenue function and desired revenue $R \in \Re_{++}$ are known, the *Revenue Indirect Input Correspondence*

$$IL : \Re_+^M \longrightarrow IL(r/R) \subseteqq \Re_+^N \tag{2.1.10}$$

can be defined. Unlike the input correspondence L, which maps output vectors into subsets of input vectors, the revenue indirect input correspondence IL maps revenue normalized output price vectors into subsets

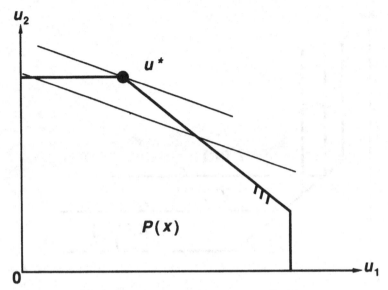

Fig. 2.4. *The Revenue Maximization Problem*

of input vectors. The *Revenue Indirect Input Set*

$$IL(r/R) = \{x : R(x,r) \geqq R\} = \{x : R(x,r/R) \geqq 1\} \qquad (2.1.11)$$

denotes the collection of all input vectors yielding at least desired revenue R with output price vector r. The revenue indirect input set is illustrated in Figure 2.5. It should be noted that the (direct) input sets $L(u^1)$ and $L(u^2)$ which satisfy the revenue target, i.e., $ru^1 \geqq R$ and $ru^2 \geqq R$, are subsets of the indirect input set $IL(r/R)$.

It can be shown that

(2.1.12)   **Proposition**: $\{x : R(x,r) \geqq R\} = \{x : x \in L(u), ru \geqq R\}$.

Proof: Suppose that $x \in \{x : R(x,r) \geqq R\}$, then there exists a $u \in P(x)$ such that $R(x,r) = ru$. Since $u \in P(x)$, $x \in L(u)$ and since $R(x,r) = ru$, $ru \geqq R$, thus $x \in \{x : x \in L(u), ru \geqq R\}$. Conversely suppose that $x \in \{x : x \in L(u), ru \geqq R\}$, then $x \in L(u)$ and $ru \geqq R$, thus $u \in P(x)$ and $R(x,r) \geqq ru \geqq R$. Therefore $x \in \{x : R(x,r) \geqq R\}$.

Q.E.D.

Suppose again that the revenue function $R(x,r)$ and desired revenue $R \in \Re_{++}$ are known, then the *Dual Output Correspondence*

$$DP : \Re_+^N \longrightarrow DP(x) \subseteq \Re_+^M \qquad (2.1.13)$$

can be defined. Unlike the output correspondence P, which maps input vectors into subsets of output vectors, the dual output correspondence

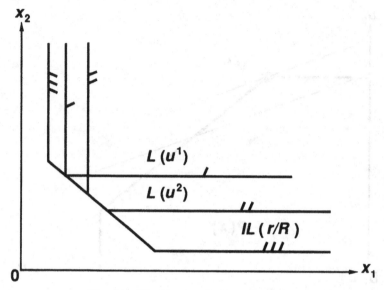

Fig. 2.5. *The Revenue Indirect Input Set*

DP maps input vectors into subsets of revenue deflated output price vectors. The *Dual Output Set*

$$DP(x) = \{r/R : R(x, r/R) \leqq 1\} \qquad (2.1.14)$$

denotes the collection of all revenue deflated output price vectors for which the revenue function does not exceed one for input vector x.

Suppose now that in addition to the input sets $L(u)$, input prices $p \in \Re_{++}^{N}$ are known. If $L(u)$ is nonempty and closed, the *Cost Function*

$$
\begin{aligned}
Q(u, p) &= \min_{x}\{px : x \in L(u)\} \qquad (2.1.15) \\
&= \min_{x}\{\sum_{n=1}^{N} p_n x_n : (x_1, x_2, \cdots, x_N) \in L(u)\}
\end{aligned}
$$

provides an input price-dependent characterization of technology. It shows the minimum expenditure required to produce output vector u at input prices p. If input prices are not strictly positive, the minimum in (2.1.15) may not exist. However, if we assume that the efficient subset $Eff\, L(u) = \{x : x \in L(u), y \leq x \implies y \notin L(u)\}$ is bounded, then even if some input prices are zero, the minimum exists. We also note that the cost function is homogeneous of degree +1 in input prices. The cost minimization problem is illustrated in Figure 2.6. In Figure 2.6 two

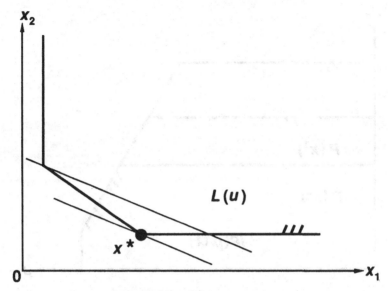

Fig. 2.6. *The Cost Minimization Problem*

isocost lines are indicated. The lower one represents cost minimization relative to $L(u)$, and the minimum is achieved at x^*.

If the cost function $Q(u, p)$ and target cost $Q \in \Re_{++}$ are known, the *Cost Indirect Output Correspondence*

$$IP : \Re_+^N \longrightarrow IP(p/Q) \subseteq \Re_+^M \qquad (2.1.16)$$

can be defined. Unlike the output correspondence P, which maps input vectors into subsets of output vectors, the cost indirect output correspondence maps normalized input price vectors into subsets of output vectors. The *Cost Indirect Output Set*

$$IP(p/Q) = \{u : Q(u, p) \leqq Q\} = \{u : Q(u, p/Q) \leqq 1\} \qquad (2.1.17)$$

denotes the collection of all output vectors obtainable at input price vector p and at cost not exceeding Q. The cost indirect output set is illustrated in Figure 2.7. It should be noted that the (direct) output sets $P(x^1)$ and $P(x^2)$ for which the cost px^1 and px^2 does not exceed target cost Q, are subsets of the indirect output set $IP(p/Q)$.

It can be shown that if $p \in \Re_{++}^N$, i.e., prices are strictly positive, or if $p \in \Re_+^N$ and the efficient subset $Eff\ L(u)$ is bounded, then

$$IP(p/Q) = \{u : Q(u, p) \leqq Q\} = \{u : u \in P(x), px \leqq Q\}. \qquad (2.1.18)$$

Suppose again that the cost function $Q(u, p)$ and target cost $Q \in \Re_{++}$

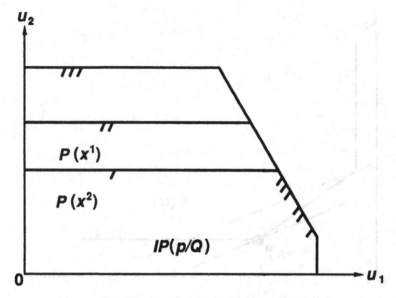

Fig. 2.7. *The Cost Indirect Output Set*

are known. Then the *Dual Input Correspondence*

$$DL : \Re_+^M \longrightarrow DL(u) \subseteqq \Re_+^N \qquad (2.1.19)$$

can be defined. Unlike the input correspondence L, which maps output vectors into subsets of input vectors, the dual input correspondence maps output vectors into subsets of cost deflated input price vectors. The *Dual Input Set*

$$DL(u) = \{p/Q : Q(u, p/Q) \geqq 1\} \qquad (2.1.20)$$

denotes the collection of all cost deflated input price vectors for which the minimum cost of producing output vector u is at least one.

Figure 2.8 summarizes the relationships among the various production correspondences introduced above.

2.2 Returns to Scale and Diversification

The purpose of this section is to introduce two sets of notions that model change in size of operation. The first set consists of various definitions of returns to scale, which model proportional changes in size of the technology, i.e., existing activities are scaled. Returns to scale is a characteristic of the surface of the graph. For observations interior to the

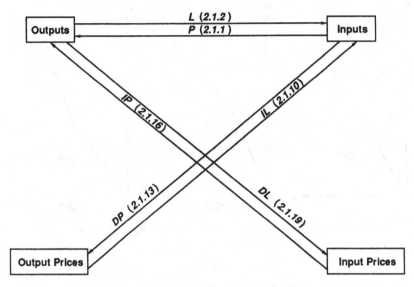

Fig. 2.8. *Relationships Among Six Production Correspondences*

graph, returns to scale is measured at a corresponding boundary point. The second set of notions of size consists of models of diversification, which model addition of productive units, e.g., additional activities may be added to existing activities. Diversification is also a feature of the surface of the graph. Thus both scaling and addition are modeled in this section.

We begin with scale properties. Since the graph of the technology highlights input–output transformation, we begin by defining returns to scale in terms of the graph. The following types of global scale behavior are illustrated in Figure 2.9. Local scale behavior is discussed in Section 2.4.

(2.2.1) **Proposition**: The technology exhibits *Constant Returns to Scale (CRS)* if $\mu GR = GR, \mu > 0$; it exhibits *Non Increasing Returns to Scale (NIRS)* if $\lambda GR \subseteqq GR, 0 < \lambda \leqq 1$, or equivalently if $GR \subseteqq \theta GR, \theta \geqq 1$; it exhibits *Non Decreasing Returns to Scale (NDRS)* if $\theta GR \subseteqq GR, \theta \geqq 1$, or equivalently if $GR \subseteqq \lambda GR, 0 < \lambda \leqq 1$.

If the technology exhibits *CRS, NIRS*, or *NDRS*, then all representations of technology, including P, DP, IP, L, IL and DL, exhibit equivalent properties, i.e., any of the six representations may be used to model returns to scale. To show this, we prove the equivalences for

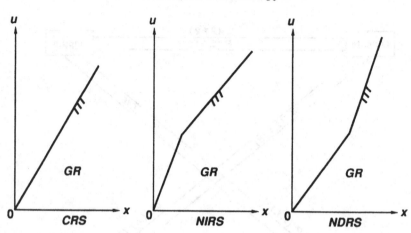

Fig. 2.9. *Returns to Scale Characterized by the Graph of the Technology*

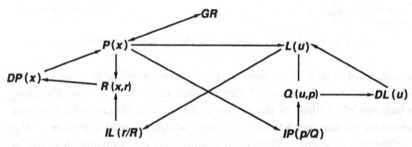

Fig. 2.10. *Returns to Scale in Terms of Various Representations of Technology*

NIRS and then state the equivalence theorem. A flow diagram of the proof is provided in Figure 2.10; readers not interested in the details of the proof may proceed to Propositions (2.2.14) – (2.2.16) for a summary of these results.

(2.2.2)   **Proposition:** Let $\theta \geqq 1$. $GR \subseteqq \theta GR \Longleftrightarrow P(\theta x) \subseteqq \theta P(x)$, $\forall x \in \Re_+^N$.

Proof: ($\Longrightarrow$) Assume $GR \subseteqq \theta GR$, i.e., $(1/\theta)GR \subseteqq GR$. Then by (2.1.6), $(1/\theta)P(\theta x) = \{u : (x,u) \in (1/\theta)GR\} \subseteqq \{u : (x,u) \in GR\} = P(x)$. Thus $P(\theta x) \subseteqq \theta P(x)$. ($\Longleftarrow$) Assume $P(\theta x) \subseteqq \theta P(x)$, i.e., $(1/\theta)P(\theta x) \subseteqq P(x)$. Then by (2.1.5), $(1/\theta)GR = \{(x,u) : u \in (1/\theta)P(\theta x), \theta x \in \Re_+^N\} \subseteqq \{(x,u) : u \in P(x), x \in \Re_+^N\} = GR$. Thus $GR \subseteqq \theta GR$.

Q.E.D.

(2.2.3)   **Proposition:** Let $\theta \geqq 1$. If $P(\theta x) \subseteqq \theta P(x)$, then $\theta R(x,r)$ $\geqq R(\theta x, r), \forall r \in \Re_+^M$.

Proof: Apply Definition (2.1.9). Since $(1/\theta)P(\theta x) \subseteq P(x)$, $R(x,r) = \max\{ru : u \in P(x)\} \geq \max\{ru : u \in (1/\theta)P(\theta x)\} = (1/\theta)\max\{rv : v \in P(\theta x)\} = (1/\theta)R(\theta x, r)$. Thus $\theta R(x,r) \geq R(\theta x, r)$.

Q.E.D.

(2.2.4)   **Proposition:** Let $\theta \geq 1$. If $\theta R(x,r) \geq R(\theta x, r)$, then $(1/\theta)DP(x) \subseteq DP(\theta x)$.

Proof: Without loss of generality, we let $R = 1$ in Definition (2.1.14). Thus $DP(x) = \{r : R(x,r) \leq 1\} \subseteq \{r : (1/\theta)R(\theta x, r) \leq 1\} = \theta DP(\theta x)$, since $R(x,r)$ is homogeneous of degree $+1$ in R. Thus $(1/\theta)DP(x) \subseteq DP(\theta x)$.

Q.E.D.

To prove the next result we recall that for the duality theorem

$$P(x) = \{u : ru \leq 1, \forall r \in DP(x)\}$$

to apply, $P(x)$ must be convex.

(2.2.5)   **Proposition:** Let $\theta \geq 1$. If $(1/\theta)DP(x) \subseteq DP(\theta x)$, then $P(\theta x) \subseteq \theta P(x)$.

Proof: $(1/\theta)P(\theta x) = \{u : ru \leq 1, \forall r \in \theta DP(\theta x)\} \subseteq \{u : ru \leq 1, \forall r \in DP(x)\} = P(x)$. Thus $P(\theta x) \subseteq \theta P(x)$.

Q.E.D.

(2.2.6)   **Proposition:** Let $\theta \geq 1$. If $P(\theta x) \subseteq \theta P(x)$, then $L(\theta u) \subseteq \theta L(u)$.

Proof: It follows from (2.1.4) that $L(u) = \{x : u \in P(x)\}$. Thus since $P(\theta x) \subseteq \theta P(x)$, $L(\theta u) \subseteq \theta L(u)$.

Q.E.D.

(2.2.7)   **Proposition:** Let $\theta \geq 1$. If $L(\theta u) \subseteq \theta L(u)$, then $IL(r/\theta R) \subseteq \theta IL(r/R)$.

Proof: Apply expression (2.1.12) to obtain $(1/\theta)IL(r/\theta R) = (1/\theta)\{x : x \in L(\theta u), r\theta u \geq \theta R\} \subseteq \{x : x \in L(u), ru \geq R\} = IL(r/R)$. Thus $IL(r/\theta R) \subseteq \theta IL(r/R)$.

Q.E.D.

(2.2.8)   **Proposition:** Let $\theta \geq 1$. If $IL(r/\theta R) \subseteq \theta IL(r/R)$, then $\theta R(x,r) \geq R(\theta x, r)$.

Proof: We note that $\max\{R : x \in IL(r/R)\} = \max\{R : R(x,r) \geq R\} = R(x,r)$. Then since $(1/\theta)IL(r/\theta R) \subseteq IL(r/R)$, $R(x,r) \geq \max\{R : x \in (1/\theta)IL(r/\theta R)\} = (1/\theta)R(\theta x, r)$. Thus $\theta R(x,r) \geq R(\theta x, r)$.

Q.E.D.

(2.2.9)   **Proposition:** Let $\theta \geq 1$. If $L(\theta u) \subseteq \theta L(u)$, then $\theta Q(u,p) \leq Q(\theta u, p), \forall p \in \Re_{++}^N$.

Proof: By Definition (2.1.15), $Q(u,p) = \min\{px : x \in L(u)\}$. Thus since $(1/\theta)L(\theta u) \subseteq L(u)$, $Q(u,p) \leq \min\{px : x \in (1/\theta)L(\theta u)\} = (1/\theta) Q(\theta u, p)$, and $\theta Q(u,p) \leq Q(\theta u, p)$.

Q.E.D.

(2.2.10)   **Proposition:** Let $\theta \geq 1$. If $\theta Q(u,p) \leq Q(\theta u, p)$, then $(1/\theta)DL(u) \subseteq DL(\theta u)$.

Proof: Without loss of generality, we may take $Q = 1$ in Definition (2.1.20). Thus $DL(\theta u) = \{p : Q(\theta u, p) \geq 1\}$ and $(1/\theta)DL(u) = \{p : \theta Q(u,p) \geq 1\} \subseteq DL(\theta u)$, since $Q(u,p)$ is homogeneous of degree $+1$ in p.

Q.E.D.

To prove the next result we recall that for the duality theorem

$$L(u) = \{x : px \geq 1, \forall p \in DL(u)\}$$

to hold, $L(u)$ must be convex.

(2.2.11)   **Proposition:** Let $\theta \geq 1$. If $(1/\theta)DL(u) \subseteq DL(\theta u)$, then $L(\theta u) \subseteq \theta L(u)$.

Proof: $(1/\theta)L(\theta u) = \{x : px \geq 1, \forall p \in \theta DL(\theta u)\} \subseteq \{x : px \geq 1, \forall p \in DL(u)\} = L(u)$, thus $L(\theta u) \subseteq \theta L(u)$.

Q.E.D.

(2.2.12)   **Proposition:** Let $\theta \geq 1$. If $P(\theta x) \subseteq \theta P(x)$, then $IP(p/\theta Q) \subseteq \theta IP(p/Q)$.

Proof: Apply expression (2.1.18) to obtain $(1/\theta)IP(p/\theta Q) = (1/\theta)\{u : u \in P(\theta x), p\theta x \leq \theta Q\} \subseteq \{u : u \in P(x), px \leq Q\} = IP(p/Q)$.

Q.E.D.

(2.2.13)   **Proposition:** Let $\theta \geq 1$. If $IP(p/\theta Q) \subseteq \theta IP(p/Q)$, then $\theta Q(u,p) \leq Q(\theta u, p)$.

Proof: We note that $\min\{Q : u \in IP(p/Q)\} = \min\{Q : Q(u,p) \leq Q\} = Q(u,p)$. Then since $(1/\theta)IP(p/\theta Q) \subseteq IP(p/Q)$, $Q(u,p) \leq \min\{Q : u \in (1/\theta)IP(p/\theta Q)\} = (1/\theta)Q(\theta u, p)$. Thus $\theta Q(u,p) \leq Q(\theta u, p)$.

Q.E.D.

Propositions (2.2.2)–(2.2.13) establish an equivalence among the characterizations of *NIRS* provided by the seven representations of technology. This equivalence is summarized in

(2.2.14)   **Proposition:** The technology exhibits *NIRS* $\Longleftrightarrow$ $(GR \subseteq \theta GR) \Longleftrightarrow (P(\theta x) \subseteq \theta P(x)) \Longleftrightarrow (IP(p/\theta Q) \subseteq$

$\theta IP(p/Q)) \iff ((1/\theta)DP(x) \subseteqq DP(\theta x)) \iff (L(\theta u) \subseteqq \theta L(u)) \iff (IL(r/\theta R) \subseteqq \theta IL(r/R)) \iff ((1/\theta)DL(u) \subseteqq DL(\theta u)), \theta \geqq 1.$

Propositions similar to (2.2.2)–(2.2.13) apply to prove the next two propositions, which establish an equivalence among the characterizations of *NDRS* and *CRS*, respectively, for the seven representations of technology.

(2.2.15)   **Proposition:** The technology exhibits *NDRS* $\iff$ $(\theta GR \subseteqq GR) \iff (\theta P(x) \subseteqq P(\theta x)) \iff (\theta IP(p/Q) \subseteqq IP(p/\theta Q)) \iff (DP(\theta x) \subseteqq (1/\theta)DP(x)) \iff (\theta L(u) \subseteqq L(\theta u)) \iff (\theta IL(r/R) \subseteqq IL(r/\theta R)) \iff (DL(\theta u) \subseteqq (1/\theta)DL(u)), \theta \geqq 1.$

(2.2.16)   **Proposition:** The technology exhibits *CRS* $\iff$ $(\mu GR = GR) \iff (P(\mu x) = \mu P(x)) \iff (IP(p/\mu Q) = \mu IP(p/Q)) \iff ((1/\mu)DP(x) = DP(\mu x)) \iff (L(\mu u) = \mu L(u)) \iff (IL(r/\mu R) = \mu IL(r/R)) \iff ((1/\mu)DL(u) = DL(\mu u)),$ $\mu > 0.$

The second topic of this section is economies of diversification. Here the thought that it may be efficient to combine two or more firms into one is investigated. Our notion of gains from diversification is more general than sub/superadditivity where each plant or firm is associated with the same cost function or input correspondence. To be explicit, suppose that individual firms $j = 1, 2, \cdots, J$ produce specialized output u^j at the minimum cost of $Q^j(u^j, p)$. It is now of interest to investigate if the cost of a diversified technology $Q^D(\sum_{j=1}^{J} u^j, p)$ is smaller or larger than the cost of the sum of the specialized individual technologies, i.e., $\sum_{j=1}^{J} Q^j(u^j, p)$. If

$$Q^D \left(\sum_{j=1}^{J} u^j, p \right) < \sum_{j=1}^{J} Q^j(u^j, p), \qquad (2.2.17)$$

we say that there are gains from diversification. If the inequality in (2.2.17) is reversed, we say that there are diseconomies of diversification. Note that this notion differs from that of subadditivity in the sense that subadditivity requires that the cost functions for the diversified and specialized firms be the same, while here they may differ. Thus the traditional notions of sub- and superadditivity of costs (and the related notion of economies of scope) may be thought of as special cases of our notion of economies of diversification. We treat this subject in more detail in Section 4 of Chapter 10.

2.3   Disposability

The purpose of this section is to introduce the notion of disposability as
a feature of technology. Disposability generally refers to the ability to
stockpile or discard or dispose of unwanted commodities. The private
disposal cost distinguishes two types of disposability of interest. Strong
disposability refers to the ability to dispose of an unwanted commodity
with no private cost. Weak disposability refers to the ability to dispose
of an unwanted commodity at positive private cost. A treatment of the
two types of disposability is most usefully developed in terms of the
input sets and output sets introduced in Section 2.1.

It is useful to divide the sets introduced in Section 2.1 into *More Sets*
(*MS*) and *Less Sets* (*LS*) . More sets have their feasible vectors bounded
below, and include the input sets $L(u), DL(u)$ and $IL(r/R)$. Less sets
have their feasible vectors bounded above, and include the output sets
$P(x), DP(x)$ and $IP(p/Q)$. We are interested in certain subsets of the
lower boundaries of *MS* and the upper boundaries of *LS*. To that end
we first introduce the notions of weak and strong disposability of both
MS and *LS*.

Regarding a more set, if $m \in MS \subseteq \Re_+^N, 0 \notin MS$, and $\lambda m \in MS, \lambda \geq$
1, we say that *MS* exhibits *Weak Disposability*. If $m \in MS$ and $m' \geq m$
$\implies m' \in MS$ we say that *MS* exhibits *Strong Disposability*. Clearly
strong disposability implies weak disposability, but the converse does
not hold.

Strong disposability is also termed free disposability, and if the more
set is an input set, strong disposability models the situation in which
inputs can be increased without reducing output. This excludes "upward
sloping" isoquants and noneconomic regions. If, however, one wishes to
explicitly model congestion or noneconomic regions, weak disposability
but not strong disposability of inputs is appropriate since "backward
bending" isoquants are feasible. Disposability of *MS* is illustrated in
Figure 2.11.

Regarding a less set, if $\ell \in LS \subseteq \Re_+^M, LS \neq \{0\}$, and $\theta\ell \in LS, 0 <$
$\theta \leq 1$, we say that *LS* exhibits *Weak Disposability*. If $\ell \in LS$ and
$0 \leq \ell' \leq \ell \implies \ell' \in LS$ we say that *LS* exhibits *Strong Disposability*.

Suppose a less set is an output set as in Section 2.1. Then if some
outputs are "bads" one should not impose strong or free disposability
of outputs on the technology, because then a firm may dispose of such
outputs without opportunity cost. When "bads" are a part of the production technology and are not to be freely disposed or emitted, then

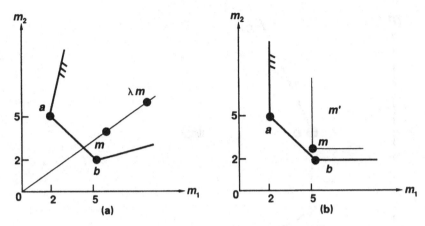

Fig. 2.11. *Disposability Properties of More Sets*

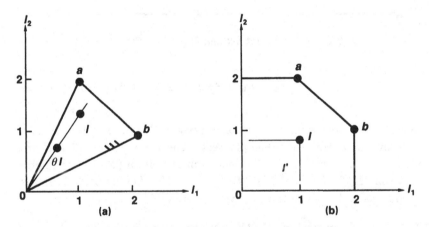

Fig. 2.12. *Disposability Properties of Less Sets*

weak (and not strong) disposability of outputs is appropriate, since weak disposability allows for "costly" disposal. These notions are illustrated in Figure 2.12.

We are now prepared to introduce three important subsets of the boundaries of more sets and less sets. These subsets form the reference sets relative to which efficiency is measured.

(2.3.1)   **Definition**: The *MS Isoquant Set* is $Isoq\ MS = \{m \in MS : \lambda m \notin MS$ if $\lambda < 1\}$. The *MS Weak Efficiency Set* is $WEff\ MS = \{m \in MS : m' \overset{*}{\geq} m \implies m' \notin MS\}$. The

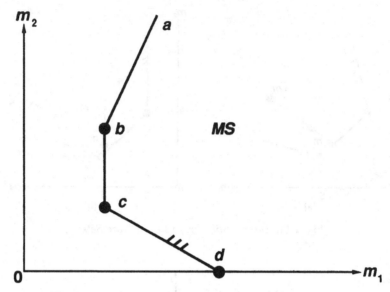

Fig. 2.13. *MS Isoquant Set and MS Weak Efficiency Set*

MS *Efficiency Set* is $Eff\ MS = \{m \in MS : m' \leq m \implies$ $m' \notin MS\}$.

Since all MS are assumed to be nonempty and closed, $Isoq\ MS, WEff$ MS and $Eff\ MS$ are nonempty sets. The three subsets of MS are illustrated in Figure 2.13. It is clear from Definition (2.3.1) and Figure 2.13 that $Eff\ MS \subseteq WEff\ MS \subseteq Isoq\ MS$. The next result shows conditions under which the last two subsets of MS coincide.

(2.3.2)   **Proposition:** If MS exhibits strong disposability, then $Isoq\ MS = WEff\ MS$.

Proof: Since in general $WEff\ MS \subseteq Isoq\ MS$, we only have to show that $Isoq\ MS \subseteq WEff\ MS$. Let $m \in Isoq\ MS$ and consider $\{m' : m' \leq m\} \cap MS$. Without loss of generality let $m_n > 0, n = 1, 2, \cdots, k$, and $m_n = 0, n = k+1, \cdots, N$. If there does not exist an $m^\circ \in \{m' : m' \leq m\} \cap MS$, such that $m_n^\circ < m_n, n = 1, 2, \cdots, k$, then $m \in WEff\ MS$ and the Proposition is proved. Thus assume that there exists such an m°. Then $\exists \lambda < 1$, such that $(m^\circ + \Re_+^N) \cap \{\lambda m : \lambda < 1\} \neq \emptyset$. Clearly by strong disposability, $(m^\circ + \Re_+^N) \subseteq MS$, and since $\lambda < 1, m \notin Isoq\ MS$. This contradiction completes the proof.

                                                   Q.E.D.

The following result on weak and strong disposability of MS sets is required in upcoming chapters.

(2.3.3)   **Proposition**: For some data set, suppose $(MS \mid W)$ satisfies weak disposability and $(MS \mid S)$ satisfies strong disposability. Then $Isoq(MS \mid W) \cap WEff(MS \mid S) = WEff(MS \mid W)$.

Proof: Clearly $WEff(MS \mid W) \subseteq WEff(MS \mid S)$, and since $WEff(MS \mid W) \subseteq Isoq(MS \mid W)$ it follows that $WEff(MS \mid W) \subseteq Isoq(MS \mid W) \cap WEff(MS \mid S)$. To prove the converse, suppose $x \in (MS \mid W)$ but $x \notin WEff(MS \mid W)$ and $x \in Isoq(MS \mid W)$. Then $\exists y \in (MS \mid W)$ such that $y \overset{*}{>} x$, thus $x \notin Isoq(MS \mid W) \cap WEff(MS \mid S)$. Hence assume $x \notin WEff(MS \mid W)$ and $x \notin Isoq(MS \mid W)$ but $x \in WEff(MS \mid S)$. Then $\exists \lambda > 1$ such that $\lambda x \in (MS \mid W)$ thus $x \notin WEff(MS \mid S)$.

$$Q.E.D.$$

We provide a final illustration of weak and strong disposability of inputs in Figure 2.14, which expands on ideas developed in Figure 2.11. In Figure 2.14 two inputs are used to produce one output. Starting at point b, an increase in x_1 causes a reduction in output when x_2 is held fixed ($b \longrightarrow c$), or requires an increase in x_2 in order to maintain constant output ($b \longrightarrow d$), and so input x_1 is weakly disposable. Starting at point a, an increase in x_2 can be disposed of freely, without cost calculated as reduced output or increased use of x_1. The generalization of these notions to many inputs and many outputs is straightforward.

(2.3.4)   **Definition**: The *LS Isoquant Set* is $Isoq\ LS = \{\ell \in LS : \theta\ell \notin LS$ if $\theta > 1\}$. The *LS Weak Efficiency Set* is $WEff\ LS = \{\ell \in LS : \ell' \overset{*}{>} \ell \Longrightarrow \ell' \notin LS\}$. The *LS Efficiency Set* is $Eff\ LS = \{\ell \in LS : \ell' \geq \ell \Longrightarrow \ell' \notin LS\}$.

Since all LS are assumed to be nonempty and closed, $Isoq\ LS, WEff\ LS$, and $Eff\ LS$, are nonempty sets. The three subsets of LS are illustrated in Figure 2.15. It is clear from Definition (2.3.4) and Figure 2.15 that $Eff\ LS \subseteq WEff\ LS \subseteq Isoq\ LS$.

(2.3.5)   **Proposition**: If LS exhibits strong disposability, then $Isoq\ LS = WEff\ LS$.

The proof of Proposition (2.3.5) is similar to that of Proposition (2.3.2) and is omitted. Also similar to Proposition (2.3.3) one can prove the following

Production Technology

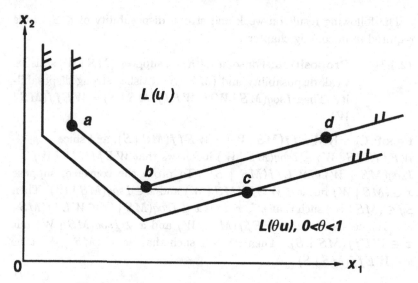

Fig. 2.14. *Weak and Strong Disposability of Inputs*

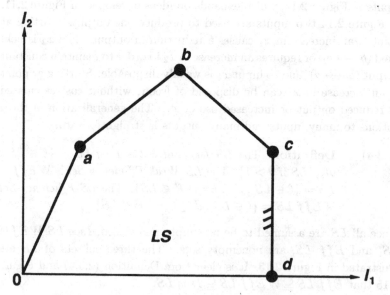

Fig. 2.15. *LS Isoquant Set and LS Weak Efficiency Set*

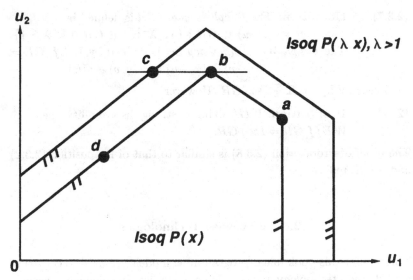

Fig. 2.16. *Weak and Strong Disposability of Outputs*

(2.3.6) **Proposition**: Suppose $(LS \mid W)$ satisfies weak disposability and $(LS \mid S)$ satisfies strong disposability. Then $Isoq(LS \mid W) \cap WEff(LS \mid S) = WEff(LS \mid W)$.

Weak and strong output disposability are illustrated in Figure 2.16, in which input x is used to produce two outputs. Starting at point b, a reduction in u_1 requires a reduction in u_2 when input is held fixed ($b \longrightarrow d$), or requires an increase in input usage to maintain the same output of u_2 ($b \longrightarrow c$). Hence output u_1 is weakly disposable; to dispose of it from b is costly, either in terms of sacrificed u_2 or in terms of increased input requirements. Starting at point a, however, a reduction in u_2 can be achieved at no cost to the producer, either in terms of sacrificed u_1 or in terms of increased input requirement, and so output u_2 is strongly disposable.

It is also possible to analyze disposability notions in terms of the graph of the technology. The graph GR is said to exhibit *Weak Disposability of Inputs and Outputs* if $(x, u) \in GR$ and $(\lambda x, \lambda^{-1} u) \in GR$ when $\lambda \geqq 1$. The graph exhibits *Strong Disposability of Inputs and Outputs* if $(x, u) \in GR$ and $y \geqq x, 0 \leqq v \leqq u \implies (y, v) \in GR$. Thus disposability of the graph is defined in terms of the more set $L(u)$ and the less set $P(x)$.

As in the cases of more sets and less sets, it is useful to define two subsets of the boundary of the graph of the technology.

(2.3.7)   **Definition**: The *Graph Isoquant Set* is defined by
$Isoq\ GR = \{(x, u) \in GR : (\lambda x, \lambda^{-1} u) \notin GR, 0 < \lambda \leq 1\}$.
The *Graph Weak Efficiency Set* is defined by $WEffGR = \{(x, u) \in GR : (y, -v) \overset{*}{<} (x, -u) \Longrightarrow (y, v) \notin GR\}$.

Obviously $WEff\ GR \subsetneq Isoq\ GR$. However

(2.3.8)   **Proposition**: If GR exhibits strong disposability, then
$WEff\ GR = Isoq\ GR$.

The proof of Proposition (2.3.8) is similar to that of Proposition (2.3.2) and is omitted.

2.4   Piecewise Technologies

Throughout this book linear programming models are used to construct a production technology and to calculate a variety of efficiency measures relative to that technology. All the efficiency measures have in common the feature that they gauge the efficiency of individual producers relative to a 'best practice' frontier constructed as a piecewise linear envelopment of the data generated by the set of all producers in the reference group. The best practice frontier is a subset of the (piecewise linear) boundary of the technology as represented by GR, or by one of the three MS sets, or by one of the three LS sets. The purpose of this section is to show how to construct piecewise linear envelopments of the various representations of technology introduced in Section 2.1.

We begin with the basic notation and terminology. Suppose we observe the activities of J producers, each using N inputs to produce M outputs. Let M denote the $(J \times M)$ matrix of observed outputs, and let N denote the $(J \times N)$ matrix of observed inputs. Individual elements of M, denoted u_{jm}, measure the quantity of the mth output produced by the jth producer, while individual elements of N, denoted x_{jn}, measure the employment level of the nth input by the jth producer.

The matrices M and N are assumed to satisfy

(i) $u_{jm} \geq 0, x_{jn} \geq 0$,

(ii) $\sum_{j=1}^{J} u_{jm} > 0, m = 1, 2, \cdots, M$,

(iii) $\sum_{n=1}^{N} x_{jn} > 0, j = 1, 2, \cdots, J$,

(iv) $\quad \sum_{j=1}^{J} x_{jn} > 0, n = 1, 2, \cdots, N,$

(v) $\quad \sum_{m=1}^{M} u_{jm} > 0, j = 1, 2, \cdots, J.$ $\qquad$ (2.4.1)

Assumption (i) requires each producer to use nonnegative amounts of each input to produce nonnegative amounts of each output. Assumptions (ii) and (iv) require aggregate production of positive amounts of every output, and aggregate employment of positive amounts of every input. Assumptions (iii) and (v) require each producer to employ a positive amount of at least one input, and to produce a positive amount of at least one output. Note that the requirements on the input and output matrices allow for some elements to be zero.

Finally, let the vector $z = (z_1, z_2, \cdots, z_J) \in \Re_+^J$ denote the intensity levels at which each of the J activities are (or might conceivably be) conducted. This vector enables us to shrink or expand individual observed activities, for the purpose of constructing unobserved but nonetheless feasible activities. It thus provides weights which facilitate the construction of the linear segments of the piecewise linear boundary of the technology.

We now introduce the piecewise linear representation of the graph of the technology. We begin by assuming that technology satisfies both constant returns to scale and strong disposability of inputs and outputs. Thus

$$(GR \mid C, S) = \{(x, u) : \quad u \le zM, zN \le x, z \in \Re_+^J\} \qquad (2.4.2)$$

$$= \{(x, u) : \quad u_m \le \sum_{j=1}^{J} z_j u_{jm}, m = 1, 2, \cdots, M,$$

$$\sum_{j=1}^{J} z_j x_{jn} \le x_n, n = 1, 2, \cdots, N, z \in \Re_+^J\},$$

where C denotes constant returns to scale and S denotes strong disposability.

In order to guarantee existence of various efficiency measures to be calculated relative to GR, we need to ensure that this set is closed.

(2.4.3) **Proposition:** $(GR \mid C, S)$ is closed.

Proof: Let x^ℓ and u^ℓ be sequences in $(GR \mid C, S)$ such that $x^\ell \longrightarrow x^\circ$ and $u^\ell \longrightarrow u^\circ$. Then there exists a sequence z^ℓ such that $u^\ell \le z^\ell M$, $z^\ell N \le x^\ell$ for all ℓ. Since x^ℓ and u^ℓ are convergent, the sequences are bounded. This implies that there exists $(\overline{x}, \overline{u})$ such that $\overline{u} \leq u^\ell$ and $\overline{x} \geq x^\ell$ for all ℓ. Consider the set $\{z \in \Re_+^J : \overline{u} \leq zM, zN \leq \overline{x}\}$. This set is compact, which implies that there exists a subsequence z^{ℓ_k} such that $z^{\ell_k} \longrightarrow z^\circ$ and $\overline{u} \leq z^{\ell_k}M, z^{\ell_k}N \leq \overline{x}$ for all ℓ_k. Since zM and zN are continuous functions, $u^\circ \leq z^\circ M, z^\circ N \leq x^\circ$.

$$Q.E.D.$$

We now introduce the piecewise linear construction of the output set representation of the same constant returns, strong disposability technology. Consider

$$P(x \mid C, S) = \{u : u \leq zM, zN \leq x, z \in \Re_+^J\} \qquad (2.4.4)$$

$$= \{u : u_m \leq \sum_{j=1}^{J} z_j u_{jm}, m = 1, 2, \cdots, M,$$

$$\sum_{j=1}^{J} z_j x_{jn} \leq x_n, n = 1, 2, \cdots, N, z \in \Re_+^J\}.$$

It is clear that (2.4.4) and (2.4.2) share the same constraints, as they must in light of Definitions (2.1.5) and (2.1.6) and Proposition (2.1.8). Consequently we can state the following

(2.4.5)   **Proposition:** $P(x \mid C, S)$ is closed and bounded.

Proof: Closure follows from the proof of Proposition (2.4.3). Boundedness follows from the nature of the inequalities in the constraints of (2.4.4) and from the fact that all elements of M and N are finite, and that no row or column of either M or N consists solely of zeros.

$$Q.E.D.$$

The third price-independent representation of technology is the input set. The piecewise linear formulation of the input set representation of the same constant returns, strong disposability technology is given by

$$L(u \mid C, S) = \{x : u \leq zM, zN \leq x, z \in \Re_+^J\} \qquad (2.4.6)$$

$$= \{x : u_m \leq \sum_{j=1}^{J} z_j u_{jm}, m = 1, 2, \cdots, M,$$

$$\sum_{j=1}^{J} z_j x_{jn} \leq x_n, n = 1, 2, \cdots, N, z \in \Re_+^J\}.$$

In light of Definitions (2.1.5) and (2.1.7), and Propositions (2.1.8), (2.4.3), and (2.4.5), we can state without proof the following

(2.4.7)   **Proposition:** $L(u \mid C, S)$ is closed and
       $Eff\ L(u \mid C, S)$ is bounded.

Next we introduce piecewise linear formulations of the indirect output and input sets, which are merely modifications of $P(x)$ and $L(u)$ restricted to satisfy cost and revenue constraints, respectively. Recall from (2.1.17) and (2.1.18) that the cost indirect output set $IP(p/Q)$ can be expressed as

$$IP(p/Q) = \{u : u \in P(x), px \leq Q\}, \tag{2.4.8}$$

where $p \in \Re_{++}^N$ is an input price vector and $Q \in \Re_{++}$ is target cost. By using (2.2.4) this set is constructed in piecewise linear form for a constant returns, strong disposability technology as

$$IP((p/Q) \mid C, S) = \{u : u \leq zM, zN \leq x, z \in \Re_+^J, \tag{2.4.9}$$
$$(p/Q)x \leq 1\}$$
$$= \{u : u_m \leq \sum_{j=1}^{J} z_j u_{jm}, m = 1, 2, \cdots, M,$$
$$\sum_{j=1}^{J} z_j x_{jn} \leq x_n, n = 1, 2, \cdots, N, z \in \Re_+^J,$$
$$\sum_{n=1}^{N} (p_n/Q)x_n \leq 1\}$$

where (p/Q) is the normalized (by target cost) input price vector. The first three constraints in (2.4.9) are the same as the constraints used to construct $P(x \mid C, S)$ in (2.4.4). The final constraint in (2.4.9) forms a compact set. These facts, in conjunction with the proof of Proposition (2.4.5), provide the proof of

(2.4.10)   **Proposition**: $IP((p/Q) \mid C, S)$ is closed and bounded.

We now construct a revenue-indirect input set in similar fashion. From (2.1.11) and (2.1.12) we have

$$IL(r/R) = \{x : x \in L(u), ru \geq R\}, \tag{2.4.11}$$

where $r \in \Re_+^M, r \neq 0$, is an output price vector and $R \in \Re_{++}$ is desired revenue. The piecewise linear formulation of (2.4.11) satisfying constant returns and strong disposability is given by

$$IL((r/R) \mid C, S) = \{x : u \leq zM, zN \leq x, z \in \Re_+^J, \tag{2.4.12}$$
$$(r/R)u \geq 1\}$$
$$= \{x : u_m \leq \sum_{j=1}^{J} z_j u_{jm}, m = 1, 2, \cdots, M,$$

$$\sum_{j=1}^{J} z_j x_{jn} \leqq x_n, n = 1, 2, \cdots, N, z \in \Re_+^J,$$

$$\sum_{m=1}^{M} (r_m/R) u_m \geqq 1\}$$

where (r/R) is a normalized (by desired revenue) output price vector. Previously developed arguments can be applied to prove the following

(2.4.13)   **Proposition**: $IL((r/R) \mid C, S)$ is closed and
$Eff\ IL((r/R)|C, S)$ is bounded.

Next we introduce piecewise linear formulations of the dual output set and the dual input set. Information required for the dual output set $DP(x)$ consists of data on revenue, output prices and input quantities. Denote the vector of normalized output prices for producer j as $\hat{r}^j = (r^j/R^j) = (r_{j1}/R^j, r_{j2}/R^j, \cdots, r_{jM}/R^j), j = 1, 2, \cdots, J$, and call the matrix of normalized output prices DM (i.e., the "dual" of the output matrix M), where DM is of dimension $(J \times M)$. Denote the vector of reciprocal input quantities for producer j as $(1/x^j) = (1/x_{j1}, 1/x_{j2}, \cdots, 1/x_{jN}), j = 1, \cdots, J$, and call the matrix of reciprocal inputs N^- (i.e., the "reciprocal" of N), where N^- is of dimension $(J \times N)$. The matrix N^- is needed to construct $DP(x)$ as an LS rather than an MS set, and its construction requires $x_{jn} > 0$ for all $j = 1, \cdots, J$ and for all $n = 1, \cdots, N$.

We are now prepared to write the piecewise linear formulation of the dual output set for a technology satisfying constant returns and strong disposability as

$$DP(x \mid C, S) = \{\hat{r} : \hat{r} \leqq zDM, zN^- \leqq (1/x), z \in \Re_+^J\} \quad (2.4.14)$$

$$= \{\hat{r} : \hat{r}_m \leqq \sum_{j=1}^{J} z_j \hat{r}_{jm}, m = 1, 2, \cdots, M,$$

$$\sum_{j=1}^{J} z_j/x_n \leqq 1/x_{jn}, n = 1, 2, \cdots, N, z \in \Re_+^J\}.$$

Note the structural similarity between $DP(x \mid C, S)$ and $P(x \mid C, S)$ in (2.4.4). Normalized output prices and output quantities switch roles, as do reciprocal inputs and inputs. Since we will be seeking maxima over this set in the calculation of dual price efficiency measures, we need the following

(2.4.15)   **Proposition**: $DP(x \mid C, S)$ is closed and bounded.

The proof is similar to the proof of Proposition (2.4.5) and is omitted.

Construction of the dual input set $DL(u)$ requires information on cost, input prices, and output quantities. Denote the vector of normalized input prices as $atp^j = (p_j/Q^j) = (p_{j1}/Q^j, p_{j2}/Q^j, \cdots, p_{jN}/Q^j), j = 1, \cdots, J$, and write the $(J \times N)$ matrix of normalized input prices $\boldsymbol{DN}$. Denote the vector of reciprocal output quantities as $(1/u^j) = (1/u_{j1}, 1/u_{j2}, \cdots, 1/u_{jM}), j = 1, \cdots, J$, and write the $(J \times M)$ matrix of reciprocal outputs $\boldsymbol{M}^-$. The matrix $\boldsymbol{M}^-$ is required to define $DL(u)$ as an MS set, and its construction requires that $u_{jm} > 0$ for all $j = 1, \cdots, J$ and for all $m = 1, \cdots, M$.

The piecewise linear formulation of the dual input set for a technology satisfying constant returns and strong disposability can now be expressed as

$$DL(u \mid C, S) = \{\hat{p} : (1/u) \leqq z\boldsymbol{M}^-, z\boldsymbol{DN} \leqq \hat{p}, \qquad (2.4.16)$$
$$z \in \Re_+^J\}$$
$$= \{\hat{p} : (1/u_m) \leqq \sum_{j=1}^J z_j/u_{jm}, m = 1, 2, \cdots, M,$$
$$\sum_{j=1}^J z_j\hat{p}_{jn} \leqq \hat{p}_n, n = 1, 2, \cdots, N, z \in \Re_+^J\}.$$

Since we will be seeking minima over this set in order to calculate dual price efficiency measures, we need the following

(2.4.17)   **Proposition:** $DL(u \mid C, S)$ is closed.

The proof is similar to the proof of Proposition (2.4.5) and is omitted.

Up to this point all seven of the piecewise linear formulations of production technology have been restricted to satisfy both constant returns to scale and strong disposability of inputs and outputs. Since many of the efficiency measures to be developed require less restrictive technologies, we now show how to relax each of the two assumptions.

We begin with returns to scale, and we employ the graph as the representation of technology. Once it is seen how the piecewise linear formulation of the graph is affected by changing assumptions concerning returns to scale, it will be apparent how piecewise linear formulations of other representations of technology are affected.

Definition (2.2.1) characterizes the scale notions of *CRS*, *NIRS*, and *NDRS* in terms of the graph of the technology. If a technology satisfies none of these conditions globally, because it satisfies at least two of them in different regions, the technology is said to exhibit *Variable Returns to Scale* (*VRS*). We are particularly interested in *CRS*, *NIRS*, and *VRS*. These three scale properties can be imposed on the piecewise linear formulation of the graph of the technology very easily by varying the restrictions on the intensity vector z. Assuming strong disposability of inputs and outputs, the three formulations are

$$(GR \mid C, S) = \{(x, u) : u \leq zM, zN \leq x, z \in \Re_+^J\}, \qquad (2.4.18)$$

$$(GR \mid N, S) = \{(x, u) : u \leq zM, zN \leq x, z \in \Re_+^J,$$

$$\sum_{j=1}^{J} z_j \leq 1\},$$

$$(GR \mid V, S) = \{(x, u) : u \leq zM, zN \leq x, z \in \Re_+^J, \sum_{j=1}^{J} z_j = 1\}.$$

Here N stands for *NIRS* and V for *VRS*. Heuristically, in the *CRS* case the restriction on z allows observed activities to be radially expanded and contracted to form other feasible activities. In the *NIRS* case z is further restricted to prohibit unbounded expansion of observed activities, while in the *VRS* case radial expansion is restricted and radial contraction to the origin is prohibited.

To illustrate the distinctions among *CRS*, *NIRS*, and *VRS*, suppose we consider the following example involving two producers, each using a single input to produce a single output

$$M = \begin{bmatrix} 1 \\ 2 \end{bmatrix}, N = \begin{bmatrix} 2 \\ 5 \end{bmatrix}, z = (z_a, z_b).$$

The piecewise linear graphs $(GR \mid C, S), (GR \mid N, S)$ and $(GR \mid V, S)$ are portrayed in Figure 2.17. Point a denotes the activity of the first producer, and point b denotes the activity of the second producer. In $(GR \mid C, S)$, the intensity variables can take on any nonnegative values, including zero. Thus both activities a and b can be scaled (radially) up or down. Consequently if *CRS* is assumed, the feasible activity b is inefficient in a sense to be made clear in later chapters, although it is clear now that activity a is on the boundary of $(GR \mid C, S)$ and activity b is interior to the boundary of $(GR \mid C, S)$. In $(GR \mid N, S)$, however, the elements of the nonnegative intensity variables cannot sum to more than one. Thus activities a and b can be contracted feasibly, but not expanded feasibly. They can be combined. Consequently in the *NIRS* case both a and b are efficient in a sense and both are located on the boundary of $(GR \mid N, S)$. Finally, in $(GR \mid V, S)$, the components of the nonnegative intensity variables must sum to one. Activities cannot be expanded or contracted radially without limit, and the feasible set of activities consists of the set of all convex combinations of observed activities a and b, both of which are located on the boundary of $(GR \mid V, S)$, as well

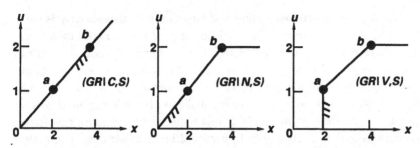

Fig. 2.17. *Piecewise Linear Graphs for* CRS, NIRS, *and* VRS *Technologies*

as extensions southeast of those points (a consequence of the inequalities in the constraints). Note finally that $(GR \mid V, S) \subseteqq (GR \mid N, S) \subseteqq (GR \mid C, S)$.

We now turn our attention to disposability, and we first use the graph to represent technology in order to summarize disposability in a compact way. We will subsequently illustrate these notions on the more sets and the less sets as well. Constant returns to scale is assumed, although *NIRS* or *VRS* can be used instead, simply by varying restrictions on z. The difference between strong and weak disposability is independent of restrictions on z. It depends instead on the nature of the relationship between hypothetical but feasible outputs and observed outputs (i.e., between u and zM), and on the nature of the relationship between hypothetical but feasible inputs and observed inputs (i.e., between x and zN).

Piecewise linear formulations of the graph of a *CRS* technology having four different disposability features – strong disposability of outputs and inputs, weak disposability of outputs and strong disposability of inputs, strong disposability of outputs and weak disposability of inputs, and weak disposability of outputs and inputs – are summarized in

$$(GR \mid C, S) = \{(x, u) : u \leqq zM, zN \leqq x, z \in \Re_+^J\},$$
$$(GR \mid C, SW) = \{(x, u) : u = \mu zM, zN \leqq x, 0 \leqq \mu \leqq 1,$$
$$z \in \Re_+^J\},$$
$$(GR \mid C, WS) = \{(x, u) : u \leqq zM, zN = \sigma x, 0 < \sigma \leqq 1,$$
$$z \in \Re_+^J\},$$
$$(GR \mid C, W) = \{(x, u) : u = \mu zM, zN = \sigma x, 0 \leqq \mu \leqq 1,$$
$$0 < \sigma \leqq 1, z \in \Re_+^J\}, \qquad (2.4.19)$$

respectively.

The difference between strong and weak output disposability is captured by the parameter μ; the condition $u \leqq zM$ is replaced by a more restrictive condition $u = \mu zM, 0 \leqq \mu \leqq 1$. Figure 2.12(a) illustrates. The entire feasible set is described by μzM, $0 \leqq \mu \leqq 1$. For points on the isoquant of this set (in this case the segment ab), $\mu = 1$. The difference between strong and weak input disposability is captured by the parameter σ; the condition $zN \leqq x$ is replaced by the more restrictive conditions $zN = \sigma x, 0 < \sigma \leqq 1$. Figure 2.11(a) illustrates. The entire feasible set is described by $zN/\sigma, 0 < \sigma \leqq 1$. For points on the isoquant of this set (in this case ab), $\sigma = 1$.

To illustrate the difference between strong and weak disposability of inputs we consider the following example involving two producers, each using two inputs to produce one output

$$M = \begin{bmatrix} 1 \\ 1 \end{bmatrix}, N = \begin{bmatrix} 2 & 5 \\ 5 & 2 \end{bmatrix}, z = (z_a, z_b).$$

If inputs and outputs are strongly disposable we use either $(GR \mid C, S)$ or $L(u \mid C, S)$, for which the restrictions for the piecewise linear representation are identical. Refer to panel (b) of Figure 2.11, and let observations a and b correspond to the information contained in N above. The line segment ab represents the set of all convex combinations of points a and b. The constraint $zN \leqq x$ in $(GR \mid C, S)$ allows for vertical and horizontal extensions of a and b and their convex combinations. Thus all input combinations northeast of (ab) are feasible. If inputs are weakly disposable the constraint $zN = \sigma x, 0 < \sigma \leqq 1$ in $(GR \mid C, W)$ prohibits unlimited vertical and horizontal extensions of a and b and their convex combinations. In panel (a) of Figure 2.11 only radial extensions of a and b and their convex combinations are feasible. Clearly some input combinations that are feasible under strong disposability of inputs are not feasible under weak disposability of inputs.

Weak and strong disposability of outputs can be treated in a similar way. In this case we use either $(GR \mid C, S)$ or $P(x \mid C, S)$ in conjunction with Figure 2.12 and the data contained in M below. By varying output constraints from $u \leqq zM$ to $u = \mu zM, 0 \leqq \mu \leqq 1$, we reveal output combinations that are feasible under strong disposability of outputs and not feasible under weak disposability of outputs.

$$M = \begin{bmatrix} 1 & 2 \\ 2 & 1 \end{bmatrix}, N = \begin{bmatrix} 2 \\ 2 \end{bmatrix}, z = (z_a, z_b).$$

We demonstrate next that the piecewise linear technology discussed above is a particular member in a wider class of piecewise technologies.

As before, let $z = (z_1, z_2, \cdots, z_J)$ denote the intensity vector, and let u_{jm} and x_{jn} denote the mth output produced and the nth input employed by the jth producer, respectively. Here we assume that u_{jm} and x_{jn} are positive for all j, m, and n. The graph of the general piecewise technology with variable returns to scale is written as

$$[GR \mid \delta, \gamma] = \{(x, u) : u_m \leq \left(\sum_{j=1}^{J} z_j (u_{jm})^{\delta} \right)^{1/\delta}, m = 1, \cdots, M,$$
$$\left(\sum_{j=1}^{J} z_j (x_{jn})^{\gamma} \right)^{1/\gamma} \leq x_n, n = 1, \cdots, N,$$
$$\sum_{j=1}^{J} z_j = 1, z \in \Re_+^J, \delta \text{ and } \gamma \in \Re\}.$$

(2.4.20)

This model consists of two parts: the output part which is characterized by a *Constant Elasticity of Transformation* formula and the input part which is characterized by a *Constant Elasticity of Substitution* formula. We note that the $(GR \mid V, S)$ model given by expression (2.4.18) equals $[GR \mid \delta = 1, \gamma = 1]$ and that (2.4.20) exhibits variable returns to scale and strong disposability of inputs and outputs. If $\delta \geq 1$ and $\gamma \leq 1$ then $[GR \mid \delta, \gamma]$ is a convex set, and so are its input sets and its output sets.

We may derive additional piecewise models by varying the two parameters δ and γ. In particular if $\delta \longrightarrow 0$ and $\gamma \longrightarrow 0$, a piecewise *Cobb–Douglas* model is obtained, namely

$$[GR \mid 0, 0] = \{(x, u) : \ln u_m \leq \sum_{j=1}^{J} z_j \ln u_{jm}, m = 1, 2, \cdots, M,$$
$$\sum_{j=1}^{J} z_j \ln x_{jn} \leq \ln x_n, n = 1, 2, \cdots, N,$$
$$\sum_{j=1}^{J} z_j = 1, z \in \Re_+^J\}.$$

(2.4.21)

This model has convex input sets, but its output sets are not convex, and so $[GR \mid 0, 0]$ is not a convex set.

There is one more special case that can be derived from (2.4.20). This is called the *FDH (Free Disposal Hull)* model. Again, let $\delta = \gamma = 1$ and let $z_j = 1$ for some $j \varepsilon \{1, \cdots, J\}$ and $z_i = 0$, $i \neq j$. Then (2.4.20) becomes

$$\{(x, u) : x_{nj} \leq x_n, n = 1, \cdots, N, u_{mj} \geq u_m, m = 1, \cdots, M, j = 1, \cdots, J\}.$$

(2.4.22)

The *FDH* model exhibits strong disposability of inputs and outputs. It imposes no restriction on returns to scale. Its input sets, its outputs sets, and consequently its graph, are non-convex.

2.5   Construction of Artificial Data for Computational Examples

One of our objectives is to provide computational examples that illustrate the construction of various representations of technology and the measurement of various types of efficiency relative to the constructed technology. We use a standard linear programming package to construct a technology and calculate efficiency, and we use artificial data. In this section we describe how the artificial data set is constructed.

The benchmark technology we use to construct the artificial data is a technology characterized by *Constant Elasticity of Transformation* (CET) on the output side and log-linear *Cobb–Douglas* (CD) on the input side. If we express *Isoq GR* as the function $g(u, x) = h(u) - f(x) = 0$, where

$$h(u) = (\frac{1}{2}u_1^2 + \frac{1}{2}u_2^2)^{1/2}, \qquad \text{(CET)} \qquad (2.5.1)$$

$$f(x) = (x_1^{1/2}x_2^{1/2})^\delta, \delta > 0, \qquad \text{(CD)} \qquad (2.5.2)$$

then varying the parameter δ allows for variable returns to scale (*VRS*). This form is consistent with the required convexity of $L(u)$ and $P(x)$.

We constructed a sample of 20 observations on (u_1, u_2, x_1, x_2). These appear in Table 2.1, collected into four groups of five observations. For the first group of "small" producers $h(u) = 25, f(x) = 25$ and $\delta = 0.898$. For the next two groups of "medium-size" producers, $h(u) = f(x) = 50$ or 75 and $\delta = 1.000$. The last group of "large-size" producers, $h(a) = 100, f(x) = 144$, and $\delta = 0.927$. Thus the artificial technology exhibits regions of increasing, constant and decreasing returns to scale. Isoquants *Isoq L(h(u))* $= f(x)$ and *Isoq P(f(x))* $= h(u)$ are displayed graphically in Figures 2.18 and 2.19. The graph of this CET-CD technology is displayed in Figure 2.20.

Throughout the book all artificial data used to construct other representations of technology will include the artificial data collected in Table 2.1 and illustrated in Figures 2.18–2.20. Other artificial data are required as well, however, including data on input prices and cost, and output prices and revenue, and these data must be consistent with the quantity data in Table 2.1. Consistency is assured as follows. In generating artificial input price data we begin by deriving the cost function consistent with the technology described in Equations (2.5.1) and (2.5.2). This cost function is self-dual, and so

$$Q(u, p) = 2(\frac{1}{2}u_1^2 + \frac{1}{2}u_2^2)^{1/2\delta}(p_1p_2)^{1/2}. \qquad (2.5.3)$$

Using Shephard's Lemma to solve for $x_1(u,p), x_2(u,p)$ and inverting to solve for input prices gives

$$p_1 = Q/2x_1, \qquad\qquad p_2 = Q/2x_2. \qquad (2.5.4)$$

Without loss of generality we specify $Q = 36$ or 50 or 75 or 144. The 20 observations on cost and input prices are collected in Table 2.2.

We also use the revenue function to construct output prices. The revenue function consistent with the CET-CD technology described in Equations (2.5.1) and (2.5.2) is

$$R(x,r) = (2x_1^\delta x_2^\delta)^{1/2}(r_1^2 + r_2^2)^{1/2} \qquad (2.5.5)$$

from which output supply equations may be derived. Inverting them to solve for output prices gives

$$r_1 = u_1 R/(2x_1^\delta x_2^\delta), \qquad\qquad r_2 = u_2 R/(2x_1^\delta x_2^\delta). \qquad (2.5.6)$$

Setting $R = 25$ or 50 or 75 or 100 generates 20 observations on output prices consistent with the input quantity data and output quantity data in Table 2.1. These revenue and output price data appear in Table 2.2.

The artificial data in Tables 2.1 and 2.2 are used throughout the text to illustrate the calculation of various efficiency measures.

2.6   References to the Literature

The direct models of production were developed by Shephard (1953, 1970) and extended by Färe (1988a). The indirect models of production were also developed by Shephard (1974), and have been examined in detail by Färe and Grosskopf (1990a). Duality theorems and envelope properties may be found in the above references, and in McFadden (1978), Blackorby, Primont, and Russell (1978), Diewert (1982), and Färe and Primont (1990).

During the past decade a huge literature has developed exploring economies of size in multi-output production. It is convenient to decompose "size" into scale and diversification. An early analysis of economies of scale by Hall (1973) has been followed by Panzar and Willig (1977); by Färe, Grosskopf, and Lovell (1986, 1987a) and Fukuyama (1987), who focus on various dual representations of scale economies; and also by Färe and Mitchell (1990), who focus exclusively on the meaning of homotheticity in multi-output production. A pioneering analysis of economies of diversification by Pfouts (1961) has been sadly neglected. A very restricted form of diversification has come to be known as economies of scope, and is analyzed in detail in Baumol, Panzar, and Willig (1982).

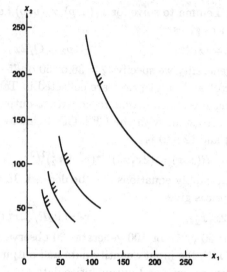

Fig. 2.18. *Isoq L(h(u)) for the CET-CD Technology*

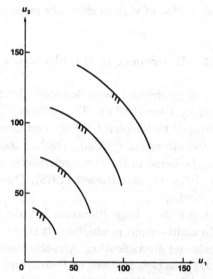

Fig. 2.19. *Isoq P(f(x)) for the CET-CD Technology*

Table 2.1. *Artificial Data Set: Input Quantities and Output Quantities*

Activity	x_1	x_2	u_1	u_2
1	36	36	25	25
2	28.8	45	30	18.71
3	21.6	60	20	29.15
4	19.98	65	15	32.02
5	43.2	30	12	33.26
6	50	50	50	50
7	45	55.56	40	58.31
8	60	41.67	60	37.42
9	30	83.33	30	64.03
10	70	35.71	20	67.82
11	75	75	75	75
12	45	125	30	101.7
13	60	93.75	50	93.54
14	105	53.57	80	69.64
15	85	66.18	90	56.12
16	144	144	100	100
17	115.2	180	115	82.31
18	86.4	240	80	116.62
19	172.8	120	65	125.6
20	201.6	102.86	60	128.06

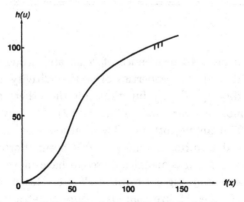

Fig. 2.20. *GR of the CET-CD Technology*

Table 2.2. *Artificial Data Set: Cost, Input Prices, Revenue and Output Prices*

Activity	Q	p_1	p_2	R	r_1	r_2
1	36	0.50000	0.50000	25	0.50088	0.50088
2	36	0.62500	0.40000	25	0.60105	0.37486
3	36	0.83333	0.30000	25	0.40070	0.58402
4	36	0.90090	0.24692	25	0.29996	0.64032
5	36	0.41667	0.60000	25	0.24042	0.66637
6	50	0.50000	0.50000	50	0.50000	0.50000
7	50	0.55556	0.44996	50	0.39997	0.58305
8	50	0.41667	0.59995	50	0.59995	0.37417
9	50	0.83333	0.30001	50	0.30001	0.64033
10	50	0.35714	0.70008	50	0.20002	0.67828
11	75	0.50000	0.50000	75	0.50000	0.50000
12	75	0.83333	0.30000	75	0.20000	0.67800
13	75	0.62500	0.40000	75	0.33333	0.62360
14	75	0.35714	0.70002	75	0.53335	0.46428
15	75	0.44118	0.56664	75	0.59997	0.37411
16	144	0.50000	0.50000	100	0.49816	0.49816
17	144	0.62500	0.40000	100	0.57288	0.41003
18	144	0.83333	0.30000	100	0.39853	0.58095
19	144	0.41667	0.60000	100	0.32380	0.62568
20	144	0.35714	0.69998	100	0.29889	0.63792

The relationship between economies of scale and economies of scope on the one hand, and the properties of superadditivity of production sets and subadditivity of cost functions on the other, has been explored by Baumol, Panzar, and Willig (1982), Sharkey (1982), and Lloyd (1984, 1989) among others. The mathematical foundations of subadditivity are due to Rosenbaum (1950). Recent efforts to avoid the stringent requirements of economies of scope have moved Färe (1986, 1988b) back toward the original work of Pfouts. Recent empirical applications of economies of size that use nonparametric techniques include Byrnes, Färe, Grosskopf, and Kraft (1987) (Illinois grain farms), Grosskopf, Hayes, and Yaisawarng (1989) (Illinois grain farms again), Ferrier, Grosskopf, Hayes, and Yaisawarng (1990) (banking), Ferrier and Lovell (1990) (banking again), Førsund and Kittelsen (1992) (Norwegian district courts), and Hjalmarsson and Veiderpass (1992) (Swedish electricity distribution).

Most early studies of weak and strong (free) disposability focused on inputs. Borts and Mishan (1962) modeled technologies with backward bending isoquants, and Maxwell (1965) attempted to diminish the practical significance of weak disposability by attributing it to indivisibility and distinguishing indivisibility in purchase from divisibility in use. Sitorus (1966) discussed redundant, but still strongly disposable, inputs in an explicit linear programming framework. McFadden (1978; 8-10) has a nice treatment of weak disposability of inputs, in which he makes the telling point that the standard assumption of strong disposability is invoked more for its analytic convenience than for its economic realism, despite the fact that it is unnecessary for most economic analysis. More recently, Färe and Svensson (1980) have introduced concepts of congestion to characterize technologies in which inputs are not strongly disposable. These ideas have been extended by Färe and Grosskopf (1983a), and Färe, Grosskopf, and Lovell (1983). They have been translated into an analogous problem of output congestion and weak disposability of outputs by Färe, Grosskopf, and Lovell (1985). Evidence of congestion and its effects can be found in the literature on agricultural production (Färe and Jansson (1976)) and traffic flow (Inman (1978) and Färe, Grosskopf, and Yoon (1982)), and there is a large literature on job scheduling and lot sizing in the presence of bottlenecks, queuing and congestion in the management science literature (Yao and Kim (1987)). Nonparametric tests of input and output disposability, and associated nonparametric input and output congestion measures, appear in Färe, Grosskopf, and Lovell (1987b). Empirical applications of these nonparametric tests can be found in Färe, Grosskopf, and Logan (1983) (electric utilities), Byrnes, Färe, and Grosskopf (1984) (coal mining), Färe, Grosskopf, and Pasurka (1986, 1989) (regulated electric utilities), Byrnes, Färe, Grosskopf, and Lovell (1988) (coal mining again), and Färe, Grosskopf, Lovell, and Pasurka (1989) (paper production). In some of these applications the weakly disposable output is an undesirable output such as pollution; see Section 8.3 for a model of this problem.

Piecewise linear representations, or activity analysis models, date back at least to von Neumann (1938 [1945]). Other early presentations are in Koopmans (1951, 1957) and Karlin (1959). Explorations of economies of size within the piecewise linear framework can be found in Afriat (1972), Banker (1984), Banker, Charnes, and Cooper (1984), Färe, Grosskopf, and Lovell (1985), and Grosskopf (1986). Skepticism concerning our ability to correctly identify the nature of scale economies in a piecewise linear model has been expressed by Maindiratta (1990), Chang and Guh (1991), and Banker and Thrall (1992). Weak and strong disposability are modeled within a piecewise linear framework by Shephard (1974) for inputs, and by Grosskopf (1986) and Zhu (1991) for both inputs and outputs.

Piecewise representations of technology that are not necessarily piecewise linear, piecewise log-linear, for example, date back to Charnes, Cooper, Seiford, and Stutz (1982, 1983). They have been further investigated by Banker and Maindiratta (1986a, 1986b), and strongly criticized by Chang and Guh (1989). The piecewise CET-CES model was introduced by Färe, Grosskopf, and Njinkeu (1988).

The nonparametric models introduced in Chapter 2 and used throughout the book envelop the input–output data, in a piecewise linear fashion, as tightly as possible consistent with the assumptions made concerning scale economies and disposability. Convexity of production sets is a maintained hypothesis. But convexity can also be relaxed, enabling the nonparametric model to envelop the data more closely still. Dugger (1974), citing inspiration from unpublished work of Afriat, constructs piecewise linear technologies that satisfy strong disposability but not convexity, since they are nondecreasing but not necessarily increasing. They take the form of step functions. Later Deprins, Simar, and Tulkens (1984) relaxed Dugger's model with a "free disposal hull" (FDH) model in which only strong disposability of inputs and outputs is imposed. The FDH model is by now widely used, if not universally accepted, and has been applied to Belgian Post Offices by Deprins, Simar, and Tulkens (1984), Tulkens (1986a, 1986b, 1989b), and Thiry and Tulkens (1988), to urban transit in Belgium by Nollet, Thiry, and Tulkens (1988) and Tulkens (1990), to Belgian banks by Respaut (1989) and Tulkens (1990), to Belgian municipalities by Vanden Eeckaut and Tulkens (1989) and Tulkens (1990), and to Belgian courts by Jamar and Tulkens (1990) and Tulkens (1990). An alternative approach to relaxing the convexity postulate in piecewise linear models has been developed by Petersen (1990).

3

Input-Based Efficiency Measurement

3.0 Introduction

In this chapter we model technology with the input correspondence $u \longrightarrow L(u)$. We assume that $x \in L(u)$ and measure production efficiency by calculating where in the input set $L(u)$ the input vector x is located. Thus we take the observed output vector u as given and adopt a resource conservation approach toward efficiency measurement. We refer to this approach as input based, since inputs are the choice variables, and we measure efficiency in terms of maximum feasible shrinkage of an observed input vector, feasibility being determined by the input set $L(u)$.

Shrinkage can be given many interpretations. Throughout most of the chapter shrinkage is accomplished radially, i.e., by an equiproportionate reduction in all inputs. In Section 3.1 input-based efficiency measures that are radial and independent of prices are introduced. We obtain a measure of technical efficiency, and show how it can be decomposed into three components that measure the separate contributions of scale efficiency, congestion of inputs, and "pure" technical efficiency. Each of these measures is calculated relative to the input set $L(u)$ that takes output as given.

In Section 3.2 we introduce input prices and develop a radial, price dependent measure of cost efficiency. This measure is then decomposed into two parts, technical efficiency (which itself has three components) and allocative efficiency. This enables us to attribute potential cost saving to elimination of waste and adjustments to the input mix.

A difficulty with radial measurement of technical efficiency is that a radially shrunken input vector need not necessarily belong to the efficient subset of the input set. That is, a radial measure of technical efficiency projects an input vector onto the isoquant of the input set, and not necessarily onto the (generally smaller) efficient subset of the input set. Since membership in the efficient subset is a compelling notion of technical efficiency, there is reason to develop a measure that projects an input vector onto the efficient subset of the input set. We do this in Section 3.3 by developing a nonradial input-based measure of technical efficiency. It turns out that the measure of cost efficiency is unaffected; only the decomposition of cost efficiency into technical and allocative components is affected by replacing a radial measure of technical efficiency with a nonradial measure.

In Section 3.4 we return to radial input efficiency measurement, and we develop an alternative measure of scale efficiency. In Section 3.1 scale efficiency is measured using data on input quantities and output quantities. In Section 3.4 we assume that data on output quantities and input cost are available. Thus the data requirements are different, and less stringent in the sense that N input quantities are replaced with one cost figure. We conclude this section by comparing the two types of scale efficiency measures.

In Section 3.5 we present a numerical example of the calculation of some of the input-based efficiency measures using the artificial data set introduced in Chapter 2.

3.1   Radial Efficiency Measures Requiring Input Quantity and Output Quantity Data: The Decomposition of Technical Efficiency

The purpose of this section is to obtain and analyze a family of measures of the efficiency of an input vector used to produce an output vector. Since the output vector is considered to be predetermined, by whatever means, the efficiency measures are called "input based" measures, and the appropriate representation of technology is the input set.

Suppose that the input matrix N and the output matrix M are given. The input sets satisfying the strong properties of constant returns to scale and strong disposability of inputs are formed from M and N as (see (2.4.6))

$$L(u \mid C, S) = \{x : u \leqq zM, zN \leqq x, z \in \Re_+^J\}, u \in \Re_+^M. \qquad (3.1.1)$$

We refer to these sets as (C, S) input sets, C for constant returns to scale and S for strong disposability of inputs. That $L(u \mid C, S)$ satisfies these properties is proved in the following:

(3.1.2) **Proposition:** The (C, S) input sets $L(u \mid C, S)$ satisfy

(i) $L(\theta u \mid C, S) = \theta L(u \mid C, S), \theta > 0,$

(ii) $x \geqq y \in L(u \mid C, S) \Longrightarrow x \in L(u \mid C, S).$

Proof: (i) Let $\theta > 0$ and consider

$$
\begin{aligned}
L(\theta u \mid C, S) &= \{x : \theta u \leqq zM, zN \leqq x, z \in \Re_+^J\} \\
&= \theta\{x/\theta : u \leqq (z/\theta)M, (z/\theta)N \leqq x/\theta, \\
&\qquad (z/\theta) \in (1/\theta)\Re_+^J\} \\
&= \theta L(u \mid C, S).
\end{aligned}
$$

(ii) This property follows from the nature of the inequality $zN \leqq x$.

Q.E.D.

Now let (x^j, u^j) represent the input–output vector, or the "activity," of the jth producer. In (3.1.1) we may take $z \in \Re_+^J$ such that $z_i = 1$ if $i = j$ and $z_i = 0$ otherwise, guaranteeing that $x^j \in L(u^j \mid C, S)$. Where in the input set x^j is located, i.e., how close to the lower boundary, is another matter. An indication of the proximity of x^j to the lower boundary of $L(u^j \mid C, S)$ is provided by the following efficiency measure.

(3.1.3) **Definition:** The function

$$F_i(u^j, x^j \mid C, S) = \min\{\lambda : \lambda x^j \in L(u^j \mid C, S)\},$$
$$j = 1, 2, \cdots, J,$$

is called the (C, S) *Input Measure of Technical Efficiency.*

The (C, S) measure $F_i(u^j, x^j \mid C, S)$, which is illustrated in Figure 3.1 for a piecewise linear technology, measures the efficiency of x^j in the production of u^j when technology is assumed to satisfy (C, S). It does so by computing the ratio of the largest feasible contraction of x^j in $L(u^j \mid C, S)$ to itself, i.e., $F_i(u^j, x^j \mid C, S) = \parallel F_i(u^j, x^j \mid C, S) \cdot x^j \parallel$ $/ \parallel x^j \parallel$. The measure $F_i(u^j, x^j \mid C, S)$ is homogeneous of degree -1 in x^j, homogeneous of degree $+1$ in u^j, and consequently homogeneous of degree zero in (u^j, x^j). Its value is bounded by zero and unity, and it attains its upper bound if, and only if, x^j belongs to the weak efficient subset of the (C, S) input set. The measure is also independent of unit of measurement, i.e., if, for example, one changes the measure of labor from labor-hours to labor-years, the measure is not affected. These properties are proved in the following

(3.1.4) **Proposition:** Given $L(u^j \mid C, S)$, then for each
$$j = 1, 2, \cdots, J,$$

$F_i.1 \quad F_i(u^j, \delta x^j \mid C, S) = \delta^{-1} F_i(u^j, x^j \mid C, S), \delta > 0,$

$F_i.2 \quad F_i(\theta u^j, x^j \mid C, S) = \theta F_i(u^j, x^j \mid C, S), \theta > 0,$

$F_i.3 \quad 0 < F_i(u^j, x^j \mid C, S) \leqq 1,$

$F_i.4 \quad x^j \in WEff\, L(u^j \mid C, S) \Longleftrightarrow F_i(u^j, x^j \mid C, S) = 1,$

$F_i.5 \quad F_i(u^j, x^j \mid C, S)$ is independent of unit of measurement.

Proof:

($F_i.1$)
$$F_i(u^j, \delta x^j \mid C, S) = \min\{\lambda : \lambda \delta x^j \in L(u^j \mid C, S)\}$$
$$= \delta^{-1} \min\{\lambda \delta : \lambda \delta x^j \in L(u^j \mid C, S)\}$$
$$= \delta^{-1} F_i(u^j, x^j \mid C, S).$$

($F_i.2$)   From Proposition (3.1.2(i))
$$F_i(\theta u^j, x^j \mid C, S) = \min\{\lambda : \lambda x^j \in L(\theta u^j \mid C, S)\}$$
$$= \min\{\lambda : \lambda x^j \in \theta L(u^j \mid C, S)\}$$
$$= \theta F_i(u^j, x^j \mid C, S).$$

($F_i.3$)   Follows from the fact that for each observation j, $x^j \in L(u^j \mid C, S)$, and $0 \notin L(u^j \mid C, S), u^j \geqq 0$.

($F_i.4$)   As a radial input measure, $F_i(u^j, x^j \mid C, S) = 1 \Longleftrightarrow$ $F_i(u^j, x^j \mid C, S) \cdot x^j \in Isoq\, L(u^j \mid C, S)$. However, since inputs are strongly disposable (3.1.2(ii)), $WEff\, L(u) = Isoq\, L(u)$, see (2.3.2). Thus $F_i.4$ applies.

($F_i.5$)   Let us consider just the nth input constraint $\sum_{j=1}^{J} z_j x_{jn} \leqq \lambda x_{jn}$. If the unit of measurement is changed, so that $\hat{x}_{jn} = \nu x_{jn}, j = 1, 2, \cdots, J, \nu > 0$, then clearly λ and $z_j, j = 1, 2, \cdots, J$, are not affected.

$$\text{Q.E.D.}$$

Using the piecewise linear (C, S) technology given by (3.1.1), the (C, S) input measure of technical efficiency can be calculated for activity j as the solution to the linear programming problem

$$F_i(u^j, x^j \mid C, S) = \min_{\lambda, z} \lambda \qquad (3.1.5)$$

$$\text{s.t. } u^j \leqq zM$$

$$zN \leqq \lambda x^j$$

$$z \in \Re_+^J$$

or

$$\min_{\lambda, z} \lambda$$

$$\text{s.t. } u_{jm} \leqq \sum_{j=1}^{J} z_j u_{jm}, m = 1, 2, \cdots, M,$$

$$\sum_{j=1}^{J} z_j x_{jn} \leqq \lambda x_{jn}, n = 1, 2, \cdots, N,$$

$$z_j \geqq 0, j = 1, 2, \cdots, J.$$

The (C, S) input measure of technical efficiency is illustrated twice

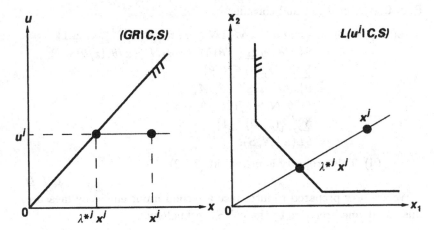

Fig. 3.1. *The (C, S) Input Measure of Technical Efficiency*

in Figure 3.1. In the second panel it is assumed that $N = 2$, and $L(u^j, x^j \mid C, S)$ is used. In the first panel it is assumed that $M = N = 1$, and $(GR \mid C, S)$ is used. In both panels λ^{*j} is the minimizing value of λ, and $\lambda^{*j} x^j = F_i(u^j, x^j \mid C, S) \cdot x^j$ is technically efficient relative to the (C, S) technology.

We now repeat the whole exercise on the assumption that technology satisfies nonincreasing returns to scale and strong disposability of inputs. The purpose is to compare efficiency measures based on different assumptions concerning scale economies. The input sets satisfying nonincreasing returns to scale and strong disposability are obtained from M and N as

$$L(u \mid N, S) = \{x : u \leq zM, zN \leq x, z \in \Re_+^J, \sum_{j=1}^{J} z_j \leq 1\}, u \in \Re_+^M.$$

(3.1.6)

These sets are referred to as (N, S) input sets, N for nonincreasing returns to scale and S for strong disposability of inputs. Since the intensity vector is more constrained in (3.1.6) than in (3.1.1) it follows directly that

$$L(u \mid N, S) \subseteq L(u \mid C, S). \tag{3.1.7}$$

Also, satisfaction of nonincreasing returns to scale and strong disposability of inputs is proved in

(3.1.8)   **Proposition:** The (N, S) input sets satisfy
       (i) $L(\theta u \mid N, S) \subseteq \theta L(u \mid N, S), \theta \geq 1,$
       (ii) $x \geq y \in L(u \mid N, S) \Longrightarrow x \in L(u \mid N, S).$

Proof: (i) Let $\theta \geq 1$ and consider

$$
\begin{aligned}
L(\theta u \mid N, S) &= \{x : \theta u \leq zM, zN \leq x, z \in \Re^J_+, \sum_{j=1}^J z_j \leq 1\} \\
&= \theta\{x/\theta : u \leq (z/\theta)M, (z/\theta)N \leq x/\theta, (z/\theta) \in \Re^J_+, \\
&\quad \sum_{j=1}^J (z_j/\theta) \leq 1/\theta\} \\
&\subseteq \theta\{x/\theta : u \leq (z/\theta)M, \\
&\quad (z/\theta)N \leq x/\theta, (z/\theta) \in \Re^J_+, \\
&\quad \sum_{j=1}^J (z_j/\theta) \leq 1\} \\
&= \theta L(u \mid N, S).
\end{aligned}
$$

(ii) This property is proved in (3.1.2).

Q.E.D.

We are now prepared to introduce a second input efficiency measure, this one defined relative to the (N, S) technology.

(3.1.9)   **Definition:** The function
$$
F_i(u^j, x^j \mid N, S) = \min\{\lambda : \lambda x^j \in L(u^j \mid N, S)\}, j = 1, 2, \cdots, J,
$$
is called the (N,S) *Input Measure of Technical Efficiency.*

$F_i(u^j, x^j \mid N, S)$, which is illustrated in Figure 3.2 for a piecewise linear technology, measures the efficiency of x^j in the production of u^j on the assumption that technology satisfies nonincreasing returns to scale and strong disposability. It satisfies properties similar to those satisfied by $F_i(u^j, x^j \mid C, S)$. Minor but significant differences arise because of the difference between nonincreasing and constant returns to scale. The properties satisfied by $F_i(u^j, x^j \mid N, S)$ are summarized in the following proposition (proofs are similar to those of Proposition (3.1.4) and are omitted).

(3.1.10)   **Proposition:** Given $L(u^j \mid N, S)$, then for each
$j = 1, 2, \cdots, J$,

$F_i.1$ $F_i(u^j, \delta x^j \mid N, S) = \delta^{-1} F_i(u^j, x^j \mid N, S), \delta > 0,$

$F_i.2$ $F_i(\theta u^j, x^j \mid N, S) \geq \theta F_i(u^j, x^j \mid N, S), \theta \geq 1,$

$F_i.3$ $0 < F_i(u^j, x^j \mid N, S) \leq 1,$

$F_i.4$ $x^j \in WEff\ L(u^j \mid N, S) \iff F_i(u^j, x^j \mid N, S) = 1,$

$F_i.5$ $F_i(u^j, x^j \mid N, S)$ is independent of unit of measurement.

The (N, S) input measure of technical efficiency is calculated for activity j, using the piecewise linear (N, S) technology (3.1.6), as the solution to the linear programming problem

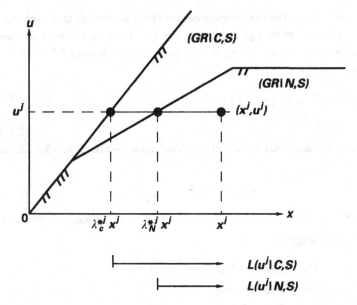

Fig. 3.2. *A Comparison of $F_i(u^j, x^j \mid C, S)$ and $F_i(u^j, x^j \mid N, S)$*

$$F_i(u^j, x^j \mid N, S) = \min_{\lambda, z} \lambda \qquad (3.1.11)$$

$$\text{s.t. } u^j \leq zM$$

$$zN \leq \lambda x^j$$

$$z \in \Re_+^J$$

$$\sum_{j=1}^{J} z_j \leq 1$$

or

$$\min_{\lambda, z} \lambda$$

$$\text{s.t. } u_{jm} \leqq \textstyle\sum_{j=1}^{J} z_j u_{jm}, m = 1, 2, \cdots, M,$$

$$\textstyle\sum_{j=1}^{J} z_j x_{jn} \leqq \lambda x_{jn}, n = 1, 2, \cdots, N,$$

$$z_j \geqq 0, j = 1, 2, \cdots, J,$$

$$\textstyle\sum_{j=1}^{J} z_j \leqq 1.$$

In light of (3.1.7) it is clear that

$$1 \geqq F_i(u^j, x^j \mid N, S) \geqq F_i(u^j, x^j \mid C, S) > 0, \qquad (3.1.12)$$

a result that is illustrated in Figure 3.2 for the $M = N = 1$ case.

We now repeat the entire exercise, on the assumption that technology satisfies the still weaker properties of variable returns to scale and strong disposability of inputs. The (V, S) input sets are obtained from M and N as

$$L(u \mid V,S) = \{x : u \leqq zM, zN \leqq x, z \in \Re_+^J, \sum_{j=1}^J z_j = 1\}, u \in \Re_+^M.$$

(3.1.13)

Comparing the restrictions on the intensity vector z in (3.1.13) and (3.1.6), it follows that

$$L(u \mid V,S) \subseteqq L(u \mid N,S).$$ 　　　　(3.1.14)

The third input efficiency measure can now be defined relative to the (V, S) technology (3.1.13) as

(3.1.15)　　**Definition**: The function $F_i(u^j, x^j \mid V,S) = \min\{\lambda : \lambda x^j \in L(u^j \mid V,S)\}$,

　　　　$j = 1, 2, \cdots, J$,

　　　　is called the (V,S) *Input Measure of Technical Efficiency.*

$F_i(u^j, x^j \mid V,S)$, which is illustrated in Figure 3.3, measures the efficiency of x^j in the production of u^j given that technology satisfies variable returns to scale and strong disposability of inputs. It satisfies properties analogous to $F_i.1, F_i.3, F_i.4$ and $F_i.5$ in Propositions (3.1.4) and (3.1.10), but because it exhibits variable returns to scale it satisfies no property like $F_i.2$. However from (3.1.14) it follows that

$$1 \geqq F_i(u^j, x^j \mid V,S) \geqq F_i(u^j, x^j \mid N,S) > 0, j = 1, 2, \cdots, J, \quad (3.1.16)$$

a result that is illustrated in Figure 3.3 for the $M = N = 1$ case.

The (V, S) input measure of technical efficiency is calculated for activity j using the piecewise linear (V, S) technology (3.1.13) as the solution to the linear programming problem

$$F_i(u^j, x^j \mid V,S) = \min_{\lambda, z} \lambda$$ 　　　　(3.1.17)

$$\text{s.t. } u^j \leqq zM$$

$$zN \leqq \lambda x^j$$

$$z \in \Re_+^J$$

$$\sum_{j=1}^J z_j = 1$$

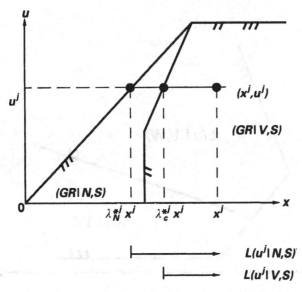

Fig. 3.3. *A Comparison of* $F_i(u^j, x^j \mid N, S)$ *and* $F_i(u^j, x^j \mid V, S)$

or

$$\min_{\lambda, z} \lambda$$
$$\text{s.t. } u_{jm} \leqq \sum_{j=1}^{J} z_j u_{jm}, m = 1, 2, \cdots, M,$$
$$\sum_{j=1}^{J} z_j x_{jn} \leqq \lambda x_{jn}, n = 1, 2, \cdots, N,$$
$$z_j \geqq 0, j = 1, 2, \cdots, J,$$
$$\sum_{j=1}^{J} z_j = 1.$$

Definitions (3.1.3), (3.1.9) and (3.1.15) describe input-based technical efficiency measures relative to a technology that satisfies strong disposability of inputs and three different types of scale behavior. We now change the focus of the analysis from scale economies to input disposability. We do so by constructing input-based technical efficiency measures relative to a technology that satisfies variable returns to scale and three types of input disposability behavior. Variable returns to scale and strong disposability of inputs has already been described in Definition (3.1.15). We proceed by relaxing the assumption that all inputs are strongly disposable. We do so by restricting a subvector of inputs to be only weakly disposable. We then show how this relaxation modifies the piecewise linear input set (3.1.13), and how this in turn leads to yet another input efficiency measure. Suppose that the input matrix N can be decomposed so that $N = (N^\alpha, N^{\hat{\alpha}})$, where $\alpha \subseteq \{1, 2, \cdots, N\}$ and

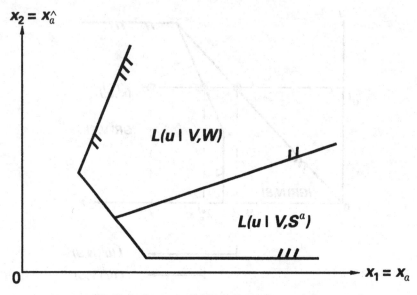

Fig. 3.4. *Strong and Weak Input Disposability*

$\hat{\alpha} = \{1, 2, \cdots, N\} \setminus \alpha$. Correspondingly write $x = (x_\alpha, x_{\hat{\alpha}})$. We may now form piecewise linear input sets allowing variable returns to scale, and strong disposability of input subvector x_α combined with weak disposability of input subvector $x_{\hat{\alpha}}$, as

$$L(u \mid V, S^\alpha) = \{x : u \leqq zM, zN^{\hat{\alpha}} = \sigma x_{\hat{\alpha}}, 0 < \sigma \leqq 1, \quad (3.1.18)$$

$$zN^\alpha \leqq x_\alpha, z \in \Re_+^J, \sum_{j=1}^J z_j = 1\}, u \in \Re_+^M.$$

If $x \in L(u \mid V, S^\alpha)$, then clearly $\lambda x \in L(u \mid V, S^\alpha), \lambda \geqq 1$, i.e., inputs are weakly disposable. However inputs are not necessarily strongly disposable because the equality $zN^{\hat{\alpha}} = \sigma x_{\hat{\alpha}}$ may make $y_{\hat{\alpha}} \geqq x_{\hat{\alpha}}$ infeasible. In Figure 3.4 input x_1 is strongly disposable, but input x_2 is only weakly disposable.

In general, we have

$$L(u \mid V, S^\alpha) \subseteqq L(u \mid V, S). \qquad (3.1.19)$$

A radial efficiency measure can now be defined relative to the (V, S^α) technology (3.1.18) as

(3.1.20)   **Definition:** The function
$$F_i(u^j, x^j \mid V, S^\alpha) = \min\{\lambda : \lambda x^j \in L(u^j \mid V, S^\alpha)\},$$

$$j = 1, 2, \cdots, J,$$

is called the (V, S^α) *Input Measure of Technical Efficiency.*

$F_i(u^j, x^j \mid V, S^\alpha)$ measures the efficiency of x^j in the production of u^j when technology satisfies variable returns to scale, and a combination of strong input disposability with respect to the input subvector x_α and weak input disposability with respect to the input subvector $x_{\hat{\alpha}}$. This measure is useful chiefly to determine which input subvector, if any, is responsible for a failure of strong disposability, i.e., for congestion. (We eventually show how to identify congesting input subvectors.) The measure satisfies $0 < F_i(u^j, x^j \mid V, S^\alpha) \leqq 1$, and by virtue of (3.1.19) it is clear that

$$1 \geqq F_i(u^j, x^j \mid V, S^\alpha) \geqq F_i(u^j, x^j \mid V, S) > 0. \tag{3.1.21}$$

The (V, S^α) input measure of technical efficiency is calculated using technology (3.1.18) as the solution to the nonlinear programming problem

$$F_i(u^j, x^j \mid V, S^\alpha) = \min_{\lambda, z, \sigma} \lambda \tag{3.1.22}$$

$$\text{s.t. } u^j \leqq z\boldsymbol{M}$$
$$z\boldsymbol{N}^\alpha \leqq \lambda x_\alpha^j$$
$$z\boldsymbol{N}^{\hat{\alpha}} = \lambda \sigma x_{\hat{\alpha}}^j$$
$$0 < \sigma \leqq 1$$
$$z \in \Re_+^J$$
$$\sum_{j=1}^J z_j = 1$$

or

$$\min_{\lambda, z, \sigma} \lambda$$
$$\text{s.t. } u_{jm} \leqq \sum_{j=1}^J z_j u_{jm}, m = 1, 2, \cdots, M,$$
$$\sum_{j=1}^J z_j x_{jn} \leqq \lambda x_{jn}, n = 1, 2, \cdots, N^\alpha,$$
$$\sum_{j=1}^J z_j x_{jn} = \lambda \sigma x_{jn}, n = N^\alpha + 1, N^\alpha + 2, \cdots, N,$$
$$0 < \sigma \leqq 1,$$
$$z_j \geqq 0, j = 1, 2, \cdots, J,$$
$$\sum_{j=1}^J z_j = 1.$$

The nonlinear programming problem (3.1.22) may be converted into a linear programming problem by taking $\sigma = 1$. Since F_i is a radial measure, this conversion does not change the optimal value of the measure.

We now consider the most general input sets considered here, those satisfying variable returns to scale and weak input disposability. Piecewise linear input sets satisfying these weak properties may be formed from M and N as

$$L(u \mid V,W) = \{x : u \leqq zM, zN = \sigma x, 0 < \sigma \leqq 1, \quad (3.1.23)$$

$$z \in \Re^J_+, \sum_{j=1}^{J} z_j = 1\}, u \in \Re^M_+.$$

A radial efficiency measure can be defined relative to $L(u \mid V,W)$ as

(3.1.24) **Definition**: The function

$$F_i(u^j, x^j \mid V,W) = \min\{\lambda : \lambda x^j \in L(u^j \mid V,W)\},$$

$$j = 1, 2, \cdots, J,$$

is called the (V,W) *Input Measure of Technical Efficiency.*

$F_i(u^j, x^j \mid V,W)$ measures the efficiency of x^j in the production of u^j when the least restrictive assumptions (V,W) are imposed on technology. Proofs similar to those of Proposition (3.1.4) can be used to obtain the following properties of $F_i(u^j, x^j \mid V,W)$.

(3.1.25) **Proposition**: Given $L(u^j \mid V,W)$, then for each
$j = 1, 2, \cdots, J,$

$F_i.1 \quad F_i(u^j, \delta x^j \mid V,W) = \delta^{-1} F_i(u^j, x^j \mid V,W), \delta > 0,$

$F_i.2 \quad 0 < F_i(u^j, x^j \mid V,W) \leqq 1,$

$F_i.3 \quad x^j \in Isoq\, L(u^j \mid V,W) \Longleftrightarrow F_i(u^j, x^j \mid V,W) = 1,$

$F_i.4 \quad F_i(u^j, x^j \mid V,W)$ is independent of unit of measurement.

Moreover, since

$$L(u \mid V,W) \subseteqq L(u \mid V, S^\alpha) \quad (3.1.26)$$

it follows that

$$1 \geqq F_i(u^j, x^j \mid V,W) \geqq F_i(u^j, x^j \mid V, S^\alpha) > 0. \quad (3.1.27)$$

The (V,W) efficiency measure may be calculated relative to the piecewise linear technology (3.1.23) as the solution to the nonlinear programming problem

$$F_i(u^j, x^j \mid V,W) = \min_{\lambda, z, \sigma} \lambda \quad (3.1.28)$$

$$\text{s.t. } u^j \leqq zM$$

$$zN = \lambda \sigma x^j$$

$$0 < \sigma \leqq 1$$

$$z \in \Re^J_+$$

$$\sum_{j=1}^{J} z_j = 1$$

or

$$\min_{\lambda, z, \sigma} \lambda$$

$$\text{s.t. } u_{jm} \leq \sum_{j=1}^{J} z_j u_{jm}, m = 1, 2, \cdots, M,$$
$$\sum_{j=1}^{J} z_j x_{jn} = \lambda \sigma x_{jn}, n = 1, 2, \cdots, N,$$
$$0 < \sigma \leq 1,$$
$$z_j \geq 0, j = 1, 2, \cdots, J,$$
$$\sum_{j=1}^{J} z_j = 1.$$

This problem can be converted into a linear programming problem by taking $\alpha = 1$ as before, without changing the value of (λ, z).

At this point it is useful to summarize the relationships among the five input measures of technical efficiency. Because it measures the efficiency of input vector x^j in the production of output vector u^j under the least restrictive assumptions concerning the structure of technology, the (V, W) input measure assigns the highest efficiency score. From equations (3.1.12), (3.1.16), (3.1.21), and (3.1.27) and Propositions (3.1.4) and (3.1.25) it follows that

$$0 < F_i(u^j, x^j \mid C, S) \leq F_i(u^j, x^j \mid N, S) \leq F_i(u^j, x^j \mid V, S)$$
$$\leq F_i(u^j, x^j \mid V, S^\alpha) \leq F_i(u^j, x^j \mid V, W) \leq 1. \tag{3.1.29}$$

The ordering of technical efficiencies in (3.1.29) is useful primarily because its components can be converted into ratios, and ratios of (or differences between) efficiency measures provide information concerning scale economies and input disposability. The first step is to decompose the most restrictive (C, S) input measure of technical efficiency into component measures of input scale efficiency, input congestion, and the least restrictive (V, W) input measure of technical efficiency. We begin by proposing a measure of input scale efficiency.

(3.1.30) **Definition:** The function
$$S_i(u^j, x^j) = F_i(u^j, x^j \mid C, S)/F_i(u^j, x^j \mid V, S),$$
$$j = 1, 2, \cdots, J,$$
is called the *Input Scale Efficiency Measure.*

Clearly activity j is input scale efficient if $F_i(u^j, x^j \mid C, S) = F_i(u^j, x^j \mid V, S)$, or if it is equally efficient relative to (C, S) and (V, S) technologies. This point is illustrated in Figure 3.5. Activity (u^j, x^j) is input scale efficient because it is equally (technically) efficient relative to (C, S) and (V, S) technologies. Input vector x^j is producing a scale efficient output vector u^j. However neither activity (u^k, x^k) nor activity (u^ℓ, x^ℓ) is input scale efficient because each is more (technically) efficient relative to the (V, S) technology than to the (C, S) technology. Input vector x^k is producing output vector u^k which is too small to be scale efficient, while x^ℓ is producing u^ℓ which is too large to be scale efficient. The properties of $S_i(u^j, x^j)$ are summarized in

(3.1.31)   **Proposition**: Given $S_i(u^j, x^j)$, then for each
$$j = 1, 2, \cdots, J,$$

S$_i$.1 $0 < S_i(u^j, x^j) \leqq 1$,

S$_i$.2 $S_i(u^j, x^j) = 1 \iff F_i(u^j, x^j \mid V, S) \cdot x^j$, exhibits *CRS*,
          or equivalently $F_i(u^j, x^j \mid V, S) \cdot x^j \in Isoq\, L(u^j \mid C, S)$,

S$_i$.3 $S_i(u^j, \lambda x^j) = S_i(u^j, x^j), \lambda > 0$,

S$_i$.4 $S_i(u^j, x^j)$ is independent of unit of measurement.

Proof: S$_i$.1 follows from (3.1.30) and (3.1.29). S$_i$.3 is a consequence of the input homogeneity properties of $F_i(u^j, x^j \mid C, S)$ and $F_i(u^j, x^j \mid V, S)$, and S$_i$.4 follows from (3.1.4) and (3.1.25). To prove S$_i$.2 assume $S_i(u^j, x^j) = 1$, so that $F_i(u^j, x^j \mid C, S) = F_i(u^j, x^j \mid V, S)$ and $F_i(u^j, x^j \mid V, S) \cdot x^j \in Isoq\, L(u^j \mid C, S)$, i.e., $F_i(u^j, x^j \mid V, S) \cdot x^j$ exhibits *CRS*. Conversely if $F_i(u^j, x^j \mid V, S) \cdot x^j$ exhibits *CRS*, then $F_i(u^j, x^j \mid V, S) \cdot x^j \in Isoq\, L(u^j \mid C, S) \implies F_i(u^j, x^j \mid V, S) = F_i(u^j, x^j \mid C, S) \implies S_i(u^j, x^j) = 1$.

Q.E.D.

Suppose now that $S_i(u^j, x^j) < 1$. We want to determine whether the source of input scale inefficiency is production of an inefficiently small output vector in a region of increasing returns to scale (as with (x^k, u^k) in Figure 3.5), or production of an inefficiently large output vector in a region of decreasing returns to scale (as with (x^ℓ, u^ℓ) in Figure 3.5). The determination is based on a comparison of $F_i(u^j, x^j \mid C, S)$ with $F_i(u^j, x^j \mid N, S)$. If $S_i(u^j, x^j) < 1$ and $F_i(u^j, x^j \mid C, S) = F_i(u^j, x^j \mid N, S)$, input scale inefficiency is due to increasing returns to scale. If $S_i(u^j, x^j) < 1$ and $F_i(u^j, x^j \mid C, S) < F_i(u^j, x^j \mid N, S)$, input scale inefficiency is due to decreasing returns to scale. Figure 3.5 illustrates. The input scale inefficiency of activity (x^k, u^k) is due to increasing returns to scale because $F_i(u^k, x^k \mid C, S) = F_i(u^k, x^k \mid N, S)$. The input scale inefficiency of activity (x^ℓ, u^ℓ) is due to decreasing returns to scale because $F_i(u^\ell, x^\ell \mid C, S) < F_i(u^\ell, x^\ell \mid N, S)$.

We continue to decompose the (C, S) input measure of technical efficiency by focusing on input disposability. We begin by proposing a measure of input congestion in terms of the (V, S) and (V, W) technologies.

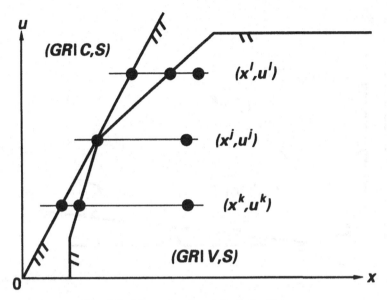

Fig. 3.5. *Measuring Input Scale Inefficiency*

(3.1.32) **Definition**: The function
$$C_i(u^j, x^j) = F_i(u^j, x^j \mid V, S)/F_i(u^j, x^j \mid V, W),$$
$$j = 1, 2, \cdots, J,$$
is called the *Input Congestion Measure*.

The input congestion measure provides a comparison of the feasible proportionate reduction in inputs required to maintain output when technology satisfies weak versus strong input disposability. We say that input vector x^j is not congested for output vector u^j if $C_i(u^j, x^j) = 1$, i.e., if $F_i(u^j, x^j \mid V, S) = F_i(u^j, x^j \mid V, W)$. In Figure 3.6, input vector x^k does not congest output vector $u^k = u^j$ because $F_i(u^k, x^k \mid V, S) = F_i(u^k, x^k \mid V, W)$. However x^j congests u^j because $F_i(u^j, x^j \mid V, S) < F_i(u^j, x^j \mid V, W)$. The properties of the input congestion measure are summarized in

(3.1.33) **Proposition**: Given $C_i(u^j, x^j)$, then for each
$$j = 1, 2, \cdots, J,$$

C$_i$.1 $0 < C_i(u^j, x^j) \leqq 1$,

C$_i$.2 $C_i(u^j, x^j) = 1 \Longleftrightarrow F_i(u^j, x^j \mid V, W) \cdot x^j \in WEff\, L(u^j \mid V, W)$,

C$_i$.3 $C_i(u^j, \lambda x^j) = C_i(u^j, x^j), \lambda > 0$,

C$_i$.4 $C_i(u^j, x^j)$ is independent of unit of measurement.

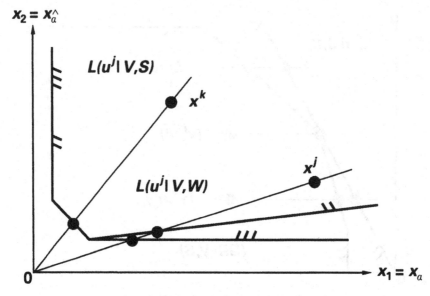

Fig. 3.6. *Measuring Input Congestion*

Proof: $C_i.1$, $C_i.3$ and $C_i.4$ are proved like $S_i.1$, $S_i.3$ and $S_i.4$. To prove $C_i.2$, suppose that $C_i(u^j, x^j) = 1$, then $F_i(u^j, x^j \mid V, S) \cdot x^j = F_i(u^j, x^j \mid V, W) \cdot x^j \in Isoq\ L(u^j \mid V, S) \cap Isoq\ L(u^j \mid V, W)$. Thus by Propositions (2.3.2) and (2.3.3), $F_i(u^j, x^j \mid V, W) \cdot x^j \in WEff\ L(u^j \mid V, W)$. Conversely, if $F_i(u^j, x^j \mid V, W) \cdot x^j \in WEff\ L(u^j \mid V, W)$, then since $WEff\ L(u^j \mid V, W) \subseteq WEff\ L(u^j \mid V, S)$, $F_i(u^j, x^j \mid V, W) = F_i(u^j, x^j \mid V, S)$ and $C_i(u^j, x^j) = 1$.

$$Q.E.D.$$

Suppose that $C_i(u^j, x^j) < 1$. This tells us that congestion is present, but it does not tell us where it is coming from. Thus the next step is to determine the source of the congestion, the identity of the subvector of inputs that is obstructing production. In Figure 3.6 it is clear that x^j congests u^j, and that the subvector responsible for the congestion is x_1. We now develop a strategy to generalize this simple example; the strategy is logically the same as the strategy developed above to determine the source of scale inefficiency. If $C_i(u^j, x^j) < 1$, the subsets of congesting inputs are determined as follows. First, compare $F_i(u^j, x^j \mid V, S)$ and $F_i(u^j, x^j \mid V, S^\alpha)$ for each $\alpha \subseteq \{1, 2, \cdots, N\}$. If $C_i(u^j, x^j) < 1$ and $F_i(u^j, x^j \mid V, S) = F_i(u^j, x^j \mid V, S^\alpha)$, the subvector $x_{\hat{\alpha}}$ obstructs production. Of course $x_{\hat{\alpha}}$ may not be unique, and the exercise may produce a set of congesting subvectors, each of which can account for $C_i(u^j, x^j) < 1$.

Thus the magnitude and source of input congestion can be determined by solving the programming problems (3.1.17), (3.1.22), and (3.1.28). Note that the latter two problems are nonlinear, but easily made linear, and that (3.1.22) must be solved one time for every partition $(\alpha, \hat{\alpha})$ of N.

We conclude this section with a statement of the desired decomposition of the (C, S) input measure of technical efficiency. Using Definitions (3.1.30) and (3.1.32) we have

$$F_i(u^j, x^j \mid C, S) = F_i(u^j, x^j \mid V, W) \cdot S_i(u^j, x^j) \cdot C_i(u^j, x^j). \quad (3.1.34)$$

The input measure of technical efficiency relative to the constant returns to scale, strong disposability of inputs technology is equal to the product of three components: a measure of input scale efficiency, a measure of input congestion, and an input measure of technical efficiency relative to a variable returns to scale, weak input disposability technology. $F_i(u^j, x^j \mid C, S) = 1$ if, and only if, all three components have a value of unity.

3.2 Radial Efficiency Measures Requiring Input Price, Input Quantity, and Output Quantity Data: The Decomposition of Cost Efficiency

In the previous section we concluded by decomposing a (C, S) input measure of technical efficiency into measures of scale efficiency, congestion, and what might be called "pure" technical efficiency. The (C, S) measure and its three components are all physical measures, in the sense that they are derived from input and output quantity data only. They are price-independent efficiency measures. In this section we augment, rather than decompose, the (C, S) measure of technical efficiency with an input price-dependent measure of input mix efficiency. We then show how these two measures combine to form an input price-dependent measure of cost efficiency. Finally, it follows that the cost efficiency measure decomposes into four components, an input mix efficiency measure and the three components of the (C, S) technical efficiency measure.

Suppose that in addition to the input and output matrices N and M, input prices $p \in \Re_+^N, p \neq 0$, are given for each activity $j = 1, 2, \cdots, J$. Since the piecewise linear technology has a bounded efficient subset, we can relax the requirement that $p \in \Re_{++}^N$ and allow for some zero input prices. Then we can compute for each activity the minimum expenditure required to produce output vector u^j at input prices p^j, and this calculation can be performed relative to any of the technologies considered in Section 3.1.

Let us consider cost minimization relative to the input set $L(u \mid C, S)$. For activity j we have

$$Q(u^j, p^j \mid C, S) = \min_{z,x} \{p^j x : x \in L(u^j \mid C, S)\}, j = 1, 2, \cdots, J. \quad (3.2.1)$$

This cost may be calculated as the solution to the linear programming problem

$$Q(u^j, p^j \mid C, S) = \min_{z,x} p^j x \qquad (3.2.2)$$

$$\text{s.t. } u^j \leq zM$$
$$zN \leq x$$
$$z \in \Re_+^J$$

or

$$\min_{z,x} \sum_{n=1}^N p_{jn} x_n$$
$$\text{s.t. } u_{jm} \leq \sum_{j=1}^J z_j u_{jm}, m = 1, 2, \cdots, M,$$
$$\sum_{j=1}^J z_j x_{jn} \leq x_n, n = 1, 2, \cdots, N,$$
$$z_j \geq 0, j = 1, 2, \cdots, J.$$

It is supposed that p^j and x^j are known, and we assume that observed total cost $p^j x^j > 0$. This suggests

(3.2.3)   **Definition:** The function
$$O_i(u^j, p^j, x^j \mid C, S) = Q(u^j, p^j \mid C, S)/p^j x^j, j = 1, 2, \cdots, J,$$
is called the (C,S) *Input Cost Efficiency Measure.*

The (C, S) input cost efficiency measure is given by the ratio of minimum cost obtainable from the (C, S) technology to observed cost. The measure satisfies properties described in

(3.2.4)   **Proposition:** Given $L(u^j \mid C, S)$, then for each
$j = 1, 2, \cdots, J,$

O$_i$.1 $O_i(u^j, p^j, \delta x^j \mid C, S) = \delta^{-1} O_i(u^j, p^j, x^j \mid C, S), \delta > 0,$

O$_i$.2 $O_i(\theta u^j, p^j, x^j \mid C, S) = \theta O_i(u^j, p^j, x^j \mid C, S), \theta > 0,$

O$_i$.3 $O_i(u^j, \lambda p^j, x^j \mid C, S) = O_i(u^j, p^j, x^j \mid C, S), \lambda > 0,$

O$_i$.4 $0 < O_i(u^j, p^j, x^j \mid C, S) \leq 1,$

O$_i$.5 x^j solves (3.2.1) $\Longleftrightarrow O_i(u^j, p^j, x^j \mid C, S) = 1,$

O$_i$.6 $O_i(u^j, p^j, x^j \mid C, S)$ is independent of unit of measurement.

The proof of this proposition is left to the reader.

Suppose $O_i(u^j, p^j, x^j \mid C, S) < 1$. Activity j is spending more on inputs than is required to produce output vector u^j at input prices p^j. This excess must logically be due to either or both of two factors (i) using proportionately too much of all inputs, and (ii) using inputs in the wrong mix. The first factor has already been discussed, and a measure obtained. Technical efficiency relative to a (C, S) technology is measured by $F_i(u^j, x^j \mid C, S)$. The second factor is obtained residually from $O_i(u^j, p^j, x^j \mid C, S)$ and $F_i(u^j, x^j \mid C, S)$.

(3.2.5)   **Definition:** The function
$$A_i(u^j, p^j, x^j \mid C, S) = O_i(u^j, p^j, x^j \mid C, S)/F_i(u^j, x^j \mid C, S),$$
$$j = 1, 2, \cdots, J,$$
is called the (C, S) *Input Allocative Efficiency Measure.*

The (C, S) input allocative efficiency measure satisfies properties summarized in

(3.2.6)   **Proposition:** Given $L(u^j \mid C, S)$, then for each
$$j = 1, 2, \cdots, J,$$

A$_i$.1 $A_i(u^j, p^j, \delta x^j \mid C, S) = A_i(u^j, p^j, x^j \mid C, S), \delta > 0,$

A$_i$.2 $A_i(\theta u^j, p^j, x^j \mid C, S) = A_i(u^j, p^j, x^j \mid C, S), \theta > 0,$

A$_i$.3 $A_i(u^j, \lambda p^j, x^j \mid C, S) = A_i(u^j, p^j, x^j \mid C, S), \lambda > 0,$

A$_i$.4 $0 < A_i(u^j, p^j, x^j \mid C, S) \leqq 1,$

A$_i$.5 $\exists \lambda \in (0, 1]$ such that λx^j solves (3.2.1)
            $\iff A_i(u^j, p^j, x^j \mid C, S) = 1,$

A$_i$.6 $A_i(u^j, p^j, x^j \mid C, S)$ is independent of unit of measurement.

Proof: The proofs of A$_i$.1 $-$ A$_i$.4 and A$_i$.6 are left to the reader. To prove A$_i$.5, assume $\exists \lambda \in (0, 1]$ such that λx^j solves (3.2.1). Then $Q(u^j, p^j \mid C, S) = p^j \lambda x^j$, thus from Definition (3.2.5), $A_i(u^j, p^j, x^j \mid C, S) = 1$. Conversely, assume $A_i(u^j, p^j, x^j \mid C, S) = 1$. Then $Q(u^j, p^j \mid C, S) = p^j(F_i(u^j, x^j \mid C, S) \cdot x^j)$. Since $F_i(u^j, x^j \mid C, S) \in (0, 1], A_i$.5 holds.

Q.E.D.

From Definitions (3.2.3) and (3.2.5) we obtain the following decomposition of the (C, S) input cost efficiency measure.

$$O_i(u^j, p^j, x^j \mid C, S) = A_i(u^j, p^j, x^j \mid C, S) \cdot F_i(u^j, x^j \mid C, S). \quad (3.2.7)$$

This decomposition is illustrated in Figure 3.7, where the cost-minimizing input vector is labelled x^{*j}. The observed input vector is technically inefficient, since it can be contracted radially to $F_i(u^j, x^j \mid C, S) \cdot x^j$

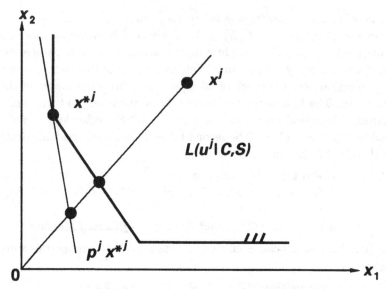

Fig. 3.7. *The Decomposition of Input Cost Efficiency*

with no loss in output. It is also allocatively inefficient, using too large an x_1/x_2 mix in light of observed input prices p^j, and moving to x^{*j} would eliminate allocative inefficiency, reducing cost to $p^j \cdot O_i(u^j, x^j, p^j \mid C, S) \cdot x^j = Q(u^j, p^j \mid C, S)$.

By solving the linear programming problems (3.1.5) and (3.2.2), we can decompose the (C, S) input cost efficiency measure (3.2.3) into its (C, S) input allocative efficiency (3.2.5) and (C, S) technical efficiency (3.1.5) components. If in addition we apply the decomposition (3.1.34) of $F_i(u^j, x^j \mid C, S)$ we obtain

$$O_i(u^j, p^j, x^j \mid C, S) = A_i(u^j, p^j, x^j \mid C, S) \cdot S_i(u^j, x^j) \cdot C_i(u^j, x^j)$$
$$\cdot F_i(u^j, x^j \mid V, W). \tag{3.2.8}$$

Thus input cost inefficiency must be due to selection of the wrong input mix $(A_i(u^j, p^j, x^j \mid C, S))$, to the adoption of an inefficiently small or large scale $(S_i(u^j, x^j))$, to input congestion $(C_i(u^j, x^j))$, or to "purely" technical inefficiency $(F_i(u^j, x^j \mid V, W))$.

As with (3.1.34), $O_i(u^j, p^j, x^j \mid C, S) = 1$ if, and only if, every one of its components has a value of unity.

Finally we note that the double decomposition in (3.2.8) can be applied to technologies more general than a (C, S) technology, with the result that the decomposition simplifies because one or more components become unity. For more general technologies the decomposition is given below

$$O_i(u^j, p^j, x^j \mid C, W) = A_i(u^j, p^j, x^j \mid C, S) \cdot S_i(u^j, x^j) \quad (3.2.9)$$
$$\cdot F_i(u^j, x^j \mid V, W)$$
$$O_i(u^j, p^j, x^j \mid V, S) = A_i(u^j, p^j, x^j \mid C, S) \cdot S_i(u^j, x^j)$$
$$\cdot F_i(u^j, x^j \mid V, W)$$
$$O_i(u^j, p^j, x^j \mid V, W) = A_i(u^j, p^j, x^j \mid V, W) \cdot F_i(u^j, x^j \mid V, W).$$

Results (3.2.8) and (3.2.9) are interpreted as follows. (3.2.8) states that cost inefficiency calculated relative to a restrictive (C, S) technology might be allocative inefficiency or scale inefficiency or congestion or purely technical inefficiency. The first part of (3.2.9) states that cost inefficiency calculated relative to a somewhat less restrictive (C, W) technology might in fact be allocative inefficiency or scale inefficiency or purely technical inefficiency, but it cannot really be congestion because the technology allows for weak disposability of inputs. The second and third parts of (3.2.9) are interpreted in a similar manner.

3.3   Nonradial Efficiency Measurement: The Russell Measure

In Sections 3.1 and 3.2 efficiency is measured radially, from input vector $x^j \in L(u^j \mid C, S)$ back toward the origin. As Proposition (3.1.4) notes, the input measure of technical efficiency calls an input vector efficient if, and only if, it is an element of $WEff\ L(u^j \mid C, S)$. However, since $Eff\ L(u^j \mid C, S) \subsetneqq WEff\ L(u^j \mid C, S)$, this means that an input vector x^j can be called technically efficient by $F_i(u^j, x^j \mid C, S)$ even though it is not an element of $Eff\ L(u^j \mid C, S)$. We would like a measure to call an input vector technically efficient if, and only if, it belongs to the efficient subset. For this purpose we propose a nonradial measure of technical efficiency.

Suppose that the input matrix N and the output matrix M are given and that $x_{jn} > 0, j = 1, 2, \cdots, J$, and $n = 1, 2, \cdots, N$. Then a nonradial measure of technical efficiency that satisfies our criteria of accurate labeling is provided by

(3.3.1)   **Definition:** The function
$$RM_i(u^j, x^j \mid C, S) = \min\{\textstyle\sum_{n=1}^{N} \lambda_n/N :$$
$$(\lambda_1 x_{j1}, \cdots, \lambda_N x_{jN}) \in L(u^j \mid C, S), \lambda_N \geqq 0, n = 1, 2, \cdots, N\},$$
$$j = 1, 2, \cdots, J,$$

is called the (C,S) *Russell Input Measure of Technical Efficiency.*

The Russell measure can be calculated for positive inputs as the solution to the programming problem

$$RM_i(u^j, x^j \mid C, S) = \frac{1}{N} \min_{\lambda, z} \sum_{n=1}^{N} \lambda_n \qquad (3.3.2)$$

$$\text{s.t. } u_{jm} \leqq \sum_{j=1}^{J} z_j u_{jm}, m = 1, 2, \cdots, M,$$

$$\sum_{j=1}^{J} z_j x_{jn} \leqq \lambda_n x_{jn}, n = 1, 2, \cdots, N,$$

$$z_j \geqq 0, j = 1, 2, \cdots, J.$$

If some inputs x_{jn} are zero, then we modify the measure and set $\lambda_n = 1$ for those n with $x_{jn} = 0$.

The Russell measure allows for non-proportional reductions in each positive input, and this is what permits it to shrink an input vector all the way back to the efficient subset. The nonradial Russell measure collapses to the radial measure defined in (3.1.3) when $\lambda_n = \lambda$, for all λ_n corresponding to $x_{jn} > 0$. However, since the Russell measure can shrink an input vector at least as far as the radial measure can, we have the result that

$$0 < RM_i(u^j, x^j \mid C, S) \leqq F_i(u^j, x^j \mid C, S) \leqq 1. \qquad (3.3.3)$$

The Russell measure is illustrated in Figure 3.8, where it is compared with the radial measure given by Definition (3.1.3). For observation $x^k \in L(u^j \mid C, S)$ the two efficiency measures coincide since there is no slack in the reference point $F_i(u^j, x^k \mid C, S) \cdot x^k$. However for observation $x^j \in L(u^j \mid C, S)$ the radial measure compares x^j to $F_i(u^j, x^j \mid C, S) \cdot x^j \in WEff\ L(u^j \mid C, S)$, which has slack in input x_2. The Russell measure eliminates this slack by comparing x^j to $(\lambda_1^* x_{j1}, \lambda_2^* x_{j2}, \ldots, \lambda_N^* x_{jN}) \in Eff\ L(u^j \mid C, S)$, and it is clear geometrically that in general $0 < RM_i(u^j, x^j \mid C, S) \leqq F_i(u^j, x^j \mid C, S) \leqq 1$.

By imposing restrictions on the intensity vector in the piecewise linear technology, the Russell measure can also be calculated for (N, S) and (V, S) technologies and inferences concerning the nature of scale economies can be made. This derivation of a Russell measure of scale efficiency is left to the reader.

It should be apparent from Figure 3.8 that a measure of the overall cost efficiency of some $x^j \in L(u^j \mid C, S)$ is independent of whether the

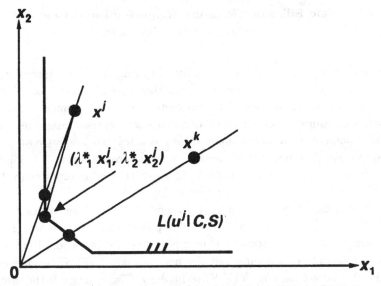

Fig. 3.8. *A Comparison of $RM_i(u^j, x^j \mid C, S)$ and $F_i(u^j, x^j \mid C, S)$*

technical efficiency component of the cost efficiency measure is calculated radially using $F_i(u^j, x^j \mid C, S)$ or nonradially using $RM_i(u^j, x^j \mid C, S)$. This leads to the following

(3.3.4)   **Definition**: The function
$$RMA_i(u^j, p^j, x^j \mid C, S) = O_i(u^j, p^j, x^j \mid C, S)/$$
$$RM_i(u^j, x^j \mid C, S), j = 1, 2, \cdots, J, \text{ is called the } (C, S) \text{ Russell}$$
Input Measure of Allocative Efficiency.

Since $0 < RM_i(u^j, x^j \mid C, S) \leqq F_i(u^j, x^j \mid C, S) \leqq 1$ it follows immediately that

$$1 \geqq RMA_i(u^j, p^j, x^j \mid C, S) \geqq A_i(u^j, p^j, x^j \mid C, S) > 0. \qquad (3.3.5)$$

The decompositions of overall input efficiency using the radial and nonradial measure of technical efficiency are illustrated in Figure 3.9. The difference between the two decompositions could be used to provide a measure of input slack, which is called allocative inefficiency by the radial measure and technical inefficiency by the nonradial Russell measure. We leave this exercise for the reader.

3.4   Scale Efficiency Measure Requiring Input Cost and Output Quantity Data

We have measured input scale efficiency in terms of a departure of observed output, however produced, from that rate of output for which returns to scale are constant. In this method the measurement of scale efficiency requires data on input quantities and output quantities. It is also possible to measure input scale efficiency using input cost and output quantity data. The advantage of this approach is that it requires less data ($(M+1)$ variables instead of $(M+N)$) since an input quantity vector is replaced with an input cost scalar.

Suppose that the output matrix M and the input cost vector $Q = (Q_1, Q_2, \cdots, Q_J)$ are known. The first step in the formulation of a scale efficiency measure is to solve two linear programming problems. Both are cost minimization problems, but the first assumes a (C, S) technology while the second assumes a (V, S) technology. The strategy is the same as in Sections 3.1 and 3.2: comparing efficiency scores obtained relative to (C, S) and (V, S) technologies reveals the nature of scale economies. Note however that the objective is to minimize input cost rather than to minimize the cost of input usage as in Section 3.2. The two problems are

$$F_Q(u^j \mid C, S) \;=\; \min_z zQ \qquad\qquad (3.4.1)$$
$$\text{s.t. } u^j \leqq zM$$
$$z \in \Re_+^J$$

or

$$\min_z \sum_{j=1}^J z_j Q_j$$
$$\text{s.t. } u_{jm} \leqq \sum_{j=1}^J z_j u_{jm}, m = 1, 2, \cdots, M,$$
$$z_j \geqq 0, j = 1, 2, \cdots, J,$$

and

$$F_Q(u^j \mid V, S) \;=\; \min_z zQ \qquad\qquad (3.4.2)$$
$$\text{s.t. } u^j \leqq zM$$
$$z \in \Re_+^J$$
$$\sum_{j=1}^J z_j = 1$$

or

$$\min_z \sum_{j=1}^J z_j Q_j$$
$$\text{s.t. } u_{jm} \leq \sum_{j=1}^J z_j u_{jm}, m = 1, 2, \cdots, M,$$
$$z_j \geq 0, j = 1, 2, \cdots, J,$$
$$\sum_{j=1}^J z_j = 1.$$

The solutions to these problems will differ unless the (V, S) technology in (3.4.2) coincides with the (C, S) technology in (3.4.1), or unless technology satisfies constant returns to scale. This suggests the following

(3.4.3) **Definition:** The function
$$S_Q(u^j) = F_Q(u^j \mid C, S)/F_Q(u^j \mid V, S), j = 1, 2, \cdots, J,$$
is called the *Input Cost Scale Efficiency Measure.*

Activity j is input cost scale efficient if $S_Q(u^j) = 1$, or if $F_Q(u^j \mid C, S) = F_Q(u^j \mid V, S)$. If $S_Q(u^j) < 1$ activity j is input cost scale inefficient, and we want to determine whether the inefficiency is due to increasing returns to scale or decreasing returns to scale. To do so it is necessary to solve a third linear programming problem, a cost minimization problem defined on an (N, S) technology. This problem can be written

$$F_Q(u^j \mid N, S) = \min_z zQ \qquad (3.4.4)$$
$$\text{s.t. } u^j \leq z\boldsymbol{M}$$
$$z \in \Re_+^J$$
$$\sum_{j=1}^J z_j \leq 1$$

or

$$\min_z \sum_{j=1}^J z_j Q_j$$
$$\text{s.t. } u_{jm} \leq \sum_{j=1}^J z_j u_{jm}, m = 1, 2, \cdots, M$$
$$z_j \geq 0, j = 1, 2, \cdots, J,$$
$$\sum_{j=1}^J z_j \leq 1.$$

The next step is to compare the solutions to the three problems (3.4.1), (3.4.2), and (3.4.4). If $S_Q(u^j) < 1$ and $F_Q(u^j \mid N, S) = F_Q(u^j \mid C, S)$, scale inefficiency is due to increasing returns to scale, while if $S_Q(u^j) < 1$ and $F_Q(u^j \mid C, S) < F_Q(u^j \mid N, S)$, scale inefficiency is due to decreasing returns to scale.

We have developed two different measures of input scale efficiency. In Section 3.2 we obtained $S_i(u^j, x^j)$ using input quantity and output quantity data. In this section we obtained $S_Q(u^j)$ using input cost and

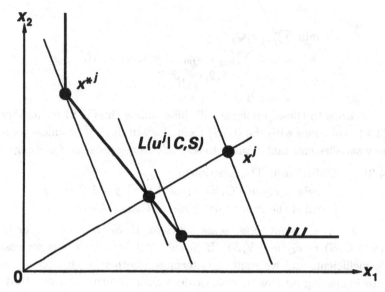

Fig. 3.9. *Radial and Nonradial Decompositions of Input Cost Efficiency*

output quantity data. Now we would like to determine the conditions under which the two measures coincide. That the two do not necessarily coincide is apparent from the fact that the second method uses observed, possibly inefficient, cost rather than minimum cost.

In order to demonstrate the conditions under which the two measures of scale efficiency $S_i(u^j, x^j)$ and $S_Q(u^j)$ yield the same result, we first introduce a third (intermediate) method of computing scale efficiency. Suppose that M and N as well as input prices are known. Under this condition, we may calculate the (C, S) Farrell decomposition (3.2.8). In addition to this (C, S) Farrell decomposition, we may also compute a (V, S) Farrell decomposition as given in (3.2.9). The ratio of the two is

$$\frac{O_i(u^j, p^j, x^j \mid C, S)}{O_i(u^j, p^j, x^j \mid V, S)} = \frac{A_i(u^j, p^j, x^j \mid C, S) \cdot S_i(u^j, x^j)}{A_i(u^j, p^j, x^j \mid V, S)}. \qquad (3.4.5)$$

Thus if $A_i(u^j, p^j, x^j \mid C, S) = A_i(u^j, p^j, x^j \mid V, S)$ then

$$S_i(u^j, x^j) = \frac{O_i(u^j, p^j, x^j \mid C, S)}{O_i(u^j, p^j, x^j \mid V, S)} = \frac{Q(u^j, p^j \mid C, S)}{Q(u^j, p^j \mid V, S)}. \qquad (3.4.6)$$

Expression (3.4.6) shows that if an observation has the same allocative efficiencies for the (C, S) and (V, S) technologies, the input scale efficiency measure $S_i(u^j, x^j)$ can be calculated as the ratio of the two minimum cost functions obtained from the (C, S) and the (V, S) technologies. However input prices appear on the right side of (3.4.6), and they do not appear in the input cost measure of scale efficiency $S_Q(u^j)$. Thus another restriction is required. This restriction is obtained by assuming that $p \in \Re_+^N$ is a common input price vector faced by all producers. Now consider the linear programming problem

$$Q(u^j, p \mid C, S) = \min_{z,x} px \qquad (3.4.7)$$

$$\text{s.t. } u^j \leq zM$$

$$zN \leq x$$

$$z \in \Re_+^J.$$

At optimum, $zN = x$, enabling us to write

$$Q(u^j, p \mid C, S) = \min_z zpN \qquad (3.4.8)$$

$$\text{s.t. } u^j \leq zM$$

$$z \in \Re_+^J.$$

Now $pN = Q$, and so $Q(u^j, p \mid C, S) = F_Q(u^j \mid C, S)$. Applying the same logic to the (V, S) technology we obtain $Q(u^j, p \mid V, S) = F_Q(u^j \mid V, S)$. Thus from expression (3.3.6) and Definition (3.3.3) we obtain

$$S_i(u^j, x^j) = \frac{F_Q(u^j \mid C, S)}{F_Q(u^j \mid V, S)} = S_Q(u^j), j = 1, 2, \cdots, J. \qquad (3.4.9)$$

Consequently, if all activities face the same input price vector, and if technology is such that allocative efficiency is the same for (C, S) and (V, S) versions (that is, if allocative efficiency is independent of the scale structure of technology), then $S_i(u^j, x^j) = S_Q(u^j)$. If either condition fails, then measuring scale economies using input quantities and output quantities may give different results from using input cost and output quantities.

3.5   A Numerical Example: Input-Based Efficiency Measurement

In this section we provide numerical examples of some of the input-based efficiency measures introduced in this chapter using the artificial data described in Section 5 of Chapter 2. Specifically, we include calculations of the measures included in the decomposition (3.2.7)

$$O_i(u^j, p^j, x^j \mid C, S) = A_i(u^j, p^j, x^j \mid C, S) \cdot F_i(u^j, x^j \mid C, S),$$

in (3.1.34)

$$F_i(u^j, x^j \mid C, S) = F_i(u^j, x^j \mid V, W) \cdot S_i(u^j, x^j) \cdot C_i(u^j, x^j),$$

and, for purposes of comparison with $F_i(u^j, x^j \mid C, S)$, the Russell measure $RM_i(u^j, x^j \mid C, S)$, from which the reader may calculate $RMA_i(u^j, p^j, x^j \mid C, S)$ using Definition (3.3.4).

The efficiency measures are calculated using SAS linear programming software, specifically, the PROC LP procedure found in SAS/OR. In this section we provide a detailed description of two of the linear programming problems used here to illustrate the general setup of the two major types of problems used throughout this book, namely: (1) cost function type problems (i.e., those in which the problem is to find a hyperplane to support an element of the reference more or less set) and (2) distance function type problems (i.e., those in which an observation is radially contracted/expanded to the boundary of the reference more or less set).

We begin with the cost function problem used to calculate $Q(u^j, p^j \mid C, S)$, i.e., problem (3.2.2), which in turn is used to calculate $O_i(u^j, p^j, x^j \mid C, S)$, (3.2.3). We begin by restating (3.2.2):

$$Q(u^j, p^j \mid C, S) = \min_{z,x} p^j x$$

$$\text{s.t. } u^j \leqq zM$$

$$zN \leqq x$$

$$z \in \Re_+^J,$$

where z and x are the variables over which the minimization occurs. Written in (approximately) canonical form, the problem becomes

$$Q(u^j, p^j \mid C, S) = \min_{z,x} p_{j1}x_1 + p_{j2}x_2 + \cdots + p_{JN}x_N$$

s.t.

$$
\begin{array}{ccccccc}
u_{11}z_1 & + & u_{21}z_2 & + & \cdots & + & u_{J1}z_J & \geqq & u_{j1} \\
u_{12}z_1 & + & u_{22}z_2 & + & \cdots & + & u_{J2}z_J & \geqq & u_{j2} \\
\vdots & & \vdots & & & & \vdots & & \vdots \\
u_{1M}z_1 & + & u_{2M}z_2 & + & \cdots & + & u_{JM}z_J & \geqq & u_{jM} \\
\\
x_{11}z_1 & + & x_{21}z_2 & + & \cdots & + & x_{J1}z_J - x_1 & \leqq & 0 \\
x_{12}z_1 & + & x_{22}z_2 & + & \cdots & + & x_{J2}z_J - x_2 & \leqq & 0 \\
\vdots & & \vdots & & & & \vdots & & \vdots \\
x_{1N}z_1 & + & x_{2N}z_2 & + & \cdots & + & x_{JN}z_J - x_N & \leqq & 0
\end{array}
$$

$$x_1 \geqq 0, x_2 \geqq 0, \cdots, x_N \geqq 0; z_1 \geqq 0, z_2 \geqq 0, \cdots, z_J \geqq 0.$$

Written in this form it becomes obvious that observed outputs and inputs serve as coefficients to the intensity variables (the z_js) and that the constraints form the technology through linear combinations of observed inputs and outputs. The solution yields $Q(u^j, p^j \mid C, S)$, i.e., minimal cost (labeled "objective value" in the PROC LP output) as well as optimal values of the x and z variables (labeled "activity" in the variable summary in SAS). We note that the nonzero optimal z values represent basic solutions, i.e., the corresponding observations or activities are used to form the part of the reference frontier relative to which observation (u^j, p^j) is being evaluated. These can be interpreted as model firms for the observation being evaluated. The solution values for the xs represent optimal (cost minimal) input usage given observed relative input prices and technology.

Additional information concerning the sensitivity of the solution to the constraints is contained in the dual solution variables (labeled "dual activity" under the constraint summary in the SAS output). These capture the sensitivity of the optimal value of the objective function to changes in the right hand side constants of the individual constraints. For our example, the dual variables associated with the output constraints yield "shadow" output marginal cost, and the dual variables associated with the input constraints yield "shadow" prices of the inputs; all are analogous to Lagrange multipliers in the differentiable case. We also note that if a dual variable is nonzero, then the corresponding constraint is binding, i.e., it holds at the optimum with strict equality (there is no slack or surplus).

Next we consider a distance function type efficiency problem, specifically, the computation of the $F_i(u^j, x^j \mid C, S)$ measure. We begin by writing out (3.1.5), namely

$$
\begin{aligned}
F_i(u^j, x^j \mid C, S) \;=\; & \min_{z, \lambda} \lambda \\
\text{s.t. } & u^j \leq zM \\
& zN \leq \lambda x^j \\
& z \in \Re^J_+,
\end{aligned}
$$

where z and λ are the variables over which minimization occurs. Rewriting this problem in (approximately) canonical form yields:

$$
F_i(u^j, x^j \mid C, S) = \min_{z, \lambda} \lambda
$$

s.t.

$$
\begin{array}{ccccccc}
u_{11}z_1 & + & u_{21}z_2 & + & \cdots & + & u_{J1}z_J & \geqq & u_{j1} \\
u_{12}z_1 & + & u_{22}z_2 & + & \cdots & + & u_{J2}z_J & \geqq & u_{j2} \\
\vdots & & \vdots & & & & \vdots & & \vdots \\
u_{1M}z_1 & + & u_{2M}z_2 & + & \cdots & + & u_{JM}z_J & \geqq & u_{jM}
\end{array}
$$

$$
\begin{aligned}
x_{11}z_1 &+ x_{21}z_2 + \cdots + x_{J1}z_J - x_{j1}\lambda \leqq 0 \\
x_{12}z_1 &+ x_{22}z_2 + \cdots + x_{J2}z_J - x_{j2}\lambda \leqq 0 \\
&\;\;\vdots \qquad\qquad\qquad\qquad\quad\vdots \qquad\quad\; \vdots \\
x_{1N}z_1 &+ z_{2N}z_2 + \cdots + x_{JN}z_J - x_{jN}\lambda \leqq 0
\end{aligned}
$$

$$ z_1 \geqq 0, z_2 \geqq 0, \cdots, z_J \geqq 0, \lambda \geqq 0. $$

This problem appears to be somewhat untraditional due to the objective function, which has only one variable. Note also that the λ variable is multiplied by all of observation j's inputs, i.e., it proportionally or radially contracts them until they are on the boundary of the technology.

Again the solution values of the z variables can be used to identify basic solutions/model firms, and the dual variables can be used for sensitivity analysis. We note that if a dual variable is nonzero, the associated slack/surplus is zero, i.e., the constraint is binding. Note that solution values of 1.000 do not guarantee minimum feasible input use, since $x^j \cdot F_i(u^j, x^j \mid C, S) \in WEff\, L(u^j \mid C, S)$, but $x^j \cdot F_i(u^j, x^j \mid C, S) \notin Eff\, L(u^j \mid C, S)$.

The dual to $F_i(u^j, x^j \mid C, S)$ is the following problem

$$ \max_{y,v} \; \sum_{m=1}^{M} y_m u_{jm} $$

$$ \text{s.t.} \; \sum_{m=1}^{M} y_m u_{jm} - \sum_{n=1}^{N} v_n x_{jn} \leqq 0, j = 1, 2, \ldots, J, $$

$$ \sum_{n=1}^{N} v_n \leqq 1. $$

Again, coefficients in the objective function for $F_i(u^j, x^j \mid C, S)$ become right hand side constants in the dual and vice versa. The coefficient matrix is also transposed.

We now turn to the results. We first calculate $Q(u^j, p^j \mid C, S)$ from (3.2.2) and divide the solution by observed cost. We thereby arrive at $O_i(u^j, p^j, x^j \mid C, S)$, see (3.2.3). Next we calculate $F_i(u^j, x^j \mid C, S)$ from (3.1.5) which is then also used to calculate $A_i(u^j, p^j, x^j \mid C, S) = O_i(u^j, p^j, x^j \mid C, S)/F_i(u^j, x^j \mid C, S)$, see (3.2.5). In order to decompose $F_i(u^j, x^j \mid C, S)$ into its components, we calculate $F_i(u^j, x^j \mid V, S)$ from (3.1.17) and use the definition (3.1.30) to calculate $S_i(u^j, x^j)$. We calculate $F_i(u^j, x^j \mid V, W)$ from (3.1.28) and use definition (3.1.32) to yield $C_i(u^j, x^j)$.

We calculate $RM_i(u^j, x^j \mid C, S)$ based on (3.3.2). We note that the problem is quite similar to $F_i(u^j, x^j \mid C, S)$, although λ is a vector in the former and a scalar in the latter. In that sense $RM_i(u^j, x^j \mid C, S)$ will appear as a more traditional linear programming problem than $F_i(u^j, x^j \mid C, S)$. In computing the Russell measure we use the following as the objective function

$$\min \sum_{n=1}^{N} \lambda_n$$

in order to make the problem linear. We then divide the solution value by N to arrive at $RM_i(u^j, x^j \mid C, S)$.

Solution values for these various measures are collected in Table 3.1 for our 20 observations of artificial data. Recall that by construction our data are "efficient" in the sense that they are on the frontier of a CES-CET technology, and prices and cost have been constructed to be consistent with the associated cost function. The data were constructed to exhibit varying returns to scale: observations 1-5 satisfy increasing returns to scale, observations 6-15 satisfy constant returns to scale, and observations 16-20 satisfy decreasing returns to scale. These varying returns to scale are picked up in our efficiency measures; observations 1-5 and 16-20 are not scale efficient, and that is also reflected in all of the measures which are constructed relative to a constant returns to scale technology. Perhaps the most interesting result is that the Russell measure and the C, S measure of input cost efficiency yield identical results.

3.6   References to the Literature

Radial input-based technical efficiency measures were developed by Debreu (1951) and Farrell (1957), the latter with empirical application to agricultural production. Consequently the technical efficiency measure (3.1.3) is frequently referred to as the (input-based) Debreu–Farrell measure. Neither Farrell nor Farrell and Fieldhouse (1962) were able to write down and solve the efficiency measurement problem as a linear programming problem, although Farrell and Fieldhouse clearly saw that it could be done. Apparently Boles (1966) was the first to develop a code for solving the appropriate linear programming problem for obtaining a technically efficient unit isoquant in the single output CRS case (he also suggests how to deal with multiple outputs). His

Table 3.1. *Input-Based Efficiency Measures Using Artificial Data*

Obs	$O_i(u^j, p^j, x^j \mid C, S)$	$A_i(u^j, p^j, x^j \mid C, S)$	$F_i(u^j, x^j \mid C, S)$
1	0.694	1.000	0.694
2	0.737	0.749	0.984
3	0.749	0.830	0.903
4	0.699	0.931	0.751
5	0.712	0.990	0.719
6	1.000	1.000	1.000
7	1.000	1.000	1.000
8	1.000	1.000	1.000
9	1.000	1.000	1.000
10	1.000	1.000	1.000
11	1.000	1.000	1.000
12	1.000	1.000	1.000
13	1.000	1.000	1.000
14	1.000	1.000	1.000
15	1.000	1.000	1.000
16	0.694	1.000	0.694
17	0.734	0.776	0.946
18	0.749	0.830	0.903
19	0.724	0.998	0.725
20	0.717	1.000	0.717

Obs	$S_i(u^j, x^j)$	$C_i(u^j, x^j)$	$RM_i(u^j, x^j \mid C, S)$	$F_i(u^j, x^j \mid V, S)$
1	0.694	1.000	0.694	1.000
2	0.984	1.000	0.737	1.000
3	0.903	1.000	0.749	1.000
4	0.751	1.000	0.696	1.000
5	0.719	1.000	0.712	1.000
6	1.000	1.000	1.000	1.000
7	1.000	1.000	1.000	1.000
8	1.000	1.000	1.000	1.000
9	1.000	1.000	1.000	1.000
10	1.000	1.000	1.000	1.000
11	1.000	1.000	1.000	1.000
12	1.000	1.000	1.000	1.000
13	1.000	1.000	1.000	1.000
14	1.000	1.000	1.000	1.000
15	1.000	1.000	1.000	1.000
16	0.694	1.000	0.694	1.000
17	0.946	1.000	0.734	1.000
18	0.903	1.000	0.749	1.000
19	0.725	1.000	0.724	1.000
20	0.717	1.000	0.717	1.000

technique was immediately applied to the calculation of Debreu–Farrell input-based efficiency scores in Philippine agriculture by Sitorus (1966), and in U.S. steam-electric generating plants by Seitz (1966). This work was continued by Seitz (1968, 1970, 1971) (more electricity generation), Carlson (1972) (U.S. higher education), and Dugger (1974) (banking), among others.

The formulation of the Debreu–Farrell input-based technical efficiency measurement problem as a set of linear programming problems was introduced into the OR/MS literature several years later by Charnes, Cooper, and Rhodes (1978). A great virtue of this and all subsequent OR/MS models is the ability to accommodate multiple outputs, although Boles had already shown how this could be done. OR/MS models analogous to our models in equations (3.1.5), (3.1.11), and (3.1.17) are occasionally referred to as CCR models, or BCC models, depending on their exact formulation, after Charnes, Cooper, and Rhodes (1978) and Banker, Charnes, and Cooper (1984), respectively. Details of these and other similar OR/MS formulations of the radial input-based technical efficiency measurement model can be found in Banker, Charnes, Cooper, Swarts, and Thomas (1989) and Seiford and Thrall (1990). Computational aspects are discussed by Adolphson, Cornia, and Walters (1990), Ali (1991), Boyd and Färe (1984), Färe and Hunsaker (1986), Charnes, Cooper, Golany, Seiford and Stutz (1985), Sueyoshi (1990), and Sueyoshi and Chang (1989).

The decomposition (3.2.7) of cost efficiency into its technical and allocative components was first obtained from Farrell (1957). An early linear programming application of the decomposition is found in Seitz (1966) (electricity generation). A recent nonparametric application of the decomposition is Ferrier and Porter (1989) (cooperatives and other producers in U.S. agriculture).

Absence of reliable input price data has forced much research to concentrate on the technical component of cost efficiency; this has been particularly true in the public sector applications so prevalent in the OR/MS literature, and for which DEA was originally developed. However the existence of price data motivated a large body of agricultural economics and economic development literature in the 1950s and 1960s. This literature used parametric techniques to test the "poor but efficient" hypothesis by testing for satisfaction of the first-order conditions for cost minimizing input allocation or for profit maximizing input and output allocation. Here the focus has been primarily, but not exclusively, on price efficiency. Influential early contributions include Tax (1953),

Hopper (1965), and Schultz (1964); more recent contributions include Wise and Yotopoulos (1969), Shapiro (1982), and Junankar (1989).

The ordering (3.1.29) of technical efficiency measures according to scale and disposability properties of the technology is due to Afriat (1972) and Grosskopf (1986). One use of this ordering is the development of measures of scale efficiency and congestion. Another use is in the nonparametric testing of regularity conditions.

Input-based measures of scale efficiency were anticipated by Farrell and Fieldhouse (1962). Their ideas were further developed in a parametric framework by Nerlove (1963), and in a nonparametric framework by Bressler (1966) and Seitz (1966). More recent treatments of input-based scale efficiency measurement include Førsund and Hjalmarsson (1979a) in a parametric framework, and Banker (1984), Banker, Charnes, and Cooper (1984), Chang and Guh (1991), and Maindiratta (1990) in a nonparametric framework.

Measures of input congestion developed by Färe and Jansson (1974, 1975, 1976) and Färe and Svensson (1980) were given nonparametric representations by Färe, Grosskopf, and Lovell (1985,1987b).

Recent nonparametric decompositions of overall input cost efficiency into technical, scale, congestion, and allocative components include Färe, Grosskopf, and Logan (1983) (electric utilities), Byrnes, Färe, Grosskopf, and Lovell (1988) (coal mining), Field (1990) (British building societies), and Byrnes and Valdmanis (1989) (hospitals).

The Russell measure described in Section 3.3 was introduced by Färe and Lovell (1978). It is a generalization of both the Debreu–Farrell measures and the single-factor or partial efficiency measures (e.g., labor productivity) discussed in Färe (1975), Kopp (1981), and Färe, Lovell, and Zieschang (1983). An application of the Russell measure to highway maintenance is provided by Deller and Nelson (1989, 1991). An alternative to the Russell measure, a two-step measure that removes slack left by the radial Debreu–Farrell measure, has been proposed by Zieschang (1984).

Scale efficiency measures requiring input cost and output quantity data were proposed by Färe and Grosskopf (1985), and have been implemented by Vanden Eeckaut, Tulkens, and Jamar (1993).

4

Output-Based Efficiency Measurement

4.0 Introduction

In Chapter 3 we modeled technology in terms of the input correspondence and measured efficiency relative to the input set, i.e., output quantities were taken as given and inefficiency identified by feasible reductions in input quantities or cost. In this chapter we measure efficiency relative to the output set $P(x)$, i.e., we take input quantities as given and judge performance by the ability to increase output quantities or revenue. As such the topic of this chapter is very much in the spirit of the neoclassical production functions defined as maximum achievable output given input quantities and technology, although we generalize here to the case of multiple rather than scalar output.

In Section 4.1 output-based measures which are independent of prices, i.e., technical in nature, are introduced, and we show how overall technical efficiency can be decomposed into three component measures – scale, congestion, and purely technical efficiency. All of these measures of technical efficiency take input quantities as given and measure efficiency as feasible proportional expansion of all outputs.

In Section 4.2 we turn to output price-dependent measures of efficiency, the goal being to maximize revenue rather than to proportionally increase outputs. Here it becomes relevant to alter the output mix in light of existing output prices. In particular, we show how to decompose overall revenue efficiency (defined as the ratio of maximum to observed revenue) into technical and allocative components.

Sections 4.1 and 4.2 focus on what we call radial measures of output efficiency. One of the drawbacks of these radial measures is that they project an observation onto the isoquant of the output set, and not necessarily onto the efficient subset of the output set. In particular, the overall technical efficiency measure judges an observation which is on a horizontal or vertical segment of the frontier of the output set to be efficient (no further proportional increases in all outputs are feasible), yet increases in a subset of the output vector are still feasible. In Section 4.3 we introduce a nonradial measure of output efficiency which judges activities as efficient if and only if they are members of the efficient subset.

In Section 4.4 we return to radial measures of output efficiency. Specifically, we introduce an alternative formulation of scale efficiency which has different data requirements than the measure of scale efficiency in Section 4.1. Here scale efficiency is measured using data on revenue (instead of output quantities) and input quantities. We also show that this revenue measure of scale efficiency coincides with the quantity-based measure only if all activities face the same output price vector and allocative efficiency is independent of the scale of technology.

Section 4.5 provides a comparison of the input-based measures introduced in Chapter 3 and the output-based measures discussed in this chapter. We show that under constant returns to scale, the overall measure of technical input efficiency yields an efficiency value which is equal to the reciprocal of the overall measure of technical output efficiency. We also discuss the relationship between output and input measures of scale efficiency, i.e., when their values are reciprocals and when they give the same inferences concerning returns to scale. There is, however, no necessary relationship between input-based and output-based measures of allocative efficiency, overall efficiency, or congestion.

Section 4.6 includes a numerical example of some of the output-based efficiency measures introduced in this chapter using our artificial data set.

4.1   Radial Efficiency Measures Requiring Input Quantity and Output Quantity Data: The Decomposition of Technical Efficiency

This section is identical in format to Section 3.1 of Chapter 3. The data requirements are the same. However the roles of inputs and outputs are reversed in the analysis. Consequently we seek a family of measures of the efficiency with which an output vector is produced with an input vector. It is the input vector that is predetermined, and the output vector whose size is to be evaluated. The efficiency measures obtained are referred to as "output-based" measures, and output sets are used to represent technology. Reversing the order of inputs and outputs has two consequences of particular interest. First, technical and scale efficiency refer to the same phenomena as in Section 3.1, although output-based measures of technical and scale efficiency may have different numerical values than input-based measures. Second, congestion refers to output congestion, a totally different phenomenon than input congestion introduced in Section 3.1. Thus numerical values for the two types of congestion measure bear no necessary relation to one another. Consequently the output-based decompositions obtained at the end of Section 4.1, while similar in appearance to the input-based decompositions at the end of Section 3.1, refer to fundamentally different phenomena and can have very different numerical elements.

Suppose the input matrix N and the output matrix M are given. The output reference set satisfying constant returns to scale and strong disposability of outputs can be formed from N and M as

$$P(x \mid C, S) = \{u : u \leq zM, zN \leq x, z \in \Re_+^J\}, x \in \Re_+^N, \qquad (4.1.1)$$

where z denotes the vector of intensity variables, C denotes a constant returns to scale technology as before, and S refers to strong disposability of outputs (see also (2.4.4)). The fact that $P(x \mid C, S)$ describes a constant returns to scale, strong disposability of outputs technology is verified by the following:

(4.1.2)   **Proposition:** The (C, S) output sets $P(x \mid C, S)$ satisfy

(i) $P(\lambda x \mid C, S) = \lambda P(x \mid C, S), \lambda > 0$,

(ii) $u \leq v \in P(x \mid C, S) \implies u \in P(x \mid C, S)$.

Proof: (i) Let $\lambda > 0$ and consider

$$\begin{aligned}
P(\lambda x \mid C, S) &= \{u : u \leq zM, zN \leq \lambda x, z \in \Re_+^J\} \\
&= \lambda\{u/\lambda : u/\lambda \leq (z/\lambda)M, (z/\lambda)N \leq \\
&\qquad x, (z/\lambda) \in (1/\lambda)\Re_+^J\} \\
&= \lambda P(x \mid C, S).
\end{aligned}$$

(ii) This property follows from the inequality $u \leq zM$.

Q.E.D.

Let $u^j \in P(x^j \mid C, S)$. We want to know how efficient the feasible u^j is, i.e., how close u^j is to the upper boundary of $P(x^j \mid C, S)$. A measure is provided by

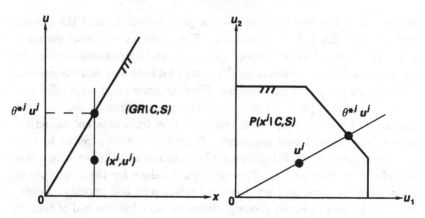

Fig. 4.1. *The (C,S) Output Measure of Technical Efficiency*

(4.1.3)   **Definition**: The function
$$F_o(x^j, u^j \mid C, S) = \max\{\theta : \theta u^j \in P(x^j \mid C, S)\}, j = 1, 2, \cdots, J,$$
is called the (C,S) *Output Measure of Technical Efficiency.*

The measure $F_o(x^j, u^j \mid C, S)$, which is illustrated in Figure 4.1 for a piecewise linear technology, measures the efficiency of u^j produced from x^j when technology is assumed to satisfy (C,S). It does so by radially expanding u^j as much as technologically possible, and then by computing the ratio of the expanded to the observed outputs. Thus $F_o(x^j, u^j \mid C, S) = \parallel F_o(x^j, u^j \mid C, S) \cdot u^j \parallel / \parallel u^j \parallel$. The properties of the (C,S) output measure of technical efficiency are summarized in

(4.1.4)   **Proposition**: Given $P(x^j \mid C, S)$, then for each
$j = 1, 2, \cdots, J,$

$F_o.1$ $F_o(x^j, \delta u^j \mid C, S) = \delta^{-1} F_o(x^j, u^j \mid C, S), \delta > 0,$

$F_o.2$ $F_o(\lambda x^j, u^j \mid C, S) = \lambda F_o(x^j, u^j \mid C, S), \lambda > 0,$

$F_o.3$ $1 \le F_o(x^j, u^j \mid C, S) < +\infty,$

$F_o.4$ $u^j \in WEff\ P(x^j \mid C, S) \iff F_o(x^j, u^j \mid C, S) = 1,$

$F_o.5$ $F_o(x^j, u^j \mid C, S)$ is independent of unit of measurement.

Proof:

$(F_o.1)$ $F_o(x^j, \delta u^j \mid C, S) = \max\{\theta : \theta \delta u^j \in P(x^j \mid C, S)\}$
$$= \max\{\delta^{-1}\theta\delta : \theta\delta u^j \in P(x^j \mid C, S)\}$$
$$= \delta^{-1} F_o(x^j, u^j \mid C, S).$$

(F_o.2)   Using (4.1.2(i)),

$$F_o(\lambda x^j, u^j \mid C, S) = \max\{\theta : \theta u^j \in P(\lambda x^j \mid C, S)\}$$
$$= \lambda F_o(x^j, u^j \mid C, S).$$

(F_o.3)   Follows from the fact that for each j, $u^j \in P(x^j \mid C, S)$.

(F_o.4)   As a radial measure, $F_o(x^j, u^j \mid C, S) = 1 \iff F_o(x^j, u^j \mid C, S) \cdot u^j \in Isoq\ P(x^j \mid C, S)$. Since we have strong disposability of outputs from (4.1.2(ii)), $WEff\ P(x^j \mid C, S) = Isoq\ P(x^j \mid C, S)$, and F_o.4 holds.

(F_o.5)   Consider just the mth output constraint $\theta u_{jm} \leq \sum_{j=1}^{J} z_j u_{jm}$. If the unit of measurement is changed, so that $\hat{u}_{jm} = \nu u_{jm}, j = 1, 2, \cdots, J$, then clearly θ and z are not affected.

$$Q.E.D.$$

The (C, S) output measure of technical efficiency can be evaluated for any observation j as the solution to the following linear programming problem.

$$F_o(x^j, u^j \mid C, S) = \max_{\theta, z} \theta$$
$$\text{s.t.}\ \theta u^j \leq zM$$
$$zN \leq x^j \qquad (4.1.5)$$
$$z \in \Re_+^J,$$

or

$$\max_{\theta, z} \theta$$
$$\text{s.t.}\ \theta u_{jm} \leq \sum_{j=1}^{J} z_j u_{jm}, m = 1, 2, \cdots, M,$$
$$\sum_{j=1}^{J} z_j x_{jn} \leq x_{jn}, n = 1, 2, \cdots, N,$$
$$z_j \geq 0, j = 1, 2, \cdots, J.$$

The measure $F_o(x^j, u^j \mid C, S)$ is illustrated using a piecewise linear technology in Figure 4.1. In the first panel $M = N = 1$, and $(GR \mid C, S)$ is used, while in the second panel $M = 2$, $N = 1$, and $P(x^j \mid C, S)$ is used. In both panels u^j is produced from x^j, and $\theta^{*j} u^j = F_o(x^j, u^j \mid C, S) \cdot u^j$ is technically efficient relative to the (C, S) technology, where θ^{*j} is the maximizing value of θ.

The next output measure of technical efficiency is defined relative to a slightly less restrictive technology than that defined in (4.1.1). In particular, instead of constant returns to scale, the output reference set will now be required to satisfy nonincreasing returns to scale. Strong disposability of outputs is, however, maintained. This new output reference technology can be described from the input matrix N and output matrix M as

$$P(x \mid N, S) = \{u : u \leqq zM, zN \leqq x, z \in \Re_+^J, \sum_{j=1}^J z_j \leqq 1\}, x \in \Re_+^N,$$

(4.1.6)

where z is the activity vector as before, and has the same restriction as on the corresponding input technology defined in (3.1.6). (4.1.6) is related to (4.1.1) as follows

$$P(x \mid N, S) \subseteqq P(x \mid C, S), \tag{4.1.7}$$

and

(4.1.8)   **Proposition:** Let P be the output correspondence defined in (4.1.6). It satisfies

(i) $P(\lambda x \mid N, S) \subseteqq \lambda P(x \mid N, S), \lambda \geqq 1$,

(ii) $u \leqq v \in P(x \mid N, S) \Longrightarrow u \in P(x \mid N, S)$.

Proof: (i) Assume $\lambda \geqq 1$ and consider

$$
\begin{aligned}
P(\lambda x \mid N, S) &= \{u : u \leqq zM, zN \leqq \lambda x, z \in \Re_+^J, \sum_{j=1}^J z_j \leqq 1\}, \\
&= \lambda\{u/\lambda : u/\lambda \leqq (z/\lambda)M, (z/\lambda)N \leqq x, \\
&\qquad (z/\lambda) \in \Re_+^J, \sum_{j=1}^J (z_j/\lambda) \leqq 1/\lambda\} \\
&\subseteqq \lambda\{u/\lambda : u/\lambda \leqq (z/\lambda)M, (z/\lambda)N \leqq x, \\
&\qquad (z/\lambda) \in \Re_+^J, \sum_{j=1}^J (z_j/\lambda) \leqq 1\} \\
&= \lambda P(x \mid N, S).
\end{aligned}
$$

(ii) This is left to the reader.

Q.E.D.

Next, we can introduce a new (but still radial) output measure of technical efficiency relative to the (N, S) technology defined in (4.1.6).

(4.1.9)   **Definition:** The function

$F_o(x^j, u^j \mid N, S) = \max\{\theta : \theta u^j \in P(x^j \mid N, S)\}, j = 1, 2, \cdots, J,$

is called the (N,S) *Output Measure of Technical Efficiency.*

The (N, S) output measure of technical efficiency computes the efficiency of u^j produced from x^j by taking the ratio of the greatest feasible radial expansion of u^j given the (N, S) technology to u^j itself. Thus $F_o(x^j, u^j \mid N, S) = \parallel F_o(x^j, u^j \mid N, S) \cdot u^j \parallel / \parallel u^j \parallel$. The properties satisfied by $F_o(x^j, u^j \mid N, S)$ are very similar to those satisfied by $F_o(x^j, u^j \mid C, S)$, the only differences arising from the different scale properties assumed for the two technologies. The properties of $F_o(x^j, u^j \mid N, S)$ are summarized in the following proposition, stated without proof because these proofs are so similar to those of Proposition (4.1.4).

(4.1.10)   **Proposition:** Given $P(x^j \mid N, S)$, then for each $j = 1, 2, \cdots, J$,

$F_o.1$ $F_o(x^j, \delta u^j \mid N, S) = \delta^{-1} F_o(x^j, u^j \mid N, S), \delta > 0,$

$F_o.2$ $F_o(\lambda x^j, u^j \mid N, S) \leq \lambda F_o(x^j, u^j \mid N, S), \lambda \geq 1,$

$F_o.3$ $1 \leq F_o(x^j, u^j \mid N, S) < +\infty,$

$F_o.4$ $u^j \in WEff\, P(x^j \mid N, S) \iff F_o(x^j, u^j \mid N, S) = 1,$

$F_o.5$ $F_o(x^j, u^j \mid N, S)$ is independent of unit of measurement.

The (N, S) output measure of technical efficiency can be calculated for observation j using the (N, S) piecewise linear technology (4.1.6) as the solution to the following linear programming problem

$$F_o(x^j, u^j \mid N, S) = \max_{\theta, z} \theta \qquad (4.1.11)$$

$$\text{s.t. } \theta u^j \leq zM$$

$$zN \leq x^j$$

$$z \in \Re_+^J$$

$$\sum_{j=1}^J z_j \leq 1$$

or

$$\max_{\theta, z} \theta$$

$$\text{s.t. } \theta u_{jm} \leq \sum_{j=1}^J z_j u_{jm}, m = 1, 2, \cdots, M,$$

$$\sum_{j=1}^J z_j x_{jn} \leq x_{jn}, n = 1, 2, \cdots, N,$$

$$z_j \geq 0, j = 1, 2, \cdots, J,$$

$$\sum_{j=1}^J z_j \leq 1.$$

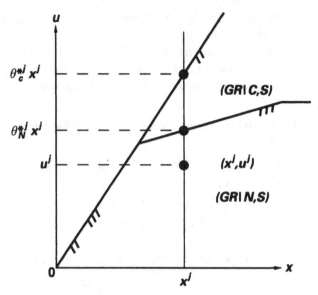

Fig. 4.2. *A Comparison of $F_o(x^j, u^j \mid C, S)$ and $F_o(x^j, u^j \mid N, S)$*

In light of (4.1.7) it is clear that

$$1 \leqq F_o(x^j, u^j \mid N, S) \leqq F_o(x^j, u^j \mid C, S), \qquad (4.1.12)$$

so that output technical efficiency measured relative to an (N, S) technology is no more than (i.e., is at least as close to its minimum value of unity) output technical efficiency measured relative to a (C, S) technology. Figure 4.2 illustrates for the $M = N = 1$ case, using the graph, where θ_c^{*j} and θ_N^{*j} are the maximum feasible expansions of u^j given (C, S) and (N, S) technology, respectively.

We now repeat the exercise, this time on the assumption that technology satisfies the still weaker scale property of variable returns to scale. Strong disposability of outputs is maintained. The (V, S) output sets are obtained from the data matrices M and N by means of

$$P(x \mid V, S) = \{u : u \leqq zM, zN \leqq x, z \in \Re_+^J, \sum_{j=1}^{J} z_j = 1\}, x \in \Re_+^N.$$

$$(4.1.13)$$

We note that the intensity vector z is now restricted to sum to unity. Consequently

$$P(x \mid V, S) \subseteqq P(x \mid N, S). \qquad (4.1.14)$$

We can now define a radial measure of output technical efficiency relative to the (V, S) technology in (4.1.13).

(4.1.15)   **Definition**: The function
$$F_o(x^j, u^j \mid V, S) = \max\{\theta : \theta u^j \in P(x^j \mid V, S)\},$$
$$j = 1, 2, \cdots, J,$$
is called the (V,S) *Output Measure of Technical Efficiency*.

The (V, S) output measure satisfies properties analogous to $F_o.1$, $F_o.3$, $F_o.4$ and $F_o.5$ in Propositions (4.1.4) and (4.1.10). It satisfies no property like $F_o.2$, however, since it obeys variable returns to scale. However, from (4.1.14) we have

$$1 \leqq F_o(x^j, u^j \mid V, S) \leqq F_o(x^j, u^j \mid N, S), j = 1, 2, \cdots, J, \qquad (4.1.16)$$

a result that is illustrated in Figure 4.3 for the $M = N = 1$ case using the graph.

The (V, S) Output Measure of Technical Efficiency is calculated for observation j using the piecewise linear (V, S) technology (4.1.13) as the solution to the linear programming problem

$$F_o(x^j, u^j \mid V, S) = \max_{\theta, z} \theta \qquad (4.1.17)$$

$$\text{s.t. } \theta u^j \leqq z M$$
$$z N \leqq x^j$$
$$z \in \Re_+^J$$
$$\sum_{j=1}^{J} z_j = 1$$

or

$$\max_{\theta, z} \theta$$

$$\text{s.t. } \theta u_{jm} \leqq \sum_{j=1}^{J} z_j u_{jm}, m = 1, 2, \cdots, M,$$

$$\sum_{j=1}^{J} z_j x_{jn} \leqq x_{jn}, n = 1, 2, \cdots, N,$$

$$z_j \geqq 0, j = 1, 2, \cdots, J,$$

$$\sum_{j=1}^{J} z_j = 1.$$

We now have three output technical efficiency measures, calculated relative to technologies satisfying three scale properties and the same strong disposability of output property. We next maintain the variable returns to scale property and relax the strong output disposability prop-

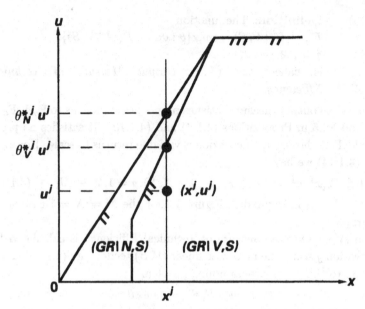

Fig. 4.3. *A Comparison of $F_o(x^j, u^j \mid N, S)$ and $F_o(x^j, u^j \mid V, S)$*

erty, in two stages. We begin by allowing a subvector of outputs to be weakly disposable, while its complement is restricted to be strongly disposable. This will generate a fourth output technical efficiency measure. We then allow all outputs to be weakly disposable, which generates a fifth output technical efficiency measure.

We begin by partitioning the matrix of observed outputs. Let $M = (M^\alpha, M^{\hat\alpha})$ where $\alpha \subseteq \{1, 2, \cdots, M\}$ and $\hat\alpha = \{1, \cdots, M\}\backslash\alpha$. Correspondingly, we partition the vector of outputs as $u = (u_\alpha, u_{\hat\alpha})$. We can now define an output reference set which does not restrict scale properties and relaxes strong disposability to weak disposability for output subvector $u_{\hat\alpha}$, while maintaining strong disposability for output subvector u_α. We have

$$P(x \mid V, S^\alpha) = \{u : u_\alpha \leqq zM^\alpha, u_{\hat\alpha} = \mu zM^{\hat\alpha}, \qquad (4.1.18)$$

$$0 \leqq \mu \leqq 1, zN \leqq x, z \in \Re_+^J, \sum_{j=1}^J z_j = 1\}, x \in \Re_+^N.$$

If $u \in P(x \mid V, S^\alpha)$ then so is $\delta u, \delta \in [0, 1]$, so that outputs are weakly disposable. However only a subset of outputs u_α remains strongly disposable; the equality $u_{\hat\alpha} = \mu zM^{\hat\alpha}$ implies that outputs in $u_{\hat\alpha}$ are not necessarily strongly disposable. In Figure 4.4 output u_1 is weakly and

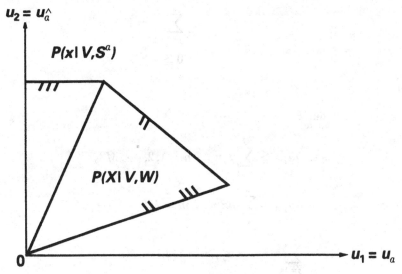

Fig. 4.4. *Strong and Weak Output Disposability*

strongly disposable and output u_2 is weakly (but not strongly) disposable.

We can now define an output technical efficiency measure on the technology defined by the output set $P(x \mid V, S^\alpha)$ in (4.1.18).

(4.1.19)   **Definition:** The function

$$F_o(x^j, u^j \mid V, S^\alpha) = \max\{\theta : \theta u^j \in P(x^j \mid V, S^\alpha)\}, j = 1, 2, \cdots, J,$$

is called the (V, S^α) *Output Measure of Technical Efficiency.*

$F_o(x^j, u^j \mid V, S^\alpha)$ measures the efficiency of u^j obtained from x^j when technology satisfies variable returns to scale, weak disposability with respect to output subvector $u_{\hat{\alpha}}$ and strong disposability with respect to output subvector u_α. It is calculated, using the piecewise linear (V, S^α) technology (4.1.18), as the solution to the nonlinear programming problem

$$F_o(x^j, u^j \mid V, S^\alpha) = \max_{\theta, z, \mu} \theta \qquad (4.1.20)$$

$$\text{s.t. } \theta u_\alpha^j \leqq z M^\alpha$$

$$\theta u_{\hat{\alpha}}^j = \mu z M^{\hat{\alpha}}$$

$$z N \leqq x^j$$

$$z \in \Re_+^J$$

$$\sum_{j=1}^{J} z_j = 1$$

$$0 \leqq \mu \leqq 1$$

or

$$\max_{\theta, z, \mu} \theta$$

$$\text{s.t. } \theta u_{jm} \leqq \sum_{j=1}^{J} z_j u_{jm}, m = 1, 2, \cdots, M^{\alpha},$$

$$\theta u_{jm} = \sum_{j=1}^{J} \mu z_j u_{jm}, m = M^{\alpha} + 1, \cdots, M,$$

$$\sum_{j=1}^{J} z_j x_{jn} \leqq x_{jn}, n = 1, 2, \cdots, N,$$

$$0 \leqq \mu \leqq 1,$$

$$z_j \geqq 0, j = 1, 2, \cdots, J,$$

$$\sum_{j=1}^{J} z_j = 1.$$

This problem can be converted into a linear programming problem by setting $\mu = 1$. Such a procedure leaves the maximizing (θ, z) values unchanged.

Since $P(x^j \mid V, S^{\alpha}) \subseteqq P(x^j \mid V, S)$ it follows that

$$1 \leqq F_o(x^j, u^j \mid V, S^{\alpha}) \leqq F_o(x^j, u^j \mid V, S), j = 1, \cdots, J. \qquad (4.1.21)$$

We now construct the most general output set: that satisfying variable returns to scale and weak disposability of outputs. No subvector of outputs is required to be strongly disposable. The piecewise linear (V, W) output set is given by

$$P(x \mid V, W) = \{u : u = \mu z M, z N \leqq x, 0 \leqq \mu \leqq 1, z \in \Re_+^J,$$

$$\sum_{j=1}^{J} z_j = 1\}, x \in \Re_+^N, \qquad (4.1.22)$$

where W refers to weak disposability of outputs (see Figure 4.4).

We measure output technical efficiency relative to this technology by means of

(4.1.23) **Definition:** The function

$$F_o(x^j, u^j \mid V, W) = \max\{\theta : \theta u^j \in P(x^j \mid V, W)\}, j = 1, 2, \cdots, J,$$

is called the (V, W) *Output Measure of Technical Efficiency.*

The (V, W) measure calculates the efficiency of u^j obtained from x^j when the least restrictive assumptions concerning both scale and output disposability are imposed on technology. Proofs similar to those of Proposition (4.1.4) can be used to verify the following properties of $F_o(x^j, u^j \mid V, W)$.

(4.1.24) **Proposition:** Given $P(x^j \mid V, W)$, then for each $j = 1, 2, \cdots, J,$

$F_o.1$ $F_o(x^j, \delta u^j \mid V, W) = \delta^{-1} F_o(x^j, u^j \mid V, W), \delta > 0,$

$F_o.2$ $1 \leq F_o(x^j, u^j \mid V, W) < +\infty,$

$F_o.3$ $u^j \in Isoq\, P(x^j \mid V, W) \Longleftrightarrow F_o(x^j, u^j \mid V, W) = 1,$

$F_o.4$ $F_o(x^j, u^j \mid V, W)$ is independent of unit of measurement.

Since $P(x \mid V, W) \subseteq P(x \mid V, S^\alpha)$ we also have

$$1 \leq F_o(x^j, u^j \mid V, W) \leq F_o(x^j, u^j \mid V, S^\alpha), j = 1, 2, \cdots, J. \qquad (4.1.25)$$

The (V, W) Output Measure of Technical Efficiency can be calculated relative to the piecewise linear (V, W) technology (4.1.22) as the solution to the nonlinear programming problem

$$F_o(x^j, u^j \mid V, W) = \max_{\theta, z, \mu} \theta \qquad (4.1.26)$$

$$\text{s.t. } \theta u^j = \mu z M$$

$$z N \leq x^j$$

$$0 \leq \mu \leq 1$$

$$z \in \Re_+^J$$

$$\sum_{j=1}^J z_j = 1$$

or

$$\max_{\theta, z, \mu} \theta$$

$$\text{s.t. } \theta u_{jm} = \mu \sum_{j=1}^J z_j u_{jm}, m = 1, 2, \cdots, M,$$

$$\sum_{j=1}^J z_j x_{jn} \leq x_{jn}, n = 1, 2, \cdots, N,$$

$$0 \leqq \mu \leqq 1,$$
$$z_j \geqq 0, j = 1, 2, \cdots, J,$$
$$\sum_{j=1}^{J} z_j = 1.$$

This problem can be linearized by setting $\mu = 1$ as before, without altering the maximizing values (θ, z).

We now collect results concerning the five output measures of technical efficiency. From equations (4.1.12), (4.1.16), (4.1.21), and (4.1.25) relating them, and Propositions (4.1.4) and (4.1.24) bounding them, we have

$$1 \leqq F_o(x^j, u^j \mid V, W) \leqq F_o(x^j, u^j \mid V, S^\alpha) \leqq F_o(x^j, u^j \mid V, S)$$
$$\leqq F_o(x^j, u^j \mid N, S) \leqq F_o(x^j, u^j \mid C, S) < +\infty. \qquad (4.1.27)$$

This relationship demonstrates that because the technologies relative to which these functions are measured are nested, these efficiency measures can be ordered. This string of inequalities could be extended by allowing for all possible combinations of returns to scale and disposability properties, an exercise we leave for the reader. We turn our attention instead to exploiting the relationships summarized in (4.1.27).

We do so by noting that the first three measures in (4.1.27) capture variations in technology due to variations in the ability to freely dispose of outputs. Starting from the right hand side, the last three measures capture variations in technology due to variations in scale properties. Because the underlying technologies are nested and these measures reflect that relationship, we can construct new measures as ratios of these measures of technical efficiency which allow us to identify output congestion and deviations from efficient scale, and which provide a decomposition of $F_o(x^j, u^j \mid C, S)$ into three mutually exclusive and exhaustive components: congestion, scale efficiency, and purely technical efficiency. We begin by examining departures from constant returns to scale, and we propose the measure of output scale efficiency given in

(4.1.28)   **Definition:** The function
$$S_o(x^j, u^j) = \frac{F_o(x^j, u^j \mid C, S)}{F_o(x^j, u^j \mid V, S)}, j = 1, 2, \cdots, J,$$
is called the *Output Scale Efficiency Measure.*

We say that observation j is output scale efficient if $S_o(x^j, u^j) = 1$, or if it is equally technically efficient relative to the (C, S) and (V, S) output sets. The properties of $S_o(x^j, u^j)$ are summarized in

(4.1.29)   **Proposition:** Given $S_o(x^j, u^j)$, then for each
$$j = 1, 2, \cdots, J,$$

$S_o.1$ $1 \leq S_o(x^j, u^j) < +\infty,$

$S_o.2$ $S_o(x^j, u^j) = 1 \iff F_o(x^j, u^j \mid V, S) \cdot u^j$ exhibits CRS, or equivalently $F_o(x^j, u^j \mid V, S) \cdot u^j \in$ $Isoq\ P(x^j \mid C, S),$

$S_o.3$ $S_o(x^j, \delta u^j) = S_o(x^j, u^j), \delta > 0,$

$S_o.4$ $S_o(x^j, u^j)$ is independent of unit of measurement.

Proof:

$(S_o.1)$ This follows from (4.1.27) and (4.1.28).

$(S_o.2)$ Assume that $S_o(x^j, u^j) = 1$. Then $F_o(x^j, u^j \mid C, S) = F_o(x^j, u^j \mid V, S)$ and $F_o(x^j, u^j \mid V, S) \cdot u^j \in Isoq\ P(x^j \mid C, S)$. Thus CRS prevails at $F_o(x^j, u^j \mid V, S) \cdot u^j$. Conversely, if CRS prevails at $F_o(x^j, u^j \mid V, S) \cdot u^j$ then $F_o(x^j, u^j \mid V, S) \cdot u^j \in Isoq\ P(x^j \mid C, S)$. Hence $F_o(x^j, u^j \mid V, S) = F_o(x^j, u^j \mid C, S)$ and $S_o(x^j, u^j) = 1$.

$(S_o.3)$ This follows from the homogeneity properties of $F_o(x^j, u^j \mid C, S)$ and $F_o(x^j, u^j \mid V, S)$.

$(S_o.4)$ This follows from the fact that $F_o(x^j, u^j \mid V, S)$ and $F_o(x^j, u^j \mid C, S)$ are independent of unit of measurement.

$$Q.E.D.$$

Output scale efficiency is illustrated in Figure 4.5. Observation (x^j, u^j) is output scale efficient, as are all feasible $(x^j, \delta u^j), \delta > 0$, because it is equally technically efficient relative to (C, S) and (V, S) technologies. All other observations are either too large or too small to be output scale efficient. For example, observation (x^k, u^k) operates at an inefficiently small scale. For this observation $F_o(x^k, u^k \mid C, S) > F_o(x^k, u^k \mid V, S)$, which demonstrates output scale inefficiency, and also $F_o(x^k, u^k \mid C, S) = F_o(x^k, u^k \mid N, S)$, which demonstrates inefficiently small scale. Observation (x^k, u^k) is operating in the region of increasing returns to scale. Just the opposite holds for observation (x^ℓ, u^ℓ). For this observation $F_o(x^\ell, u^\ell \mid C, S) > F_o(x^\ell, u^\ell \mid V, S)$, which demonstrates output scale inefficiency, and $F_o(x^\ell, u^\ell \mid C, S) > F_o(x^\ell, u^\ell \mid N, S)$, which demonstrates inefficiently large scale, or operation in the region of decreasing returns to scale.

The magnitude and nature of output scale efficiency depends entirely on the relationships among the three output measures of technical efficiency, $F_o(x^j, u^j \mid C, S), F_o(x^j, u^j \mid N, S)$, and $F_o(x^j, u^j \mid V, S)$. Consequently an operational test for the nature of scale efficiency is based on the solutions to the three programming problems (4.1.5), (4.1.11), and (4.1.17). Aside from calculating ratios, once the three output measures of technical efficiency have been calculated no additional calculations are required in order to calculate output scale efficiency measures.

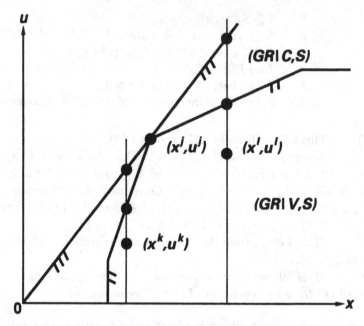

Fig. 4.5. *Measuring Output Scale Efficiency*

We continue the decomposition process by turning to the issue of output congestion, or the loss of potential output due to the lack of strong disposability of outputs. In terms of the string of inequalities in (4.1.27), we have finished with the three measures at the right end of the string of inequalities; differences among them involve scale differences among technologies having strong output disposability. We turn our attention to the three measures at the left end of the string of inequalities; differences among these involve output disposability differences among technologies satisfying variable returns to scale.

A measure of the loss in potential output due to the lack of strong output disposability is provided by

(4.1.30)   **Definition:** The function

$$C_o(x^j, u^j) = \frac{F_o(x^j, u^j | V, S)}{F_o(x^j, u^j | V, W)}, j = 1, 2, \cdots, J,$$

is called the *Output Congestion Measure.*

The properties of the output congestion measure are given in

(4.1.31)   **Proposition:** Given $C_o(x^j, u^j)$, then for each

$$j = 1, 2, \cdots, J,$$

     $C_o.1$ $1 \leqq C_o(x^j, u^j) < +\infty,$

$C_o.2 \quad C_o(x^j, u^j) = 1 \Longleftrightarrow F_o(x^j, u^j \mid V, W) \cdot u^j \in$
$WEff\ P(x^j \mid V, W),$

$C_o.3 \quad C_o(x^j, \delta u^j) = C_o(x^j, u^j), \delta > 0,$

$C_o.4 \quad C_o(x^j, u^j)$ is independent of unit of measurement.

Proof: $(C_o.1), (C_o.3),$ and $(C_o.4)$ are proved using arguments similar to those used in Proposition (4.1.29), parts $(S_o.1), (S_o.3),$ and $(S_o.4)$. To prove $(C_o.2)$, assume that $C_o(x^j, u^j) = 1$, then $F_o(x^j, u^j \mid V, S) \cdot u^j = F_o(x^j, u^j \mid V, W) \cdot u^j \in Isoq\ P(x^j \mid V, S) \cap Isoq\ P(x^j \mid V, W)$. Thus by Propositions (2.3.5) and (2.3.6), $F_o(x^j, u^j \mid V, W) \cdot u^j \in WEff\ P(x^j \mid V, W)$. Conversely, if $F_o(x^j, u^j \mid V, W) \cdot u^j \in WEff\ P(x^j \mid V, W)$ then since $WEff\ P(x^j \mid V, W) \subseteq WEff\ P(x^j \mid V, S), F_o(x^j, u^j \mid V, S) = F_o(x^j, u^j \mid V, W)$ and $C_o(x^j, u^j) = 1$.

$$Q.E.D.$$

The output congestion measure is illustrated in Figure 4.6. There is no output congestion for observation u^ℓ, since technical efficiency relative to the (V, W) technology is the same as technical efficiency relative to the (V, S) technology. However observation u^k encounters output congestion since it is more technically efficient relative to the (V, W) technology than the (V, S) technology. In the case of observation u^k the congesting output is u_1.

More generally, if output congestion occurs at (x^j, u^j), the congesting output subvectors can be determined by comparing $F_o(x^j, u^j \mid V, S)$ with $F_o(x^j, u^j \mid V, S^\alpha)$, for each $\alpha \subseteq \{1, 2, \cdots, M\}$. If $C_o(x^j, u^j) > 1$ and $F_o(x^j, u^j \mid V, S) = F_o(x^j, u^j \mid V, S^\alpha)$, then the subvector $u^j_{\bar{\alpha}}$ obstructs the production of outputs. Comparing the measures for each subvector yields the set of subvectors which are not strongly disposable. Operationally, this information is available from the results of programming problems (4.1.17), (4.1.20), and (4.1.26).

We are now able to decompose the (C, S) output measure of technical efficiency. Using (4.1.28) and (4.1.30) we have

$$F_o(x^j, u^j \mid C, S) = F_o(x^j, u^j \mid V, W) \cdot S_o(x^j, u^j) \cdot C_o(x^j, u^j). \quad (4.1.32)$$

The output measure of technical efficiency relative to the constant returns to scale, strong disposability of outputs technology decomposes into the product of three terms: a measure of output technical efficiency relative to the least restrictive variable returns to scale, weak output disposability technology, a measure of output scale efficiency, and a measure of output congestion.

If the output measure of technical efficiency for activity j relative to the (C, S) technology is equal to one, i.e., activity j is efficient relative

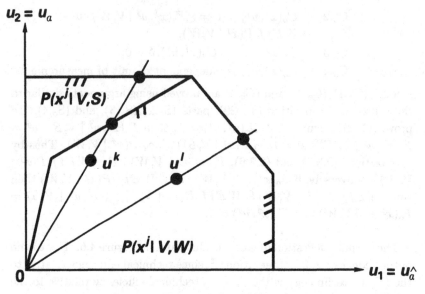

Fig. 4.6. *Measuring Output Congestion*

to the (C, S) technology, then it also is necessarily technically efficient relative to the (V, W) technology as well as being congestion free and scale efficient. The converse is also true.

4.2 Radial Efficiency Measures Requiring Output Price, Output Quantity, and Input Quantity Data: The Decomposition of Revenue Efficiency

In Section 4.1 we decomposed an output measure of technical efficiency into three components. All three components, and hence their product, are purely technical measures of the efficiency of the input–output transformation process. All four require data on input quantities and output quantities only. We now augment these measures of technical efficiency with a measure of output mix efficiency and a measure of revenue efficiency. The latter two measures require output price data not required of the four technical efficiency measures.

Suppose that in addition to the input and output matrices N and M, output prices $r^j \in \Re_+^M$ are given for each observation $j = 1, 2, \cdots, J$. With these additional data we can compute the maximal revenue that can be obtained given x^j, relative to each of the reference technologies introduced in Section 4.1.

Consider revenue maximization relative to the output set $P(x \mid C, S)$. For observation j we have

$$R(x^j, r^j \mid C, S) = \max\{r^j u : u \in P(x^j \mid C, S)\}. \qquad (4.2.1)$$

This revenue may be calculated as the solution to the linear programming problem

$$R(x^j, r^j \mid C, S) = \max_{z, u} r^j u \qquad (4.2.2)$$

$$\text{s.t. } u \leqq zM$$
$$zN \leqq x^j$$
$$z \in \Re_+^J$$

or

$$\max_{z, u} \sum_{m=1}^{M} r_{jm} u_m$$

$$\text{s.t. } u_m \leqq \sum_{j=1}^{J} z_j u_{jm}, m = 1, 2, \cdots, M,$$

$$\sum_{j=1}^{J} z_j x_{jn} \leqq x_{jn}, n = 1, 2, \cdots, N,$$

$$z_j \geqq 0, j = 1, 2, \cdots, J.$$

Given our additional data on output prices and, through (4.2.2), on maximal revenue and assuming that observed revenue $r^j u^j > 0$, we can now state the following:

(4.2.3)   **Definition**: The function
$$O_o(x^j, r^j, u^j \mid C, S) = \frac{R(x^j, r^j \mid C, S)}{r^j u^j}$$
is called the (C, S) *Output Revenue Efficiency Measure*.

The (C, S) output revenue efficiency measure is given by the ratio of maximum possible revenue obtainable from (x^j, r^j) and the (C, S) technology to observed revenue. The properties of this measure are given by

(4.2.4)   **Proposition**: Given $P(x^j \mid C, S)$, for each $j = 1, 2, \cdots, J$,

$O_o.1 \qquad O_o(x^j, r^j, \delta u^j \mid C, S) = \delta^{-1} O_o(x^j, r^j, u^j \mid C, S)$,
$\delta > 0$,

$O_o.2 \qquad O_o(\lambda x^j, r^j, u^j \mid C, S) = \lambda O_o(x^j, r^j, u^j \mid C, S), \lambda > 0$,

$O_o.3$ $\quad O_o(x^j, \theta r^j, u^j \mid C, S) = O_o(x^j, r^j, u^j \mid C, S), \theta > 0,$

$O_o.4$ $\quad 1 \leqq O_o(x^j, r^j, u^j \mid C, S) < +\infty,$

$O_o.5$ $\quad u^j$ solves (4.2.1) $\Longleftrightarrow O_o(x^j, r^j, u^j \mid C, S) = 1,$

$O_o.6$ $\quad O_o(x^j, r^j, u^j)$ is independent of unit of measurement.

The proof of this proposition is left to the reader.

Suppose $O_o(x^j, r^j, u^j \mid C, S) > 1$, so that observed revenue is not maximal. The shortfall can be attributed to either of two sources: producing proportionately too little of each output from given inputs and the (C, S) technology, or producing the wrong mix of outputs in light of prevailing output prices. The first source has already been explored, and the second can be measured residually by

(4.2.5) **Definition:** The function
$$A_o(x^j, r^j, u^j \mid C, S) = \frac{O_o(x^j, r^j, u^j \mid C, S)}{F_o(x^j, u^j \mid C, S)}, j = 1, 2, \cdots, J,$$
is called the (C, S) *Output Allocative Efficiency Measure.*

The properties of the (C, S) output allocative efficiency measure are given in

(4.2.6) **Proposition:** Given $P(x^j \mid C, S)$, then for each $j = 1, 2, \cdots, J$,

$A_o.1$ $\quad A_o(x^j, r^j, \delta u^j \mid C, S) = A_o(x^j, r^j, u^j \mid C, S), \delta > 0,$

$A_o.2$ $\quad A_o(\lambda x^j, r^j, u^j \mid C, S) = A_o(x^j, r^j, u^j \mid C, S), \lambda > 0,$

$A_o.3$ $\quad A_o(x^j, \theta r^j, u^j \mid C, S) = A_o(x^j, r^j, u^j \mid C, S), \theta > 0,$

$A_o.4$ $\quad 1 \leqq A_o(x^j, r^j, u^j \mid C, S) < +\infty,$

$A_o.5$ $\quad \exists \delta \in [1, +\infty)$ such that δu^j solves (4.2.1) $\Longleftrightarrow$ $A_o(x^j, r^j, u^j \mid C, S) = 1,$

$A_o.6$ $\quad A_o(x^j, r^j, u^j \mid C, S)$ is independent of unit of measurement.

Proof: The proofs of $A_o.1 - A_o.4$ and $A_o.6$ are left to the reader. To prove $A_o.5$ assume first that $\exists \delta \in [1, +\infty)$ that solves (4.2.1). Then $R(x^j, r^j \mid C, S) = r^j \delta u^j$ and from definitions (4.2.3) and (4.2.5), $A_o(x^j, r^j, u^j \mid C, S) = 1$. Conversely, assume that $A_o(x^j, r^j, u^j \mid C, S) = 1$. It follows that $R(x^j, r^j \mid C, S) = r^j \cdot F_o(x^j, u^j \mid C, S) \cdot u^j$. Since $F_o(x^j, u^j \mid C, S) \geqq 1$, $A_o.5$ holds.

Q.E.D.

From Definitions (4.2.3) and (4.2.5) we obtain the desired decomposition of the overall revenue efficiency measure into its output price-independent technical component and its output price-dependent allocative component given by

$$O_o(x^j, r^j, u^j \mid C, S) = F_o(x^j, u^j \mid C, S) \cdot A_o(x^j, r^j, u^j \mid C, S). \quad (4.2.7)$$

The decomposition is illustrated in Figure 4.7, where the revenue maximizing output vector is labeled u^{*j}. The observed output vector u^j is both technically and allocatively inefficient. Output technical inefficiency is eliminated by an equiproportionate expansion of all outputs to $F_o(x^j, u^j \mid C, S) \cdot u^j$. Output allocative inefficiency is eliminated by reducing the u_1/u_2 mix and moving to u^{*j}. The decomposition just described can be implemented by solving programming problems (4.2.2) and (4.1.5).

If, in addition, we apply the decomposition (4.1.32) of output technical efficiency into its technical, scale, and congestion components to the decomposition (4.2.7) of output revenue efficiency into its technical and allocative components, we obtain the final decomposition

$$O_o(x^j, r^j, u^j \mid C, S) = F_o(x^j, u^j \mid V, W) \cdot S_o(x^j, u^j) \cdot C_o(x^j, u^j)$$
$$\cdot A_o(x^j, r^j, u^j \mid C, S). \tag{4.2.8}$$

Thus output revenue inefficiency has four possible sources: purely technical inefficiency, operation at the wrong scale, congestion due to a lack of strong output disposability, and operation at the wrong output mix in light of prevailing output prices. If observation j is (C, S) output revenue efficient, i.e., $O_o(x^j, r^j, u^j \mid C, S) = 1$, then it must be efficient as judged by each of the measures on the right hand side of (4.2.8) as well. The converse also holds. Finally, decompositions of output revenue efficiency may also be derived relative to the (N, S) and (V, S) technologies, along the lines of (3.2.9). These are left to the reader.

4.3 Nonradial Output Efficiency Measurement: The Russell Measure

The technical efficiency measures discussed in this chapter dub an output vector efficient if it belongs to the isoquant or weak efficient subset of the associated output set. If $u^j \in WEff\ P(x^j)$, there may exist $v^j \in P(x^j)$ such that $v^j \geq u^j$, i.e., there may be slacks or unexploited potential increases in a subvector of outputs. Here we introduce a nonradial output efficiency measure called the Russell measure, which dubs an output vector efficient only if it belongs to the efficient subset of $P(x)$, i.e., there are no slacks.

Suppose positive outputs $u^j, j = 1, 2, \cdots, J$, and inputs x^j, $j = 1, 2, \cdots, J$, which satisfy the conditions stated in Section 2.4 are known.

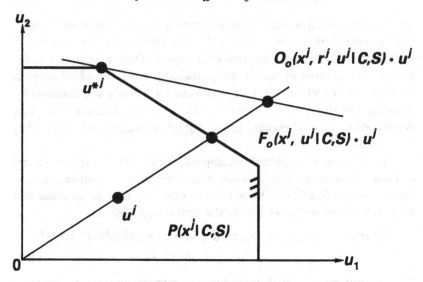

Fig. 4.7. *The Decomposition of Output Revenue Efficiency*

(4.3.1)   **Definition:** The function
$$RM_o(x^j, u^j \mid C, S) = \max\{\textstyle\sum_{m=1}^{M} \theta_m/M :$$
$$(\theta_1 u_{j1}, \cdots, \theta_M u_{jM}) \in P(x^j \mid C, S), \theta_m \geqq 0, m = 1, 2, \cdots, M\},$$
$$j = 1, 2, \cdots, J,$$
is called the (C,S) *Russell Output Measure of Technical Efficiency.*

This can be calculated as the solution to the following programming problem

$$RM_o(x^j, u^j \mid C, S) \;=\; \frac{1}{M} \max_{\theta, z} \sum_{m=1}^{M} \theta_m \qquad (4.3.2)$$

$$\text{s.t. } \theta_m u_{jm} \leqq \sum_{j=1}^{J} z_j u_{jm}, m = 1, 2, \cdots, M,$$

$$\sum_{j=1}^{J} z_j x_{jn} \leqq x_{jn}, n = 1, 2, \cdots, N,$$

$$z_j \geqq 0, j = 1, 2, \cdots, J.$$

Thus the Russell output measure of technical efficiency allows for different expansions of each output, in contrast to the radial measures which take $\theta_m = \theta, m = 1, 2, \cdots, M$. As a consequence we have the

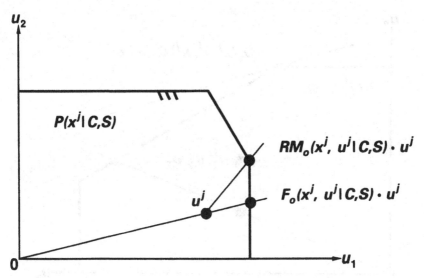

Fig. 4.8. *Comparison of* $RM_o(x^j, u^j \mid C, S)$ *and* $F_o(x^j, u^j \mid C, S)$

following relationship

$$RM_o(x^j, u^j \mid C, S) \geq F_o(x^j, u^j \mid C, S) \geq 1 \qquad (4.3.3)$$

This is illustrated in Figure 4.8, where $M = 2$.

By varying the restrictions on the intensity variable z, one can derive nonradial analogs of $F_o(x^j, u^j \mid N, S)$ and $F_o(x^j, u^j \mid V, S)$ as well as a *Russell Output Measure of Scale Efficiency*. These are left to the reader to explore.

One can also define a *(C,S) Russell Output Measure of Revenue Efficiency*, as the ratio of maximal to observed revenue as in (4.2.3). As long as output prices r^j are strictly positive, however, this measure will be identical to $O_o(x^j, r^j, u^j \mid C, S)$. This leads to the following

(4.3.4)   **Definition:** The function

$$RMA_o(x^j, r^j, u^j \mid C, S) = \frac{O_o(x^j, r^j, u^j \mid C, S)}{RM_o(x^j, u^j \mid C, S)}, j = 1, 2, \cdots, J,$$

is called the *(C,S) Russell Output Measure of Allocative Efficiency*.

Since $RM_o(x^j, u^j \mid C, S) \geq F_o(x^j, u^j \mid C, S) \geq 1$, we have the following relationship

$$1 \leq RMA_o(x^j, r^j, u^j \mid C, S) \leq A_o(x^j, r^j, u^j \mid C, S). \qquad (4.3.5)$$

We also have the following decomposition for $j = 1, 2, \cdots, J$,

$$O_o(x^j, r^j, u^j \mid C, S) = RMA_o(x^j, r^j, u^j \mid C, S) \cdot RM_o(x^j, u^j \mid C, S),$$

$$\qquad (4.3.6)$$

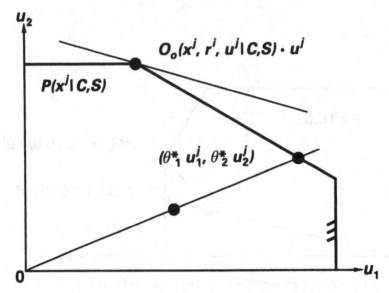

Fig. 4.9. *Russell Output Measure of Revenue Efficiency*

which is illustrated in Figure 4.9. Given observation u^j, technology $P(x^j \mid C, S)$ and relative output prices represented by the slope of $r^j r^j$, $RMA_o(x^j, r^j, u^j \mid C, S) < A_o(x^j, r^j, u^j \mid C, S)$; $RM_o(x^j, u^j \mid C, S) > F_o(x^j, u^j \mid C, S)$.

4.4   Scale Efficiency Measures Requiring Output Revenue and Input Quantity Data

We have provided a measure of output scale efficiency in Definition (4.1.28) that employs data on input quantities and output quantities. In this section we provide an alternative measure of output scale efficiency that uses input quantity data as before, but which replaces output quantity data with output revenue data.

In addition to the input matrix N, suppose that total revenues $R^j, j = 1, 2, \cdots, J$, are known. Denote the vector of observed revenues by R, and assume that all firms face the same output prices, so that $r^j = r, j = 1, 2, \cdots, J$. We begin by defining (C, S) and (V, S) measures of technical efficiency which expand revenue rather than output, and we construct our revenue based measure of scale efficiency from these two technical efficiency measures. We then show under what conditions our two measures of scale efficiency coincide, which also provides guidelines as to when value data may be substituted for quantity data.

To formulate an output scale efficiency measure using output revenue and input quantity data, we solve the following linear programming problem

$$F_R(x^j \mid C, S) = \max_z zR \qquad (4.4.1)$$

$$\text{s.t. } zN \leq x^j$$

$$z \in \Re_+^J$$

or

$$\max_z \sum_{j=1}^{J} z_j R_j$$

$$\text{s.t. } \sum_{j=1}^{J} z_j x_{jn} \leq x_{jn}, n = 1, 2, \cdots, N,$$

$$z_j \geq 0, j = 1, 2, \cdots, J,$$

and

$$F_R(x^j \mid V, S) = \max_z zR \qquad (4.4.2)$$

$$\text{s.t. } zN \leq x^j$$

$$z \in \Re_+^J$$

$$\sum_{j=1}^{J} z_j = 1$$

or

$$\max_z \sum_{j=1}^{J} z_j R_j$$

$$\text{s.t. } \sum_{j=1}^{J} z_j x_{jn} \leq x_{jn}, n = 1, 2, \cdots, N,$$

$$z_j \geq 0, j = 1, 2, \cdots, J,$$

$$\sum_{j=1}^{J} z_j = 1.$$

The solutions to these problems will differ unless the (C, S) and (V, S) technologies coincide, in which case constant returns to scale is obtained. This suggests

(4.4.3)   **Definition**: The function
$$S_R(x^j) = \frac{F_R(x^j|C,S)}{F_R(x^j|V,S)}, j = 1, 2, \cdots, J,$$
is called the *Output Revenue Scale Efficiency Measure*.

Clearly $S_R(x^j) = 1$ when constant returns to scale hold, in which case observation j is said to be output revenue scale efficient. If $S_R(x^j) > 1$ observation j is output revenue scale inefficient, the nature of the scale inefficiency can be determined from the solution to a third linear programming problem

$$F_R(x^j \mid N, S) = \max_{z} zR \qquad (4.4.4)$$

$$\text{s.t. } zN \leq x^j$$

$$z \in \Re_{+}^{J}$$

$$\sum_{j=1}^{J} z_j \leq 1$$

or

$$\max_{z} \sum_{j=1}^{J} z_j R_j$$

$$\text{s.t. } \sum_{j=1}^{J} z_j x_{jn} \leq x_{jn}, n = 1, 2, \cdots, N,$$

$$z_j \geq 0, j = 1, 2, \cdots, J,$$

$$\sum_{j=1}^{J} z_j \leq 1.$$

If $S_R(x^j) > 1$ and $F_R(x^j \mid N, S) = F_R(x^j \mid C, S)$ then scale inefficiency is due to increasing returns to scale. If $S_R(x^j) > 1$ and $F_R(x^j \mid N, S) < F_R(x^j \mid C, S)$ scale inefficiency is due to decreasing returns to scale.

We would also like to know under what conditions the two output measures of scale efficiency $S_o(x^j, u^j)$ and $S_R(x^j)$ yield the same value. We begin by introducing a third method of computing output scale efficiency assuming that N as well as M and output prices are known. Given this information we can derive the decomposition given in (4.2.7). In addition we can compute a similar decomposition for the (V, S) output reference set given in (4.1.13), which we denote as

$$O_o(x^j, r^j, u^j \mid V, S) = F_o(x^j, u^j \mid V, S) \cdot A_o(x^j, r^j, u^j \mid V, S). \quad (4.4.5)$$

The quotient of (4.2.7) and (4.4.5) is

$$\frac{O_o(x^j, r^j, u^j \mid C, S)}{O_o(x^j, r^j, u^j \mid V, S)} = \frac{A_o(x^j, r^j, u^j \mid C, S) \cdot F_o(x^j, u^j \mid C, S)}{A_o(x^j, r^j, u^j \mid V, S) \cdot F_o(x^j, u^j \mid V, S)}. \quad (4.4.6)$$

If $A_o(x^j, r^j, u^j \mid C, S) = A_o(x^j, r^j, u^j \mid V, S)$ then we have

$$S_o(x^j, u^j) = \frac{F_o(x^j, u^j \mid C, S)}{F_o(x^j, u^j \mid V, S)} = \frac{O_o(x^j, r^j, u^j \mid C, S)}{O_o(x^j, r^j, u^j \mid V, S)} \quad (4.4.7)$$

$$= \frac{R(x^j, r^j \mid C, S)}{R(x^j, r^j \mid V, S)}.$$

Expression (4.4.7) shows that if allocative efficiency for the (C, S) technology (4.1.1) and the (V, S) technology (4.1.13) are equal, output scale efficiency may be calculated as the quotient of the maximal revenue functions $R(x^j, r^j \mid C, S)$ and $R(x^j, r^j \mid V, S) = \max_u \{r^j u : u \in P(x^j \mid V, S)\}$. This method requires relatively extensive information (input quantities, output quantities and output prices), whereas the computation of $S_R(x^j)$ only requires information on revenue and input quantities.

To establish the relationship between $S_o(x^j, u^j)$ and $S_R(x^j)$, let $r \in \Re_+^M$ be a given output price vector which we assume to be identical for every observation. Now consider

$$R(x^j, r \mid C, S) = \max_{z, u} ru \quad (4.4.8)$$

$$\text{s.t. } u \leqq zM$$

$$zN \leqq x^j$$

$$z \in \Re_+^J.$$

At an optimum, $zM = u$, which allows us to write

$$R(x^j, r \mid C, S) = \max_z zrM \quad (4.4.9)$$

$$\text{s.t. } zN \leqq x^j$$

$$z \in \Re_+^J.$$

We know that $rM = R$, therefore $R(x^j, r \mid C, S) = F_R(x^j \mid C, S)$. Applying the same logic to the (V, S) reference set (4.1.13), we obtain $R(x^j, r \mid V, S) = F_R(x^j \mid V, S)$. Thus from expression (4.4.7) we have

$$S_o(x^j, u^j) = \frac{F_R(x^j \mid C, S)}{F_R(x^j \mid V, S)} = S_R(x^j), j = 1, 2, \cdots, J. \quad (4.4.10)$$

This shows that if output prices are the same for all observations and if allocative efficiencies for the reference sets (4.1.1) and (4.1.13) are equal, $S_o(x^j, u^j) = S_R(x^j)$. Otherwise $S_o(x^j, u^j)$ and $S_R(x^j)$ may provide different measures of the size and nature of scale economies.

4.5   The Relationship Between Input-Based Measures and Output-Based Measures

In Chapter 3 input-based measures of efficiency were discussed. The price-independent or technical measures gauged efficiency by contracting an input vector as much as possible while remaining feasible. In contrast, the price-independent or technical output-based measures discussed in this chapter expand an output vector as much as possible while remaining feasible. In this section we compare the input- and output-based (C, S) measures and the scale efficiency measures. Input-based and output-based measures of congestion, allocative and overall efficiency are not comparable.

We begin our comparison with the following

(4.5.1)   **Proposition:** $F_i(u^j, x^j \mid C, S) = 1/F_o(x^j, u^j \mid C, S)$.

Proof: By Definition (3.1.3),

$$
\begin{aligned}
F_i(u^j, x^j \mid C, S) &= \min\{\lambda : \lambda x^j \in L(u^j \mid C, S)\} \\
&= \min\{\lambda : u^j \in P(\lambda x^j \mid C, S)\} \\
&= \min\{\lambda : \frac{u^j}{\lambda} \in P(x^j \mid C, S)\} \\
&= 1/\max\{\theta : \theta u^j \in P(x^j \mid C, S)\} \\
&= 1/F_o(x^j, u^j \mid C, S).
\end{aligned}
$$

Q.E.D.

Thus if the technology exhibits constant returns to scale and strong disposability, either input-based or output-based measures can be used without altering the numerical value (in reciprocal terms) of technical efficiency. The reader can confirm this result by referring to Tables 3.1 and 4.1. It can also be shown that the two measures yield reciprocal values only if the technology exhibits constant returns to scale, an exercise we leave to the reader.

In a comparison of input- and output-based scale efficiency two issues must be dealt with. First, under what conditions does $S_i(u^j, x^j)$ equal the reciprocal of $S_o(x^j, u^j)$, and second, when do the two approaches yield the same qualitative result, i.e., when do they both predict CRS, DRS, or IRS, respectively? Regarding the first issue, it follows from Proposition (4.5.1) that $S_i(u^j, x^j) = 1/S_o(x^j, u^j)$ if and only if $F_i(u^j, x^j \mid V, S) = 1/F_o(x^j, u^j \mid V, S)$. Thus the two scale efficiency measures yield reciprocal values if and only if the two (V, S) measures are reciprocal, which can only occur if the observation (x^j, u^j) exhibits CRS (region (CC) in Figure 4.10), or $F_i(u^j, x^j \mid V, S) = F_o(x^j, u^j \mid V, S) = 1$ as along the upward sloping segments of the frontier of the (V, S) technology.

Turning to the second issue, identification of returns to scale, we already know that if $F_i(u^j, x^j \mid V, S) = F_i(u^j, x^j \mid C, S)$ (region $(CC) \cup (CD)$ in Figure 4.10) and $F_o(x^j, u^j \mid V, S) = F_o(x^j, u^j \mid C, S)$ (region $(CC) \cup (IC)$ in Figure 4.10), the two models both predict constant returns to scale (region (CC) in Figure 4.10). If $S_i(u^j, x^j) \neq 1$, and $S_o(x^j, u^j) \neq 1$, then if $F_i(u^j, x^j \mid N, S) = F_i(u^j, x^j \mid C, S)$ (region $(II) \cup (IC) \cup (ID)$ in Figure 4.10) and $F_o(x^j, u^j \mid N, S) = F_o(x^j, u^j \mid C, S)$ (region (II) in Figure 4.10), the two approaches predict increasing returns to scale (region (II) in Figure 4.10). Finally if both models indicate scale inefficiency the conditions $F_i(u^j, x^j \mid V, S) = F_i(u^j, x^j \mid N, S)$ (region (DD) in Figure 4.10) and $F_o(x^j, u^j \mid V, S) = F_o(x^j, u^j \mid N, S)$ (region $(ID) \cup (CD) \cup (DD)$ in Figure 4.10) suffice for the two approaches to predict decreasing returns to scale.

Thus the two measures $S_i(u^j, x^j)$ and $S_o(x^j, u^j)$ give the same qualitative information concerning scale economies for producers located in region $(II) \cup (CC) \cup (DD)$ after they have been moved to the frontier in Figure 4.10. For producers located in region $(IC) \cup (ID) \cup (CD)$ the two measures give contradictory information. Moreover, they achieve reciprocally equal numerical values only in region CC, which may be a point. The reason for the disparity is that the two measures incorporate fundamentally different notions of the "scale" of an operation. $S_i(u^j, x^j)$ defines scale in terms of output and compares two contracted input vectors. $S_o(x^j, u^j)$ defines scale in terms of input and compares two expanded output vectors. Since the two measures evaluate scale efficiency by looking in different directions toward the graph of the technology, it should not be surprising that they can provide different information concerning scale economies.

4.6 A Numerical Example: Output-Based Efficiency Measurement

In this section we provide numerical examples of some of the output-based efficiency measures introduced in this chapter using the artificial data described in Section 5 of Chapter 2. Specifically, we include calcu-

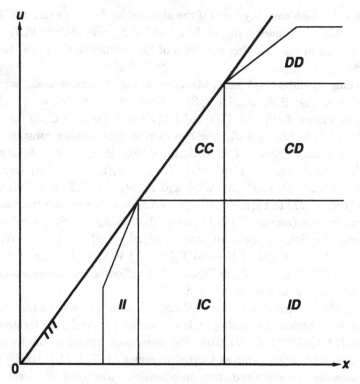

Fig. 4.10. *Comparison of* $S_i(u^j, x^j)$ *and* $S_o(x^j, u^j)$

lations of the measures included in decomposition (4.2.7):

$$O_o(x^j, r^j, u^j \mid C, S) = A_o(x^j, r^j, u^j \mid C, S) \cdot F_o(x^j, u^j \mid C, S).$$

We begin by calculating maximum revenue, i.e., $R(x^j, r^j \mid C, S)$ using (4.2.2). This is then divided by observed revenue $R_j = r^j u^j$ to arrive at $O_o(x^j, r^j, u^j \mid C, S)$, see (4.2.3). Next, we calculate $F_o(x^j, u^j \mid C, S)$ which is used to derive $A_o(x^j, r^j, u^j \mid C, S)$ via (4.2.5).

These measures are calculated for each of our 20 observations of artificial data using the SAS PROC LP procedure. The results are displayed in Table 4.1.

Table 4.1. *Output-Based Efficiency Measures Using Artificial Data*

Obs	$O_o(x^j, r^j, u^j \mid C, S)$	$A_o(x^j, r^j, u^j \mid C, S)$	$F_o(x^j, u^j \mid C, S)$
1	1.440	1.000	1.440
2	1.277	1.256	1.016
3	1.421	1.283	1.108
4	1.332	1.000	1.332
5	1.391	1.000	1.391
6	1.000	1.000	1.000
7	1.000	1.000	1.000
8	1.000	1.000	1.000
9	1.000	1.000	1.000
10	1.000	1.000	1.000
11	1.000	1.000	1.000
12	1.000	1.000	1.000
13	1.000	1.000	1.000
14	1.000	1.000	1.000
15	1.000	1.000	1.000
16	1.440	1.000	1.440
17	1.307	1.236	1.057
18	1.421	1.283	1.108
19	1.388	1.006	1.379
20	1.424	1.021	1.395

4.7   References to the Literature

In view of the structural symmetry between input-based efficiency measures and output-based efficiency measures, many of the basic references cited in Chapter 3 are equally relevant here.

Farrell (1957) recognized the structural symmetry between input-based and output-based measures, although he concentrated on the former. The first linear programming model of output-based efficiency measurement is due to Boles (1966). Soon thereafter Aigner and Chu (1968) developed linear and quadratic programming models for calculating technical efficiency relative to a parametric Cobb–Douglas production frontier. Afriat (1972) introduced non-constant returns to scale in a scalar output model, and Burley (1980) formulated a linear programming problem to calculate output-based (C, S) technical efficiency in a scalar output model. In a multiple output model Charnes, Cooper, and Rhodes (1978) employed fractional and linear programming methods to calculate output-based (C, S) technical efficiency; their work was extended to (V, S) technologies by Banker, Charnes, and Cooper (1984).

The decomposition of output-based technical efficiency into output-based measures of scale efficiency, congestion and "pure" technical efficiency was initiated by Färe and Grosskopf (1983b) and completed by Färe, Grosskopf, and Lovell (1985). Additional material on output-based measurement of scale efficiency and congestion appears in Färe, Grosskopf, and Lovell (1987a, 1987b).

The measurement of output-based overall (revenue) efficiency, and its decomposition into an output price-independent technical efficiency component and an output price-dependent allocative efficiency component, is apparently due to Färe, Grosskopf, and Lovell (1985), who also developed linear programming models to calculate overall revenue efficiency as well as the elements of the output technical efficiency decomposition.

The nonradial Russell output-based measure of technical efficiency was apparently first proposed by Deprins and Simar (1983). Additional analysis can be found in Färe, Grosskopf, and Lovell (1985).

Analysis of the relationship between input-based and output-based efficiency measures has a long history. Farrell (1957) recognized that under constant returns to scale input-based and output-based measures of technical efficiency are equal. That constant returns to scale is both necessary and sufficient for equality of the two measures was proved by Färe and Lovell (1978) and Deprins and Simar (1983). See also Banker, Charnes, and Cooper (1984) and Førsund and Hjalmarsson (1987). The relationship between $S_i(u, x)$ and $S_o(u, x)$, and Frisch's (1965) passus coefficient, or scale elasticity, was established for the scalar output case by Førsund and Hjalmarsson (1979a), and extended to the multiple output case by Färe, Grosskopf, and Lovell (1987a). A comparison of input-based and output-based measures makes sense only for technical and scale efficiency. Although there are many papers on scale efficiency, we are not aware of any that make the comparison suggested by Figure 4.10.

Empirical applications of output-based efficiency measurement are far fewer in number than applications of input-based efficiency measurement. This we attribute to two causes: a preponderance of settings in which input conservation for given outputs seems to be the appropriate orientation (e.g., public utilities required to meet demand), and a relative paucity of multiple output data sets available for empirical analysis.

Nonetheless, a sampling of the extant studies reveals a diversity comparable to that of the input-based efficiency measurement applications.

Perhaps the first use of linear programming techniques to calculate output-based measures of technical efficiency was by Carlson (1972), in his study of the performance of U.S. institutions of higher education. In a multiple input, multiple output framework Carlson calculated both output-based technical efficiency and input-based overall cost efficiency. Subsequently Bessent, Bessent, Kennington, and Reagan (1982) calculated output-based measures of technical efficiency of schools in Houston, Texas; Lewin, Morey, and Cook (1982) did likewise for courts in North Carolina; and Adolphson, Cornia, and Walters (1989) used output-based technical efficiency measures to obtain estimates of obsolescence of railroad property. Banker and Morey (1986a) showed how to adapt output-based technical efficiency measurement techniques to the presence of exogenously fixed inputs or outputs, and applied their technique to a sample of fast-food restaurants. The adaptation of linear programming models of output- (or input-) based efficiency measurement to accommodate categorical variables was initiated by Carlson (1972), who included university characteristics (public, private, and other types) in his model. More recent treatments of categorical variables include Banker and Morey (1986b) and Kamakura (1988).

Empirical calculations of output-based measures of technical efficiency and scale efficiency include Grabowski and Pasurka (1988) (antebellum farming in the U.S. south and north), Albriktsen and Førsund (1990) (Norwegian building and construction), Førsund and Hernaes (1990) (ferry transport in Norway), and Førsund and Kittelsen (1992) (Norwegian district courts).

Empirical calculations of output-based technical efficiency and output congestion include Färe, Grosskopf, and Pasurka (1986, 1989) (the impacts of environmental controls on performance in electricity generation), and Byrnes and Valdmanis (1989) (the effects of charity care provision on hospital performance).

Applications that decompose output-based technical efficiency into scale, congestion and pure technical efficiency components include Färe, Grosskopf, and Logan (1983) (electric utilities) and Byrnes, Färe, Grosskopf, and Kraft (1987) (Illinois grain farms).

5

Indirect Input-Based Efficiency Measurement

5.0 Introduction

The purpose of this chapter is to extend the radial input-based efficiency measures in Chapter 3, where efficiency of the observed input vector is judged relative to technology, given fixed outputs, to the case in which input efficiency is judged relative to the revenue indirect production technology. In this case, outputs are restricted but not fixed, and they may vary as long as their revenue meets or exceeds a prespecified target. In contrast, in Chapter 3 outputs are assumed exogenously fixed.

In Section 5.1, price-independent measures of indirect input-based technical efficiency are developed. These measures take output prices and target revenue as given and measure efficiency as proportional contraction of all inputs. The measures distinguish between scale, congestion and purely technical efficiency. Complete decomposition of the constant returns, strong disposal revenue indirect measure of technical efficiency is provided. All our technical measures are radial in nature, but it is clear that nonradial measures like the Russell measure introduced in Chapter 3 may also be considered. We leave this for the interested reader.

Price dependent input-based measures are discussed in Section 5.2. We introduce input prices and consider the objective of shrinking expenditure on input. This leads to revenue indirect measures of input cost efficiency and input allocative efficiency which, together with one of our technical measures, yields a decomposition of revenue indirect cost efficiency.

In Section 5.3 we discuss measures of benefit effectiveness by comparing the minimum cost with the target revenue it generates. In Section 5.4 comparisons between direct and indirect measures are discussed. Our artificial data set is used in Section 5.4 to illustrate the different measures developed in the chapter.

5.1 Radial Indirect Efficiency Measures Requiring Input Quantity, Output Quantity, and Output Price Data: The Decomposition of Indirect Technical Efficiency

The purpose of this section is to derive a family of measures of the efficiency of an input vector used to generate at least a certain revenue. Here we assume that output prices and target revenue are both known, and we wish to evaluate production efficiency on the basis of input usage. For this purpose technology is most usefully represented by the revenue indirect input correspondence, and efficiency measurement is input-based. Thus the structure of this section is similar to that of Section 1 of Chapter 3, but since the standard relative to which input efficiency is measured is changed from outputs to revenue, the representation of technology is also changed from input sets to revenue indirect input sets.

Suppose that, in addition to the input matrix N and the output matrix M, output prices $r \in \Re_+^M$ with $r \neq 0$ and target revenue $R \in \Re_{++}$ are given. The initial revenue indirect input sets are formed from the data by means of

$$IL(r/R \mid C, S) = \{x : u \leq zM, zN \leq x, ru \geq R\}, z \in \Re_+^J, (r/R) \neq 0,$$
(5.1.1)

where z denotes the intensity vector. As the notation suggests, the revenue indirect input sets defined in (5.1.1) satisfy the important properties of constant returns to scale and strong disposability of inputs. This is proved in the following

(5.1.2) **Proposition:** The (C, S) revenue indirect input sets $IL(r/R \mid C, S)$ satisfy
  (i) $IL(r/\theta R \mid C, S) = \theta IL(r/R \mid C, S), \theta > 0,$
  (ii) $x \geq y \in IL(r/R \mid C, S) \Longrightarrow x \in IL(r/R \mid C, S).$

Proof: (i) Let $\theta > 0$. Then from (5.1.1)

$$
\begin{aligned}
IL(r/\theta R \mid C, S) &= \{x : u \leq zM, zN \leq x, ru \geq \theta R, z \in \Re_+^J\} \\
&= \theta\{x/\theta : u/\theta \leq (z/\theta)M, (z/\theta)N \leq x/\theta, \\
&\qquad r(u/\theta) \geq R, (z/\theta) \in \Re_+^J\}
\end{aligned}
$$

$$= \theta IL(r/R \mid C, S).$$

(ii) This property follows from the nature of the inequality $zN \leqq x$.

Q.E.D.

Now let $(x^j, u^j, r^j/R^j)$ be an observation. We may take $z \in \Re_+^J$ such that $z_i = 1$ for $i = j$ and $z_i = 0$ otherwise, which guarantees that $x^j \in IL(r^j/R^j \mid C, S)$, i.e., that x^j is feasible. The efficiency of feasible x^j is measured by

(5.1.3)   **Definition**: The function
$$IF_i(r^j/R^j, x^j \mid C, S) = \min\{\lambda : \lambda x^j \in IL(r^j/R^j \mid C, S)\},$$
$$j = 1, 2, \cdots, J,$$
is called the (C, S) *Revenue Indirect Input Measure of Technical Efficiency.*

$IF_i(r^j/R^j, x^j \mid C, S)$ provides a measure of the efficiency of input vector x^j in the generation of revenue R^j at output prices r^j when production technology satisfies (C, S). It does so by computing the ratio of the smallest feasible radial contraction of x^j in $IL(r^j/R^j \mid C, S)$ to itself, i.e., $IF_i(r^j/R^j, x^j \mid C, S) = \| IF_i(r^j/R^j, x^j \mid C, S) \cdot x^j \| / \| x^j \|$.

The revenue indirect input measure of technical efficiency is illustrated in Figure 5.1 for the $N = 2$ case. A (C, S) revenue indirect input set consistent with the revenue constraint is drawn, together with a (C, S) direct input set. The (C, S) revenue indirect technical efficiency of a producer using x^j to generate revenue of at least R^j by producing output for sale at price r^j is given by $\| Ox^{*j} \| / \| Ox^j \|$. We observe from the figure that the indirect measure is less than or equal to the corresponding direct measure.

The properties satisfied by $IF_i(r^j/R^j, x^j \mid C, S)$ are summarized in the following

(5.1.4)   **Proposition**: Given $IL(r^j/R^j \mid C, S)$, then for each $j = 1, 2, \cdots, J$,

IF$_i$.1 $IF_i(r^j/R^j, \delta x^j \mid C, S) = \delta^{-1} IF_i(r^j/R^j, x^j \mid C, S)$, $\delta > 0$,

IF$_i$.2 $IF_i(r^j/\theta R^j, x^j \mid C, S) = \theta IF_i(r^j/R^j, x^j \mid C, S)$, $\theta > 0$,

IF$_i$.3 $0 < IF_i(r^j/R^j, x^j \mid C, S) \leqq 1$,

IF$_i$.4 $x^j \in WEff\ IL(r^j/R^j \mid C, S) \Longleftrightarrow IF_i(r^j/R^j, x^j \mid C, S) = 1$,

IF$_i$.5 $IF_i(r^j/R^j, x^j \mid C, S)$ is independent of unit of measurement.

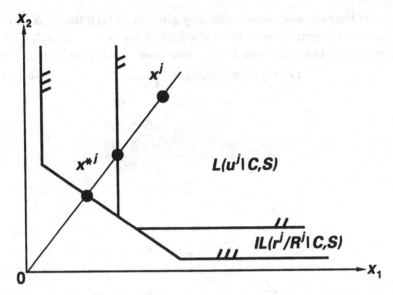

Fig. 5.1. *The (C,S) Revenue Indirect Input Measure of Technical Efficiency*

Proof:

(IF$_i$.1)
$$IF_i(r^j/R^j, \delta x^j \mid C, S) = \min\{\lambda : \lambda \delta x^j \in IL(r^j/R^j \mid C, S)\}$$
$$= \delta^{-1} \min\{\lambda \delta : \lambda \delta x^j \in IL(r^j/R^j \mid C, S)\}$$
$$= \delta^{-1} IF_i(r^j/R^j, x^j \mid C, S).$$

(IF$_i$.2)   From Proposition (5.1.2(i)),
$$IF_i(r^j/\theta R^j, x^j \mid C, S) = \min\{\lambda : \lambda x^j \in IL(r^j/\theta R^j \mid C, S)\}$$
$$= \min\{\lambda : \lambda x^j \in \theta IL(r^j/R^j \mid C, S)\}$$
$$= \theta IF_i(r^j/R^j, x^j \mid C, S).$$

(IF$_i$.3)   Follows from the fact that $x^j \in IL(r^j/R^j \mid C, S)$ for each $j = 1, 2, \cdots, J$.

(IF$_i$.4)   Since it is a radial measure, $IF_i(r^j/R^j, x^j \mid C, S) = 1 \Longleftrightarrow x^j \in Isoq\ IL(r^j/R^j \mid C, S)$. But since inputs are strongly disposable from Proposition (5.1.2(ii)), $Isoq\ IL(r^j/R^j \mid C, S) = WEff\ IL(r^j/R^j \mid C, S)$, see Proposition (2.3.2).

(IF$_i$.5)   Let us consider just the nth input restriction $\sum_{j=1}^{J} z_j x_{jn} \leqq \lambda x_{jn}$. If the unit of measurement is changed and $\hat{x}_{jn} = \nu x_{jn}$, $j = 1, 2, \cdots, J$, then clearly it does not affect λ or z_j, $j = 1, 2, \cdots, J$.

$Q.E.D.$

Using the piecewise linear technology given by (5.1.1), the (C, S) revenue indirect input measure of technical efficiency can be calculated for observation j as the solution to the linear programming problem

$$IF_i(r^j/R^j, x^j \mid C, S) = \min_{\lambda, z, u} \lambda \qquad (5.1.5)$$

$$\text{s.t. } u \leq zM$$

$$zN \leq \lambda x^j$$

$$r^j u \geq R^j$$

$$z \in \Re_+^J$$

or

$$\min_{\lambda, z, u} \lambda$$

$$\text{s.t. } u_m \leq \sum_{j=1}^{J} z_j u_{jm}, m = 1, 2, \cdots, M,$$

$$\sum_{j=1}^{J} z_j x_{jn} \leq \lambda x_{jn}, n = 1, 2, \cdots, N,$$

$$\sum_{m=1}^{M} r_{jm} u_m \geq R^j,$$

$$z_j \geq 0, j = 1, 2, \cdots, J.$$

In Figure 5.1 the minimizing value of λ is given by the ratio $\parallel 0x^{*j} \parallel / \parallel 0x^j \parallel$.

Suppose next that technology satisfies strong disposability of inputs as before, and a relaxed scale property of nonincreasing returns to scale. The revenue indirect input sets satisfying these two properties are obtained from M, N, r and $\cdot R$ as

$$IL(r/R \mid N, S) = \{x : u \leq zM, zN \leq x, ru \geq R, z \in \Re_+^J, (5.1.6)$$

$$\sum_{j=1}^{J} z_j \leq 1\}, (r/R) \in \Re_+^M, (r/R) \neq 0.$$

Since the elements of the intensity vector are constrained to sum to no more than one, it follows that

$$IL(r/R \mid N, S) \subseteq IL(r/R \mid C, S). \qquad (5.1.7)$$

The claim that the revenue indirect input sets defined in (5.1.6) satisfy nonincreasing returns to scale and strong disposability is proved in

(5.1.8)   **Proposition:** The (N, S) revenue indirect input sets $IL(r/R \mid N, S)$ satisfy

$\quad$ (i) $\quad IL(r/\theta R \mid N, S) \subseteq \theta IL(r/R \mid N, S), \theta \geqq 1,$

$\quad$ (ii) $\quad x \geqq y \in IL(r/R \mid N, S) \Longrightarrow x \in IL(r/R \mid N, S).$

Proof: $\quad$ (i) Let $\theta \geqq 1$. Then from (5.1.6)

$$IL(r/\theta R \mid N, S) = \{x : u \leqq zM, zN \leqq x, ru \geqq \theta R, z \in \Re_+^J,$$

$$\sum_{j=1}^{J} z_j \leqq 1\}$$

$$= \theta\{(x/\theta) : (u/\theta) \leqq (z/\theta)M, (z/\theta)N \leqq (x/\theta),$$

$$(ru/\theta) \geqq R, (z/\theta) \in \Re_+^J, \sum_{j=1}^{J}(z_j/\theta) \leqq (1/\theta)\}$$

$$\subseteq \theta\{(x/\theta) : (u/\theta) \leqq (z/\theta)M, (z/\theta)N \leqq (x/\theta),$$

$$(ru/\theta) \geqq R, (z/\theta) \in \Re_+^J, \sum_{j=1}^{J}(z_j/\theta) \leqq 1)\}$$

$$= \theta IL(r/R \mid N, S).$$

$\quad$ (ii) Follows the proof of Proposition (5.1.2(ii)).

$$Q.E.D.$$

We are now ready to introduce a second technical efficiency measure, this one relative to the (N, S) technology.

(5.1.9) $\quad$ **Definition:** The function

$\quad\quad IF_i(r^j/R^j, x^j \mid N, S) = \min\{\lambda : \lambda x^j \in IL(r^j/R^j \mid N, S)\},$

$\quad\quad j = 1, 2, \cdots, J,$

$\quad\quad$ is called the (N,S) *Revenue Indirect Input Measure of Technical Efficiency.*

Like the (C, S) measure defined in (5.1.3), the (N, S) revenue indirect input measure of technical efficiency provides a measure of the efficiency of input vector x^j in the generation of revenue R^j at output prices r^j. Unlike the (C, S) measure, the (N, S) measure does so relative to a technology that satisfies nonincreasing returns to scale. The properties of $IF_i(r^j/R^j, x^j \mid N, S)$ are summarized in the following proposition, the proof of which is sufficiently similar to the proof of Proposition (5.1.4) to be left to the reader.

(5.1.10) $\quad$ **Proposition:** Given $IL(r^j/R^j \mid N, S)$, then for each $j = 1, 2, \cdots, J,$

$\quad$ IF$_i$.1 $\quad IF_i(r^j/R^j, \delta x^j \mid N, S) = \delta^{-1}IF_i(r^j/R^j, x^j \mid N, S),$

$\quad\quad\quad \delta > 0,$

$\quad$ IF$_i$.2 $\quad IF_i(r^j/\theta R^j, x^j \mid N, S) \geqq \theta IF_i(r^j/R^j, x^j \mid N, S),$

$\quad\quad\quad \theta \geqq 1,$

IF$_i$.3 $0 < IF_i(r^j/R^j, x^j \mid N, S) \leqq 1,$

IF$_i$.4 $x^j \in WEff\ IL(r^j/R^j \mid N, S) \Longleftrightarrow IF_i(r^j/R^j, x^j \mid N, S) = 1,$

IF$_i$.5 $IF_i(r^j/R^j, x^j \mid N, S)$ is independent of unit of measurement.

The (N, S) revenue indirect input measure of technical efficiency is calculated for observation j as the solution to the linear programming problem

$$IF_i(r^j/R^j, x^j \mid N, S) = \min_{\lambda, z, u} \lambda \qquad (5.1.11)$$

$$\text{s.t. } u \leq zM$$
$$zN \leq \lambda x^j$$
$$r^j u \geq R^j$$
$$z \in \Re_+^J$$
$$\sum_{j=1}^{J} z_j \leqq 1$$

or

$$\min_{\lambda, z, u} \lambda$$

$$\text{s.t. } u_m \leqq \sum_{j=1}^{J} z_j u_{jm}, m = 1, 2, \cdots, M,$$

$$\sum_{j=1}^{J} z_j x_{jn} \leqq \lambda x_{jn}, n = 1, 2, \cdots, N,$$

$$\sum_{m=1}^{M} r_{jm} u_m \geqq R^j,$$

$$z_j \geqq 0, j = 1, 2, \cdots, J,$$

$$\sum_{j=1}^{J} z_j \leqq 1.$$

Comparing the constraints of (5.1.11) and (5.1.5) for the piecewise linear case, or directly from (5.1.7) for the general case, it follows that

$$IF_i(r^j/R^j, x^j \mid N, S) \geq IF_i(r^j/R^j, x^j \mid C, S), j = 1, 2, \cdots, J, \quad (5.1.12)$$

a result that is illustrated in Figure 5.2 for the piecewise linear $M = N = 1$ case. This figure should be compared with Figure 3.2. The (C, S) revenue indirect technical efficiency measure for observation j

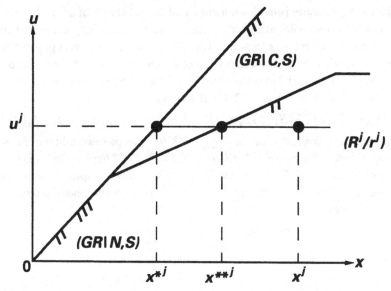

Fig. 5.2. *A Comparison of* $IF_i(r^j/R^j, x^j \mid C, S)$ *and* $IF_i(r^j/R^j, x^j \mid N, S)$

is $0x^{*j}/0x^j$, and the (N, S) measure is $0x^{**j}/0x^j$. Clearly the (N, S) measure must always be at least as great as the (C, S) measure.

By further restricting the intensity vector we can construct revenue indirect input sets that still satisfy strong disposability, but that satisfy a weakened scale property of variable returns to scale. Such input sets are formed from the data M, N, r and R as

$$IL(r/R \mid V, S) = \{x : u \leqq zM, zN \leqq x, ru \geqq R, \qquad (5.1.13)$$

$$z \in \Re_+^J, \sum_{j=1}^{J} z_j = 1\}, (r/R) \in \Re_+^M, (r/R) \neq 0.$$

Since the intensity variables are constrained to sum to unity, it follows from (5.1.13) and (5.1.6) that

$$IL(r/R \mid V, S) \subseteqq IL(r/R \mid N, S). \qquad (5.1.14)$$

We can now define an efficiency measure relative to the (V, S) revenue indirect inputs sets (5.1.13) by means of

(5.1.15)   **Definition**: The function

$IF_i(r^j/R^j, x^j \mid V, S) = \min\{\lambda : \lambda x^j \in IL(r^j/R^j \mid V, S)\},$
$j = 1, 2, \cdots, J,$

is called the *(V,S) Revenue Indirect Input Measure of Technical Efficiency*.

The (V, S) measure provides a measure of the efficiency of x^j in the generation of revenue R^j at output prices r^j when technology is allowed to exhibit variable returns to scale. The (V, S) measure satisfies properties similar to $IF_i.1, IF_i.3, IF_i.4$ and $IF_i.5$ of Propositions (5.1.4) and (5.1.8). However due to variable returns to scale, the (V, S) measure satisfies no property like $IF_i.2$. From (5.1.14) it follows that

$$IF_i(r^j/R^j, x^j \mid V, S) \geqq IF_i(r^j/R^j, x^j \mid N, S), j = 1, 2, \cdots, J, \quad (5.1.16)$$

a result that is illustrated in Figure 5.3 for the piecewise linear $M = N = 1$ case. There $IF_i(r^j/R^j, x^j \mid V, S) = 0x^{**j}/0x^j > 0x^{*j}/0x^j = IF_i(r^j/R^j, x^j \mid N, S)$. The (V, S) revenue indirect input measure of technical efficiency is calculated as the solution to the linear programming problem

$$IF_i(r^j/R^j, x^j \mid V, S) = \min_{\lambda, z, u} \lambda \qquad (5.1.17)$$

$$\text{s.t.} \quad u \leqq zM$$

$$zN \leqq \lambda x^j$$

$$r^j u \geqq R^j$$

$$z \in \Re_+^J$$

$$\sum_{j=1}^{J} z_j = 1$$

or

$$\min_{\lambda, z, u} \lambda$$

$$\text{s.t.} \quad u_m \leqq \sum_{j=1}^{J} z_j u_{jm}, m = 1, 2, \cdots, M,$$

$$\sum_{j=1}^{J} z_j x_{jn} \leqq \lambda x_{jn}, n = 1, 2, \cdots, N,$$

$$\sum_{m=1}^{M} r_{jm} u_m \geqq R^j,$$

$$z_j \geqq 0, j = 1, 2, \cdots, J,$$

$$\sum_{j=1}^{J} z_j = 1.$$

Having relaxed the scale property imposed on technology from constant to nonincreasing to variable returns to scale, we now maintain variable returns to scale and consider a relaxation of the disposability property

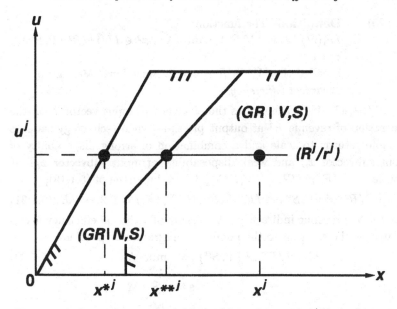

Fig. 5.3. *A Comparison of* $IF_i(r^j/R^j, x^j \mid N, S)$ *and* $IF_i(r^j/R^j, x^j \mid V, S)$

from strong disposability of inputs to weak disposability of inputs. In order to do so we partition the input matrix N so that $N = (N^\alpha, N^{\hat{\alpha}})$ where $\alpha \subseteq \{1, 2, \cdots, N\}$ and $\hat{\alpha} = \{1, 2, \cdots, N\}\backslash\alpha$. Also $x = (x_\alpha, x_{\hat{\alpha}})$. We can now form revenue indirect input sets that impose strong disposability only on the input subvector x_α by means of

$$IL(r/R \mid V, S^\alpha) = \{x : u \leqq zM, zN^{\hat{\alpha}} = \sigma x_{\hat{\alpha}}, 0 < \sigma \leqq 1, \quad (5.1.18)$$

$$zN^\alpha \leqq x_\alpha, ru \geqq R, z \in \Re_+^J, \sum_{j=1}^{J} z_j = 1\},$$

$$(r/R) \in \Re_+^M, (r/R) \neq 0.$$

To verify that inputs are weakly disposable in (5.1.18), suppose $x \in IL(r/R \mid V, S^\alpha)$ and let $\lambda \geqq 1$. We need to show that $\lambda x \in IL(r/R \mid V, S^\alpha)$. Clearly $\lambda x_\alpha \geqq x_\alpha$. By taking $\sigma = \lambda^{-1}$ we have $zN^{\hat{\alpha}} = \lambda \sigma x_{\hat{\alpha}}$ with $0 < \lambda \sigma \leqq 1$, which shows that inputs are weakly disposable. The equality $zN^{\hat{\alpha}} = \sigma x_{\hat{\alpha}}$ shows that inputs need not be strongly disposable. Consequently

$$IL(r/R \mid V, S^\alpha) \subseteq IL(r/R \mid V, S). \quad (5.1.19)$$

A radial efficiency measure may be defined relative to the (V, S^α) revenue indirect inputs sets (5.1.18) by means of

(5.1.20)   **Definition:** The function
$$IF_i(r^j/R^j, x^j \mid V, S^\alpha) = \min\{\lambda : \lambda x^j \in IL(r^j/R^j \mid V, S^\alpha)\},$$
$j = 1, 2, \cdots, J,$
is called the (V, S^α) *Revenue Indirect Input Measure of Technical Efficiency.*

$IF_i(r^j/R^j, x^j \mid V, S^\alpha)$ measures the efficiency of input vector x^j in the generation of revenue R^j at output prices r^j when technology satisfies variable returns to scale and a combination of strong disposability of input subvector x_α and weak disposability of input subvector $x_{\hat{\alpha}}$. It satisfies $0 < IF_i(r^j/R^j, x^j \mid V, S^\alpha) \leq 1$ and, by virtue of (5.1.19),

$$IF_i(r^j/R^j, x^j \mid V, S^\alpha) \geqq IF_i(r^j/R^j, x^j \mid V, S), j = 1, 2, \cdots, J. \quad (5.1.21)$$

The (V, S^α) revenue indirect input measure of technical efficiency is calculated as the solution to the nonlinear programming problem

$$IF_i(r^j/R^j, x^j \mid V, S^\alpha) = \min_{\lambda, z, u, \sigma} \lambda \qquad (5.1.22)$$

$$\text{s.t.} \ u \leqq zM$$
$$zN^\alpha \leqq \lambda x_\alpha^j$$
$$zN^{\hat{\alpha}} = \lambda \sigma x_{\hat{\alpha}}^j$$
$$0 < \sigma \leqq 1$$
$$r^j u \geqq R^j$$
$$z \in \Re_+^J$$
$$\sum_{j=1}^{J} z_j = 1$$

or

$$\min_{\lambda, z, u, \sigma} \lambda$$

$$\text{s.t.} \ u_m \leqq \sum_{j=1}^{J} z_j u_{jm}, m = 1, 2, \cdots, M,$$

$$\sum_{j=1}^{J} z_j x_{jn} \leqq \lambda x_{jn}, n = 1, 2, \cdots, N^\alpha,$$

$$\sum_{j=1}^{J} z_j x_{jn} = \lambda \sigma x_{jn}, n = N^\alpha + 1, \cdots, N,$$

$$0 < \sigma \leqq 1,$$

$$\sum_{m=1}^{M} r_{jm} u_m \geqq R^j,$$

$$z_j \geqq 0, j = 1, 2, \cdots, J,$$

$$\sum_{j=1}^{J} z_j = 1.$$

In the calculations one may convert (5.1.22) into a linear programming problem by taking $\sigma = 1$, without changing the result.

We now consider the most general revenue indirect input sets, those satisfying variable returns to scale and weak disposability of inputs. Such sets are formed from the data M, N, r and R as

$$IL(r/R \mid V, W) = \{x : u \leqq zM, zN = \sigma x, 0 < \sigma \leqq 1, \quad (5.1.23)$$

$$ru \geqq R, z \in \Re_+^J, \sum_{j=1}^{J} z_j = 1\}, (r/R) \in \Re_+^M,$$

$$(r/R) \neq 0.$$

A radial measure of the efficiency of input vector x^j in the generation of revenue R^j at output prices r^j can be defined on the (V, W) revenue indirect input sets as

(5.1.24)   **Definition**: The function
$IF_i(r^j/R^j, x^j \mid V, W) = \min\{\lambda : \lambda x^j \in IL(r^j/R^j \mid V, W)\},$
$j = 1, 2, \cdots, J,$
is called the (V, W) *Revenue Indirect Input Measure of Technical Efficiency*.

Proofs similar to those of Proposition (5.1.4) suffice to establish the following properties of $IF_i(r^j/R^j, x^j \mid V, W)$.

(5.1.25)   **Proposition**: Given $IL(r^j/R^j \mid V, W)$, then for each $j = 1, 2, \cdots, J,$

IF$_i$.1 $IF_i(r^j/R^j, \delta x^j \mid V, W) = \delta^{-1} IF_i(r^j/R^j, x^j \mid V, W), \delta > 0,$

IF$_i$.2 $0 < IF_i(r^j/R^j, x^j \mid V, W) \leqq 1,$

IF$_i$.3 $x^j \in Isoq \, IL(r^j/R^j \mid V, W) \Longleftrightarrow IF_i(r^j/R^j, x^j \mid V, W) = 1,$

IF$_i$.4 $IF_i(r^j/R^j, x^j \mid V, W)$ is independent of unit of measurement.

Moreover, since it follows from (5.1.18) and (5.1.23) that

$$IL(r/R \mid V, W) \subseteqq IL(r/R \mid V, S^\alpha), \quad (5.1.26)$$

we have also

$$IF_i(r^j/R^j, x^j \mid V, W) \geqq IF_i(r^j/R^j, x^j \mid V, S^\alpha), j = 1, 2, \cdots, J. \quad (5.1.27)$$

The (V, W) revenue indirect input efficiency measure may be calculated

as the solution to the nonlinear programming problem (which can be
converted to a linear programming problem by setting $\sigma = 1$)

$$IF_i(r^j/R^j, x^j \mid V, W) = \min_{\lambda, z, u} \lambda \qquad (5.1.28)$$

$$\text{s.t. } u \leqq zM$$

$$zN = \lambda \sigma x^j$$

$$0 < \sigma \leqq 1$$

$$r^j u \geqq R^j$$

$$z \in \Re_+^J$$

$$\sum_{j=1}^{J} z_j = 1$$

or

$$\min_{\lambda, z, u} \lambda$$

$$\text{s.t. } u_m \leqq \sum_{j=1}^{J} z_j u_{jm}, m = 1, 2, \cdots, M,$$

$$\sum_{j=1}^{J} z_j x_{jn} = \lambda \sigma x_{jn}, n = 1, 2, \cdots, N,$$

$$0 < \sigma \leqq 1,$$

$$\sum_{m=1}^{M} r_{jm} u_m \geqq R^j,$$

$$z_j \geqq 0, j = 1, 2, \cdots, J,$$

$$\sum_{j=1}^{J} z_j = 1.$$

At this point it is useful to summarize the relationship among the five
revenue indirect input measures of technical efficiency. Because it measures the efficiency of input vector x^j in the generation of revenue R^j
at output prices r^j under the most restrictive assumptions concerning
the structure of technology, the (C, S) revenue indirect input measure
assigns the lowest efficiency score. From equations (5.1.12), (5.1.16),
(5.1.21), (5.1.27) and Propositions (5.1.4), (5.1.25) it follows that

$$0 < IF_i(r^j/R^j, x^j \mid C, S) \leqq IF_i(r^j/R^j, x^j \mid N, S) \qquad (5.1.29)$$

$$\leqq IF_i(r^j/R^j, x^j \mid V, S) \leqq IF_i(r^j/R^j, x^j \mid V, S^\alpha)$$

$$\leqq IF_i(r^j/R^j, x^j \mid V, W) \leqq 1.$$

The next objective is to introduce a decomposition of the (C, S) revenue indirect input measure of technical efficiency into component measures of revenue indirect input scale efficiency, revenue indirect input congestion, and a (V, W) revenue indirect input measure of technical efficiency. We begin by proposing a measure of revenue indirect input scale efficiency.

(5.1.30)   **Definition:** The function

$$IS_i(r^j/R^j, x^j) = IF_i(r^j/R^j, x^j \mid C, S)/IF_i(r^j/R^j, x^j \mid V, S), j = 1, 2, \cdots, J,$$

is called the *Revenue Indirect Input Scale Efficiency Measure.*

Observation j is revenue indirect input scale efficient if $IF_i(r^j/R^j, x^j \mid C, S) = IF_i(r^j/R^j, x^j \mid V, S)$, or if it is equally efficient relative to (C, S) and (V, S) revenue indirect input sets.

This point is illustrated in Figure 5.4. Observation j is revenue indirect input scale efficient because it is equally (technically) efficient relative to (C, S) and (V, S) revenue indirect technologies. Input vector x^j is producing a scale-efficient output vector u^j. However neither observation k nor observation ℓ is revenue indirect input scale efficient because each is more (technically) efficient relative to the (V, S) revenue indirect technology than to the (C, S) revenue indirect technology. Input vector x^k is producing output vector u^k which is too small to be revenue indirect input scale efficient, while x^ℓ is producing u^ℓ which is too large to be revenue indirect input scale efficient. The properties of $IS_i(r^j/R^j, x^j)$ are summarized in

(5.1.31)   **Proposition:** Given $IS_i(r^j/R^j, x^j)$, then for each $j = 1, 2, \cdots, J,$

IS$_i$.1 $0 < IS_i(r^j/R^j, x^j) \leq 1,$

IS$_i$.2 $IS_i(r^j/R^j, x^j) = 1 \iff IF_i(r^j/R^j, x^j \mid V, S) \cdot x^j$ exhibits CRS, or equivalently $IF_i(r^j/R^j, x^j \mid V, S) \cdot x^j \in Isoq\ IL(r^j/R^j \mid C, S),$

IS$_i$.3 $IS_i(r^j/R^j, \lambda x^j) = IS_i(r^j/R^j, x^j), \lambda > 0,$

IS$_i$.4 $IS_i(r^j/R^j, x^j)$ is independent of unit of measurement.

Proof: IS$_i$.1 follows from (5.1.29). IS$_i$.3 is a consequence of the homogeneity of degree -1 of both numerator and denominator of the right side of Definition (5.1.30), and IS$_i$.4 is obvious. To prove IS$_i$.2 assume that $IS_i(r^j/R^j, x^j) = 1$. Then $IF_i(r^j/R^j, x^j \mid C, S) = IF_i(r^j/R^j, x^j \mid V, S)$ and $IF_i(r^j/R^j, x^j \mid V, S) \cdot x^j \in Isoq\ IL(r^j/R^j \mid C, S)$, i.e., $IF_i(r^j/R^j, x^j \mid V, S) \cdot x^j$ exhibits CRS. Conversely if $IF_i(r^j/R^j, x^j \mid$

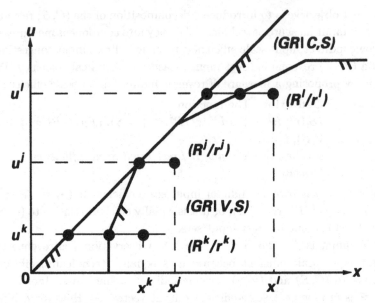

Fig. 5.4. *Measuring Revenue Indirect Input Scale Efficiency*

$V, S) \cdot x^j$ exhibits CRS, then $IF_i(r^j/R^j, x^j \mid V, S) \cdot x^j \in Isoq\ IL(r^j/R^j \mid C, S)$, and $IF_i(r^j/R^j, x^j \mid V, S) = IF_i(r^j/R^j, x^j \mid C, S)$, so that $IS_i(r^j/R^j, x^j) = 1$.

Q.E.D.

Suppose now that $IS_i(r^j/R^j, x^j) < 1$. We want to determine whether the source of revenue indirect input scale inefficiency is utilization of an inefficiently small input vector in a region of increasing returns to scale (as with x^k in Figure 5.4), or utilization of an inefficiently large input vector in a region of decreasing returns to scale (as with x^ℓ in Figure 5.4). The determination is based on a comparison of $IF_i(r^j/R^j, x^j \mid C, S)$ with $IF_i(r^j/R^j, x^j \mid N, S)$. If $IS_i(r^j/R^j, x^j) < 1$ and $IF_i(r^j/R^j, x^j \mid C, S) = IF_i(r^j/R^j, x^j \mid N, S)$, revenue indirect input scale inefficiency is due to increasing returns to scale. If $IS_i(r^j/R^j, x^j) < 1$ and $IF_i(r^j/R^j, x^j \mid C, S) < IF_i(r^j/R^j, x^j \mid N, S)$, revenue indirect input scale inefficiency is due to decreasing returns to scale. Figure 5.4 illustrates. The revenue indirect input scale inefficiency of activity k is due to increasing returns to scale because $IF_i(r^k/R^k, x^k \mid C, S) = IF_i(r^k/R^k, x^k \mid N, S)$. The revenue indirect input scale inefficiency of activity ℓ is due to decreasing returns to scale because $IF_i(r^\ell/R^\ell, x^\ell \mid C, S) < IF_i(r^\ell/R^\ell, x^\ell \mid N, S)$.

Thus a determination of existence and nature of revenue indirect input

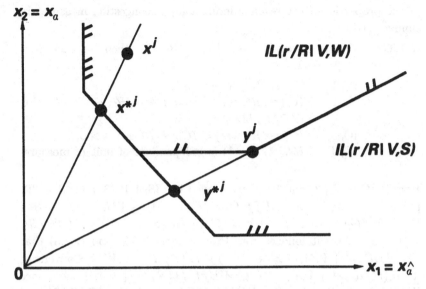

Fig. 5.5. *The Revenue Indirect Input Congestion Measure*

scale inefficiency can be made simply by solving programming problems (5.1.5), (5.1.11), and (5.1.17). The solutions provide the three measures required to calculate revenue indirect input scale efficiency measures for every observation.

We continue the decomposition of the (C, S) revenue indirect input measure of technical efficiency by considering input congestion. We begin by proposing a measure of revenue indirect input congestion.

(5.1.32)   **Definition**: The function
$$IC_i(r^j/R^j, x^j) = IF_i(r^j/R^j, x^j \mid V, S)/IF_i(r^j/R^j, x^j \mid V, W), j = 1, 2, \cdots, J,$$
is called the *Revenue Indirect Input Congestion Measure*.

The revenue indirect input congestion measure provides a comparison of the feasible proportionate reduction in inputs achievable maintaining revenue at given output prices when technology satisfies weak instead of strong input disposability. We say that input vector x^j is not congesting for normalized output price vector r^j/R^j if $IC_i(r^j/R^j, x^j) = 1$, i.e., if $IF_i(r^j/R^j, x^j \mid V, S) = IF_i(r^j/R^j, x^j \mid V, W)$. Figure 5.5 illustrates, with two indirect input sets $IL(r/R \mid V, S)$ and $IL(r/R \mid V, W)$. The input vector x^j is not congesting, since x^{*j} belongs to the boundary of both sets. Input vector y^j is congesting though, since y^{*j} is not on the boundary of both sets.

The properties of the revenue indirect input congestion measure are summarized in

(5.1.33)   **Proposition**: Given $IC_i(r^j/R^j, x^j)$, then for each $j = 1, 2, \cdots, J$,

IC$_i$.1 $0 < IC_i(r^j/R^j, x^j) \leqq 1$,

IC$_i$.2 $IC_i(r^j/R^j, x^j) = 1 \iff IF_i(r^j/R^j, x^j \mid V, W) \cdot x^j \in WEff\ IL(r^j/R^j \mid V, W)$,

IC$_i$.3 $IC_i(r^j/R^j, \lambda x^j) = IC_i(r^j/R^j, x^j), \lambda > 0$,

IC$_i$.4 $IC_i(r^j/R^j, x^j)$ is independent of unit of measurement.

Proof: IC$_i$.1, IC$_i$.3, and IC$_i$.4 are proved like IS$_i$.1, IS$_i$.3, and IS$_i$.4. To prove IC$_i$.2, recall that $WEff\ IL(r^j/R^j \mid V, W) \subseteqq WEff\ IL(r^j/R^j \mid V, S)$. If $IC_i(r^j/R^j, x^j) = 1$ then $IF_i(r^j/R^j, x^j \mid V, W) = IF_i(r^j/R^j, x^j \mid V, S)$. Now it follows from Propositions (2.3.2) and (2.3.3) that $IF_i(r^j/R^j, x^j \mid V, W) \cdot x^j \in WEff\ IL(r^j/R^j \mid V, W)$. Conversely, if $IF_i(r^j/R^j, x^j \mid V, W) \cdot x^j \in WEff\ IL(r^j/R^j \mid V, W)$ then since $WEff\ IL(r^j/R^j \mid V, W) \subseteqq WEff\ IL(r^j/R^j \mid V, S)$, $IF_i(r^j/R^j, x^j \mid V, W) = IF_i(r^j/R^j, x^j \mid V, S)$ and $IC_i(r^j/R^j, x^j) = 1$.

$$Q.E.D.$$

Suppose that $IC_i(r^j/R^j, x^j) < 1$. The next step is to determine the source of the congestion, i.e., the subvector of inputs that is obstructing revenue generation. The subset of congesting inputs is determined as follows. First, compare $IF_i(r^j/R^j, x^j \mid V, W)$ and $IF_i(r^j/R^j, x^j \mid V, S^\alpha)$ for each $\alpha \subseteqq \{1, 2, \cdots, N\}$. If $IC_i(r^j/R^j, x^j) < 1$ and $IF_i(r^j/R^j, x^j \mid V, W) = IF_i(r^j/R^j, x^j \mid V, S^\alpha)$, the subvector $x_{\hat\alpha}$ is the source of the congestion. Of course $x_{\hat\alpha}$ may not be unique, and the exercise may produce a set of congesting subvectors, each of which can account for $IC_i(r^j/R^j, x^j) < 1$.

Thus the magnitude and source of revenue indirect input congestion can be determined by solving the programming problems (5.1.17), (5.1.22), and (5.1.28). Note that the latter two problems are nonlinear (but can be rendered linear by setting $\sigma = 1$), and that (5.1.22) must be solved one time for every partition $(\alpha, \hat\alpha)$ of $\boldsymbol{N}$.

We conclude this section with a statement of the desired decomposition of the (C, S) revenue indirect input measure of technical efficiency. Using Definitions (5.1.30) and (5.1.32) we have

$$IF_i(r^j/R^j, x^j \mid C, S) = IF_i(r^j/R^j, x^j \mid V, W) \cdot IS_i(r^j/R^j, x^j) \cdot IC_i(r^j/R^j, x^j). \qquad (5.1.34)$$

The revenue indirect input measure of technical efficiency relative to the constant returns to scale, strong disposability of inputs technology is the product of three components: a revenue indirect measure of input scale efficiency, a revenue indirect measure of input congestion, and a revenue indirect input measure of technical efficiency relative to a variable returns to scale, weak disposability of inputs technology.

5.2 Radial Indirect Efficiency Measures Requiring Input Quantity, Input Price, Output Quantity, and Output Price Data: The Decomposition of Indirect Cost Efficiency

The revenue indirect input measures introduced in the previous section are all measures of technical efficiency. This is because they focus on the effectiveness of an input vector in generating revenue, without regard for the prices of the inputs being evaluated. The object is to (radially) shrink the input vector. In this section, however, we introduce input prices and consider the objective of shrinking expenditure on inputs. This leads to a (revenue indirect) measure of input mix efficiency, which in turn interacts with the technical (C, S) measure previously introduced to generate a (revenue indirect) measure of input cost efficiency.

Suppose that in addition to the input matrix N, the output matrix M, the output price vector $r \in \Re_+^M, r \neq 0$, and desired revenue $R \in \Re_{++}$, input prices $p \in \Re_+^N, p \neq 0$, are known. Then for each observation we can compute the minimal cost of obtaining revenue R, relative to each of the reference technologies introduced in Section 5.1.

Let us consider cost minimization relative to the revenue indirect input set $IL(r/R \mid C, S)$. For observation j we define the minimum cost required to obtain revenue R^j given output prices r^j and input prices p^j as

$$IQ(r^j/R^j, p^j \mid C, S) = \min_x \{p^j x : x \in IL(r^j/R^j \mid C, S)\}. \qquad (5.2.1)$$

This cost can be calculated as the solution to

$$IQ(r^j/R^j, p^j \mid C, S) = \min_{z,x,u} p^j x \qquad (5.2.2)$$

$$\text{s.t. } u \leqq zM$$

$$zN \leqq x$$

$$r^j u \geqq R^j$$

$$z \in \Re_+^J$$

or

$$\min_{z,x,u} \sum_{n=1}^{N} p_{jn} x_n$$

$$\text{s.t.} \quad u_m \leq \sum_{j=1}^{J} z_j u_{jm}, m = 1, 2, \cdots, M,$$

$$\sum_{j=1}^{J} z_j x_{jn} \leq x_n, n = 1, 2, \cdots, N,$$

$$\sum_{m=1}^{M} r_{jm} u_m \geq R^j,$$

$$z_j \geq 0, j = 1, 2, \cdots, J.$$

Both input prices p^j and input quantities x^j are assumed known, and so total realized cost $p^j x^j$ is known. Assuming that $p^j x^j > 0$, we may now introduce

(5.2.3)   **Definition**: The function
$$IO_i(r^j/R^j, p^j, x^j \mid C, S) = IQ(r^j/R^j, p^j \mid C, S)/p^j x^j, j = 1, 2, \cdots, J,$$
is called the *(C,S) Revenue Indirect Input Cost Efficiency Measure.*

The (C, S) revenue indirect input cost efficiency measure computes the ratio of minimum cost to actual cost. Its properties are summarized in

(5.2.4)   **Proposition**: Given $IL(r^j/R^j \mid C, S)$, then for each $j = 1, 2, \cdots, J$,

$IO_i.1$ $IO_i(r^j/R^j, p^j, \delta x^j \mid C, S) = \delta^{-1} IO_i(r^j/R^j, p^j, x^j \mid C, S), \delta > 0,$

$IO_i.2$ $IO_i(r^j/\theta R^j, p^j, x^j \mid C, S) = \theta IO_i(r^j/R^j, p^j, x^j \mid C, S), \theta > 0,$

$IO_i.3$ $IO_i(r^j/R^j, \lambda p^j, x^j \mid C, S) = IO_i(r^j/R^j, p^j, x^j \mid C, S), \lambda > 0,$

$IO_i.4$ $0 < IO_i(r^j/R^j, p^j, x^j \mid C, S) \leq 1,$

$IO_i.5$ x^j solves (5.2.1) $\iff IO_i(r^j/R^j, p^j, x^j \mid C, S) = 1,$

$IO_i.6$ $IO_i(r^j/R^j, p^j, x^j \mid C, S)$ is independent of unit of measurement.

The proof of this proposition is left for the reader.

(5.2.5) **Definition:** The function
$$IA_i(r^j/R^j, p^j, x^j \mid C, S) = IO_i(r^j/R^j, p^j, x^j \mid C, S)/$$
$$IF_i(r^j/R^j, x^j \mid C, S), j = 1, 2, \cdots, J,$$
is called the (C, S) *Revenue Indirect Input Allocative Efficiency Measure*.

The revenue indirect input allocative efficiency measure provides an indication of how the chosen input intensity $(x/ \parallel x \parallel)$ deviates from the optimal intensity. The properties of this measure are listed in

(5.2.6) **Proposition:** Given $IL(r^j/R^j \mid C, S)$, then for each $j = 1, 2, \cdots, J,$

IA$_i$.1 $IA_i(r^j/R^j, p^j, \delta x^j \mid C, S) = IA_i(r^j/R^j, p^j, x^j \mid C, S), \delta > 0,$

IA$_i$.2 $IA_i(r^j/\theta R^j, p^j, x^j \mid C, S) = IA_i(r^j/R^j, p^j, x^j \mid C, S), \theta > 0,$

IA$_i$.3 $IA_i(r^j/R^j, \lambda p^j, x^j \mid C, S) = IA_i(r^j/R^j, p^j, x^j \mid C, S), \lambda > 0,$

IA$_i$.4 $0 < IA_i(r^j/R^j, p^j, x^j \mid C, S) \leq 1,$

IA$_i$.5 $\exists \lambda \in (0, 1]$ such that λx^j solves (5.2.1)
$$\Longleftrightarrow IA_i(r^j/R^j, p^j, x^j \mid C, S) = 1,$$

IA$_i$.6 $IA_i(r^j/R^j, p^j, x^j \mid C, S)$ is independent of unit of measurement.

Proof: We only prove IA$_i$.5. Thus assume $\exists \lambda \in (0, 1]$, such that λx^j solves (5.2.1). Then $IQ(r^j/R^j, p^j \mid C, S) = p^j \lambda x^j$, and by Definition (5.2.5), $IA_i(r^j/R^j, p^j, x^j \mid C, S) = 1$. Conversely, if $IA_i(r^j/R^j, p^j, x^j \mid C, S) = 1$, then $IQ(r^j/R^j, p^j \mid C, S) = p^j \cdot IF_i(r^j/R^j, x^j) \cdot x^j$ and since $IF_i(r^j/R^j, x^j) \in (0, 1]$, IA$_i$.5 holds.

$$Q.E.D.$$

From Definitions (5.1.3) and (5.2.5) we obtain the following decomposition of revenue indirect input cost efficiency

$$IO_i(r^j/R^j, p^j, x^j \mid C, S) = IA_i(r^j/R^j, p^j, x^j \mid C, S) \quad (5.2.7)$$
$$\cdot IF_i(r^j/R^j, x^j \mid C, S).$$

We note that if $IO_i(r^j/R^j, p^j, x^j \mid C, S) = 1$ then the other measures are also one.

Finally, a grand decomposition is obtained by combining (5.1.32) and (5.2.7)

$$IO_i(r^j/R^j, p^j, x^j \mid C, S) = IA_i(r^j/R^j, p^j, x^j \mid C, S) \quad (5.2.8)$$
$$\cdot IS_i(r^j/R^j, x^j) \cdot IC_i(r^j/R^j, x^j)$$
$$\cdot IF_i(r^j/R^j, x^j \mid V, W).$$

Thus revenue indirect input cost inefficiency is due to some combination of a selection of an inappropriate input mix, an inappropriately small or large scale of production, the presence of input congestion, and waste, or purely technical inefficiency.

5.3 Measures of Benefit Effectiveness

Departure from revenue indirect minimum cost given by $IQ(r^j/R^j, p^j \mid C, S)$ in (5.2.1) is either technical or allocative in nature, and the decomposition is given by (5.2.7). The revenue indirect efficiency measure $IO_i(r^j/R^j, p^j, x^j \mid C, S)$ provides an *ex post* evaluation of a firm's performance by comparing revenue constrained minimum cost to observed cost. Sometimes it may be preferable to conduct an *ex ante* comparison of revenue constrained minimum cost to target revenue R and to rank firms on the basis of benefit effectiveness ratios

$$IQ(r^j/R^j, p^j \mid C, S)/R^j, j = 1, 2, \cdots, J. \tag{5.3.1}$$

In particular this ratio will show if an activity j can be performed without loss, i.e., with a ratio less than or equal to one, since then

$$R^j - IQ(r^j/R^j, p^j \mid C, S) \geqq 0. \tag{5.3.2}$$

The revenue indirect cost function $IQ(r^j/R^j, p^j \mid C, S)$ is defined relative to constant returns to scale, which implies that (the proof is obtained from (5.1.2) and (5.2.1))

$$IQ(r^j/R^j, p^j \mid C, S) = R^j IQ(r^j, p^j \mid C, S). \tag{5.3.3}$$

Thus the expression (5.3.2) takes the simple form

$$1 - IQ(r^j, p^j \mid C, S) \geqq 0. \tag{5.3.4}$$

This expression is independent of R^j, thus we can only compare costs to target revenue equal one. However if the revenue indirect costs are computed relative to the $IL(r^j/R^j \mid N, S)$ or $IL(r^j/R^j \mid V, S)$ technologies, our comparison between revenue constrained cost and target revenue becomes more useful. Thus firms or activities may be ranked on the basis of

$$IQ(r^j/R^j, p^j \mid N, S)/R^j, j = 1, 2, \cdots, J, \tag{5.3.5}$$

or

$$IQ(r^j/R^j, p^j \mid V, S)/R^j, j = 1, 2, \cdots, J. \tag{5.3.6}$$

5.4   The Relationship Between Direct and Indirect Measures

In Chapter 3 direct input-based measures were discussed. The technical measures took outputs as given and gauged efficiency by proportionally contracting inputs as much as possible while remaining feasible. In this chapter revenue deflated output prices, rather than outputs, are assumed given.

In general, given an observation (x^j, u^j) with $r^j u^j \geqq R^j$, we have the following relation between the direct and indirect measures;

$$F_i(u^j, x^j \mid C, S) \geqq IF_i(r^j/R^j, x^j \mid C, S) > 0 \qquad (5.4.1)$$

since

$$
\begin{aligned}
F_i(u^j, x^j \mid C, S) &= \min\{\lambda : \lambda x^j \in L(u^j \mid C, S)\} \\
&\geqq \min\{\lambda : \lambda x^j \in IL(r^j/R^j \mid C, S)\} \\
&= IF_i(r^j/R^j, x^j \mid C, S),
\end{aligned}
$$

where the inequality follows from the fact that

$$L(u^j \mid C, S) \subseteqq IL(r^j/R^j \mid C, S). \qquad (5.4.2)$$

Clearly, one may also prove that

$$Q(u^j, p^j \mid C, S) \geqq IQ(r^j/R^j, p^j \mid C, S) \qquad (5.4.3)$$

if $r^j u^j \geqq R^j$. Therefore it is also true that

$$O_i(u^j, p^j, x^j \mid C, S) \geqq IO_i(r^j/R^j, p^j, x^j). \qquad (5.4.4)$$

5.5   A Numerical Example: Indirect Input-Based Efficiency Measurement

In this section we provide numerical examples of some of the indirect input-based efficiency measures introduced in this chapter using the artificial data described in Section 5 of Chapter 2. More specifically, we include calculations of the measures included in the decomposition (5.2.8)

$$
\begin{aligned}
IO_i(r^j/R^j, p^j, x^j \mid C, S) &= IA_i(r^j/R^j, p^j, x^j \mid C, S) \cdot IS_i(r^j/R^j, x^j) \\
&\quad \cdot IC_i(r^j/R^j, x^j) \cdot IF_i(r^j/R^j, x^j \mid V, W).
\end{aligned}
$$

These efficiency measures are calculated using the PROC LP procedures available in SAS/OR. We begin by calculating revenue indirect minimum cost $IQ(r^j/R^j, p^j \mid C, S)$ using (5.2.2), the solution to which is used to calculate $IO_i(r^j/R^j, p^j, x^j \mid C, S)$, see (5.2.3). The linear programming problem used to solve for $IQ(r^j/R^j, p^j \mid C, S)$ is closely related to the familiar cost minimization problem. The reader is referred to Section 4 of Chapter 3 for a statement of this problem in canonical form.

Next, we calculate $IF_i(r^j/R^j, x^j \mid V, W)$ as the solution to the linear programming problem stated in (5.1.28). We note that we used $r^j u^j$ as our proxy for R^j in the constraint $\sum_{m=1}^{M} r_{jm} u_m \geqq R^j, j = 1, 2, \cdots, J$, to avoid infeasibility problems which arose when we used the R^j from Table 2.2. This problem arose in this case due to rounding error (i.e., $r^j u^j$ was slightly less than R^j for some observations due to the way r^j and u^j were constructed, see Chapter 2).

We also calculated $IF_i(r^j/R^j, x^j \mid C, S)$ from (5.1.5) which was used to derive $IA_i(r^j/R^j, p^j, x^j \mid C, S)$, see Definition (5.2.5), and $IS_i(r^j/R^j, x^j)$ from Definition (5.1.30). Finally, we calculated $IF_i(r^j/R^j, x^j \mid V, S)$ from (5.1.17) which was used with $IF_i(r^j/R^j, x^j \mid V, W)$ to derive $IC_i(r^j/R^j, x^j)$ from Definition (5.1.32).

The results are collected and displayed in Table 5.1. As discussed in Chapter 2 our artificial data were constructed to include increasing returns to scale (observations 1-5), constant returns to scale (observations 6-15), and decreasing returns to scale. This is reflected in the results for $IS_i(r^j/R^j, x^j)$ and naturally in the overall revenue indirect measure $IO_i(r^j/R^j, p^j, x^j \mid C, S)$. It is also of interest to compare $IF_i(r^j/R^j, x^j \mid V, S)$ to $F_i(u^j, x^j \mid V, S)$ from Chapter 3. Since the revenue indirect measures of input efficiency allow outputs to vary (as long as they satisfy the revenue constraint), whereas outputs are taken as given and only inputs are allowed to vary in the standard input-based efficiency measures introduced in Chapter 3, the relevant more than sets will be nested: the revenue indirect more than sets contain the standard more than sets. Correspondingly, $IF_i(r^j/R^j, x^j \mid V, S) \leqq F_i(u^j, x^j \mid V, S)$. It follows that $IF_i(r^j/R^j, x^j \mid C, S) \leqq F_i(u^j, x^j \mid C, S)$ and $IF_i(r^j/R^j, x^j \mid N, S) \leqq F_i(u^j, x^j \mid N, S)$ and consequently $IS_i(r^j/R^j, x^j) \gtreqqless S_i(r^j/R^j, x^j)$.

5.6   References to the Literature

The theoretical framework for revenue indirect input-based efficiency measurement was established by Shephard (1974) and Shephard and Färe (1980). A complete treatment of revenue indirect production is provided by Färe and Grosskopf (1990a). The piecewise linear formulation of the model is due to Färe, Grosskopf, and Lovell (1988), who also

Table 5.1. *Indirect Input-Based Efficiency Measures Using Artificial Data*

Obs	$IO_i(r^j/R^j, p^j, x^j \mid C, S)$	$IA_i(r^j/R^j, p^j, x^j \mid C, S)$
1	0.694	1.000
2	0.731	0.933
3	0.704	1.000
4	0.696	0.927
5	0.704	0.979
6	1.000	1.000
7	1.000	1.000
8	1.000	1.000
9	1.000	1.000
10	1.000	1.000
11	1.000	1.000
12	1.000	1.000
13	1.000	1.000
14	1.000	1.000
15	1.000	1.000
16	0.694	1.000
17	0.722	0.943
18	0.704	1.000
19	0.716	0.994
20	0.702	1.000

Obs	$IS_i(r^j/R^j, x^j)$	$IC_i(r^j/R^j, x^j)$	$IF_i(r^j/R^j, x^j \mid V, W)$
1	0.694	1.000	1.000
2	0.783	1.000	1.000
3	0.704	1.000	1.000
4	0.751	1.000	1.000
5	0.719	1.000	1.000
6	1.000	1.000	1.000
7	1.000	1.000	1.000
8	1.000	1.000	1.000
9	1.000	1.000	1.000
10	1.000	1.000	1.000
11	1.000	1.000	1.000
12	1.000	1.000	1.000
13	1.000	1.000	1.000
14	1.000	1.000	1.000
15	1.000	1.000	1.000
16	0.694	1.000	1.000
17	0.765	1.000	1.000
18	0.704	1.000	1.000
19	0.720	1.000	1.000
20	0.702	1.000	1.000

obtained the decomposition (5.2.8) of overall revenue indirect efficiency into its technical and allocative components.

A stochastic parametric application of the revenue indirect production model to the measurement of the efficiency of municipal government service provision can be found in Färe, Grosskopf, and Hayes (1990).

6

Indirect Output-Based Efficiency Measurement

6.0 Introduction

The purpose of this chapter is to extend the radial output-based efficiency measures in Chapter 4, where efficiency of the observed output vector is judged relative to technology with fixed inputs, to the case in which outputs are judged relative to the cost indirect production technology. In this case, inputs are restricted but not fixed, they may vary as long as their cost does not exceed a prespecified target. In contrast, in Chapter 4, inputs are assumed exogenously given and fixed.

In Section 6.1, measures of indirect output-based technical efficiency are developed. These measures take input prices and planned cost as given and measure efficiency as proportional expansion of all outputs. The (C, S) measure is then decomposed into component measures of scale efficiency, congestion, and purely technical efficiency, all relative to the cost indirect technology.

In Section 6.2 we introduce output prices and obtain a cost indirect output revenue efficiency measure. This measure gauges the extent to which a producer succeeds in maximizing output revenue when constrained by output prices, input prices, and an input budget. This cost indirect revenue efficiency measure is then decomposed into technical and allocative components, the technical component being the measure introduced in Section 6.1.

In Section 6.3 we present a measure of revenue effectiveness, which shows the ability of a producer to convert an input budget into revenue.

In Section 6.4 our artificial data set is used to illustrate some of the cost indirect output efficiency measures developed in this chapter.

6.1 Radial Indirect Efficiency Measures Requiring Output Quantity, Input Quantity, and Input Price Data: The Decomposition of Indirect Technical Efficiency

The objective of this section is to derive a family of measures of the efficiency of an output vector produced given a fixed budget, input prices, and production technology. Thus we assume that input prices and the budget are both known and production efficiency is gauged on the basis of outputs produced. For this purpose technology is most usefully represented by the cost indirect output correspondence, and efficiency measurement is output-based. Thus the structure of this section is similar to that of Chapter 4 in the sense the efficiency measurement is output-based. It is also similar to that of Chapter 5 in the sense that efficiency is measured relative to an indirect production correspondence.

Suppose that, in addition to the input matrix N and the output matrix M, input prices $p \in \Re_+^N, p \neq 0$, and planned cost $Q \in \Re_{++}$ are known. Then the initial cost indirect output sets are formed from the data by means of

$$IP(p/Q \mid C, S) = \{u : u \leq zM, zN \leq x, px \leq Q, z \in \Re_+^J\}, (p/Q) \neq 0,$$
$$\tag{6.1.1}$$

where z denotes the intensity vector. These (C, S) output sets satisfy the strong properties of constant returns to scale and strong disposability of outputs. This is proved in the following

(6.1.2)   **Proposition:** The (C, S) cost indirect output sets $IP(p/Q \mid C, S)$ satisfy

(i) $IP(p/Q\lambda \mid C, S) = \lambda IP(p/Q \mid C, S), \lambda > 0,$

(ii) $u \leq v \in IP(p/Q \mid C, S) \Longrightarrow u \in IP(p/Q \mid C, S).$

Proof: (i) Let $\lambda > 0$. Then from (6.1.1)

$$IP(p/Q\lambda \mid C, S) = \{u : u \leq zM, zN \leq x, px \leq Q\lambda, z \in \Re_+^J\}$$
$$= \lambda\{u/\lambda : (u/\lambda) \leq (z/\lambda)M, (z/\lambda)N \leq (x/\lambda),$$
$$p(x/\lambda) \leq Q, (z/\lambda) \in \Re_+^J\}$$
$$= \lambda IP(p/Q \mid C, S).$$

(ii) This property follows from the nature of the inequality $u \leq zM$.

Q.E.D.

We can now define the efficiency of an output vector relative to the cost indirect output correspondence by means of

(6.1.3)   **Definition**: The function
$$IF_o(p^j/Q^j, u^j \mid C, S) = \max\{\theta : \theta u^j \in IP(p^j/Q^j \mid C, S)\},$$
$$j = 1, 2, \cdots, J,$$
is called the (C, S) *Cost Indirect Output Measure of Technical Efficiency*.

$IF_o(p^j/Q^j, u^j \mid C, S)$ measures the efficiency of output vector u^j in the presence of budget-deflated input prices p^j/Q^j and subject to the restrictions of a (C, S) technology. It does so by calculating the ratio of the largest feasible expansion of u^j to u^j itself, feasibility being defined relative to $IP(p^j/Q^j \mid C, S)$.

The measurement of cost indirect technical efficiency is illustrated in Figure 6.1 for the $M = 2$ case. A (C, S) cost indirect output set consistent with the cost constraint $px \leq Q$ is drawn along with a (C, S) direct output set. The (C, S) cost indirect technical efficiency of producing outputs u^j at input cost not greater than Q^j when input prices are p^j is given by $\| \, 0u^{*j} \, \| \, / \, \| \, 0u^j \, \|$. It is clear from Figure 6.1 that the cost indirect measure is at least as great as the corresponding direct measure.

The properties satisfied by $IF_o(p^j/Q^j, u^j \mid C, S)$ are summarized in the following

(6.1.4)   **Proposition**: Given $IP(p^j/Q^j \mid C, S)$, then for each $j = 1, 2, \cdots, J$,

$IF_o.1$ $IF_o(p^j/Q^j, \delta u^j \mid C, S) = \delta^{-1} IF_o(p^j/Q^j, u^j \mid C, S)$, $\delta > 0$,

$IF_o.2$ $IF_o(p^j/Q^j\lambda, u^j \mid C, S) = \lambda IF_o(p^j/Q^j, u^j \mid C, S)$, $\lambda > 0$,

$IF_o.3$ $1 \leq IF_o(p^j/Q^j, u^j \mid C, S) < +\infty$,

$IF_o.4$ $u^j \in WEff \, IP(p^j/Q^j \mid C, S) \Longleftrightarrow IF_o(p^j/Q^j, u^j \mid C, S) = 1$,

$IF_o.5$ $IF_o(p^j/Q^j, u^j \mid C, S)$ is independent of unit of measurement.

Proof:
$(IF_o.1)$

$$\begin{aligned} IF_o(p^j/Q^j, \delta u^j \mid C, S) &= \max\{\theta : \theta\delta u^j \in IP(p^j/Q^j \mid C, S)\} \\ &= \delta^{-1} \max\{\theta\delta : \theta\delta u^j \in IP(p^j/Q^j \mid C, S)\} \\ &= \delta^{-1} IF_o(p^j/Q^j, u^j \mid C, S). \end{aligned}$$

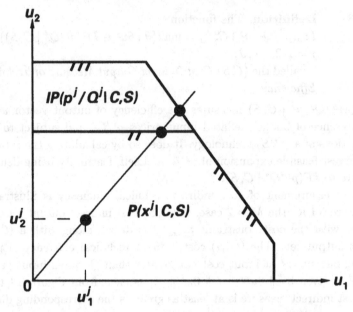

Fig. 6.1. *The (C, S) Cost Indirect Output Measure of Technical Efficiency*

(IF$_o$.2)   From Proposition (6.1.2(i)),

$$IF_o(p^j/Q^j\lambda, u^j \mid C, S) = \max\{\theta : \theta u^j \in IP(p^j/Q^j\lambda \mid C, S)\}$$
$$= \max\{\theta : \theta u^j \in \lambda IP(p^j/Q^j \mid C, S)\}$$
$$= \lambda IF_o(p^j/Q^j, u^j \mid C, S).$$

(IF$_o$.3)   Follows from the fact that $u^j \in IP(p^j/Q^j \mid C, S)$ for each $j = 1, 2, \cdots, J$.

(IF$_o$.4)   Since it is a radial measure, $IF_o(p^j/Q^j, u^j \mid C, S) = 1 \Longleftrightarrow u^j \in Isoq\ IP(p^j/Q^j \mid C, S)$. But since outputs are strongly disposable from Proposition (6.1.2(ii)), $Isoq\ IP(p^j/Q^j \mid C, S) = WEff\ IP(p^j/Q^j \mid C, S)$.

(IF$_o$.5)   Let us consider just the mth output constraint $\theta u_{jm} \leq \sum_{j=1}^{J} z_j u_{jm}$. If the unit of measurement is changed, so that $\hat{u}_{jm} = \nu u_{jm}, j = 1, 2, \cdots, J$, then clearly θ and $z_j, j = 1, 2, \cdots, J$, are not affected.

Q.E.D.

The (C, S) cost indirect output measure of technical efficiency can be calculated for observation j using the piecewise linear technology given by (6.1.1) as the solution to the linear programming problem

$$IF_o(p^j/Q^j, u^j \mid C, S) = \max_{\theta, z, x} \theta \qquad (6.1.5)$$

$$\text{s.t. } \theta u^j \leqq zM$$

$$zN \leqq x$$

$$p^j x \leqq Q^j$$

$$z \in \Re_+^J$$

or

$$\max_{\theta, z, x} \theta$$

$$\text{s.t. } \theta u_{jm} \leqq \sum_{j=1}^{J} z_j u_{jm}, m = 1, 2, \cdots, M,$$

$$\sum_{j=1}^{J} z_j x_{jn} \leqq x_n, n = 1, 2, \cdots, N,$$

$$\sum_{n=1}^{N} p_{jn} x_n \leqq Q^j,$$

$$z_j \geqq 0, j = 1, 2, \cdots, J.$$

Suppose now that production technology satisfies strong disposability of outputs and nonincreasing returns to scale. The appropriate cost indirect output sets are obtained from the data M, N, p and Q as

$$IP(p/Q \mid N, S) = \{u : u \leqq zM, zN \leqq x, px \leqq Q, z \in \Re_+^J,$$

$$\sum_{j=1}^{J} z_j \leqq 1\}, (p/Q) \in \Re_+^N, (p/Q) \neq 0. \quad (6.1.6)$$

Since the elements of the intensity vector are now restricted to sum to no more than one, it follows that

$$IP(p/Q \mid N, S) \subseteq IP(p/Q \mid C, S). \qquad (6.1.7)$$

The claim that the cost indirect output sets defined in (6.1.6) satisfy nonincreasing returns to scale and strong disposability of outputs is proved in

(6.1.8) **Proposition:** The (N, S) cost indirect output sets $IP(p/Q \mid N, S)$ satisfy

(i) $IP(p/Q\lambda \mid N, S) \subseteq \lambda IP(p/Q \mid N, S), \lambda \geq 1,$

(ii) $u \leqq v \in IP(p/Q \mid N, S) \Longrightarrow u \in IP(p/Q \mid N, S).$

Proof: (i) If $\lambda \geqq 1$ then

$$IP(p/Q\lambda \mid N, S) = \{u : u \leqq zM, zN \leqq x, px \leqq Q\lambda, z \in \Re_+^J,$$

$$\sum_{j=1}^{J} z_j \leqq 1\}$$

$$= \lambda\{u/\lambda : (u/\lambda) \leqq (z/\lambda)M, (z/\lambda)N \leqq (x/\lambda),$$

$$p(x/\lambda) \leqq Q, (z/\lambda) \in \Re_+^J, \sum_{j=1}^{J}(z_j/\lambda) \leqq 1/\lambda\}$$

$$\subseteqq \lambda\{u/\lambda : (u/\lambda) \leqq (z/\lambda)M, (z/\lambda)N \leqq (x/\lambda),$$

$$p(x/\lambda) \leqq Q, (z/\lambda) \in \Re_+^J, \sum_{j=1}^{J}(z_j/\lambda) \leqq 1\}$$

$$= \lambda IP(p/Q \mid N, S).$$

(ii) Follows the proof of Proposition (6.1.2(ii)).

$$Q.E.D.$$

We can now introduce a second cost indirect output measure of technical efficiency, which is defined relative to the (N, S) technology.

(6.1.9) **Definition:** The function

$$IF_o(p^j/Q^j, u^j \mid N, S) = \max\{\theta : \theta u^j \in IP(p^j/Q^j \mid N, S)\},$$
$$j = 1, 2, \cdots, J,$$

is called the (N,S) *Cost Indirect Output Measure of Technical Efficiency.*

The (N, S) cost indirect output measure of technical efficiency measures the efficiency of output vector u^j produced in the presence of budget-deflated input prices p^j/Q^j and with an (N, S) technology. The properties of $IF_o(p^j/Q^j, u^j \mid N, S)$ are summarized in

(6.1.10) **Proposition:** Given $IP(p^j/Q^j \mid N, S)$, then for each $j = 1, 2, \cdots, J,$

$IF_o.1$ $IF_o(p^j/Q^j, \delta u^j \mid N, S) = \delta^{-1}IF_o(p^j/Q^j, u^j \mid N, S),$
$\delta > 0,$

$IF_o.2$ $IF_o(p^j/Q^j\lambda, u^j \mid N, S) \leqq \lambda IF_o(p^j/Q^j, u^j \mid N, S),$
$\lambda \geqq 1,$

$IF_o.3$ $1 \leqq IF_o(p^j/Q^j, u^j \mid N, S) < +\infty,$

$IF_o.4$ $u^j \in WEff\, IP(p^j/Q^j \mid N, S) \iff IF_o(p^j/Q^j, u^j \mid N, S) = 1,$

$IF_o.5$ $IF_o(p^j/Q^j, u^j \mid N, S)$ is independent of unit of measurement.

The proof of Proposition (6.1.10) is similar to that of Proposition (6.1.4) and is left to the reader. The (N, S) cost indirect output measure of technical efficiency is calculated for observation j as the solution to the linear programming problem

$$IF_o(p^j/Q^j, u^j \mid N, S) = \max_{\theta, z, x} \theta \qquad (6.1.11)$$

$$\text{s.t. } \theta u^j \leqq zM$$

$$zN \leqq x$$

$$p^j x \leqq Q^j$$

$$z \in \Re_+^J$$

$$\sum_{j=1}^{J} z_j \leqq 1$$

or

$$\max_{\theta, z, x} \theta$$

$$\text{s.t. } \theta u_{jm} \leqq \sum_{j=1}^{J} z_j u_{jm}, m = 1, 2, \cdots, M,$$

$$\sum_{j=1}^{J} z_j x_{jn} \leqq x_n, n = 1, 2, \cdots, N,$$

$$\sum_{n=1}^{N} p_{jn} x_n \leqq Q^j,$$

$$z_j \geqq 0, j = 1, 2, \cdots, J,$$

$$\sum_{j=1}^{J} z_j \leqq 1.$$

For a piecewise linear representation of technology it follows from the constraints of (6.1.11) and (6.1.5), and for the general case it follows from (6.1.7), that

$$IF_o(p^j/Q^j, u^j \mid N, S) \leqq IF_o(p^j/Q^j, u^j \mid C, S), j = 1, 2, \cdots, J. \quad (6.1.12)$$

The result that an observation will be judged at least as technically efficient relative to (N, S) cost indirect output sets as to (C, S) cost indirect output sets is illustrated for the $M = N = 1$ case in Figure 6.2. There the (C, S) cost indirect output efficiency of observation j is given by the ratio $0u^{**j}/0u^j$, and the (N, S) cost indirect output efficiency is $0u^{*j}/0u^j < 0u^{**j}/0u^j$.

By further restricting the intensity vector we can construct cost indirect output sets satisfying strong disposability of outputs and variable

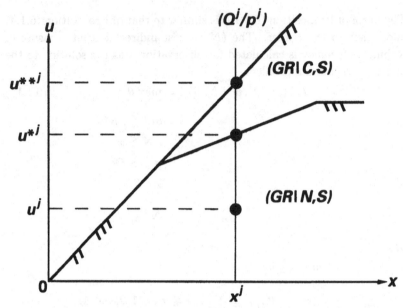

Fig. 6.2. *A Comparison of* $IF_o(p^j/Q^j, u^j \mid C, S)$ *and* $IF_o(p^j/Q^j, u^j \mid N, S)$

returns to scale. These output sets are formed from the data M, N, p and Q by means of

$$IP(p/Q \mid V, S) = \{u : u \leqq zM, zN \leqq x, px \leqq Q, z \in \Re_+^J, \sum_{j=1}^{J} z_j = 1\}.$$
$$(6.1.13)$$

Comparing the constraints of (6.1.13) with those of (6.1.6) shows the nesting property

$$IP(p/Q \mid V, S) \subseteqq IP(p/Q \mid N, S). \qquad (6.1.14)$$

We now define a cost indirect output measure of technical efficiency relative to the (V, S) technology.

(6.1.15) **Definition**: The function
$$IF_o(p^j/Q^j, u^j \mid V, S) = \max\{\theta : \theta u^j \in IP(p^j/Q^j \mid V, S)\},$$
$$j = 1, 2, \cdots, J,$$
is called the (V,S) *Cost Indirect Output Measure of Technical Efficiency.*

The (V, S) cost indirect output measure of technical efficiency provides a measure of the efficiency of output vector u^j produced in the presence of budget-deflated input prices p^j/Q^j and with a (V, S) technology. $IF_o(p^j/Q^j, u^j \mid V, S)$ satisfies properties like IF$_o$.1, IF$_o$.3, IF$_o$.4,

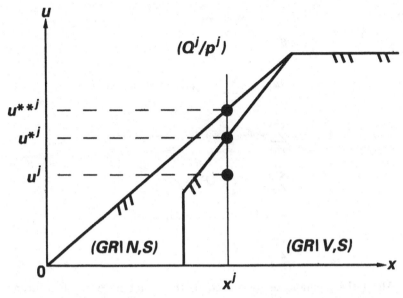

Fig. 6.3. *A Comparison of* $IF_o(p^j/Q^j, u^j \mid N, S)$ *and* $IF_o(p^j/Q^j, u^j \mid V, S)$

and IF$_o$.5 of Propositions (6.1.4) and (6.1.10). It does not satisfy a property analogous to IF$_o$.2 because of variable returns to scale. However from the nesting property (6.1.14), or in the piecewise linear case from the constraints of (6.1.17) below and (6.1.11), we have the ordering property

$$IF_o(p^j/Q^j, u^j \mid V, S) \leqq IF_o(p^j/Q^j, u^j \mid N, S), j = 1, 2, \cdots, J, \quad (6.1.16)$$

a result that is illustrated in Figure 6.3 for the piecewise linear $M = N = 1$ case, where $IF_o(p^j/Q^j, u^j \mid V, S) = 0u^{*j}/0u^j < 0u^{**j}/0u^j = IF_o(p^j/Q^j, u^j \mid N, S)$.

The (V, S) cost indirect output measure of technical efficiency is calculated as the solution to the linear programming problem

$$IF_o(p^j/Q^j, u^j \mid V, S) = \max_{\theta, z, x} \theta \qquad (6.1.17)$$

$$\text{s.t. } \theta u^j \leqq z M$$

$$z N \leqq x$$

$$p^j x \leqq Q^j$$

$$z \in \Re_+^J$$

$$\sum_{j=1}^{J} z_j = 1$$

or

$$\max_{\theta, z, x} \theta$$

$$\text{s.t. } \theta u_{jm} \leqq \sum_{j=1}^{J} z_j u_{jm}, m = 1, 2, \cdots, M,$$

$$\sum_{j=1}^{J} z_j x_{jn} \leqq x_n, n = 1, 2, \cdots, N,$$

$$\sum_{n=1}^{N} p_{jn} x_n \leqq Q^j,$$

$$z_j \geqq 0, j = 1, 2, \cdots, J,$$

$$\sum_{j=1}^{J} z_j = 1.$$

All of the technologies discussed to this point have satisfied strong disposability of outputs; only their returns to scale behavior has been altered. We now maintain the assumption of variable returns to scale and relax the assumption of strong disposability of outputs. In order to do so we partition the output matrix so that $M = (M^\alpha, M^{\hat{\alpha}})$ where $\alpha \subseteqq \{1, 2, \cdots, M\}$ and $\hat{\alpha} = \{1, 2, \cdots, M\} \backslash \alpha$. Corresponding to this partition of M is the partition $u = (u_\alpha, u_{\hat{\alpha}})$. We now form a cost indirect output correspondence satisfying strong disposability only for the output subvector u_α by means of

$$IP(p/Q \mid V, S^\alpha) = \{u : u_\alpha \leqq z M^\alpha, u_{\hat{\alpha}} = \mu z M^{\hat{\alpha}}, \tag{6.1.18}$$

$$0 \leqq \mu \leqq 1, z N \leqq x, p x \leqq Q, z \in \Re_+^J, \sum_{j=1}^{J} z_j = 1\},$$

$$(p/Q) \in \Re_+^N, (p/Q) \neq 0.$$

In this formulation the output vector u is weakly disposable since if $u \in IP(p/Q \mid V, S^\alpha)$ then $\theta u \in IP(p/Q \mid V, S^\alpha)$ for $\theta \in [0, 1]$. However the equality $u_{\hat{\alpha}} = \mu z M^{\hat{\alpha}}, 0 \leqq \mu \leqq 1$, implies that the output subvector $u_{\hat{\alpha}}$ is not necessarily strongly disposable. Thus we have another nesting property

$$IP(p/Q \mid V, S^\alpha) \subseteqq IP(p/Q \mid V, S). \tag{6.1.19}$$

We now define a cost indirect output measure of technical efficiency relative to the (V, S^α) technology by means of

(6.1.20)   **Definition**: The function

$$IF_o(p^j/Q^j, u^j \mid V, S^\alpha) = \max\{\theta : \theta u^j \in IP(p^j/Q^j \mid V, S^\alpha)\},$$
$$j = 1, 2, \cdots, J,$$

is called the (V, S^α) *Cost Indirect Output Measure of Technical Efficiency.*

The (V, S^α) cost indirect output measure of technical efficiency measures the efficiency of output vector u^j produced in the presence of budget-deflated input prices p^j/Q^j and with a variable returns to scale technology in which only a subset of outputs is necessarily strongly disposable. From the nesting property (6.1.19),

$$1 \leqq IF_o(p^j/Q^j, u^j \mid V, S^\alpha) \leqq IF_o(p^j/Q^j, u^j \mid V, S), j = 1, 2, \cdots, J.$$
$$(6.1.21)$$

For a piecewise linear technology the (V, S^α) measure is calculated as the solution to the nonlinear programming problem

$$IF_o(p^j/Q^j, u^j \mid V, S^\alpha) = \max_{\theta, z, x, \mu} \theta \qquad (6.1.22)$$

$$\text{s.t.} \quad \theta u_\alpha^j \leqq zM^\alpha$$
$$\theta u_{\hat\alpha}^j = \mu z M^{\hat\alpha}$$
$$zN \leqq x$$
$$p^j x \leqq Q^j$$
$$0 \leqq \mu \leqq 1$$
$$z \in \Re_+^J$$
$$\sum_{j=1}^{J} z_j = 1$$

or

$$\max_{\theta, z, x, \mu} \theta$$

$$\text{s.t.} \quad \theta u_{jm} \leqq \sum_{j=1}^{J} z_j u_{jm}, m = 1, 2, \cdots, M^\alpha,$$

$$\theta u_{jm} = \sum_{j=1}^{J} \mu z_j u_{jm}, m = M^\alpha + 1, \cdots, M,$$

$$\sum_{j=1}^{J} z_j x_{jn} \leqq x_n, n = 1, 2, \cdots, N,$$

$$\sum_{n=1}^{N} p_{jn} x_n \leqq Q^j,$$

$$0 \leqq \mu \leqq 1,$$

$$z_j \geqq 0, j = 1, 2, \cdots, J,$$

$$\sum_{j=1}^{J} z_j = 1.$$

As with previous nonlinear programming problems, in the calculations one may impose $\mu = 1$ to convert (6.1.22) into a linear programming problem.

We now consider the least restrictive cost indirect output sets considered here, those satisfying variable returns to scale and weak disposability of outputs. We form these sets from the data M, N, p and Q by means of

$$IP(p/Q \mid V, W) = \{u : u = \mu z M, 0 \leqq \mu \leqq 1, z N \leqq x, \quad (6.1.23)$$

$$px \leqq Q, z \in \Re_+^J, \sum_{j=1}^{J} z_j = 1\},$$

$$(p/Q) \in \Re_+^N, (p/Q) \neq 0.$$

A radial measure of the efficiency of output vector u^j relative to this (V, W) technology is provided by

(6.1.24)   **Definition:** The function
$$IF_o(p^j/Q^j, u^j \mid V, W) = \max\{\theta : \theta u^j \in IP(p^j/Q^j \mid V, W)\},$$
$$j = 1, 2, \cdots, J,$$
is called the (V, W) *Cost Indirect Output Measure of Technical Efficiency.*

Proofs similar to those of Proposition (6.1.4) establish the following properties of $IF_o(p^j/Q^j, u^j \mid V, W)$.

(6.1.25)   **Proposition:** Given $IP(p^j/Q^j \mid V, W)$, then for each $j = 1, 2, \cdots, J,$

IF$_o$.1 $IF_o(p^j/Q^j, \delta u^j \mid V, W) = \delta^{-1} IF_o(p^j/Q^j, u^j \mid V, W), \delta > 0,$

IF$_o$.2 $1 \leqq IF_o(p^j/Q^j, u^j \mid V, W) < +\infty,$

IF$_o$.3 $u^j \in Isoq\ IP(p^j/Q^j \mid V, W) \Longleftrightarrow IF_o(p^j/Q^j, u^j \mid V, W) = 1,$

IF$_o$.4 $IF_o(p^j/Q^j, u^j \mid V, W)$ is independent of unit of measurement.

Moreover, from the constraints of the two piecewise linear technologies (6.1.18) and (6.1.23) we have the nesting property

$$IP(p/Q \mid V, W) \subseteqq IP(p/Q \mid V, S^\alpha). \quad (6.1.26)$$

The nesting property (6.1.26) implies that

$$1 \leq IF_o(p^j/Q^j, u^j \mid V, W) \leq IF_o(p^j/Q^j, u^j \mid V, S^\alpha), j = 1, 2, \cdots, J.$$
(6.1.27)

The (V, W) cost indirect output measure of technical efficiency may be calculated by solving the nonlinear programming problem (which may be linearized by setting $\mu = 1$)

$$IF_o(p^j/Q^j, u^j \mid V, W) = \max_{\theta, z, x, \mu} \theta \qquad (6.1.28)$$

$$\text{s.t. } \theta u^j = \mu z M$$

$$zN \leq x$$

$$p^j x \leq Q^j$$

$$0 \leq \mu \leq 1$$

$$z \in \Re_+^J$$

$$\sum_{j=1}^{J} z_j = 1$$
(6.1.29)

or

$$\max_{\theta, z, x, \mu} \theta$$

$$\text{s.t. } \theta u_{jm} = \sum_{j=1}^{J} \mu z_j u_{jm}, m = 1, 2, \cdots, M,$$

$$\sum_{j=1}^{J} z_j x_{jn} \leq x_n, n = 1, 2, \cdots, N,$$

$$\sum_{n=1}^{N} p_{jn} x_n \leq Q^j,$$

$$0 \leq \mu \leq 1,$$

$$z_j \geq 0, j = 1, 2, \cdots, J,$$

$$\sum_{j=1}^{J} z_j = 1.$$

We can now summarize the ordering relationships among the five different cost indirect output measures of technical efficiency. Collecting results from (6.1.12), (6.1.17), (6.1.21), and (6.1.27), we have, for $j = 1, 2, \cdots, J,$

$$+\infty > IF_o(p^j/Q^j, u^j \mid C, S) \geqq IF_o(p^j/Q^j, u^j \mid N, S) \quad (6.1.30)$$
$$\geqq IF_o(p^j/Q^j, u^j \mid V, S) \geqq IF_o(p^j/Q^j, u^j \mid V, S^\alpha)$$
$$\geqq IF_o(p^j/Q^j, u^j \mid V, W) \geqq 1.$$

The meaning of the orderings summarized in (6.1.29) is that any given observation will be judged at least as efficient relative to a less restrictive technology as to a more restrictive technology. In other words, the more restrictive the assumptions made concerning production technology, the less likely it is that the technology can allow any observation to appear technically efficient.

The next step is to decompose the cost indirect output measure of technical efficiency calculated relative to the most restrictive technology, $IF_o(p^j/Q^j, u^j \mid C, S)$, into three mutually exclusive and exhaustive sources. The three components are a cost indirect output scale efficiency measure, a cost indirect measure of output congestion, and a cost indirect output measure of purely technical efficiency. We already have the latter measure; it is given by $IF_o(p^j/Q^j, u^j \mid V, W)$. We begin with a cost indirect output measure of scale efficiency.

(6.1.30) **Definition:** The function
$IS_o(p^j/Q^j, u^j) = IF_o(p^j/Q^j, u^j \mid C, S)/IF_o(p^j/Q^j, u^j \mid V, S), j = 1, 2, \cdots, J,$
is called the *Cost Indirect Output Scale Efficiency Measure.*

Observation j is cost indirect output scale efficient if $IF_o(p^j/Q^j, u^j \mid C, S) = IF_o(p^j/Q^j, u^j \mid V, S)$ or if it is equally efficient relative to the (C, S) and (V, S) indirect output sets.

This point is illustrated in Figure 6.4. Observation j is cost indirect output scale efficient since it is equally efficient relative to (C, S) and (V, S) revenue indirect technologies. Input vector x^j is affordable and it can produce a scale-efficient output vector $IF_o(p^j/Q^j, u^j \mid V, S) \mid u^j$. However, neither observation k nor observation ℓ is cost indirect output scale efficient since each is more (technically) efficient relative to the (V, S) cost indirect technology than to the (C, S) cost indirect technology. The properties of $IS_o(p^j/Q^j, u^j)$ are summarized in

(6.1.31) **Proposition:** Given $IS_o(p^j/Q^j, u^j)$, then for each $j = 1, 2, \cdots, J,$

IS$_o$.1 $\quad 1 \leqq IS_o(p^j/Q^j, u^j) < +\infty,$

IS$_o$.2 $\quad IS_o(p^j/Q^j, u^j) = 1 \iff IF_o(p^j/Q^j, u^j \mid V, S) \cdot u^j$
exhibits CRS, or equivalently
$IF_o(p^j/Q^j, u^j \mid V, S) \cdot u^j \in Isoq\ IP(p^j/Q^j \mid C, S),$

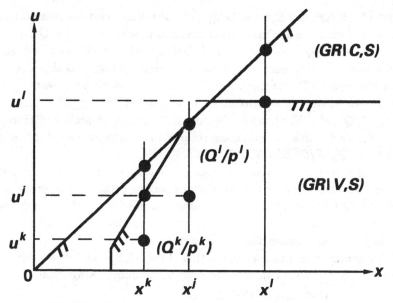

Fig. 6.4. *Measuring Cost Indirect Output Scale Efficiency*

IS$_o$.3 $IS_o(p^j/Q^j, \theta u^j) = IS_o(p^j/Q^j, u^j), \theta > 0$,

IS$_o$.4 $IS_o(p^j/Q^j, u^j)$ is independent of unit of measurement.

Proof: IS$_o$.1 follows from (6.1.29). IS$_o$.3 is a consequence of the homogeneity of degree -1 in both numerator and denominator of the right side of Definition (6.1.30), and IS$_o$.4 is obvious. To prove IS$_o$.2 assume that $IS_o(p^j/Q^j, u^j) = 1$. Then $IF_o(p^j/Q^j, u^j \mid C, S) = IF_o(p^j/Q^j, u^j \mid V, S)$ and $IF_o(p^j/Q^j, u^j \mid V, S) \cdot u^j \in Isoq\ IP(p^j/Q^j \mid C, S)$, i.e., $IF_o(p^j/Q^j, u^j \mid V, S) \cdot u^j$ exhibits CRS. Conversely, if $IF_o(p^j/Q^j, u^j \mid V, S) \cdot x^j \in Isoq\ IP(p^j/Q^j \mid C, S)$, then $IF_o(p^j/Q^j, u^j \mid C, S) \cdot x^j \in Isoq\ IP(p^j/Q^j \mid C, S)$ and $IF_o(p^j/Q^j, u^j \mid V, S) = IF_o(p^j/Q^j, u^j \mid C, S)$, so that $IS_o(p^j/Q^j, u^j) = 1$.

$Q.E.D.$

Suppose now that $IS_o(p^j/Q^j, u^j) > 1$. We want to determine whether the source of cost indirect output scale inefficiency is due to utilization of an inefficiently small input vector in a region of increasing returns to scale (as with x^k in Figure 6.4) or utilization of an inefficiently large input vector in a region of decreasing returns to scale (as with x^ℓ in Figure 6.4). The determination is based on a comparison of $IF_o(p^j/Q^j, u^j \mid C, S)$ with $IF_o(p^j/Q^j, u^j \mid N, S)$. If $IS_o(p^j/Q^j, u^j) > 1$

and $IF_o(p^j/Q^j, u^j \mid C, S) = IF_o(p^j/Q^j, u^j \mid N, S)$, cost indirect output scale inefficiency is due to increasing returns to scale. If $IS_o(p^j/Q^j, u^j) > 1$ and $IF_o(p^j/Q^j, u^j \mid C, S) > IF_o(p^j/Q^j, u^j \mid N, S)$, cost indirect output scale inefficiency is due to decreasing returns to scale. Figure 6.4 illustrates. The cost indirect output scale inefficiency of activity k is due to increasing returns to scale because $IF_o(p^k/Q^k, u^k \mid C, S) = IF_o(p^k/Q^k, u^k \mid N, S)$, while the cost indirect output scale inefficiency of activity ℓ is due to decreasing returns to scale since $IF_o(p^\ell/Q^\ell, u^\ell \mid C, S) > IF_o(p^\ell/Q^\ell, u^\ell \mid N, S)$.

Thus a determination of existence and nature of cost indirect output scale inefficiency can be made simply by solving programming problems (6.1.5), (6.1.11), and (6.1.17). The solutions provide the three measures required to compute cost indirect output scale efficiency and the nature of any scale inefficiency for each observation.

We continue with the decomposition of the (C, S) cost indirect output measure of technical efficiency by considering output congestion.

(6.1.32)   **Definition**: The function
$IC_o(p^j/Q^j, u^j) = IF_o(p^j/Q^j, u^j \mid V, S)/IF_o(p^j/Q^j, u^j \mid V, W), j = 1, 2, \cdots, J,$
is called the *Cost Indirect Output Congestion Measure*.

The cost indirect output congestion measure provides an indication of the greater proportionate increase in affordable output obtainable when outputs are strongly disposable as opposed to weakly disposable. We say that output vector u^j is not congested for cost normalized input prices p^j/Q^j if $IC_o(p^j/Q^j, u^j) = 1$, i.e., if $IF_o(p^j/Q^j, u^j \mid V, S) = IF_o(p^j/Q^j, u^j \mid V, W)$.

The properties of the cost indirect output congestion measure are summarized in

(6.1.33)   **Proposition**: Given $IC_o(p^j/Q^j, u^j)$, then for each $j = 1, 2, \cdots, J$,

$IC_o.1$ $1 \leqq IC_o(p^j/Q^j, u^j) < +\infty,$

$IC_o.2$ $IC_o(p^j/Q^j, u^j) = 1 \iff IF_o(p^j/Q^j, u^j \mid V, W) \cdot u^j \in WEff\ IP(p^j/Q^j \mid V, S),$

$IC_o.3$ $IC_o(p^j/Q^j, \theta u^j) = IC_o(p^j/Q^j, u^j), \theta > 0,$

$IC_o.4$ $IC_o(p^j/Q^j, u^j)$ is independent of unit of measurement.

Proof: $IC_o.1$, $IC_o.3$, and $IC_o.4$ are proved like $IS_o.1$, $IS_o.3$, and $IS_o.4$ in Proposition (6.1.31). To prove $IC_o.2$, recall that $WEff\ IP(p^j/Q^j \mid$

$V, W) \subseteq WEff\ IP(p^j/Q^j \mid V, S)$. If $IC_o(p^j/Q^j, u^j) = 1$, then
$IF_o(p^j/Q^j, u^j \mid V, W) \cdot u^j = IF_o(p^j/Q^j, u^j \mid V, S) \cdot u^j \in Isoq\ IP(p^j/Q^j \mid V, S) \cap Isoq\ IP(p^j/Q^j \mid V, W)$ and it follows from Propositions (2.3.5)
and (2.3.6) that $IF_o(p^j/Q^j, u^j \mid V, W) \cdot u^j \in WEff\ IP(p^j/Q^j \mid V, S)$.
Conversely, if $IF_o(p^j/Q^j, u^j \mid V, W) \cdot u^j \in WEff\ IP(p^j/Q^j \mid V, S)$,
since $WEff\ IP(p^j/Q^j \mid V, W) \subseteq WEff\ IP(p^j/Q^j \mid V, S)$, $IF_o(p^j/Q^j \mid V, W) = IF_o(p^j/Q^j \mid V, S)$ and $IC_o(p^j/Q^j, u^j) = 1$.

Q.E.D.

Suppose that $IC_o(p^j/Q^j, u^j) > 1$. The next step is to determine the
source of the congestion, the subvector of outputs that cannot be disposed of freely. In Figure 6.5 it is clear that u_2 is not congesting relative
to $IP(p^j/Q^j \mid V, W)$, since adding $(0ab)$ to the output set $IP(p^j/Q^j \mid V, W)$ does not change the solution u^{*j}. However, allowing u_1 to be freely
disposable, a new solution u^{**j} is obtained, with the property that $\|u^{**j}\| > \|u^{*j}\|$; thus the first output is congesting relative to $IP(p^j/Q^j \mid V, W)$. More generally, if $IC_o(p^j/Q^j, u^j) > 1$, the subvector of congesting outputs is determined as follows. First, compare $IF_o(p^j/Q^j, u^j \mid V, S)$ and $IF_o(p^j/Q^j, u^j \mid V, S^\alpha)$ for each $\alpha \subseteq \{1, 2, \cdots, M\}$. If $IC_o(p^j/Q^j, u^j) > 1$ and $IF_o(p^j/Q^j, u^j \mid V, S) = IF_o(p^j/Q^j, u^j \mid V, S^\alpha)$ the subvector $u_{\hat{\alpha}}$ is the source of congestion. Of course $u_{\hat{\alpha}}$ may not be unique
and the exercise may produce a set of congesting subvectors, each of
which can account for $IC_o(p^j/Q^j, u^j) > 1$.

Thus the magnitude and source of output congestion can be determined by solving the programming problems (6.1.17), (6.1.22), and
(6.1.28). Note that the latter two problems are nonlinear, but they are
easily made linear, and that (6.1.22) must be solved for every partition
$(\alpha, \hat{\alpha})$ of M.

We conclude this section with a statement of the desired decomposition of the (C, S) cost indirect output measure of technical efficiency.
Using Definitions (6.1.30) and (6.1.32) we have

$$IF_o(p^j/Q^j, u^j \mid C, S) = IF_o(p^j/Q^j, u^j \mid V, W) \cdot IS_o(p^j/Q^j, u^j)$$
$$\cdot IC_o(p^j/Q^j, u^j). \qquad (6.1.34)$$

The output measure of technical efficiency relative to the cost indirect
technology satisfying constant returns to scale and strong disposability of
output is equal to the product of three components: a measure of output
scale efficiency, a measure of output congestion, and an output measure
of technical efficiency relative to the cost indirect variable returns to
scale, weak output disposability technology.

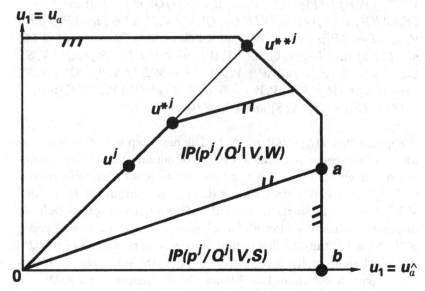

Fig. 6.5. *Cost Indirect Output Congestion*

6.2 Radial Indirect Efficiency Measures Requiring Input Quantity, Input Price, Output Quantity, and Output Price Data: The Decomposition of Indirect Revenue Efficiency

The cost indirect output measures introduced in the previous section are all measures of technical efficiency. This is because they focus on the effectiveness of an output vector that can be produced from affordable inputs, without regarding the prices of outputs being evaluated. The object is to (radially) expand the output vector. In this section, however, we introduce output prices and consider the objective of expanding revenue from outputs. This leads to a (cost indirect) measure of output mix efficiency, which in turn interacts with the technical (C, S) measure previously introduced to generate a (cost indirect) measure of output revenue efficiency.

Suppose that in addition to the input matrix N, the output matrix M, the input prices $p \in \Re_+^N, p \neq 0$, and target cost $Q \in \Re_{++}$, output prices $r \in \Re_+^M, r \neq 0$, are known. Then for each observation j we can compute the maximal revenue that can be obtained under the cost restriction of Q, relative to each of the reference technologies introduced in Section 6.1.

Let us consider revenue maximization relative to the cost indirect output set $IP(p^j/Q^j \mid C, S)$. For observation j we define the maximal revenue obtainable given target cost Q^j, input prices p^j and the output prices r^j as

$$IR(p^j/Q^j, r^j \mid C, S) = \max\{r^j u : u \in IP(p^j/Q^j \mid C, S)\}. \qquad (6.2.1)$$

This revenue can be calculated as the solution to

$$IR(p^j/Q^j, r^j \mid C, S) = \max_{z,x,u} r^j u \qquad (6.2.2)$$

$$\text{s.t. } u \leqq zM$$
$$zN \leqq x$$
$$p^j x \leqq Q^j$$
$$z \in \Re_+^J$$

or

$$\max_{z,x,u} \sum_{m=1}^{M} r_{jm} u_m$$

$$\text{s.t. } \quad u_m \leqq \sum_{j=1}^{J} z_j u_{jm}, m = 1, 2, \cdots, M,$$

$$\sum_{j=1}^{J} z_j x_{jn} \leqq x_n, n = 1, 2, \cdots, N,$$

$$\sum_{n=1}^{N} p_{jn} x_n \leqq Q^j,$$

$$z_j \geqq 0, j = 1, 2, \cdots, J.$$

Both output prices r^j and output quantities u^j are assumed known and so total realized revenue $r^j u^j$ is known. Assuming $r^j u^j > 0$, we may then introduce

(6.2.3) **Definition**: The function
$$IO_o(p^j/Q^j, r^j, u^j \mid C, S) = IR(p^j/Q^j, r^j \mid C, S)/r^j u^j, j = 1, 2, \cdots, J,$$
is called the (C,S) *Cost Indirect Output Revenue Efficiency Measure*.

The (C, S) cost indirect output revenue efficiency measure computes the ratio of maximal revenue to actual revenue. Its properties are summarized in

(6.2.4) **Proposition**: Given $IP(p^j/Q^j \mid C, S)$, then for each $j = 1, 2, \cdots, J,$

$IO_o.1$ $IO_o(p^j/Q^j, r^j, \theta u^j \mid C, S) = \theta^{-1} IO_o(p^j/Q^j, r^j, u^j \mid C, S), \theta > 0,$

$IO_o.2$ $IO_o(p^j/\lambda Q^j, r^j, u^j \mid C, S) = \lambda IO_o(p^j/Q^j, r^j, u^j \mid C, S), \lambda > 0,$

$IO_o.3$ $IO_o(p^j/Q^j, \theta r^j, u^j \mid C, S) = IO_o(p^j/Q^j, r^j, u^j \mid C, S), \theta > 0,$

$IO_o.4$ $1 \leqq IO_o(p^j/Q^j, r^j, u^j \mid C, S) < +\infty,$

$IO_o.5$ u^j solves (6.2.1) $\Longleftrightarrow IO_o(p^j/Q^j, r^j, u^j \mid C, S) = 1,$

$IO_o.6$ $IO_o(p^j/Q^j, r^j, u^j \mid C, S)$ is independent of unit of measurement.

The proof of this proposition is left for the reader.

(6.2.5)   **Definition:** The function
$$IA_o(p^j/Q^j, r^j, u^j \mid C, S) = IO_o(p^j/Q^j, r^j, u^j \mid C, S)/$$
$$IF_o(p^j/Q^j, u^j \mid C, S), j = 1, 2, \cdots, J,$$
is called the *(C,S) Cost Indirect Output Allocative Efficiency Measure.*

The cost indirect output allocative efficiency measure provides an indication of how the chosen output intensity $(u/ \parallel u \parallel)$ deviates from the optimal intensity. The properties of this measure are listed in

(6.2.6)   **Proposition:** Given $IP(p^j/Q^j \mid C, S)$, then for each $j = 1, 2, \cdots, J,$

$IA_o.1$ $IA_o(p^j/Q^j, r^j, \theta u^j \mid C, S) = IA_o(p^j/Q^j, r^j, u^j \mid C, S), \theta > 0,$

$IA_o.2$ $IA_o(p^j/\lambda Q^j, r^j, u^j \mid C, S) = IA_o(p^j/Q^j, r^j, u^j \mid C, S), \lambda > 0,$

$IA_o.3$ $IA_o(p^j/Q^j, \theta r^j, u^j \mid C, S) = IA_o(p^j/Q^j, r^j, u^j \mid C, S), \theta > 0,$

$IA_o.4$ $1 \leqq IA_o(p^j/Q^j, r^j, u^j \mid C, S) < +\infty,$

$IA_o.5$ $\exists \theta \geqq 1$ such that θu^j solves (6.2.1) $\Longleftrightarrow IA_o(p^j/Q^j, r^j, u^j \mid C, S) = 1,$

$IA_o.6$ $IA_o(p^j/Q^j, r^j, u^j \mid C, S)$ is independent of unit of measurement.

Proof: We only prove $IA_o.5$. Thus assume there exists $\theta \geqq 1$, such that θu^j solves (6.2.1). Then $IR(p^j/Q^j, r^j \mid C, S) = r^j \theta u^j$, and by Definition (6.2.5), $IA_o(p^j/Q^j, r^j, u^j \mid C, S) = 1$. Conversely, if $IA_o(p^j/Q^j, r^j, u^j \mid C, S) = 1$, then $IR(p^j/Q^j, r^j \mid C, S) = r^j \cdot IF_o(p^j/Q^j, u^j \mid C, S) \cdot u^j$ and since $IF_o(p^j/Q^j, u^j \mid C, S) \geqq 1$, $IA_o.5$ holds.

$Q.E.D.$

From Definitions (6.1.3) and (6.2.5) we obtain the following decomposition of indirect output revenue efficiency. Figure 6.6 illustrates.

$$IO_o(p^j/Q^j, r^j, u^j \mid C, S) = IA_o(p^j/Q^j, r^j, u^j \mid C, S) \quad (6.2.7)$$
$$\cdot IF_o(p^j/Q^j, u^j \mid C, S).$$

Finally, a grand decomposition is obtained by combining (6.1.34) and (6.2.7)

$$IO_o(p^j/Q^j, r^j, u^j \mid C, S) = IA_o(p^j/Q^j, r^j, u^j \mid C, S) \quad (6.2.8)$$
$$\cdot IS_o(p^j/Q^j, u^j) \cdot IC_o(p^j/Q^j, u^j)$$
$$\cdot IF_o(p^j/Q^j, u^j \mid V, W).$$

Thus cost indirect output revenue efficiency is due to some combination of a selection of an inappropriate output mix, an inappropriately small or large scale of production, the presence of output congestion, and purely technical inefficiency.

6.3   Measures of Expense Effectiveness

Departure from cost indirect maximum revenue $IR(p^j/Q^j, r^j \mid C, S)$ defined in (6.2.1) is either technical or allocative in nature, and the decomposition is given by (6.2.7). The cost indirect efficiency measure $IO_o(p^j/Q^j, r^j, u^j \mid C, S)$ evaluates an activity's performance by comparing cost constrained maximum revenue to observed revenue. Sometimes it may be preferable to compare cost constrained maximum revenue to target cost Q and to rank on the basis of expense effectiveness ratios

$$IR(p^j/Q^j, r^j \mid C, S)/Q^j, j = 1, 2, \cdots, J. \quad (6.3.1)$$

In particular this ratio will show if an activity j can be conducted without losses, i.e., with a ratio greater than or equal to one, since then

$$IR(p^j/Q^j, r^j \mid C, S) - Q^j \geqq 0. \quad (6.3.2)$$

The cost indirect revenue function $IR(p^j/Q^j, r^j \mid C, S)$ is defined relative to a constant returns to scale technology which implies that (the proof is obtained from (6.2.2))

$$IR(p^j/Q^j, r^j \mid C, S) = Q^j \cdot IR(p^j, r^j \mid C, S). \quad (6.3.3)$$

Thus the expression (6.3.2) takes the simple form

$$IR(p^j, r^j \mid C, S) - 1 \geqq 0. \quad (6.3.4)$$

This expression is independent of Q^j, thus we can only compare revenue to target cost equal to one. However, if the cost indirect revenue

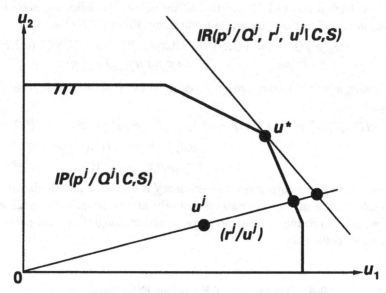

Fig. 6.6. *Decomposition of Indirect Output Revenue Efficiency*

function is computed relative to $IP(p^j/Q^j \mid N, S)$ or $IP(p^j/Q^j \mid V, S)$ technologies, our comparison between cost constrained revenue and target cost becomes more useful. Thus firms or activities may be ranked on the basis of

$$IR(p^j/Q^j, r^j \mid N, S)/Q^j, j = 1, 2, \cdots, J, \qquad (6.3.5)$$

or

$$IR(p^j/Q^j, r^j \mid V, S)/Q^j, j = 1, 2, \cdots, J. \qquad (6.3.6)$$

6.4 A Numerical Example: Indirect Output-Based Efficiency Measurement

In this section we provide numerical examples of some of the indirect output-based efficiency measures introduced in this chapter using the artificial data described in Section 5 of Chapter 2. Specifically, we include calculations of the measures included in decomposition (6.2.8)

$$IO_o(p^j/Q^j, r^j, u^j \mid C, S) = IA_o(p^j/Q^j, r^j, u^j \mid C, S) \cdot IS_o(p^j/Q^j, u^j)$$
$$\cdot IC_o(p^j/Q^j, u^j) \cdot IF_o(p^j/Q^j, u^j \mid V, W).$$

Table 6.1. *Indirect Output-Based Efficiency Measures Using Artificial Data*

Obs	$IO_o(p^j/Q^j, r^j, u^j \mid C, S)$	$IA_o(p^j/Q^j, r^j, u^j \mid C, S)$
1	1.440	1.000
2	1.369	1.009
3	1.421	1.065
4	1.437	1.000
5	1.420	1.012
6	1.000	1.000
7	1.000	1.000
8	1.000	1.000
9	1.000	1.000
10	1.000	1.000
11	1.000	1.000
12	1.000	1.000
13	1.000	1.000
14	1.000	1.000
15	1.000	1.000
16	1.440	1.000
17	1.386	1.017
18	1.421	1.065
19	1.397	1.011
20	1.424	1.021

Obs	$IS_o(p^j/Q^j, u^j)$	$IC_o(p^j/Q^j, u^j)$	$IF_o(p^j/Q^j, u^j \mid V, W)$
1	1.440	1.000	1.000
2	1.357	1.000	1.000
3	1.335	1.000	1.000
4	1.437	1.000	1.000
5	1.404	1.000	1.000
6	1.000	1.000	1.000
7	1.000	1.000	1.000
8	1.000	1.000	1.000
9	1.000	1.000	1.000
10	1.000	1.000	1.000
11	1.000	1.000	1.000
12	1.000	1.000	1.000
13	1.000	1.000	1.000
14	1.000	1.000	1.000
15	1.000	1.000	1.000
16	1.440	1.000	1.000
17	1.363	1.000	1.000
18	1.335	1.000	1.000
19	1.382	1.000	1.000
20	1.395	1.000	1.000

We begin by calculating maximum cost indirect revenue, i.e., $IR(p^j/Q^j, r^j \mid C, S)$, using (6.2.2). The solution to this problem is used to derive $IO_o(p^j/Q^j, r^j, u^j \mid C, S)$, which is the ratio of maximum cost indirect revenue to observed revenues $R^j = r^j u^j$, see (6.2.3). Next we calculate $IF_o(p^j/Q^j, u^j \mid C, S)$, which is used to derive $IA_o(p^j/Q^j, r^j, u^j \mid C, S)$ via (6.2.5). In order to calculate cost indirect output scale efficiency we need both $IF_o(p^j/Q^j, u^j \mid C, S)$ and $IF_o(p^j/Q^j, u^j \mid V, S)$, see (6.1.30). Finally, to calculate cost indirect congestion we need $IF_o(p^j/Q^j, u^j \mid V, W)$ and $IF_o(p^j/Q^j, u^j \mid V, S)$, see (6.1.32).

These measures are calculated for each of our 20 observations of artificial data using the PROC LP procedure in SAS. The results are collected in Table 6.1. We note that in order to avoid infeasible solutions, we used $p^j x^j$ as our proxy for Q^j in the cost constraints (machine rounding resulted in some observations violating the $p^j x^j \leq Q^j$ constraint when target cost from Table 2.2 was used instead of $p^j x^j$).

By construction the artificial data satisfy variable returns to scale. Observations 1-5 exhibit increasing returns to scale, 6-15 exhibit constant returns to scale (and should therefore be cost indirect output scale efficient), and observations 16-20 exhibit decreasing returns to scale. Thus, as expected, deviations from cost indirect output scale efficiency are the major sources of deviations from (C, S) overall cost indirect efficiency.

6.5   References to the Literature

The foundations of cost indirect output-based efficiency measurement are the same as those of revenue indirect input-based efficiency measurement, and so we refer the reader to Shephard (1974), Shephard and Färe (1980), Färe, Grosskopf, and Lovell (1988) and Färe and Grosskopf (1990a).

An application to performance measurement in a sample of St. Louis area public school districts appears in Färe, Grosskopf, and Lovell (1988).

7

The Measurement of Price Efficiency

7.0 Introduction

In this chapter we depart from earlier chapters in that we model technology and measure efficiency relative to what we call price sets. In contrast, Chapters 3 through 6 judged efficiency and modeled technology relative to what might be called quantity sets. These earlier chapters also had in common the assumption that input and output prices are taken as given, i.e., the individual unit is assumed to be a price taker. In this chapter we model the case in which prices are the choice variables and input and output vectors are taken as given.

In evaluating performance relative to price sets rather than quantity sets, we are departing from the usual economic approach, which generally takes quantity data as "primal." In fact, one possible interpretation of the measurement of efficiency in price space is to assume that this is an accounting model, rather than an economic model. Another interpretation is related to what has come to be known as a nonminimal cost function approach. In that approach it is assumed that firms' observed costs and observed or market prices are "distorted" – due to regulation, for example, price controls, imperfect competition, etc. Or firm managers may be utility maximizers rather than cost minimizers. In these cases, firm behavior may be consistent with shadow cost minimization with respect to shadow prices (which may deviate from observed prices). The goal of the nonminimal cost literature is to identify those shadow prices and use their deviation from observed prices as a measure of allocative efficiency. The approach offered here also identifies such shadow prices as well as corresponding efficiency measures; however, the technique provided here yields firm specific shadow prices; the nonminimal cost approach only identifies sample level information.

We note that the efficiency measures derived in price space do not correspond directly to their analogs calculated in quantity space, e.g., if an observation is judged (C, S) technically inefficient in quantity space, it does not follow that that observation is (C, S) technically inefficient in price space. However, if an activity is (C, S) cost efficient in quantity space, it is also (C, S) cost efficient in price space.

In Section 7.1 input price efficiency measures are introduced and we show how overall input price efficiency can be decomposed into technical and allocative components. Specifically, with technical price efficiency target output vector and budget (total cost) are given; the goal is to radially contract observed cost-deflated input prices until the target output is achievable, given cost. We seek cost-deflated input prices which rationalize target output (technical input price efficiency) or minimize cost (overall input price efficiency).

Section 7.2 introduces a parallel decomposition of output price efficiency measures. These take input and output as given and measure efficiency as the maximization of revenue-deflated output prices (technical price efficiency) and as revenue maximization for overall price efficiency. Specifically, a target input vector is given; the goal is to adjust revenue-deflated output prices until target or maximum revenue is achieved. The measures introduced in this chapter are applied to our artificial data set and the results are reported in Section 7.3.

7.1 Input Price Efficiency Measures Requiring Data on Input Prices, Cost, and Output Quantities: The Decomposition of (Dual) Cost Efficiency

In this section we introduce cost-deflated input price measures of efficiency. We begin with input price technical efficiency relative to a (C, S) price technology, and then turn to cost efficiency in price space and its decomposition. Again, the goal is to seek cost-deflated input (shadow) prices which allow attainment of the output target given cost.

In measuring input price efficiency, individual observations are gauged relative to the frontier of the reference set formed from observed cost-deflated input prices and (reciprocal) outputs. More formally, each observation j consists of a positive vector of observed reciprocal outputs denoted $[1/u^j] \in \Re_{++}^M$, where $[1/u^j] = (1/u_{j1}, 1/u_{j2}, \cdots, 1/u_{jM})$;

positive total minimum cost Q^j; and an input price vector $p^j \in \Re^N_+$, $p \neq 0, j = 1, 2, \cdots, J$. Denote the jth cost-deflated input price vector by $\hat{p}^j = p^j/Q^j = (p_{j1}/Q^j, p_{j2}/Q^j, \cdots, p_{jN}/Q^j), j = 1, 2, \cdots, J$ and form the matrix of observed cost-deflated input prices DN, where DN is of order $(J \times N)$, J observations and N input prices. Denote the $J \times M$ matrix of observed reciprocal outputs as M^-. We can now define a dual input price correspondence satisfying homogeneity of degree -1 in outputs and strong disposability of cost-deflated input prices as

$$DL(u \mid C, S) = \{\hat{p} : [1/u] \leqq zM^-, zDN \leqq \hat{p}, z \in \Re^J_+\}, \qquad (7.1.1)$$

where z denotes the vector of intensity variables; see also (2.4.16).

The mapping $DL : \Re^M_{++} \longrightarrow DL(u \mid C, S) \subseteq \Re^N_+$ satisfies several properties including analogs of constant returns to scale and strong disposability as stated in the following

(7.1.2)   **Proposition:** Let DL be the dual input correspondence defined by (7.1.1), then DL satisfies

(i) $DL(\theta u \mid C, S) = (1/\theta)DL(u \mid C, S), \theta > 0,$

(ii) $\hat{p} \geqq \hat{q} \in DL(u \mid C, S) \Longrightarrow \hat{p} \in DL(u \mid C, S),$

Proof: (i) Let $\theta > 0$ and consider

$$\begin{aligned}
DL(\theta u \mid C, S) &= \{\hat{p} : [1/\theta u] \leqq zM^-, zDN \leqq \hat{p}, z \in \Re^J_+\} \\
&= \{\hat{p} : [1/u] \leqq (\theta z)M^-, (\theta z)DN \leqq \theta\hat{p}, \theta z \in \Re^J_+\} \\
&= (1/\theta)\{\hat{p}' : [1/u] \leqq z'M^-, z'DN \leqq \hat{p}', z' \in \Re^J_+\} \\
&= (1/\theta)DL(u \mid C, S),
\end{aligned}$$

where $\hat{p}' = \theta\hat{p}$ and $z' = \theta z$.
(ii) This follows from the nature of the inequality $zDN \leqq \hat{p}$.
$$Q.E.D.$$

The set associated with the (C, S) dual input price correspondence is illustrated in Figure 7.1. Like $L(u \mid C, S)$, the dual input price set can be illustrated using "more" sets, although in contrast to $L(u \mid C, S)$, these are defined in terms of cost-deflated input prices instead of input quantities.   We can now define an efficiency measure relative to this technology, namely

(7.1.3)   **Definition:** The function
$$DF_i(u^j, \hat{p}^j \mid C, S) = \min\{\lambda : \lambda\hat{p}^j \in DL(u^j \mid C, S)\}, j = 1, 2, \cdots, J,$$
is called the (C, S) *Input Price Measure of Technical Efficiency.*

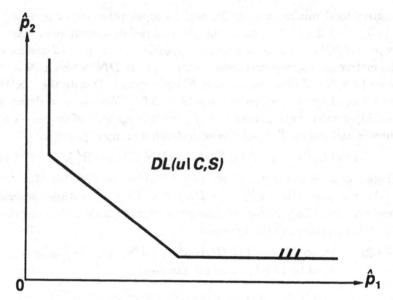

Fig. 7.1. *Dual Input Price Set*

For each observation j, the (C,S) measure $DF_i(u^j, \hat{p}^j \mid C, S)$ computes the ratio of the smallest feasible contraction of $\hat{p}^j$ in $DL(u^j \mid C, S)$ to itself, i.e., $DF_i(u^j, \hat{p}^j \mid C, S) = \| DF_i(u^j, \hat{p}^j \mid C, S) \cdot \hat{p}^j \| / \| \hat{p}^j \|$. $DF_i(u^j, \hat{p}^j \mid C, S)$ is homogeneous of degree -1 in $\hat{p}^j$ as well as in u^j. Its value is bounded by zero and unity, and it attains its upper bound if, and only if, $\hat{p}^j$ belongs to the weak efficient subset of the (C, S) input price set. The measure is also independent of unit of measurement. These properties are proved in the following

(7.1.4)   **Proposition:** Given $DL(u^j \mid C, S)$, for each $j = 1, 2, \cdots, J$,

DF$_i$.1 $DF_i(u^j, \delta\hat{p}^j \mid C, S) = \delta^{-1} DF_i(u^j, \hat{p}^j \mid C, S), \delta > 0,$

DF$_i$.2 $DF_i(\theta u^j, \hat{p}^j \mid C, S) = \theta^{-1} DF_i(u^j, \hat{p}^j \mid C, S), \theta > 0,$

DF$_i$.3 $0 < DF_i(u^j, \hat{p}^j \mid C, S) \leqq 1,$

DF$_i$.4 $\hat{p}^j \in WEffDL(u^j \mid C, S) \Longleftrightarrow DF_i(u^j, \hat{p}^j \mid C, S) = 1,$

DF$_i$.5 $DF_i(u^j, \hat{p}^j \mid C, S)$ is independent of unit of measurement.

Proof:
(DF$_i$.1)

$$DF_i(u^j, \delta\hat{p}^j \mid C, S) = \min\{\lambda : \lambda\delta\hat{p}^j \in DL(u^j \mid C, S)\}$$
$$= \min\{\delta^{-1}\lambda\delta : \lambda\delta\hat{p}^j \in DL(u^j \mid C, S)\}$$

$$= \delta^{-1} DF_i(u^j, \hat{p}^j \mid C, S).$$

(DF$_i$.2)   Since $DL(\theta u^j \mid C, S) = \theta^{-1} DL(u^j \mid C, S)$ by homogeneity of degree -1 in outputs,

$$DF_i(\theta u^j, \hat{p}^j \mid C, S) = \min\{\lambda : \lambda \hat{p}^j \in DL(\theta u^j \mid C, S)\}$$
$$= \min\{\lambda : \lambda \hat{p}^j \in \theta^{-1} DL(u^j \mid C, S)\}$$
$$= \theta^{-1} DF_i(u^j, \hat{p}^j \mid C, S).$$

(DF$_i$.3)   This follows from the fact that each observation j is an element of $DL(u^j \mid C, S)$.

(DF$_i$.4)   Since $DF_i(u^j, \hat{p}^j \mid C, S)$ is a radial measure, $DF_i(u^j, \hat{p}^j \mid C, S) = 1 \Longleftrightarrow \hat{p}^j \in IsoqDL(u^j \mid C, S)$. Since cost-deflated input prices are strongly disposable by (7.1.2), $WEffDL(u^j \mid C, S) = IsoqDL(u^j \mid C, S)$, and DF$_i$.4 holds.

(DF$_i$.5)   Consider the nth input price constraint $\sum_{j=1}^{J} z_j \hat{p}_{jn} \leqq \lambda \hat{p}_{jn}$. If the unit of measurement is changed so that $\hat{p}'_{jn} = \nu \hat{p}_{jn}, j = 1, 2, \cdots, J$, then λ and z_j are unaffected.

$$Q.E.D.$$

Using the piecewise linear (C, S) technology given by (7.1.1), the (C, S) input price measure of technical efficiency can be calculated for activity j as the solution to the linear programming problem

$$DF_i(u^j, \hat{p}^j \mid C, S) = \min_{\lambda, z} \lambda \qquad (7.1.5)$$

$$\text{s.t. } [1/u^j] \leqq zM^-$$
$$zDN \leqq \lambda \hat{p}^j$$
$$z \in \Re_+^J$$

or

$$\min_{\lambda, z} \lambda$$

$$\text{s.t. } 1/u_{jm} \leqq \sum_{j=1}^{J} z_j (1/u_{jm}), m = 1, 2, \cdots, M,$$

$$\sum_{j=1}^{J} z_j \hat{p}_{jn} \leqq \lambda \hat{p}_{jn}, n = 1, 2, \cdots, N,$$

$$z_j \geqq 0, j = 1, 2, \cdots, J.$$

The (C, S) input price measure of technical efficiency is illustrated in Figure 7.2. We assume that $N = 2$, and denote the minimizing value of λ^j as λ^{*j}. Thus $\lambda^{*j} \hat{p}^j = DF_i(u^j, \hat{p}^j \mid C, S) \cdot \hat{p}^j$ is technically efficient relative to the (C, S) technology. At $\hat{p}^j$, prices are "too high" to allow

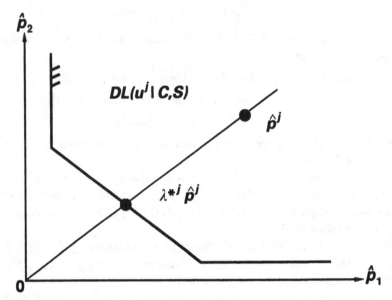

Fig. 7.2. *The* (C, S) *Input Price Measure of Technical Efficiency*

producer j to achieve output vector u^j given the budget Q^j. By reducing cost-deflated input prices to $\lambda^{*j}\hat{p}^j$, producer j can achieve the output target with budget Q^j, i.e., the producer can afford to purchase enough inputs to produce u^j.

If, in addition to input prices, cost, and output quantities, we have data on input quantities for each observation, we can develop measures analogous to overall and allocative efficiency and derive a dual representation of Farrell's original decomposition. Assume then that the input vectors $x^j \in \Re^N_+, x^j \neq 0, j = 1, 2, \cdots, J$, are known. We can define the dual cost function by

$$DQ(u^j, x^j \mid C, S) = \min\{\hat{p}x^j : \hat{p} \in DL(u^j \mid C, S)\} \qquad (7.1.6)$$

where the minimization occurs over elements of $\hat{p}$. The dual (or shadow) cost function can be calculated as the solution to the following problem

$$DQ(u^j, x^j \mid C, S) \;=\; \min_{z,\hat{p}} \; \hat{p}x^j \qquad (7.1.7)$$

$$\text{s.t. } [1/u^j] \leqq zM^-$$

$$zDN \leqq \hat{p}$$

$$z \in \Re^J_+$$

or

$$\min_{z,\hat{p}} \sum_{n=1}^{N} \hat{p}_n x_{jn}$$

$$\text{s.t. } 1/u_{jm} \leqq \sum_{j=1}^{J} z_j(1/u_{jm}), m = 1, 2, \cdots, M,$$

$$\sum_{j=1}^{J} z_j \hat{p}_{jn} \leqq \hat{p}_n, n = 1, 2, \cdots, N,$$

$$z_j \geqq 0, j = 1, 2, \cdots, J.$$

Note that as part of the solution to problem (7.1.7), we derive optimal shadow prices given the observed input mix. As mentioned in the introduction to this chapter, these are equivalent to the shadow prices which "support" the observed input mix. Such shadow prices are sought in the nonminimal cost function approach; however the techniques used to date in that literature allow identification of such (relative) shadow prices only at the sample level. The solution to (7.1.7) provides shadow price information at the firm level. Given the dual cost function and assuming observed $\hat{p}^j x^j > 0$, overall efficiency with respect to input prices can now be defined as

(7.1.8) **Definition:** The measure
$DO_i(u^j, x^j, \hat{p}^j \mid C, S) = DQ(u^j, x^j \mid C, S)/\hat{p}^j x^j$
is called the (C,S) *Overall Input Price Efficiency Measure.*

This measure computes the ratio of minimum to observed cost. Some properties of this measure are summarized (proofs are left to the reader) in the following

(7.1.9) **Proposition:** Given $DL(u^j \mid C, S)$, for each $j = 1, 2, \cdots, J$,

$DO_i.1$ $DO_i(u^j, \delta x^j, \hat{p}^j \mid C, S) = DO_i(u^j, x^j, \hat{p}^j \mid C, S)$, $\delta > 0$,

$DO_i.2$ $DO_i(\theta u^j, x^j, \hat{p}^j \mid C, S) = \theta^{-1} DO_i(u^j, x^j, \hat{p}^j \mid C, S)$, $\theta > 0$,

$DO_i.3$ $DO_i(u^j, x^j, \lambda \hat{p}^j \mid C, S) = \lambda^{-1} DO_i(u^j, x^j, \hat{p}^j \mid C, S), \lambda > 0$,

$DO_i.4$ $0 < DO_i(u^j, x^j, \hat{p}^j \mid C, S) \leqq 1$,

$DO_i.5$ $\hat{p}^j$ solves (7.1.6) $\Longleftrightarrow DO_i(u^j, x^j, \hat{p}^j \mid C, S) = 1$,

$DO_i.6$ $DO_i(u^j, x^j, \hat{p}^j \mid C, S)$ is independent of unit of measurement.

One other interesting "property" arises due to our definition of $\hat{p}^j$. Recall that $\hat{p}^j = p^j/Q^j$. If $Q^j = p^j x^j$, then $\hat{p}^j = p^j/p^j x^j$. Since $DO_i(u^j, x^j, \hat{p}^j \mid C, S) = DQ(u^j, x^j \mid C, S)/\hat{p}^j x^j$, the denominator becomes $p^j x^j/p^j x^j = 1$ and $DO_i(u^j, x^j, \hat{p}^j \mid C, S) = DQ(u^j, x^j \mid C, S)$. The intuition here is quite simple. By (7.1.6), $DQ(u^j, x^j \mid C, S)$ is defined as the minimum value of $\hat{p}x^j$ for which $\hat{p}$ is feasible. Note that $\hat{p}x^j \geqq 1$, with equality holding when observed cost equals minimum cost.

Note that if $DO_i(u^j, x^j, \hat{p}^j \mid C, S) < 1$, then activity j is spending more on inputs than is required to produce output vector u^j given inputs x^j. This excess must be due to either or both of two factors: (i) paying input prices that are proportionally too high and (ii) relative observed input prices are inconsistent with the given input mix. The first source of inefficiency is captured by $DF_i(u^j, \hat{p}^j \mid C, S)$. The second source is obtained residually from $DO_i(u^j, x^j, \hat{p}^j \mid C, S)$ and $DF_i(u^j, \hat{p}^j \mid C, S)$.

(7.1.10)   **Definition:** The measure
$$DA_i(u^j, x^j, \hat{p}^j \mid C, S) = DO_i(u^j, x^j, \hat{p}^j \mid C, S)/DF_i(u^j, \hat{p}^j \mid C, S)$$
is called the (C,S) *Allocative Input Price Efficiency Measure*.

Given the discussion above, this could also be defined in terms of $DQ(u^j, x^j \mid C, S)$, i.e., $DA_i(u^j, x^j, \hat{p}^j \mid C, S) = DQ(u^j, x^j \mid C, S)/DF_i(u^j, \hat{p}^j \mid C, S)$. Some properties which are satisfied by this measure are summarized in the following

(7.1.11)   **Proposition:** Given $DL(u^j \mid C, S)$, for each $j = 1, 2, \cdots, J$,

DA$_i$.1 $DA_i(u^j, \delta x^j, \hat{p}^j \mid C, S) = DA_i(u^j, x^j, \hat{p}^j \mid C, S)$, $\delta > 0$,

DA$_i$.2 $DA_i(\theta u^j, x^j, \hat{p}^j \mid C, S) = DA_i(u^j, x^j, \hat{p}^j \mid C, S)$, $\theta > 0$,

DA$_i$.3 $DA_i(u^j, x^j, \lambda \hat{p}^j \mid C, S) = DA_i(u^j, x^j, \hat{p}^j \mid C, S)$, $\lambda > 0$,

DA$_i$.4 $0 < DA_i(u^j, x^j, \hat{p}^j \mid C, S) \leqq 1$,

DA$_i$.5 $\exists \, \delta \in (0, 1]$ such that $\delta \hat{p}^j$ solves (7.1.6) $\iff DA_i(u^j, x^j, \hat{p}^j \mid C, S) = 1$,

DA$_i$.6 $DA_i(u^j, x^j, \hat{p}^j \mid C, S)$ is independent of unit of measurement.

Proof: The proofs of DA$_i$.1 $-$ DA$_i$.4 and DA$_i$.6 are left to the reader. To prove DA$_i$.5 assume $\exists \, \delta \in (0, 1]$ such that $\delta \hat{p}^j$ solves (7.1.6). Then $DQ(u^j, x^j \mid C, S) = \delta \hat{p}^j x^j$, and from Definition (7.1.10), $DA_i(u^j, x^j, \hat{p}^j \mid C, S) = \left[\frac{\delta \hat{p}^j x^j}{\hat{p}^j x^j}/\delta \right] = 1$. Conversely, assume that $DA_i(u^j, x^j, \hat{p} \mid C, S) =$

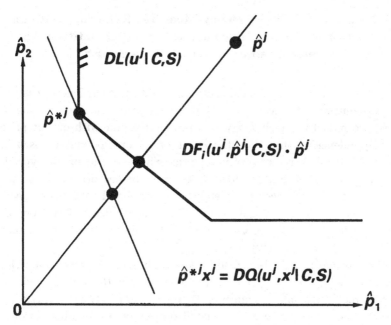

Fig. 7.3. *Dual Farrell Decomposition of Overall Input Price Efficiency*

1, then $DQ(u^j, x^j \mid C, S) = x^j DF_i(u^j, \hat{p}^j \mid C, S)\hat{p}^j$. Since $DF_i(u^j, \hat{p}^j \mid C, S) \in (0, 1], \mathrm{DA_i}.5$ holds.

Q.E.D.

Combining Definitions (7.1.8) and (7.1.10), we can obtain a dual Farrell decomposition of overall input price efficiency, i.e.,

$$DO_i(u^j, x^j, \hat{p}^j \mid C, S) = DA_i(u^j, x^j, \hat{p}^j \mid C, S) \cdot DF_i(u^j, \hat{p}^j \mid C, S).$$
$$(7.1.12)$$

Thus input price inefficiency must be due to selection of the wrong relative input prices ($DA_i(u^j, x^j, \hat{p}^j \mid C, S)$) or to "purely" technical price inefficiency ($DF_i(u^j, \hat{p}^j \mid C, S)$). Consider Figure 7.3. At $\hat{p}^j$, cost-deflated input prices are too high to allow firm j to produce u^j at Q^j, i.e., they must be reduced to $DF_i(u^j, \hat{p}^j \mid C, S) \cdot \hat{p}^j$ in order to make u^j feasible. Given input quantities x^j, minimum dual cost is achieved at $\hat{p}^{*j}$ and is equal to $DQ(u^j, x^j \mid C, S)$.

We note that the decomposition in (7.1.12) can be applied to technologies more general than the (C, S) technology, which we leave to the interested reader.

7.2 Output Price Efficiency Measures Requiring Data on Output Prices, Revenue, and Input Quantities: The Decomposition of (Dual) Revenue Efficiency

In this section we develop analogs to the input price efficiency measures for the output side, i.e., we develop output price efficiency measures. Thus we model the technology of a productive unit with output price correspondences rather than the input price correspondences used in Section 7.1. As in the case of input price efficiency, one of the byproducts of this approach is the identification of shadow prices. These are the output shadow prices which support the observed output mix, given inputs, i.e., they are virtual prices. Since they reflect relative opportunity cost, they could be used to calculate transfer prices or to gauge price distortions or market power.

More formally, each observation j consists of an observed output price vector $r^j \in \Re_+^M, r^j \neq 0$, maximum total revenue $R^j \in \Re_{++}$, and observed reciprocal input quantities $[1/x^j] = (1/x_{j1}, 1/x_{j2}, \cdots, 1/x_{jN})$. Denote the vector of revenue deflated output prices for observation j as $\hat{r}^j = r^j/R^j = (r_{j1}/R^j, r_{j2}/R^j, \cdots, r_{jM}/R^j), j = 1, 2, \cdots, J$. Denote the matrix of observed revenue-deflated output prices as DM where M is of dimension $(J \times M)$ and denote the matrix of observed reciprocal inputs as N^- where N^- is of dimension $(J \times N)$.

The next step is to introduce a piecewise linear output price reference technology. Thus define the dual output price correspondence satisfying homogeneity of degree -1 in input quantities and strong disposability of revenue-deflated output prices as

$$DP(x \mid C, S) = \{\hat{r} : \hat{r} \leq zDM, zN^- \leq [1/x], z \in \Re_+^J\}, \qquad (7.2.1)$$

where z is the vector of intensity variables.

Associated with $DP(x \mid C, S)$ are "less" sets which resemble those associated with $P(x \mid C, S)$; see Figure 7.4. Thus $DP(x^j \mid C, S)$ is the set of all revenue-deflated output prices which are feasible given x^j and target revenue R^j. Note that revenue-deflated output prices substitute for the output quantities which appear on the axes for $P(x^j \mid C, S)$. The mapping $DP : \Re_+^N \longrightarrow DP(x \mid C, S) \subseteq \Re_+^M$ satisfies several properties including analogs of constant returns to scale and strong disposability as stated in the following

(7.2.2)   **Proposition:** Let DP be the dual output correspondence defined in (7.2.1), then DP satisfies

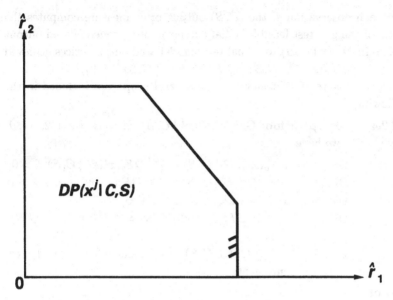

Fig. 7.4. *Dual Output Price Set*

(i) $DP(\lambda x \mid C, S) = \lambda^{-1} DP(x \mid C, S), \lambda > 0,$

(ii) $\hat{r} \leqq \hat{s} \in DP(x \mid C, S) \Longrightarrow \hat{r} \in DP(x \mid C, S).$

Proof: (i) Let $\lambda > 0$ and consider

$$
\begin{aligned}
DP(\lambda x \mid C, S) &= \{\hat{r} : \hat{r} \leqq zDM, zN^- \leqq [1/\lambda x], z \in \Re_+^J\} \\
&= \{\hat{r} : \lambda\hat{r} \leqq (\lambda z)DM, (\lambda z)N^- \leqq [1/x], \lambda z \in \Re_+^J\} \\
&= (1/\lambda)\{\hat{r}' : \hat{r}' \leqq z'DM, z'N^- \leqq [1/x], z' \in \Re_+^J\} \\
&= (1/\lambda)DP(x \mid C, S),
\end{aligned}
$$

where $\hat{r}' = \lambda\hat{r}, z' = \lambda z.$

(ii) This follows from the inequality $\hat{r} \leqq zDM.$

Q.E.D.

We can now define an efficiency measure relative to this technology, namely

(7.2.3)   **Definition:** The measure

$DF_o(x^j, \hat{r}^j \mid C, S) = \max\{\theta : \theta\hat{r}^j \in DP(x^j \mid C, S)\}, j = 1, 2, \cdots, J,$

is called the *(C,S) Output Price Measure of Technical Efficiency*.

For each observation j, the (C, S) output price measure computes the ratio of the greatest feasible radial extension of revenue-deflated output prices in $DP(x \mid C, S)$ to actual revenue-deflated output prices achieved by j, i.e., $DF_o(x^j, \hat{r}^j \mid C, S) = \parallel DF_o(x^j, \hat{r}^j \mid C, S) \cdot \hat{r}^j \parallel / \parallel \hat{r}^j \parallel$.

This measure of efficiency satisfies several properties included in the following

(7.2.4)   **Proposition**: Given $DP(x^j \mid C, S)$, for each $j = 1, 2, \cdots, J$, we have

DF$_o$.1 $DF_o(x^j, \delta \hat{r}^j \mid C, S) = \delta^{-1} DF_o(x^j, \hat{r}^j \mid C, S), \delta > 0$,

DF$_o$.2 $DF_o(\lambda x^j, \hat{r}^j \mid C, S) = \lambda^{-1} DF_o(x^j, \hat{r}^j \mid C, S), \lambda > 0$,

DF$_o$.3 $1 \leqq DF_o(x^j, \hat{r}^j \mid C, S) < +\infty$,

DF$_o$.4 $\hat{r}^j \in WEff \, DP(x^j \mid C, S) \Longleftrightarrow DF_o(x^j, \hat{r}^j \mid C, S) = 1$,

DF$_o$.5 $DF_o(x^j, \hat{r}^j \mid C, S)$ is independent of unit of measurement.

Proof:
(DF$_o$.1)

$$\begin{aligned} DF_o(x^j, \delta \hat{r}^j \mid C, S) &= \max\{\theta : \theta \delta \hat{r}^j \in DP(x^j \mid C, S)\}, \delta > 0, \\ &= \max\{\delta^{-1} \theta \delta : \theta \delta \hat{r}^j \in DP(x^j \mid C, S)\} \\ &= \delta^{-1} DF_o(x^j, \hat{r}^j \mid C, S). \end{aligned}$$

(DF$_o$.2)   By homogeneity of degree -1 in inputs of $DP(x^j \mid C, S)$

$$\begin{aligned} DF_o(\lambda x^j, \hat{r}^j \mid C, S) &= \max\{\theta : \theta \hat{r}^j \in DP(\lambda x^j \mid C, S)\}, \lambda > 0, \\ &= \max\{\theta : \theta \hat{r}^j \in \lambda^{-1} DP(x^j \mid C, S)\}, \\ &= \lambda^{-1} DF_o(x^j, \hat{r}^j \mid C, S). \end{aligned}$$

(DF$_o$.3)   Follows from the fact that for each observation j, $\hat{r}^j \in DP(x^j \mid C, S)$.

(DF$_o$.4)   As a radial efficiency measure, $DF_o(x^j, \hat{r}^j \mid C, S) = 1 \Longleftrightarrow \hat{r}^j \in Isoq \, DP(x^j \mid C, S)$. Since we have strong disposability of revenue-deflated output prices (7.2.2), $WEff \, DP(x^j \mid C, S) = Isoq \, DP(x^j \mid C, S)$; see (2.3.4).

(DF$_o$.5)   Consider the mth output price constraint $\theta \hat{r}_{jm} \leq \sum_{j=1}^{J} z_j \hat{r}_{jm}$. If the unit of measurement is changed, so that $\hat{r}_{jm} = \nu \hat{r}_{jm}, j = 1, 2, \cdots, J$, then the solution values of θ and z_j are not affected.

Q.E.D.

The (C, S) output price measure of technical efficiency can be calculated for any observation j as the solution to the following linear programming problem

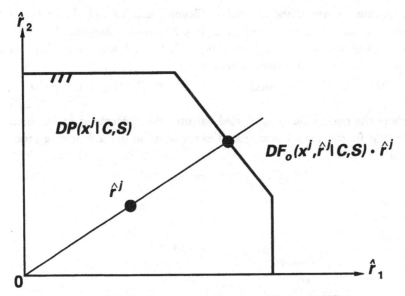

Fig. 7.5. *The* (C, S) *Output Price Measure of Technical Efficiency*

$$DF_o(x^j, \hat{r}^j \mid C, S) = \max_{\theta, z} \theta \qquad (7.2.5)$$

$$\text{s.t. } \theta \hat{r}^j \leqq zDM$$

$$zN^- \leqq [1/x^j]$$

$$z \in \Re_+^J$$

or

$$\max_{\theta, z} \theta$$

$$\text{s.t. } \theta \hat{r}_{jm} \leqq \sum_{j=1}^{J} z_j \hat{r}_{jm}, m = 1, 2, \cdots, M,$$

$$\sum_{j=1}^{J} z_j (1/x_{jn}) \leqq (1/x_{jn}), n = 1, 2, \cdots, N,$$

$$z_j \geqq 0, j = 1, 2, \cdots, J.$$

This measure is illustrated in Figure 7.5 for observation j. Observed revenue-deflated output prices $\hat{r}^j$ are too low to achieve target revenue R^j given x^j. By proportionately increasing $\hat{r}^j$ to $DF_o(x^j, \hat{r}^j \mid C, S) \cdot \hat{r}^j$, that target revenue becomes feasible.

If, in addition to output prices, revenue and input quantities, we have data on output quantities for each observation, we can develop measures analogous to overall and allocative efficiency and derive a dual revenue representation of Farrell's original decomposition. Assume then that the output vectors $u^j \in \Re_+^M$, $u^j \neq 0, j = 1, 2, \cdots, J$, are known. We can then define the dual revenue function by

$$DR(x^j, u^j \mid C, S) = \max\{\hat{r}u^j : \hat{r} \in DP(x^j \mid C, S)\}, j = 1, 2, \cdots, J,$$
$$(7.2.6)$$

where the maximization is carried out over the elements of $\hat{r}$. The dual revenue function can be calculated as the solution to the following problem

$$DR(x^j, u^j \mid C, S) = \max_{z, \hat{r}} \hat{r}u^j \qquad (7.2.7)$$

$$\text{s.t. } \hat{r} \leq zDM$$
$$zN^- \leq [1/x^j]$$
$$z \in \Re_+^J$$

or

$$\max_{z, \hat{r}} \sum_{m=1}^{M} \hat{r}_m u_{jm}$$

$$\text{s.t. } \hat{r}_m \leq \sum_{j=1}^{J} z_j \hat{r}_{jm}, m = 1, 2, \cdots, M,$$

$$\sum_{j=1}^{J} z_j(1/x_{jn}) \leq (1/x_{jn}), n = 1, 2, \cdots, N,$$

$$z_j \geq 0, j = 1, 2, \cdots, J.$$

Note that the solution to problem (7.2.7) yields information not only on maximum (shadow) revenue, but also a vector of optimal shadow prices.

Given the dual revenue function, overall output price efficiency can be defined, assuming $\hat{r}^j u^j > 0$, as

(7.2.8)   **Definition**: The measure
$$DO_o(x^j, u^j, \hat{r}^j \mid C, S) = DR(x^j, u^j \mid C, S)/\hat{r}^j u^j, j = 1, 2,$$
$$\cdots, J,$$
is called the (C, S) *Overall Output Price Efficiency Measure*.

This measure computes the ratio of maximum to observed revenue. Some properties of this measure are summarized in the following

(7.2.9)   **Proposition**: Given $DP(x^j \mid C, S)$, for each $j = 1, 2, \cdots, J$,

$DO_o.1$ $DO_o(\delta x^j, u^j, \hat{r}^j \mid C, S) = \delta^{-1} DO_o(x^j, u^j, \hat{r}^j \mid C, S)$,
$\delta > 0$,

DO$_o$.2 $DO_o(x^j, \theta u^j, \hat{r}^j \mid C, S) = DO_o(x^j, u^j, \hat{r}^j \mid C, S)$, $\theta > 0$,

DO$_o$.3 $DO_o(x^j, u^j, \lambda \hat{r}^j \mid C, S) = \lambda^{-1} DO_o(x^j, u^j, \hat{r}^j \mid C, S)$, $\lambda > 0$,

DO$_o$.4 $1 \leqq DO_o(x^j, u^j, \hat{r}^j \mid C, S) < +\infty$,

DO$_o$.5 $\hat{r}^j$ solves (7.2.6) $\Longleftrightarrow DO_o(x^j, u^j, \hat{r}^j \mid C, S) = 1$,

DO$_o$.6 $DO_o(x^j, u^j, \hat{r}^j \mid C, S)$ is independent of unit of measurement.

The proof of this proposition is left to the reader.

One other interesting "property" arises due to our definition of $\hat{r}^j = r^j/R^j = (r_{j1}/R^j, r_{j2}/R^j, \cdots, r_{jM}/R^j)$. Since $DO_o(x^j, u^j, \hat{r}^j \mid C, S) = DR(x^j, u^j \mid C, S)/\hat{r}^j u^j$, the denominator $\hat{r}^j u^j = 1$, whenever $R^j = r^j u^j$, and consequently, $DO_o(x^j, u^j, \hat{r}^j \mid C, S) = DR(x^j, u^j \mid C, S)$. This proves useful in calculating overall output price efficiency.

Next we introduce a definition of dual allocative efficiency by

(7.2.10)   **Definition**: The measure
$$DA_o(x^j, u^j, \hat{r}^j \mid C, S) = DO_o(x^j, u^j, \hat{r}^j \mid C, S)/DF_o(x^j, \hat{r}^j \mid C, S), j = 1, 2, \cdots, J,$$
is called the (C, S) *Allocative Output Price Efficiency Measure*.

Alternatively, given the discussion above, we could define allocative output price efficiency as $DA_o(x^j, u^j, \hat{r}^j \mid C, S) = DR(x^j, \hat{r}^j \mid C, S)/DF_o(x^j, \hat{r}^j \mid C, S)$. The properties of this measure are summarized in the following

(7.2.11)   **Proposition**: Given $DP(x^j \mid C, S)$, for each $j = 1, 2, \cdots, J$,

DA$_o$.1 $DA_o(\delta x^j, u^j, \hat{r}^j \mid C, S) = DA_o(x^j, u^j, \hat{r}^j \mid C, S)$, $\delta > 0$,

DA$_o$.2 $DA_o(x^j, \theta u^j, \hat{r}^j \mid C, S) = DA_o(x^j, u^j, \hat{r}^j \mid C, S)$, $\theta > 0$,

DA$_o$.3 $DA_o(x^j, u^j, \lambda \hat{r}^j \mid C, S) = DA_o(x^j, u^j, \hat{r}^j \mid C, S)$, $\lambda > 0$,

DA$_o$.4 $1 \leqq DA_o(x^j, u^j, \hat{r}^j \mid C, S) < +\infty$,

DA$_o$.5 $\exists \delta \geqq 1$ such that $\delta \hat{r}^j$ solves (7.2.6) $\Longleftrightarrow DA_o(x^j, u^j, \hat{r}^j \mid C, S) = 1$,

DA$_o$.6 $DA_o(x^j, u^j, \hat{r}^j \mid C, S)$ is independent of unit of measurement.

Proof: The proofs of DA$_o$.1 $-$ DA$_o$.4 and DA$_o$.6 are left to the reader. To prove DA$_o$.5 first assume that $\exists \delta \geqq 1$ that solves (7.2.6). Then $DR(x^j, u^j \mid C, S) = \delta \hat{r}^j u^j$ and from Definitions (7.2.8) and (7.2.10),

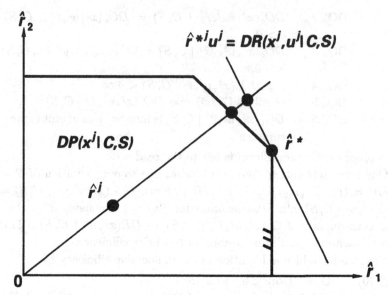

Fig. 7.6. *Dual Farrell Decomposition of Overall Output Price Efficiency*

$DA_o(x^j, u^j, \hat{r}^j \mid C, S) = (\delta \hat{r}u/\hat{r}u)/\delta = \delta/\delta = 1$. Conversely, assume that $DA_o(x^j, u^j, \hat{r}^j \mid C, S) = 1$, then $DR(x^j, u^j \mid C, S) = \hat{r}^j DF_o(x^j, \hat{r}^j \mid C, S)u^j$. Since $DF_o(x^j, \hat{r}^j \mid C, S) \geqq 1$, DA$_o$.5 holds.

Q.E.D.

Combining Definitions (7.2.8) and (7.2.10), we can now obtain a dual Farrell decomposition of overall output price efficiency, i.e.,

$$DO_o(x^j, u^j, \hat{r}^j \mid C, S) = DA_o(x^j, u^j, \hat{r}^j \mid C, S) \cdot DF_o(x^j, \hat{r}^j \mid C, S).$$
(7.2.12)

This decomposition is illustrated in Figure 7.6. Observed revenue-deflated output prices $\hat{r}^j$ are not overall output price efficient, optimal revenue-deflated output prices $\hat{r}^{*j}$ maximize dual revenues. Thus $\hat{r}^j$ is both technically and allocatively inefficient: observed prices $\hat{r}^j$ are too low to be technically efficient, and $\hat{r}_2/\hat{r}_1$ is relatively too high to maximize dual revenue.

7.3 A Numerical Example: Input and Output Price Efficiency Measurement

In this section we provide numerical examples of some of the measures introduced in this chapter using the artificial data described in Section 5 of Chapter 2. Specifically we calculate the input price efficiency measures included in decomposition (7.1.12)

$$DO_i(u^j, x^j, \hat{p}^j \mid C, S) = DA_i(u^j, x^j, \hat{p}^j \mid C, S) \cdot DF_i(u^j, \hat{p}^j \mid C, S)$$

as well as the parallel output price efficiency measures included in decomposition (7.2.12)

$$DO_o(x^j, u^j, \hat{r}^j \mid C, S) = DA_o(x^j, u^j, \hat{r}^j \mid C, S) \cdot DF_o(x^j, \hat{r}^j \mid C, S).$$

Before calculating our input and output price efficiency measures, we must first calculate minimum cost Q^j and maximum revenue R^j which are used to deflate input and output prices, respectively. We calculate Q^j as $Q(u^j, x^j \mid C, S)$ from Chapter 3 and R^j as $R(x^j, u^j \mid C, S)$ from Chapter 4.

Next we calculate dual minimum cost $DQ(u^j, x^j \mid C, S)$ from (7.1.7) and dual maximum revenue $DR(x^j, u^j \mid C, S)$ from (7.2.7) to derive $DO_i(u^j, x^j, \hat{p}^j \mid C, S)$ and as $DO_o(x^j, u^j, \hat{r}^j \mid C, S)$, respectively. These problems are very similar to their direct (quantity space) counterparts, $Q(u^j, x^j \mid C, S)$ and $R(x^j, u^j \mid C, S)$ from Chapters 3 and 4, respectively. In terms of calculation the prices and quantities reverse roles: prices are the decision variables here, whereas quantities were the choice variables in Chapters 3 and 4.

Next we calculate (C, S) input and output price measures of technical efficiency, i.e., $DF_i(u^j, \hat{p}^j \mid C, S)$ and $DF_o(x^j, \hat{r}^j \mid C, S)$ from (7.1.5) and (7.2.5), respectively, which are then used to calculate $DA_i(u^j, x^j, \hat{p}^j \mid C, S)$ and $DA_o(x^j, u^j, \hat{r}^j \mid C, S)$ see (7.1.10) and (7.2.10).

These measures are calculated for each of our 20 observations of artificial data using the PROC LP procedure in SAS. The results are displayed in Tables 7.1 and 7.2.

7.4 References to the Literature

The use of input price space and output price space to model production technology is due to Shephard (1970), as is the use of distance and value functions in price space. The notions of price efficiency and its radial measurement were introduced by Färe (1984b). Input-based overall price efficiency and its decomposition (7.1.2) into technical and allocative components were developed by Färe and Grosskopf (1988), who also developed the requisite linear programming models, and extended by Färe, Grosskopf, and Nelson (1990).

The Measurement of Price Efficiency

Table 7.1. *Dual Input Price Efficiency Measures Using Artificial Data*

Obs	$DO_i(u^j, x^j, \hat{p}^j \mid C, S)$	$DA_i(u^j, x^j, \hat{p}^j \mid C, S)$	$DF_i(u^j, \hat{p}^j \mid C, S)$
1	0.81950	0.98894	0.82867
2	1.00000	1.00000	1.00000
3	0.85286	0.86516	0.98578
4	0.84965	0.85865	0.98951
5[-1.1pt] 5	0.95034	0.97698	0.97273
6	0.81950	0.98894	0.82867
7	0.80510	0.99553	0.80871
8	1.00000	1.00000	1.00000
9	0.83858	0.92004	0.91146
10	1.00000	1.00000	1.00000
11	0.81950	0.98894	0.82867
12	1.00000	1.00000	1.00000
13	0.82107	0.97697	0.84042
14	0.87312	0.88483	0.98677
15	1.00000	1.00000	1.00000
16	0.81950	0.98894	0.82867
17	0.93546	0.99756	0.93775
18	0.85284	0.86518	0.98573
19	0.86598	0.99523	0.87013
20	0.87433	0.95378	0.91670

Dual price efficiency has been applied by Yaisawarng (1989) (electric utilities, where regulation leads one to expect a divergence between observed and shadow input price ratios), and also to electric utilities by Färe, Grosskopf, and Nelson (1990) and Färe, Grosskopf, and Yaisawarng (1989).

There is a large empirical literature on the estimation of non-minimum cost (or non-maximum revenue or profit) functions, that stresses "relative economic efficiency," and in which the source of the suboptimum is generally purely allocative. First-order optimizing conditions are not satisfied, and failure is modeled by replacing "marginal rate of substitution ≠ price ratio" conditions with "marginal rate of substitution = $\theta \cdot$ price ratio" conditions, and estimating the elements of the vector θ. Estimates of the elements of θ indicate direction and magnitude, and sometimes cost, of the allocative inefficiency. Examples of this approach to modeling include Lau and Yotopoulos (1971), Yotopoulos and Lau

Table 7.2. *Dual Output Price Efficiency Measures Using Artificial Data*

Obs	$DO_o(x^j, u^j, \hat{r}^j \mid C, S)$	$DA_o(x^j, u^j, \hat{r}^j \mid C, S)$	$DF_o(x^j, \hat{r}^j \mid C, S)$
1	1.02006	1.00214	1.01788
2	1.00000	1.00000	1.00000
3	1.03516	1.02991	1.00510
4	1.00000	1.00000	1.00000
5	1.00000	1.00000	1.00000
6	1.02006	1.00214	1.01788
7	1.01671	1.01671	1.00000
8	1.00000	1.00000	1.00000
9	1.05245	1.00165	1.05071
10	1.00000	1.00000	1.00000
11	1.02006	1.00214	1.01788
12	1.03843	1.03843	1.00000
13	1.00000	1.00000	1.00000
14	1.00000	1.00000	1.00000
15	1.00768	1.00005	1.00763
16	1.02006	1.00214	1.01788
17	1.02119	1.02119	1.00000
18	1.03518	1.02986	1.00516
19	1.00000	1.00000	1.00000
20	1.00000	1.00000	1.00000

(1973), and Sidhu (1974) (Indian agriculture), Toda (1976) (Soviet manufacturing), Trosper (1978) (U.S. Indian ranching), Yotopoulos and Lau (1979) (a collection of studies of agriculture in six countries), Atkinson and Halvorsen (1980, 1984, 1986) (electric utilities), Eakin and Kniesner (1988) and Eakin (1991) (hospitals), and Eakin (1993) (U.S. physicians engaged in group or solo practice). There is a close relationship between this literature and the approach to the measurement of price efficiency outlined in this chapter, and this relationship is discussed in Färe and Grosskopf (1990c) and Färe, Grosskopf, and Nelson (1990).

8

Graph Efficiency Measurement

8.0 Introduction

Chapters 3 and 4 of this monograph introduce and decompose cost and revenue efficiency, respectively. In this chapter we are interested in profit efficiency, which requires that we simultaneously adjust input and output quantities, given input and output prices. Since we simultaneously wish to increase output quantities and associated revenues and decrease input quantities and their associated costs, we require a different reference technology and perhaps a different means of attaining the frontier of that technology than in Chapters 3 and 4.

In order to judge adjustments of both input and output quantities simultaneously, we model technology with the graph. Specifically, we introduce a series of efficiency measures which judge performance relative to technology as described by the graph. In contrast to most of the efficiency measures introduced in earlier chapters, those introduced here are not radial contractions or expansions of observed data, but rather follow a hyperbolic path to the frontier of technology. More specifically, both inputs and outputs are allowed to vary by the same proportion, but inputs are proportionately decreased while outputs are simultaneously increased at the same proportion.

The fact that we require increases in output quantities and decreases in input quantities to occur at the same proportion or rate, yields a hyperbolic path to the frontier of the graph. One can imagine alternatives: a Russell type measure which allows variation in the rate of increase of individual outputs and in the rate of decrease of individual inputs, or a measure which increases outputs at a proportionate rate which may differ, however, from the proportionate rate of decrease of inputs. These variations are left to the interested reader.

In Section 8.1 graph measures of technical efficiency are introduced. The measures are all hyperbolic, and distinguish among scale, congestion and purely technical graph efficiency.

Price dependent measures of graph efficiency are discussed in Section 8.2, and a decomposition of overall graph efficiency is proposed. This section also includes an exposition of the relationship between overall graph efficiency and profit maximization. In particular, overall graph efficiency cannot be interpreted as the ratio of observed to maximum profit. Rather, maximum profit is equal to graph efficiency adjusted revenue less graph efficiency adjusted cost, and the two adjustments are different.

The fact that graph measures treat output quantities or revenues and input quantities or costs asymmetrically can be exploited and generalized to allow for a variety of cases in which some sort of asymmetry may be useful. For example, the graph measures of efficiency lend themselves to analysis of performance when some outputs are undesirable, i.e., when one may wish to increase some outputs and decrease others. This is discussed in Section 8.3. We conclude with an empirical example using our set of artificial data.

8.1 Hyperbolic Graph Efficiency Measures Requiring Input Quantity and Output Quantity Data

Suppose the matrix of observed inputs N and the matrix of observed outputs M are known. The reference set relative to which hyperbolic graph efficiency will be gauged is the graph, GR. As in previous chapters we develop a series of such reference sets satisfying different scale and disposability properties. Thus define the graph reference set satisfying constant returns to scale and strong disposability of inputs and outputs as

$$(GR \mid C, S) = \{(x, u) : u \leqq zM, zN \leqq x, z \in \Re_+^J\}, u \in \Re_+^M, x \in \Re_+^N,$$

$$(8.1.1)$$

where z denotes the vector of intensity variables.

We note that if $(x^j, u^j) \in (GR \mid C, S)$, then $x^j \in L(u^j \mid C, S)$ and $u^j \in P(x^j \mid C, S)$. Two of the properties of the graph reference set are constant returns to scale and strong disposability of inputs and outputs.

(8.1.2)   **Proposition:** Let GR be the graph defined in (8.1.1). It satisfies

(i) $\lambda(GR \mid C,S) = (GR \mid C,S), \lambda > 0$,

(ii) $(x,u) \in (GR \mid C,S) \implies (y,v) \in (GR \mid C,S)$ for $y \geqq x$ and $u \geqq v$.

Proof: (i)

$$(GR \mid C,S) = \{(x,u) : u \leqq zM, zN \leqq x, z \in \Re_+^J\}$$

$$= \{(\frac{\lambda}{\lambda}x, \frac{\lambda}{\lambda}u) : \frac{u}{\lambda} \leqq \frac{z}{\lambda}M, \frac{z}{\lambda}N \leqq \frac{x}{\lambda}, \frac{z}{\lambda} \in \Re_+^J\}$$

$$= \{\lambda(\frac{x}{\lambda}, \frac{u}{\lambda}) : \frac{u}{\lambda} \leqq \frac{z}{\lambda}M, \frac{z}{\lambda}N \leqq \frac{x}{\lambda}, \frac{z}{\lambda} \in \Re_+^J\}$$

$$= \lambda\{(y,v) : v \leqq z'M, z'N \leqq y, z' \in \Re_+^J\}$$

$$= \lambda(GR \mid C,S), \text{ for } \lambda > 0.$$

(ii) This follows from the inequalities, $u \leqq zM$ and $zN \leqq x$.

$$Q.E.D.$$

Relative to this technology we can now state the following

(8.1.3)   **Definition:** The function

$$F_g(x^j, u^j \mid C,S) = \min\{\lambda : (\lambda x^j, \lambda^{-1}u^j) \in (GR \mid C,S)\}, j = 1, 2, \cdots, J,$$

is called the (C,S) *Graph Measure of Technical Efficiency*.

For observation j, this measure computes the ratio of the maximum equiproportionate input reduction and output expansion in $(GR \mid C,S)$ to itself. This is illustrated in Figure 8.1 for the case $N = M = 1$. Given observed (x^j, u^j), $F_g(x^j, u^j \mid C,S)$ simultaneously expands u^j and contracts x^j at the same rate, following the hyperbolic path shown in the figure. In contrast, the (C,S) measure of input technical efficiency from Chapter 3 contracts x^j, following the horizontal path to the graph. The (C,S) measure of output technical efficiency expands u^j to the graph, holding x^j fixed, i.e., following the vertical path to the graph. The properties of $F_g(x^j, u^j \mid C,S)$ are stated in the following

(8.1.4)   **Proposition:** Given $(GR \mid C,S)$, then for each $j = 1, 2, \cdots, J$,

$F_g.1$ $F_g(\mu x^j, \mu u^j \mid C,S) = F_g(x^j, u^j \mid C,S), \mu > 0$,

$F_g.2$ $0 < F_g(x^j, u^j \mid C,S) \leqq 1$,

$F_g.3$ $(x^j, u^j) \in WEff\ (GR \mid C,S) \iff F_g(x^j, u^j \mid C,S) = 1$,

$F_g.4$ $F_g(\theta x^j, \theta^{-1}u^j \mid C,S) = \theta^{-1}F_g(x^j, u^j \mid C,S), \theta > 0$,

$F_g.5$ $F_g(x^j, u^j \mid C,S)$ is independent of unit of measurement.

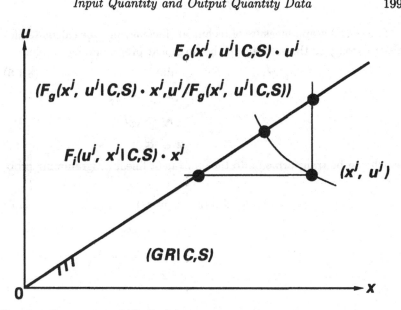

Fig. 8.1. *Comparison of (C,S) Graph, Input and Output Measures of Technical Efficiency*

Proof:

$(F_g.1)$

$$F_g(\mu x^j, \mu u^j \mid C, S) = \min\{\lambda : \lambda^{-1}\mu u^j \leqq zM, zN \leqq \lambda\mu x^j, z \in \Re_+^J\}$$

$$= \min\{\lambda : \lambda^{-1} u^j \leqq \frac{z}{\mu}M, \frac{z}{\mu}N \leqq \lambda x^j, \frac{z}{\mu} \in \Re_+^J\}$$

$$= F_g(x^j, u^j \mid C, S).$$

$(F_g.2)$ This follows from the definition of $F_g(x^j, u^j \mid C, S)$.

$(F_g.3)$ If $F_g(x^j, u^j \mid C, S) = 1$, then $(x^j, u^j) \in Isoq(GR \mid C, S)$ and with strong disposability, $Isoq\,(GR \mid C, S) = WEff\,(GR \mid C, S)$.

$(F_g.4)$ Let $\theta > 0$, and consider

$$F_g(\theta x^j, \theta^{-1}u^j \mid C, S) = \min\{\lambda : (\theta\lambda x^j, \theta^{-1}\lambda^{-1}u^j) \in (GR \mid C, S)\}$$

$$= \min\{\theta\lambda\theta^{-1} : (\theta\lambda x^j, \theta^{-1}\lambda^{-1}u^j)$$

$$\in (GR \mid C, S)\}$$

$$= \theta^{-1}\min\{\delta : (\delta x^j, \delta^{-1}u^j) \in (GR \mid C, S)\}$$

$$= \theta^{-1}F_g(x^j, u^j \mid C, S).$$

$(F_g.5)$ Consider the mth output constraint, $\lambda^{-1}u_{jm} \leqq \sum_{j=1}^J z_j$ u_{jm}. If we alter $\hat{u}^j = \mu u^j, j = 1, 2, \ldots, J$, neither the optimal zs nor the optimal λ will be affected.

$$Q.E.D.$$

The (C, S) graph measure of technical efficiency may be calculated for observation j as the solution to the nonlinear programming problem

$$F_g(x^j, u^j \mid C, S) = \min_{\lambda, z} \lambda \qquad (8.1.5)$$

$$\text{s.t. } \lambda^{-1} u^j \leqq z M$$

$$z N \leqq \lambda x^j$$

$$z \in \Re_+^J,$$

which can be transformed into the equivalent linear programming problem

$$(F_g(x^j, u^j \mid C, S))^2 = \min_{\Gamma, z'} \Gamma \qquad (8.1.6)$$

$$\text{s.t. } u^j \leqq z' M$$

$$z' N \leqq \Gamma x^j$$

$$z' \in \Re_+^J$$

or

$$\min_{\Gamma, z'} \Gamma \qquad (8.1.7)$$

$$\text{s.t. } u_{jm} \leqq \sum_{j=1}^{J} z_j' u_{jm}, m = 1, 2, \cdots, M,$$

$$\sum_{j=1}^{J} z_j' x_{jn} \leqq \Gamma x_{jn}, n = 1, 2, \cdots, N,$$

$$z_j' \geqq 0, j = 1, 2, \cdots, J,$$

where $\Gamma = \lambda^2, z' = \lambda z$, and the solution is derived by solving for $\sqrt{\Gamma}$.

We note that the formulation of the square of the (C, S) graph measure in (8.1.5) is analytically and numerically equivalent to the (C, S) input measure of technical efficiency, $F_i(u^j, x^j \mid C, S)$ given by (3.1.5). From (4.5.1) we also know that $F_i(u^j, x^j \mid C, S) = [F_o(x^j, u^j \mid C, S)]^{-1}$, which suggests an alternative formulation of $[F_g(x^j, u^j \mid C, S)]^2$, which we leave to the reader. Thus, in practice, (C, S) graph measures of technical efficiency may be calculated directly from (C, S) input or output technical efficiency measures.

Next we introduce a graph reference set satisfying nonincreasing returns to scale and strong disposability of inputs and outputs. Introduce

$$(GR \mid N, S) = \{(x, u) : u \leqq z M, z N \leqq x, z \in \Re_+^J, \sum_{j=1}^{J} z_j \leqq 1\}, \quad (8.1.8)$$

where z is the vector of intensity variables. $(GR \mid N, S)$ differs from

$(GR \mid C, S)$ in terms of the restriction on the intensity variables, which yields the following relationship

$$(GR \mid N, S) \subseteqq (GR \mid C, S). \tag{8.1.9}$$

$(GR \mid N, S)$ satisfies the properties stated in the following

(8.1.10)   **Proposition:** Let $(GR \mid N, S)$ be as defined above. It satisfies

(i) $\lambda(GR \mid N, S) \subseteqq (GR \mid N, S), 0 < \lambda \leqq 1,$

(ii) $(x, u) \in (GR \mid N, S) \Longrightarrow (y, v) \in (GR \mid N, S),$ for $y \geqq x$ and $u \geqq v.$

Proof:

$$
\begin{aligned}
\text{(i) } \lambda(GR \mid N, S) &= \lambda\{(x, u) : u \leqq zM, zN \leqq x, z \in \Re_+^J, \\
&\qquad \sum_{j=1}^{J} z_j \leqq 1\} \\
&= \{(\lambda x, \lambda u) : \lambda u \leqq \lambda z M, \lambda z N \leqq \lambda x, \lambda z \in \Re_+^J, \\
&\qquad \sum_{j=1}^{J} \lambda z_j \leqq \lambda\} \\
&= \{(y, v) : v \leqq z'M, z'N \leqq y, z' \in \Re_+^J, \\
&\qquad \sum_{j=1}^{J} z_j' \leqq \lambda\} \\
&\subseteqq \{(y, v) : v \leqq z'M, z'N \leqq y, z' \in \Re_+^J, \\
&\qquad \sum_{j=1}^{J} z_j' \leqq 1\} \\
&= (GR \mid N, S).
\end{aligned}
$$

(ii) As in proposition (8.1.2).

Q.E.D.

(8.1.11)   **Definition:** The function
$$F_g(x^j, u^j \mid N, S) = \min\{\lambda : (\lambda x^j, \lambda^{-1} u^j) \in (GR \mid N, S)\},$$
$j = 1, 2, \cdots, J,$
is called the (N, S) *Graph Measure of Technical Efficiency*.

Given observation j, the (N, S) graph measure computes the ratio of the maximum equiproportionate input reduction and output expansion in $(GR \mid N, S)$ to itself. This measure satisfies properties as stated in the following

(8.1.12)   **Proposition:** Given $(GR \mid N, S)$, then for each $j = 1, 2,$
$\cdots, J,$

$F_g.1$ $F_g(\mu x^j, \mu u^j \mid N, S) \leqq F_g(x^j, u^j \mid N, S), 0 < \mu \leqq 1,$

$F_g.2$ $0 < F_g(x^j, u^j \mid N, S) \leqq 1,$

$F_g.3$ $(x^j, u^j) \in WEff \; (GR \mid N, S) \iff F_g(x^j, u^j \mid N, S) = 1,$

$F_g.4$ $F_g(\theta x^j, \theta^{-1} u^j \mid N, S) = \theta^{-1} F_g(x^j, u^j \mid N, S), \theta > 0,$

$F_g.5$ $F_g(x^j, u^j \mid N, S)$ is independent of unit of measurement.

Proof:
$(F_g.1)$

$$
\begin{aligned}
0 < \mu \leqq 1, F_g(\mu x^j, \mu u^j \mid N, S) &= \min\{\lambda : \lambda^{-1} \mu u^j \leqq zM, \\
&\quad\quad zN \leqq \lambda \mu x^j, z \in \Re_+^J, \sum_{j=1}^{J} z_j \leqq 1\} \\
&= \min\{\lambda : \lambda^{-1} u^j \leqq \frac{z}{\mu} M, \\
&\quad\quad \frac{z}{\mu} N \leqq \lambda x^j, \frac{z}{\mu} \in \Re_+^J, \\
&\quad\quad \sum_{j=1}^{J} \frac{z_j}{\mu} \leqq \frac{1}{\mu}\} \\
&= \min\{\lambda : \lambda^{-1} u^j \leqq z'M, \\
&\quad\quad z'N \leqq \lambda x^j, z' \in \Re_+^J, \sum_{j=1}^{J} z'_j \leqq \delta\}, \\
&\quad\quad \delta \geqq 1 \\
&\leqq \min\{\lambda : \lambda^{-1} u^j \leqq z'M, \\
&\quad\quad z'N \leqq \lambda x^j, z' \in \Re_+^J, \\
&\quad\quad \sum_{j=1}^{J} z'_j \leqq 1\} \\
&= F_g(x^j, u^j \mid N, S).
\end{aligned}
$$

The proofs of $(F_g.2) - (F_g.5)$ are left to the reader.

The (N, S) graph measure of technical efficiency can be calculated as the solution to the nonlinear programming problem

$$F_g(x^j, u^j \mid N, S) = \min_{\lambda, z} \lambda \qquad (8.1.13)$$

$$\text{s.t. } \lambda^{-1} u^j \leqq zM$$

$$zN \leqq \lambda x^j$$

$$z \in \Re_+^J$$

$$\sum_{j=1}^{J} z_j \leqq 1$$

which can be transformed into the linear programming problem

$$(F_g(x^j, u^j \mid N, S))^2 = \min_{\Gamma, z', \lambda} \Gamma \qquad (8.1.14)$$

$$\text{s.t. } u^j \leqq z'M$$

$$z'N \leqq \Gamma x^j$$

$$z' \in \Re_+^J$$

$$\sum_{j=1}^{J} z_j' \leqq \lambda$$

or

$$\min_{\Gamma, z', \lambda} \Gamma$$

$$\text{s.t. } u_{jm} \leqq \sum_{j=1}^{J} z_j' u_{jm}, m = 1, 2, \cdots, M,$$

$$\sum_{j=1}^{J} z_j' x_{jn} \leqq \Gamma x_{jn}, n = 1, 2, \cdots, N,$$

$$z_j' \geqq 0, j = 1, 2, \cdots, J,$$

$$\sum_{j=1}^{J} z_j' \leqq \lambda,$$

where $z' = \lambda z$ and $\Gamma = \lambda^2$.

We note that due to the relationship between $(GR \mid C, S)$ and $(GR \mid N, S)$, for each j we have

$$F_g(x^j, u^j \mid N, S) \geqq F_g(x^j, u^j \mid C, S). \qquad (8.1.15)$$

To continue, by changing the restriction on the intensity variables, we can obtain graph reference sets that allow for varying returns to scale. Reference sets satisfying strong disposability and variable returns to scale are formed from M and N as

$$(GR \mid V, S) = \{(x, u) : u \leqq zM, zN \leqq x, z \in \Re_+^J, \sum_{j=1}^{J} z_j = 1\}. \quad (8.1.16)$$

Since the elements of z are restricted to sum to unity,

$$(GR \mid V, S) \subseteqq (GR \mid N, S). \quad (8.1.17)$$

(8.1.18)   **Definition**: The function

$F_g(x^j, u^j \mid V, S) = \min\{\lambda : (\lambda x^j, \lambda^{-1} u^j) \in (GR \mid V, S)\}, j = 1, 2, \cdots, J,$

is called the (V, S) *Graph Measure of Technical Efficiency*.

From this definition it follows that $F_g(x^j, u^j \mid V, S)$ satisfies properties similar to $F_g.2 - F_g.5$ in Propositions (8.1.4) and (8.1.2), but not necessarily $F_g.1$. Moreover, from the relationship between $(GR \mid N, S)$ and $(GR \mid V, S)$ in (8.1.16) we have

$$F_g(x^j, u^j \mid V, S) \geqq F_g(x^j, u^j \mid N, S), j = 1, 2, \cdots, J. \quad (8.1.19)$$

The (V, S) graph measure of technical efficiency can be calculated as the solution to the nonlinear programming problem

$$F_g(x^j, u^j \mid V, S) = \min_{\lambda, z} \lambda \quad (8.1.20)$$

$$\text{s.t. } \lambda^{-1} u^j \leqq zM$$

$$zN \leqq \lambda x^j$$

$$z \in \Re_+^J$$

$$\sum_{j=1}^{J} z_j = 1,$$

which can be written as

$$(F_g(x^j, u^j \mid V, S))^2 = \min_{\Gamma, z', \lambda} \Gamma \quad (8.1.21)$$

$$\text{s.t. } u^j \leqq z'M$$

$$z'N \leqq \Gamma x^j$$

$$z' \in \Re_+^J$$

$$\sum_{j=1}^{J} z_j' = \lambda$$

or

$$\min_{\Gamma, z', \lambda} \Gamma$$

$$\text{s.t. } u_{jm} \leqq \sum_{j=1}^{J} z_j' u_{jm}, m = 1, 2, \cdots, M,$$

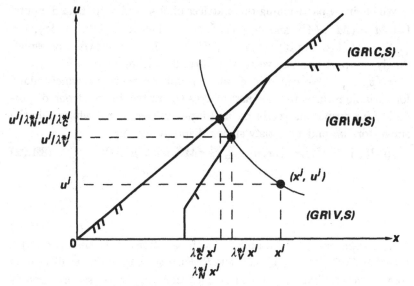

Fig. 8.2. *A Comparison of* $F_g(x^j, u^j \mid C, S), F_g(x^j, u^j \mid N, S)$, *and* $F_g(x^j, u^j \mid V, S)$

$$\sum_{j=1}^{J} z'_j x_{jn} \leqq \Gamma x_{jn}, n = 1, 2, \cdots, N,$$

$$z'_j \geqq 0, j = 1, 2, \cdots, J,$$

$$\sum_{j=1}^{J} z'_j = \lambda,$$

where $\Gamma = \lambda^2$, and $z' = \lambda z$.

In light of (8.1.14) and (8.1.18) it is clear that $F_g(x^j, u^j \mid C, S) \leqq F_g(x^j, u^j \mid N, S) \leqq F_g(x^j, u^j \mid V, S)$, which is illustrated for the case $M = N = 1$ in Figure 8.2. Notice that the "path" to the relevant technology remains hyperbolic. This is a direct result of the restriction that outputs be expanded, and inputs contracted equiproportionately.

We now turn from relaxation of scale properties to relaxation of disposability properties. Since our graph measures of efficiency allow simultaneous adjustment of input and output quantities, we will consider disposability of inputs and outputs jointly. As in previous chapters, we maintain the least restrictive scale property, namely variable returns to scale, and focus on relaxing strong disposability.

We begin by partitioning the matrices of observed outputs and inputs. Let $M = (M^\alpha, M^{\hat{\alpha}})$ and $N = (N^\beta, N^{\hat{\beta}})$, where $\alpha \subseteq \{1, 2, \cdots, M\}, \hat{\alpha} = \{1, 2, \cdots, M\}\backslash\alpha$ and $\beta \subseteq \{1, 2, \cdots, N\}, \hat{\beta} = \{1, 2, \cdots, N\}\backslash\beta$. Correspondingly, we partition the vectors of outputs and inputs as $u = (u_\alpha, u_{\hat{\alpha}})$, $x = (x_\beta, x_{\hat{\beta}})$. We can now define a graph reference set which allows for variable returns to scale and relaxes the restriction of strong disposability for output subvector $u_{\hat{\alpha}}$ and input subvector $x_{\hat{\beta}}$, where only the subvectors u_α and x_β satisfy strong disposability, as

$$(GR \mid V, S^{\alpha,\beta}) = \{(x, u) : u_\alpha \leqq zM^\alpha, u_{\hat{\alpha}} = \mu zM^{\hat{\alpha}} \qquad (8.1.22)$$

$$zN^\beta \leqq x_\beta, zN^{\hat{\beta}} = \sigma x_{\hat{\beta}}, 0 < \sigma \leqq 1, 0 \leqq \mu \leqq 1,$$

$$z \in \Re_+^J, \sum_{j=1}^J z_j = 1\}.$$

Outputs are weakly disposable for both partitions of M since if $(x, u) \in (GR \mid V, S^{\alpha,\beta}), (x, \theta u) \in (GR \mid V, S^{\alpha,\beta}), \theta \in [0, 1]$. The equality $u_{\hat{\alpha}} = \mu zM^{\hat{\alpha}}$ implies that outputs in that partition are not necessarily strongly disposable. Similarly, inputs are weakly disposable for both partitions of N and the equality $zN^{\hat{\beta}} = \sigma x_{\hat{\beta}}$ implies that inputs in that partition are not necessarily strongly disposable.

We can now define

(8.1.23)   **Definition:** The function
$F_g(x^j, u^j \mid V, S^{\alpha,\beta}) = \min\{\lambda : (\lambda x^j, \lambda^{-1} u^j) \in (GR \mid V, S^{\alpha,\beta})\}, j = 1, 2, \cdots, J,$
is called the $(V, S^{\alpha,\beta})$ *Graph Measure of Technical Efficiency.*

We ultimately use this measure to identify subvectors of outputs and inputs which create congestion. It is calculated for observation j as the solution to the nonlinear programming problem

$$F_g(x^j, u^j \mid V, S^{\alpha,\beta}) = \min_{\lambda, z, \sigma, \mu} \lambda \qquad (8.1.24)$$

$$\text{s.t. } \lambda^{-1} u_\alpha^j \leqq zM^\alpha$$

$$\lambda^{-1} u_{\hat{\alpha}}^j = \mu zM^{\hat{\alpha}}$$

$$zN^\beta \leqq \lambda x_\beta^j$$

$$zN^{\hat{\beta}} = \sigma \lambda x_{\hat{\beta}}^j$$

$$z \in \Re_+^J$$

$$\sum_{j=1}^J z_j = 1$$

$$0 < \sigma \leqq 1$$
$$0 \leqq \mu \leqq 1$$

or

$$\min_{\lambda,z,\sigma,\mu} \lambda$$

s.t. $\lambda^{-1} u_{jm} \leqq \displaystyle\sum_{j=1}^{J} z_j u_{jm}, m = 1, 2, \cdots, M^{\alpha},$

$\lambda^{-1} u_{jm} = \displaystyle\sum_{j=1}^{J} \mu z_j u_{jm}, m = M^{\alpha} + 1, M^{\alpha} + 2, \cdots, M,$

$\displaystyle\sum_{j=1}^{J} z_j x_{jn} \leqq \lambda x_{jn}, n = 1, 2, \cdots, N^{\beta},$

$\displaystyle\sum_{j=1}^{J} z_j x_{jn} = \sigma \lambda x_{jn}, n = N^{\beta} + 1, N^{\beta} + 2, \cdots, N,$

$z_j \geqq 0, j = 1, 2, \cdots, J,$

$\displaystyle\sum_{j=1}^{J} z_j = 1,$

$0 < \sigma \leqq 1,$

$0 \leqq \mu \leqq 1.$

We conjecture that this problem may be converted into a linear programming problem using the same transformations as in (8.1.4), (8.1.12), and (8.1.19). We note that $F_g(x^j, u^j \mid V, S^{\alpha,\beta}) \geq F_g(x^j, u^j \mid V, S), j = 1, 2, \cdots, J$, and $0 < F_g(x^j, u^j \mid V, S^{\alpha,\beta}) \leqq 1$.

We now introduce the most general graph reference sets used here. These allow for variable returns to scale and do not impose strong disposability of any input or output subvector. This graph reference set is given as

$$(GR \mid V, W) = \{(x, u) : u = \mu z M, z N = \sigma x, 0 < \sigma \leqq 1,$$
$$0 \leqq \mu \leqq 1, z \in \Re_+^J, \sum_{j=1}^{J} z_j = 1\}, \qquad (8.1.25)$$

where W refers to weak disposability of outputs and inputs. By extending the remarks following (8.1.21) it follows that $(GR \mid V, W)$ satisfies weak disposability of inputs and outputs.

Relative to this technology, we can now define

(8.1.26)   **Definition**: The function
$$F_g(x^j, u^j \mid V, W) = \min\{\lambda : (\lambda x^j, \lambda^{-1} u^j) \in (GR \mid$$
$$V, W)\}, \; j = 1, 2, \cdots, J,$$
is called the (V, W) *Graph Measure of Technical Efficiency.*

This measure satisfies the following properties as described in

(8.1.27)   **Proposition**: Given $(GR \mid V, W)$, then for each $j = 1, 2,$
      $\cdots, J,$

      $F_g.1$ $0 < F_g(x^j, u^j \mid V, W) \leqq 1,$

      $F_g.2$ $(x^j, u^j) \in Isoq(GR \mid V, W) \Longleftrightarrow F_g(x^j, u^j \mid$
                $V, W) = 1,$

      $F_g.3$ $F_g(\theta x^j, \theta^{-1} u^j \mid V, W) = \theta^{-1} F_g(x^j, u^j \mid V, W), \theta >$
                $0,$

      $F_g.4$ $F_g(x^j, u^j \mid V, W)$ is independent of unit of measure-
                ment.

The proofs are similar to those for the analogous properties of $F_g(x^j, u^j \mid C, S)$ and are not repeated here.

Since we know that
$$(GR \mid V, W) \subseteqq (GR \mid V, S^{\alpha, \beta}) \tag{8.1.28}$$

it follows that
$$F_g(x^j, u^j \mid V, W) \geqq F_g(x^j, u^j \mid V, S^{\alpha, \beta}), j = 1, 2, \cdots, J. \tag{8.1.29}$$

The (V, W) graph measure of technical efficiency can be calculated as the solution to the nonlinear programming problem

$$F_g(x^j, u^j \mid V, W) = \min_{\lambda, z, \mu, \sigma} \lambda \tag{8.1.30}$$

$$\text{s.t. } \lambda^{-1} u^j = \mu z M$$
$$z N = \sigma \lambda x^j$$
$$0 \leqq \mu \leqq 1$$
$$0 < \sigma \leqq 1$$
$$z \in \Re_+^J$$
$$\sum_{j=1}^{J} z_j = 1,$$

which can be transformed into the equivalent linear programming problem

$$(F_g(x^j, u^j \mid V, W))^2 = \min_{\Gamma, z', \lambda} \Gamma \tag{8.1.31}$$

$$\text{s.t. } u^j = z' M$$

$$z'N = \Gamma x^j$$
$$z' \in \Re_+^J$$
$$\sum_{j=1}^{J} z_j' = \lambda$$

or

$$\min_{\Gamma, z'} \Gamma$$

$$\text{s.t.} \quad u_{jm} = \sum_{j=1}^{J} z_j' u_{jm}, m = 1, 2, \cdots, M,$$

$$\sum_{j=1}^{J} z_j' x_{jn} = \Gamma x_{jn}, n = 1, 2, \cdots, N,$$

$$z_j' \geqq 0, j = 1, 2, \cdots, J,$$

$$\sum_{j=1}^{J} z_j' = \lambda,$$

where $\Gamma = \lambda^2, z' = z\lambda$ and $\mu = \sigma = 1$.

We can now summarize the relationship among the graph efficiency measures introduced so far. For each j we have

$$
\begin{aligned}
0 < F_g(x^j, u^j \mid C, S) &\leqq F_g(x^j, u^j \mid N, S) \\
&\leqq F_g(x^j, u^j \mid V, S) \leqq F_g(x^j, u^j \mid V, S^{\alpha,\beta}) \\
&\leqq F_g(x^j, u^j \mid V, W) \leqq 1.
\end{aligned}
\tag{8.1.32}
$$

See (8.1.14), (8.1.18), the discussion below (8.1.23), and (8.1.28). Thus we now can order the graph efficiency measures introduced up to this point, due to the nested nature of the associated technologies. These technologies differ in two ways: with respect to their scale properties and with respect to their disposability of inputs and outputs. We next turn to the construction of measures of efficiency constructed as ratios of the measures in (8.1.31) which serve to isolate graph scale efficiency, graph congestion and purely technical graph efficiency.

The next objective is to decompose the (C, S) graph measure of technical efficiency $F_g(x^j, u^j \mid C, S)$ into component measures of scale efficiency, congestion, and a graph measure of "purely" technical efficiency introduced above. The component scale and congestion measures can be derived from measures already introduced. Beginning with scale efficiency,

(8.1.33)   **Definition**: The *Graph Scale Efficiency Measure* is given
by the function
$$S_g(x^j, u^j) = F_g(x^j, u^j \mid C, S)/F_g(x^j, u^j \mid V, S), j = 1, 2, \cdots,$$
$$J.$$

We say that (x^j, u^j) is graph scale efficient if $S_g(x^j, u^j) = 1$, i.e., if
$F_g(x^j, u^j \mid C, S) = F_g(x^j, u^j \mid V, S)$. The properties of the graph scale
efficiency measure are summarized in the following

(8.1.34)   **Proposition**: Let $S_g(x^j, u^j)$ be the graph scale efficiency
measure for observation j, then

$S_g.1$ $0 < S_g(x^j, u^j) \leqq 1,$

$S_g.2$ $S_g(x^j, u^j) = 1 \iff$ constant returns to scale are
satisfied at $(F_g(x^j, u^j \mid V, S)x^j, u^j/F_g(x^j, u^j \mid V, S)),$

$S_g.3$ $S_g(\lambda x^j, \lambda^{-1} u^j) = S_g(x^j, u^j), \lambda > 0,$

$S_g.4$ $S_g(x^j, u^j)$ is independent of unit of measurement.

Proof:

($S_g.1$)   This follows from (8.1.31) and (8.1.32).

($S_g.2$)   Assume first that $S_g(x^j, u^j) = 1$, then $F_g(x^j, u^j \mid C, S) = F_g(x^j, u^j \mid V, S)$ and $(F_g(x^j, u^j \mid V, S)x^j, u^j/F_g(x^j, u^j \mid V, S)) \in Isoq(GR \mid C, S)$. That is, at that point, constant returns to scale prevail. Conversely, if constant returns prevail, $(F_g(x^j, u^j \mid V, S)x^j, u^j/F_g(x^j, u^j \mid V, S)) \in Isoq(GR \mid C, S)$. Thus $F_g(x^j, u^j \mid V, S) = F_g(x^j, u^j \mid C, S)$ and $S_g(x^j, u^j) = 1$.

($S_g.3$)   This follows from the identical homogeneity properties of $F_g(x^j, u^j \mid C, S)$ and $F_g(x^j, u^j \mid V, S)$.

($S_g.4$)   This follows from the independence of $F_g(x^j, u^j \mid C, S)$ and $F_g(x^j, u^j \mid V, S)$ from unit of measurement.

$Q.E.D.$

The graph scale efficiency measure is illustrated in Figure 8.3 for the $M = N = 1$ case. Observation j is equally graph efficient relative to $(GR \mid V, S)$ and $(GR \mid C, S)$ evaluated along the hyperbolic path to the boundary, therefore j is graph scale efficient. Note, however, that observation j is not equally efficient relative to the (C, S) and (V, S) technologies if a vertical path (as with $S_o(x^j, u^j)$) or horizontal path (as with $S_i(u^j, x^j)$) is taken to the boundary. For observations interior to $(GR \mid C, S)$ input, output and graph scale efficiency may differ, because those interior points are compared to different boundary points.

If $S_g(x^j, u^j) \neq 1$, then one would like to know whether the source of graph scale inefficiency is due to increasing or decreasing returns to

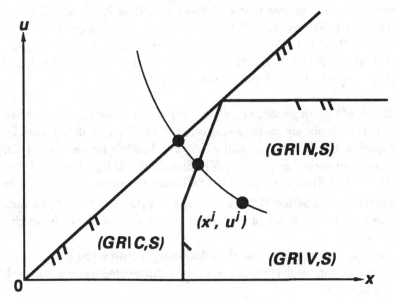

Fig. 8.3. *Graph Scale Efficiency*

scale. Our method is to compare $F_g(x^j, u^j \mid C, S)$ and $F_g(x^j, u^j \mid N, S)$ whenever $S_g(x^j, u^j) \neq 1$. If $F_g(x^j, u^j \mid C, S) = F_g(x^j, u^j \mid N, S)$ then scale inefficiency is due to increasing returns to scale. If they are not equal, then scale inefficiency is due to decreasing returns to scale.

Next we turn to the specification of the graph congestion measure.

(8.1.35)   **Definition:** For observation j, the *Graph Congestion Measure* is given by the function
$$C_g(x^j, u^j) = F_g(x^j, u^j \mid V, S)/F_g(x^j, u^j \mid V, W).$$

We say that (x^j, u^j) is congestion free if $C_g(x^j, u^j) = 1$, i.e., if $F_g(x^j, u^j \mid V, S) = F_g(x^j, u^j \mid V, W)$. Some of the properties satisfied by $C_g(x^j, u^j)$ are summarized in the following

(8.1.36)   **Proposition:** Let $C_g(x^j, u^j)$ be the graph congestion measure for observation j, then

$C_g.1$ $0 < C_g(x^j, u^j) \leqq 1,$

$C_g.2$ $C_g(x^j, u^j) = 1 \Longleftrightarrow (F_g(x^j, u^j \mid V, W)x^j, u^j/$
              $F_g(x^j, u^j \mid V, W)) \in WEff(GR \mid V, W),$

$C_g.3$ $C_g(\lambda x^j, \lambda^{-1} u^j) = C_g(x^j, u^j), \lambda > 0,$

$C_g.4$ $C_g(x^j, u^j)$ is independent of unit of measurement.

Proof: Properties $C_g.1, C_g.3$, and $C_g.4$ are proved with arguments similar to those used to prove $S_g.1, S_g.3$, and $S_g.4$, respectively. To prove $C_g.2$, first assume that $C_g(x^j, u^j) = 1$, then $F_g(x^j, u^j \mid V, W) = F_g(x^j, u^j \mid V, S)$ and thus $(F_g(x^j, u^j \mid V, W)x^j, u^j / F_g(x^j, u^j \mid V, W)) \in WEff(GR \mid V, W)$. Conversely, assume that $(F_g(x^j, u^j \mid V, W)x^j, u^j / F_g(x^j, u^j \mid V, W)) \in WEff(GR \mid V, W)$. From Chapter 2, $F_g(x^j, u^j \mid V, W) = F_g(x^j, u^j \mid V, S)$ and therefore $C_g(x^j, u^j) = 1$.

$$Q.E.D.$$

If (x^j, u^j) is congested, i.e., $C_g(x^j, u^j) < 1$, one would like to know which subvectors are causing congestion. This can be determined by comparing $F_g(x^j, u^j \mid V, S)$ and $F_g(x^j, u^j \mid V, S^{\alpha,\beta})$ for each $\alpha \subseteq \{1, 2, \cdots, M\}$ and each $\beta \subseteq \{1, 2, \cdots, N\}$. Specifically, if $C_g(x^j, u^j) < 1$ and $F_g(x^j, u^j \mid V, S) = F_g(x^j, u^j \mid V, S^{\alpha,\beta})$ then the subvectors x^j_β, u^j_α are congesting. Comparing $F_g(x^j, u^j \mid V, S)$ and $F_g(x^j, u^j \mid V, S^{\alpha,\beta})$ for each subvector yields the set of subvectors which are not freely (strongly) disposable.

Finally, we can summarize the relationship between the (C, S) graph measure of technical efficiency and its components, namely, for each $j = 1, 2, \cdots, J$,

$$F_g(x^j, u^j \mid C, S) = S_g(x^j, u^j) \cdot C_g(x^j, u^j) \cdot F_g(x^j, u^j \mid V, W). \quad (8.1.37)$$

Thus the (C, S) graph measure of technical efficiency can be decomposed into three mutually exclusive and exhaustive components: deviations from optimal scale, deviations from joint strong disposability of inputs and outputs, and deviations from (V, W) graph technical efficiency. If an observation is (C, S) graph technically efficient then it is also graph scale efficient, congestion free, and (V, W) graph technically efficient. The converse is also true.

8.2 Hyperbolic Graph Efficiency Measures Requiring Input Price, Input Quantity, Output Price, and Output Quantity Data

Suppose that, in addition to the input and output matrices N and M, output prices $r^j \in \Re_+^M$ and input prices $p^j \in \Re_+^N$ are given for each observation, $j = 1, 2, \cdots, J$. With this additional information, we can calculate the maximum profit that can be obtained given (x^j, u^j) relative to each of the reference technologies introduced in Section 8.1.

Consider profit maximization relative to the graph reference technology $(GR \mid C, S)$. For observation j we can define maximum profit as follows

$$\pi(r^j, p^j \mid C, S) = \max\{r^j u - p^j x : (x, u) \in (GR \mid C, S)\}. \qquad (8.2.1)$$

This profit may be calculated as the solution to

$$\pi(r^j, p^j \mid C, S) = \max_{z,u,x} r^j u - p^j x \qquad (8.2.2)$$

$$\text{s.t. } u \leq zM$$

$$zN \leq x$$

$$z \in \Re_+^J$$

or

$$\max_{z,u,x} \sum_{m=1}^{M} r_{jm} u_m - \sum_{n=1}^{N} p_{jn} x_n$$

$$\text{s.t. } u_m \leq \sum_{j=1}^{J} z_j u_{jm}, m = 1, 2, \cdots, M,$$

$$\sum_{j=1}^{J} z_j x_{jn} \leq x_n, n = 1, 2, \cdots, N,$$

$$z_j \geq 0, j = 1, 2, \cdots, J.$$

There are three possibilities: the optimizing input–output price hyperplane may intersect the graph at the origin, it may coincide with (part of) the boundary of the graph, or there may be no finite solution. We note that under constant returns to scale, the maximizing values x^{*j}, u^{*j} are not unique. However, the maximum feasible profit, π^{*j} in (8.2.2) is equal to zero.

We would like to derive a graph measure analog of the Farrell overall efficiency measures defined in previous chapters. For example the (radial) input measure of overall efficiency was defined as the ratio of minimum to actual cost and the (radial) output measure of overall efficiency was similarly defined as the ratio of maximum to actual revenue. Unfortunately, due to the hyperbolic rather than radial nature of the graph measures, the natural definition of overall efficiency is not the ratio of maximum to actual profit (and the graph measures of technical efficiency do not have a profit interpretation). In order to define overall graph efficiency we must first introduce the following set

$$H_g^+(x, u, p, r) = \{(y, v) : rv - py \geq ru - px\}, \qquad (8.2.3)$$

which is an upper halfspace satisfying

$$H_g^+(x, u, \lambda p, \lambda r) = H_g^+(x, u, p, r), \lambda > 0. \qquad (8.2.4)$$

We can now introduce the following

(8.2.5)   **Definition:** The function
$$O_g(x^j, u^j, p^j, r^j) = \min\{\lambda : H_g^+(\lambda x^j, \lambda^{-1} u^j, p^j, r^j) \cap GR$$
$$\neq \emptyset\}, j = 1, 2, \cdots, J,$$
is called the *Graph Measure of Overall Efficiency*.

We note that Definition (8.2.5) is relative to a general graph technology, denoted GR, that can satisfy any combination of scale and disposability properties. This measure is related to maximum profit as stated in the following

(8.2.6)   **Proposition:** $\pi(r^j, p^j) = r^j u^j / O_g(x^j, u^j, p^j, r^j)$
$$- O_g(x^j, u^j, p^j, r^j) p^j x^j, \ j = 1, 2, \cdots, J.$$

Proof: (We drop the superscript j throughout this proof.) Let $(y, v) \in H_g^+(O_g(x, u, p, r) \cdot x, [O_g(x, u, p, r)]^{-1} u) \cap GR)$, then $(y, v) \in GR$ and since $O_g(x, u, p, r)$ is a minimum, $rv - py = ([O_g(x, u, p, r)]^{-1} \cdot ru - O_g(x, u, p, r) \cdot px)$. There are three cases to consider: (1) assume $rv - py > \pi(r, p)$, then $(y, v) \notin GR$, (2) assume $rv - py < \pi(r, p)$, then $\{(z, w) : rw - pz \geq \pi(r, p)\} \subseteq \{(z, w) : rw - pz \geq rv - py\}$, and since the hyperplanes defining the two sets are parallel, $O_g(x, u, p, r)$ cannot be a minimum, that leaves (3) $rv - py = \pi(r, p)$. Thus $(O_g(x, u, p, r))^{-1} ru - O_g(x, u, p, r) px = \pi(r, p)$. Rearranging, we have $(O_g(x, u, p, r))^2 px + O_g(x, u, p, r) \pi(r, p) = ru$.

$$Q.E.D.$$

For the case in which the graph satisfies constant returns to scale (substitute $(GR \mid C, S)$ for GR in Definition (8.2.5)), we have the following simpler relationship

$$(O_g(x^j, u^j, p^j, r^j \mid C, S))^2 = r^j u^j / p^j x^j, j = 1, 2, \cdots, J, \qquad (8.2.7)$$

which follows from (8.2.6) since $\pi(r^j, p^j) = 0$ when the firm is operating at a point of constant returns to scale.

Figure 8.4 illustrates for the $M = N = 1$ case. Suppose we observe (x^j, u^j) with associated input–output price hyperplane HH. Relative to $(GR \mid C, S)$, given prices, maximum feasible profit is zero, with optimal input–output vector $(x^{*j}, u^{*j}) = (0, 0)$.

Before stating the properties satisfied by $O_g(x^j, u^j, p^j, r^j \mid C, S)$, we first need two definitions. The set of profit maximizing input and output vectors, defined relative to $(GR \mid C, S)$, is

(8.2.8)   **Definition:** $\pi M(p^j, r^j \mid C, S) = \{(x^j, u^j) \in (GR \mid C, S) : r^j u^j - p^j x^j = \pi(p^j, r^j)\}$.

(8.2.9)   **Definition:** An input–output vector $(x^j, u^j) \in (GR \mid C, S)$ is *Overall Graph Efficient* for (p^j, r^j), if $(x^j, u^j) \in \pi M(p^j, r^j \mid C, S)$.

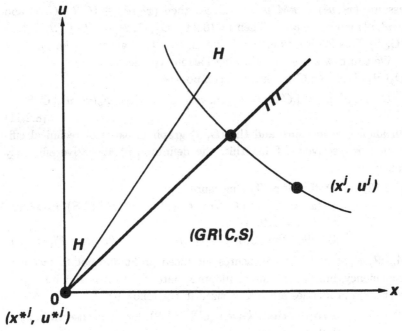

Fig. 8.4. *The (C, S) Graph Measure of Overall Efficiency*

We can now state the properties satisfied by $O_g(x^j, u^j, p^j, r^j \mid C, S)$ in the following

(8.2.10)   **Proposition:** Given $(GR \mid C, S)$, for each $j = 1, 2, \cdots, J$,

$O_g.1$ $O_g(\lambda x^j, \lambda^{-1} u^j, p^j, r^j \mid C, S) = \lambda^{-1} O_g(x^j, u^j, p^j, r^j \mid C, S), \lambda > 0,$

$O_g.2$ $O_g(x^j, u^j, \lambda p^j, \lambda r^j \mid C, S) = O_g(x^j, u^j, p^j, r^j \mid C, S), \lambda > 0,$

$O_g.3$ $0 < O_g(x^j, u^j, p^j, r^j \mid C, S) \leqq 1,$

$O_g.4$ for $(x^j, u^j) \in (GR \mid C, S), O_g(x^j, u^j, p^j, r^j \mid C, S) = 1 \iff (x^j, u^j)$ is overall graph efficient for (p^j, r^j),

$O_g.5$ $O_g(x^j, u^j, p^j, r^j \mid C, S)$ is independent of unit of measurement.

Proof:

$(O_g.1)$ This proof is similar to that for $F_g.4$ for $F_g(x^j, u^j \mid C, S)$.

$(O_g.2)$ This follows from property (8.2.4).

$(O_g.3)$ This follows from the definition of $O_g(x^j, u^j, p^j, r^j \mid C, S)$.

$(O_g.4)$ First assume that $O_g(x^j, u^j, p^j, r^j \mid C, S) = 1$, then by (8.2.6) $\pi(p^j, r^j) = r^j u^j - p^j x^j$, thus $(x^j, u^j) \in \pi M(p^j, r^j \mid C, S)$. Conversely, assume $(x^j, u^j) \in \pi M(p^j, r^j \mid C, S)$, then $(x^j, u^j) \in (GR \mid C, S)$ and $\pi(p^j, r^j) = r^j u^j - p^j x^j$. Then by (8.2.6), $O_g(x^j, u^j, p^j, r^j \mid C, S) = 1$.

(O_g.5) This follows from the definition of overall graph efficiency.

We can now state the following Farrell type decomposition of $O_g(x^j, u^j, p^j, r^j \mid C, S)$ into two components

$$O_g(x^j, u^j, p^j, r^j \mid C, S) = A_g(x^j, u^j, p^j, r^j \mid C, S) \cdot F_g(x^j, u^j \mid C, S),$$
(8.2.11)

an allocative measure and the (C, S) graph measure of technical efficiency, respectively. From this, the definition of allocative efficiency follows

(8.2.12)   **Definition:** The measure
$$A_g(x^j, u^j, p^j, r^j \mid C, S) = O_g(x^j, u^j, p^j, r^j \mid C, S)/F_g(x^j, u^j \mid C, S), j = 1, 2, \cdots, J,$$
is called the (C, S) *Graph Measure of Allocative Efficiency*.

$A_g(x^j, u^j, p^j, r^j \mid C, S)$ measures sacrificed profit due not to technical inefficiency, but rather due to inappropriate input or output mix given p^j, r^j. Its properties are summarized in the following

(8.2.13)   **Proposition:** Given $(GR \mid C, S)$, for each observation $j = 1, 2, \cdots, J$,

$A_g.1$ $A_g(\lambda x^j, \lambda^{-1} u^j, p^j, r^j \mid C, S) = A_g(x^j, u^j, p^j, r^j \mid C, S), \lambda > 0,$

$A_g.2$ $A_g(x^j, u^j, \lambda p^j, \lambda r^j \mid C, S) = A_g(x^j, u^j, p^j, r^j \mid C, S), \lambda > 0,$

$A_g.3$ $0 < A_g(x^j, u^j, p^j, r^j \mid C, S) \leqq 1,$

$A_g.4$ there exists a $\lambda \in (0, 1]$ such that $(\lambda x^j, \lambda^{-1} u^j) \in \pi M(p^j, r^j \mid C, S) \Longleftrightarrow A_g(x^j, u^j, p^j, r^j \mid C, S) = 1,$

$A_g.5$ $A_g(x^j, u^j, p^j, r^j \mid C, S)$ is independent of unit of measurement.

Proof:

($A_g.1$)   This follows from properties $O_g.1$, $F_g.4$ and Definition (8.2.12).

($A_g.2$)   This follows from property $O_g.2$.

($A_g.3$)   This follows from $F_g.3$ and the fact that if $(x^j, u^j) \in WEff(GR \mid C, S)$, then for (p^j, r^j), $O_g(x^j, u^j, p^j, r^j \mid C, S) \leqq 1$. Note also property $O_g.4$, i.e., if $O_g(x^j, u^j, p^j, r^j \mid C, S) = 1$, then $F_g(x^j, u^j \mid C, S)$ cannot be less than unity.

($A_g.4$)   Let $A_g(x^j, u^j, p^j, r^j \mid C, S) = 1$, then $O_g(x^j, u^j, p^j, r^j \mid C, S) = F_g(x^j, u^j \mid C, S) = 1$ and from (8.2.9), $(x^j, u^j) \in \pi M(p^j, r^j \mid C, S)$, i.e., $\lambda = 1$. Conversely, let $(\lambda x^j, \lambda^{-1} u^j) \in \pi M(p^j, r^j \mid C, S)$, then

both $(F_g(x^j, u^j \mid C, S) \cdot x^j, (F_g(x^j, u^j \mid C, S))^{-1} \cdot u^j)$ and $(O_g(x^j, u^j, p^j,$
$r^j \mid C, S) \cdot x^j, (O_g(x^j, u^j, p^j, r^j \mid C, S))^{-1} \cdot u^j)$ belong to $Isoq(GR \mid$
$C, S)$. Thus $O_g(x^j, u^j, p^j, r^j \mid C, S) = F_g(x^j, u^j \mid C, S)$, therefore
$A_g(x^j, u^j, p^j, r^j \mid C, S) = 1$.

(A$_g$.5)   This follows from the fact that $O_g(x^j, u^j, p^j, r^j \mid C, S)$ and
$F_g(x^j, u^j \mid C, S)$ are independent of unit of measurement.

$$Q.E.D.$$

In addition to the original graph analog of the Farrell decomposition
summarized in (8.2.11), we can also apply the decomposition (8.1.36) to
obtain

$$O_g(x^j, u^j, p^j, r^j \mid C, S) = A_g(x^j, u^j, p^j, r^j \mid C, S) \cdot S_g(x^j, u^j)$$
$$\cdot C_g(x^j, u^j) \cdot F_g(x^j, u^j \mid V, W). \quad (8.2.14)$$

An observation j is judged overall graph efficient if and only if it is
also judged efficient by all of the component measures of overall graph
efficiency on the right hand side of (8.2.14).

We note that the decomposition in (8.2.14) is defined relative to $(GR \mid$
$C, S)$. Similar decompositions can be derived for each of the graph
reference sets introduced in Section 8.1.

8.3   Graph Efficiency Measurement When Some Outputs Are Undesirable

Up to this point we have specified graph efficiency measures in which all
outputs are maximized while simultaneously minimizing inputs. In some
cases, however, one may wish to treat some output(s) or input(s) asymmetrically. As an example, consider an electric utility which produces
electricity and air pollution. The utility is subject to environmental
regulations which are designed to minimize the undesirable emissions.
Thus, one would like to treat electricity and air pollution emissions differently in gauging efficiency. This requires a nonradial efficiency measure
which expands desirable outputs and contracts undesirable outputs. It
also requires a careful treatment of the disposability properties of the
technology.

In order to treat desirable outputs and undesirable outputs differently we need to introduce a partition of the output matrix. Let $M =$
(M^g, M^b), where M^g includes all desirable ("good") outputs and M^b
consists of all undesirable ("bad") outputs. We partition the corresponding vector of outputs as $u = (u_g, u_b)$. We can now introduce a graph

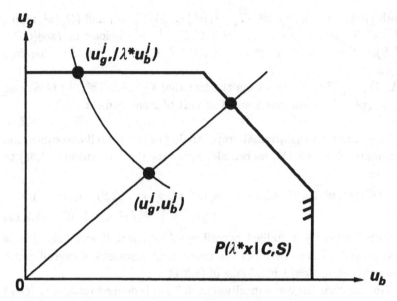

Fig. 8.5. *Comparison of (C, S) Graph Measure of Technical Efficiency With and Without Undesirable Outputs*

reference set, for example

$$(GR \mid C, S) = \{(x, u_g, u_b) : u_g \leqq zM^g, u_b \leqq zM^b, zN \leqq x, z \in \Re_+^J\}.$$
$$(8.3.1)$$

We choose the technology satisfying constant returns and strong disposability as a convenient starting point. Any of the technologies introduced in Section 8.1 could be modified and used instead of $(GR \mid C, S)$. Relative to this technology we can now define a graph measure of efficiency in which desirable outputs are expanded and undesirable outputs are contracted while simultaneously contracting inputs. Specifically

(8.3.2)   **Definition:** The measure

$$F_g(x^j, u_g^j, u_b^j \mid C, S) = \min\{\lambda : (\lambda x^j, \lambda^{-1} u_g^j, \lambda u_b^j) \in (GR \mid C, S)\}, j = 1, 2, \cdots, J,$$

is called the (C, S) *Graph Measure of Technical Efficiency When Some Outputs Are Undesirable.*

Figure 8.5 illustrates for the case of $M^g = M^b = 1$. Given observation (x^j, u_g^j, u_b^j), the (C, S) graph measure of technical efficiency when u_b^j is undesirable contracts x^j and u_b^j and expands u_g^j to $(\lambda^* x^j, u_g^j / \lambda^*, \lambda^* u_b^j)$.

The measure defined in (8.3.2) can be computed as the solution to the nonlinear programming problem

$$F_g(x^j, u_g^j, u_b^j \mid C, S) = \min_{\lambda, z} \lambda \qquad (8.3.3)$$

$$\text{s.t. } \lambda^{-1} u_g^j \leqq z M^g$$

$$\lambda u_b^j \leqq z M^b$$

$$z N \leqq \lambda x^j$$

$$z \in \Re_+^J$$

or

$$\min_{\lambda, z} \lambda$$

$$\text{s.t. } \lambda^{-1} u_{jm}^g \leqq \sum_{j=1}^{J} z_j u_{jm}^g, m = 1, 2, \cdots, M^g,$$

$$\lambda u_{jm}^b \leqq \sum_{j=1}^{J} z_j u_{jm}^b, m = 1, 2, \cdots, M^b,$$

$$\sum_{j=1}^{J} z_j x_{jn} \leqq \lambda x_{jn}, n = 1, 2, \cdots, N,$$

$$z_j \geqq 0, j = 1, 2, \cdots, J.$$

$F_g(x^j, u_g^j, u_b^j \mid C, S)$ differs from $F_g(x^j, u^j \mid C, S)$ in two ways: through the partitioning of the output matrix, and in the asymmetric treatment of u_g^j and u_b^j. Three other points are worth noting. First, we are not treating u_b like an input; u_b and u_g have the same type of disposability constraints which differ from that imposed on inputs. One may use more than observed inputs, but one may not freely produce more than observed outputs. Second, u_g and u_b are allowed to be jointly produced, but that is not required. Finally, the usual way in which bads are treated in performance measurement is that they are ignored. Here, we explicitly include bads and judge firms on their ability to decrease bads and inputs while simultaneously increasing goods.

Clearly, one could specify analogs of all of the graph measures introduced in the two previous sections which treat goods and bads asymmetrically. In addition, one could also partition the input matrix in a similar way. We note that $F_g(x^j, u_g^j, u_b^j \mid C, S)$ satisfies properties similar to $F_g.1 - F_g.5$, where those would be modified to treat undesirable outputs similar to inputs in terms of homogeneity properties.

As with the graph measures of efficiency defined in the previous sections, one can also convert the nonlinear programming problem in (8.3.3) into the linear programming problem

$$(F_g(x^j, u_g^j, u_b^j \mid C, S))^2 = \min_{\Gamma, z'} \Gamma \qquad (8.3.4)$$

$$\text{s.t. } u_g^j \leqq z' M^g$$
$$\Gamma u_b^j \leqq z' M^b$$
$$z' N \leqq \Gamma x^j$$
$$z' \in \Re_+^J$$

or

$$\min_{\Gamma, z'} \Gamma$$

$$\text{s.t. } u_{jm}^g \leqq \sum_{j=1}^{J} z_j' u_{jm}^g, m = 1, 2, \cdots, M^g,$$

$$\Gamma u_{jm}^b \leqq \sum_{j=1}^{J} z_j' u_{jm}^b, m = 1, 2, \cdots, M^b,$$

$$\sum_{j=1}^{J} z_j' x_{jn} \leqq \Gamma x_{jn}, n = 1, 2, \cdots, N,$$

$$z_j' \geqq 0, j = 1, 2, \cdots, J,$$

where $\Gamma = \lambda^2$, $z' = \lambda z$ and the solution is derived by solving for $\sqrt{\Gamma}$.

Next we turn to the case in which undesirable outputs are subject to some sort of regulation. Typically, such regulations are designed to reduce the ability of a firm to costlessly dispose of the undesirable output. Put differently, regulations require the firm to use productive resources to reduce levels of undesirable outputs. Such regulations can be modeled as deviations from strong disposability of the undesirable outputs. One way in which this can be achieved is by modeling undesirable outputs as being weakly disposable and desirable outputs as being strongly disposable. This can be achieved by modifying the technology $(GR \mid V, S^{\alpha,\beta})$ from (8.1.21) as follows

$$(GR \mid C, S^{g,b}) = \{(x, u) : u_g \leqq z M^g, u_b = \mu z M^b, z N \leqq x,$$
$$\mu \in [0, 1], z \in \Re_+^J\}, \qquad (8.3.5)$$

where the output vector is partitioned as before. Outputs are weakly disposable for both M^g and M^b since if $u \in (GR \mid C, S^{g,b})$, $\theta u \in (GR \mid C, S^{g,b})$, $\theta \in [0, 1]$. The equality $u_b = \mu z M^b$ implies that outputs in M^b are not necessarily strongly disposable.

The (C, S) and $(C, S^{g,b})$ technologies are illustrated for the case $M^g = M^b = 1$ in Figure 8.6. In order to highlight the difference in technologies

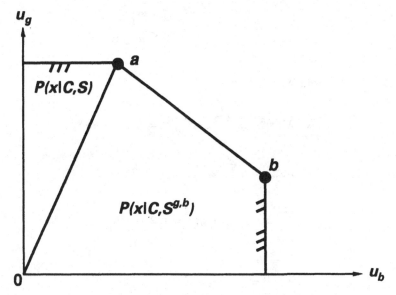

Fig. 8.6. (C,S) and $(C,S^{g,b})$ Output Sets

due to the difference in output disposability we employ the output set rather than the graph. Given two observations a and b, the (C,S) technology allows for free disposability of u_b and u_g, i.e., extensions to the west and south. In contrast, the $(C,S^{g,b})$ technology allows free disposability of u_g (extensions to the south), but only allows weak disposability of u_b, i.e., radial contractions.

We can now define

(8.3.6)   **Definition:** The function
$$F_g(x^j, u_g^j, u_b^j \mid C, S^{g,b}) = \min\{\lambda : (\lambda x^j, \lambda^{-1} u_g^j, \lambda u_b^j) \in (GR \mid C, S^{g,b})\}, j = 1, 2, \cdots, J,$$
is called the $(C,S^{g,b})$ *Graph Measure of Technical Efficiency.*

(8.3.6) differs from a similar measure defined in (8.3.2) only with respect to the difference in disposability of the technologies, with $(GR \mid C, S^{g,b})$ in the former replacing the $(GR \mid C, S)$ in the latter. The measure can be computed as the solution to the nonlinear programming problem

$$F_g(x^j, u_g^j, u_b^j \mid C, S^{g,b}) = \min_{\lambda, z, \mu} \lambda \qquad (8.3.7)$$

$$\text{s.t. } \lambda^{-1} u_g^j \leqq z M^g$$

$$\lambda u_b^j = \mu z M^b$$

$$z N \leqq \lambda x^j$$

$$z \in \Re_+^J$$
$$0 \leq \mu \leq 1$$

or

$$\min_{\lambda,z,\mu} \lambda$$

s.t. $\lambda^{-1} u_{jm}^g \leq \sum_{j=1}^{J} z_j u_{jm}^g, m = 1, 2, \cdots, M^g,$

$$\lambda u_{jm}^b = \mu \sum_{j=1}^{J} z_j u_{jm}^b, m = 1, 2, \cdots, M^b,$$

$$\sum_{j=1}^{J} z_j x_{jn} \leq \lambda x_{jn}, n = 1, 2, \cdots, N,$$

$$z_j \geq 0,$$

$$0 \leq \mu \leq 1.$$

We note that the μ parameter is redundant in this case due to the assumption of constant returns to scale. Thus, in practice one may set $\mu = 1$. The problem may also be simplified for purposes of calculation to the linear programming problem

$$(F_g(x^j, u_g^j, u_b^j \mid C, S^{g,b}))^2 = \min_{\Gamma, z'} \Gamma \qquad (8.3.8)$$

s.t. $u_g^j \leq z' M^g$

$$\Gamma u_b^j = z' M^b$$

$$z' N \leq \Gamma x^j$$

$$z' \in \Re_+^J$$

or

$$\min_{\Gamma, z'} \Gamma$$

s.t. $u_{jm}^g \leq \sum_{j=1}^{J} z_j' u_{jm}^g, m = 1, 2, \cdots, M^g,$

$$\Gamma u_{jm}^b = \sum_{j=1}^{J} z_j' u_{jm}^b, m = 1, 2, \cdots, M^b,$$

$$\sum_{j=1}^{J} z_j' x_{jn} \leq \Gamma x_{jn}, n = 1, 2, \cdots, N,$$

$$z_j' \geq 0,$$

where $\Gamma = \lambda^2$, $z' = \lambda z$ and the solution is derived by solving for $\sqrt{\Gamma}$.

We note that

$$F_g(x^j, u_g^j, u_b^j \mid C, S) \leqq F_g(x^j, u_g^j, u_b^j \mid C, S^{g,b}), \qquad (8.3.9)$$

because $(GR \mid C, S) \supseteq (GR \mid C, S^{g,b})$.

Result (8.3.9) can be used to determine the impact of regulation either in terms of potential desirable output lost or in terms of additional input required to offset the reduced disposability of the undesirable output from effective regulations. Such a measure is closely related to the graph congestion measure defined in (8.1.34).

(8.3.10)   **Definition:** For observation j, the *Graph Measure of Output Loss Due to Lack of Disposability of Undesirable Outputs* is given by the function
$$C_g(x^j, u_g^j, u_b^j) = F_g(x^j, u_g^j, u_b^j \mid C, S)/$$
$$F_g(x^j, u_g^j, u_b^j \mid C, S^{g,b}).$$

If $C_g(x^j, u_g^j, u_b^j) = 1$ then we conclude that (x^j, u_g^j, u_b^j) is freely disposable, i.e., any regulations concerning the disposability of u_b^j are ineffective. If $C_g(x^j, u_g^j, u_b^j) < 1$, then undesirable outputs u_b^j are not freely disposable, i.e., regulations are effective. The percentage by which output could have been increased (given $C_g(x^j, u_g^j, u_b^j) < 1$), can be calculated as $1 - C_g(x^j, u_g^j, u_b^j)$ and represents a measure of the opportunity cost of binding regulation to the firm.

These measures are illustrated in Figure 8.7 for the $M^g = M^b = 1$ case. In order to emphasize the output loss we use output sets rather than the graph to represent technology.

We note that $C_g(x^j, u_g^j, u_b^j)$ could be modified to satisfy nonincreasing or variable returns to scale by varying the restrictions on the z vector. Strong disposability of inputs could also be similarly relaxed.

8.4   A Numerical Example: Hyperbolic Graph Efficiency Measurement

In this section we provide numerical examples of some of the graph efficiency measures introduced in this chapter using the artificial data described in Section 5 of Chapter 2. Specifically we include calculations of the measures included in decomposition (8.2.14)

$$O_g(x^j, u^j, p^j, r^j \mid C, S) = A_g(x^j, u^j, p^j, r^j \mid C, S) \cdot S_g(x^j, u^j)$$
$$\cdot C_g(x^j, u^j) \cdot F_g(x^j, u^j \mid V, W).$$

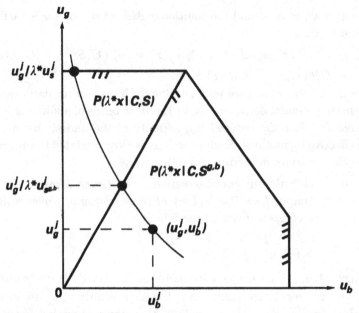

Fig. 8.7. *Comparison of* $F_g(x^j, u_g^j, u_b^j \mid C, S)$ *and* $F_g(x^j, u_g^j, u_b^j \mid C, S^{g,b})$

We begin by calculating $O_g(x^j, u^j, p^j, r^j \mid C, S)$ as the square root of $r^j u^j / p^j x^j$ from the relationship in (8.2.7). Next we calculate $F_g(x^j, u^j \mid C, S)$ from (8.1.6) and use the solution to derive $A_g(x^j, u^j, p^j, r^j \mid C, S)$ from (8.2.12). We calculate $F_g(x^j, u^j \mid V, S)$ from (8.1.20) to derive $S_g(x^j, u^j)$ from the definition in (8.1.32). Finally, we calculate $F_g(x^j, u^j \mid V, W)$ from (8.1.30), which is also used to derive $C_g(x^j, u^j)$ from (8.1.34).

These measures are calculated for each of our 20 observations of artificial data using the PROC LP procedure in SAS. The results are displayed in Table 8.1.

8.5 References to the Literature

Graph measures of technical efficiency and congestion were introduced by Färe, Grosskopf, and Lovell (1985). The graph measures of scale and "pure" technical efficiency are new, as is the price-independent decomposition (8.1.36).

The graph measures of overall efficiency and allocative efficiency were introduced by Färe, Grosskopf, and Lovell (1985), although the price-dependent decompositions (8.2.11) and (8.2.14) are new. The attempt to

Table 8.1. *Graph Efficiency Measures Using Artificial Data*

Obs	$O_g(x^j,u^j,p^j,r^j \mid C,S)$	$A_g(x^j,u^j,p^j,r^j \mid C,S)$
1	0.833	1.000
2	0.833	0.840
3	0.833	0.877
4	0.833	0.962
5	0.833	0.983
6	1.000	1.000
7	1.000	1.000
8	1.000	1.000
9	1.000	1.000
10	1.000	1.000
11	1.000	1.000
12	1.000	1.000
13	1.000	1.000
14	1.000	1.000
15	1.000	1.000
16	0.833	1.000
17	0.833	0.857
18	0.833	0.877
19	0.833	0.979
20	0.833	0.984

Obs	$S_g(x^j,u^j)$	$C_g(x^j,u^j)$	$F_g(x^j,u^j \mid V,W)$
1	0.833	1.000	1.000
2	0.992	1.000	1.000
3	0.950	1.000	1.000
4	0.866	1.000	1.000
5	0.848	1.000	1.000
6	1.000	1.000	1.000
7	1.000	1.000	1.000
8	1.000	1.000	1.000
9	1.000	1.000	1.000
10	1.000	1.000	1.000
11	1.000	1.000	1.000
12	1.000	1.000	1.000
13	1.000	1.000	1.000
14	1.000	1.000	1.000
15	1.000	1.000	1.000
16	0.833	1.000	1.000
17	0.973	1.000	1.000
18	0.950	1.000	1.000
19	0.851	1.000	1.000
20	0.847	1.000	1.000

define profit efficiency and to decompose it into technical and allocative components is not new. Nerlove (1965; Ch. 5) proposed a Farrell-like ratio measure of profit efficiency, decomposed it multiplicatively into what he called technical efficiency and price efficiency components, and illustrated the decomposition with a Cobb–Douglas production function. Nerlove's work influenced much of the "relative efficiency" literature cited in Chapter 7, which in turn has influenced recent profit efficiency studies such as Lovell and Sickles (1983) (aggregate U.S. time series), Ali and Flinn (1989) (Pakistan rice production), and Collender, Nehring, and Somwaru (1991) (Farm Credit System Associations).

The use of graph efficiency measures to analyze production in the presence of undesirable outputs originated in Färe, Grosskopf, Lovell, and Pasurka (1989), although Farrell-type desirable output-based or undesirable output-based measures would serve a similar purpose. The goal of Section 8.3 is to obtain a measure of desirable output loss, or revenue loss, due to a lack of strong disposability of the undesirable outputs. An additional objective may be to calculate abatement costs by calculating shadow price ratios along weak disposability facets of the boundary of the output set. This was the objective of the parametric analysis of Färe, Grosskopf, Lovell, and Yaisawarng (1993) (paper production and pollution generation).

9

Efficiency Measurement and Productivity Measurement

9.0 Introduction

In previous chapters we have focused on the measurement of efficiency of a set of firms observed in one time period. In this chapter we explicitly introduce multiperiod analysis, and discuss efficiency change between periods. In order to do so we introduce four measures of productivity: two direct and two indirect measures.

Each of our four productivity measures is a type of Malmquist index, actually they are geometric means of what Caves, Christensen, and Diewert (1982b) define as Malmquist productivity indexes. These indexes are based on distance functions, and hence are related to Farrell technical efficiency measures. The two direct measures are input-based and output-based measures as developed in Chapters 3 and 4, while the indirect measures are cost indirect and revenue indirect measures, as in Chapters 5 and 6.

9.1 Malmquist Input-Based Productivity Measurement

At each time period $t = 1, 2, \cdots, T$, the production technology is modeled by the graph GR^t. The graph consists of all feasible input–output vectors (x^t, u^t), i.e., $GR^t = \{(x^t, u^t) : x^t \text{ can produce } u^t\}$. For time t, $x^t \in \Re_+^{N_t}$ and $u^t \in \Re_+^{M_t}$. We define $N = \max_t\{N_t\}$ and similarly $M = \max_t\{M_t\}$. In each time period we observe $j = 1, 2, \cdots, J$ producers and we let $J = \max_t\{J_t\}$. Consequently, if $M_t \neq M_{t+1}, N_t \neq N_{t+1}$, zeros may be introduced to make $M_t = M_{t+1}, N_t = N_{t+1}$, and so on, as long as the matrices M and N meet the conditions set forth in Section 2.4.

The input distance function is defined for the (C, S) technology in period t as

$$D_i^t(u^t, x^t \mid C, S) = \min\{\lambda : (x^t/\lambda, u^t) \in (GR^t \mid C, S)\}, \qquad (9.1.1)$$

and we observe that $D_i^t(u^t, x^t \mid C, S)$ is equal to the reciprocal of the period t (C, S) input-based measure of technical efficiency; see (3.1.3). Since the productivity measures introduced in this chapter are defined in terms of distance functions, we may rely entirely on efficiency measures to compute the productivity indexes. The indexes introduced here are defined relative to (C, S) technologies only, although one may also employ less restrictive technologies.

(9.1.2)   **Definition:** The (C, S) *Malmquist Input-Based Productivity Index* is

$$M_i^{t+1}(u^{t+1}, x^{t+1}, u^t, x^t \mid C, S) = \left[\frac{D_i^t(u^{t+1}, x^{t+1} \mid C, S)}{D_i^t(u^t, x^t \mid C, S)} \right.$$
$$\left. \cdot \frac{D_i^{t+1}(u^{t+1}, x^{t+1} \mid C, S)}{D_i^{t+1}(u^t, x^t \mid C, S)} \right]^{\frac{1}{2}}.$$

In terms of input-based technical efficiency measures relative to the (C, S) technologies

$$M_i^{t+1}(u^{t+1}, x^{t+1}, u^t, x^t \mid C, S) = \left[\frac{F_i^t(u^t, x^t \mid C, S)}{F_i^t(u^{t+1}, x^{t+1} \mid C, S)} \right. \qquad (9.1.3)$$
$$\left. \cdot \frac{F_i^{t+1}(u^t, x^t \mid C, S)}{F_i^{t+1}(u^{t+1}, x^{t+1} \mid C, S)} \right]^{\frac{1}{2}},$$

where

$$F_i^t(u^t, x^t \mid C, S) = \min\{\lambda : \lambda x^t \in L^t(u^t \mid C, S)\}, \qquad (9.1.4)$$

$$F_i^t(u^{t+1}, x^{t+1} \mid C, S) = \min\{\lambda : \lambda x^{t+1} \in L^t(u^{t+1} \mid C, S)\}, \qquad (9.1.5)$$

$$F_i^{t+1}(u^t, x^t \mid C, S) = \min\{\lambda : \lambda x^t \in L^{t+1}(u^t \mid C, S)\}, \qquad (9.1.6)$$

and

$$F_i^{t+1}(u^{t+1}, x^{t+1} \mid C, S) = \min\{\lambda : \lambda x^{t+1} \in L^{t+1}(u^{t+1} \mid C, S)\}. \qquad (9.1.7)$$

In Figure 9.1, the input vectors x^t and x^{t+1} are feasible, i.e., $x^t \in L^t(u^t \mid C, S)$ and $x^{t+1} \in L^{t+1}(u^{t+1} \mid C, S)$, respectively. The technology change is drawn such that $L^{t+1}(u^{t+1} \mid C, S) \supseteq L^t(u^t \mid C, S)$. In terms of the distances in Figure 9.1 where we assume $u^t = u^{t+1}$, the productivity index can be written as

$$M_i^{t+1}(u^{t+1}, x^{t+1}, u^t, x^t \mid C, S) = \left[\frac{0e}{0d} \bigg/ \frac{0c}{0b} \cdot \frac{0f}{0d} \bigg/ \frac{0a}{0b} \right]^{\frac{1}{2}}. \qquad (9.1.8)$$

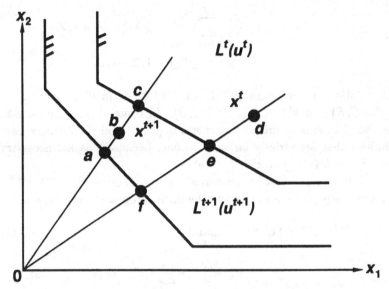

Fig. 9.1. *The (C, S) Malmquist Input-Based Productivity Index*

The two measures (9.1.4) and (9.1.7) are virtually the same as the measure (3.1.3). The only difference is that in (9.1.4) and (9.1.7), observations are dated in the sense that the input correspondences L^t and L^{t+1} are formed by observations from periods t and $t+1$, respectively, while in (3.1.3) no such distinction is made. These two measures may be calculated for each observation j as the solution to the linear programming problems

$$F_i^t(u^{t,j}, x^{t,j} \mid C, S) = \min_{\lambda, z} \lambda \qquad (9.1.9)$$

$$\text{s.t. } u_{jm}^t \leqq \sum_{j=1}^{J} z_j u_{jm}^t, m = 1, 2, \cdots, M,$$

$$\sum_{j=1}^{J} z_j x_{jn}^t \leqq \lambda x_{jn}^t, n = 1, 2, \cdots, N,$$

$$z_j \geqq 0, j = 1, 2, \cdots, J$$

and

$$F_i^{t+1}(u^{t+1,j}, x^{t+1,j} \mid C, S) = \min_{\lambda, z} \lambda \qquad (9.1.10)$$

$$\text{s.t. } u_{jm}^{t+1} \leqq \sum_{j=1}^{J} z_j u_{jm}^{t+1}, m = 1, 2, \cdots, M,$$

$$\sum_{j=1}^{J} z_j x_{jn}^{t+1} \leqq \lambda x_{jn}^{t+1}, n = 1, 2, \cdots, N,$$

$$z_j \geqq 0, j = 1, 2, \cdots, J.$$

The solutions to problems (9.1.4) and (9.1.7) lie in $(0, 1]$, since $x^t \in L(u^t \mid C, S)$ and $x^{t+1} \in L(u^{t+1} \mid C, S)$. In contrast, the solutions to the two problems of mixed time periods (9.1.5) and (9.1.6) may have solutions that are strictly larger than one, because it is *not* necessary that $x^{t+1} \in L^t(u^{t+1})$ or $x^t \in L^{t+1}(u^t)$.

We compute the first of the mixed period measures $F_i^t(u^{t+1}, x^{t+1} \mid C, S)$ for each j as the solution to the linear programming problem

$$F_i^t(u^{t+1,j}, x^{t+1,j} \mid C, S) = \min_{\lambda, z} \lambda \tag{9.1.11}$$

$$\text{s.t. } u_{jm}^{t+1} \leqq \sum_{j=1}^{J} z_j u_{jm}^t, m = 1, 2, \cdots, M,$$

$$\sum_{j=1}^{J} z_j x_{jn}^t \leqq \lambda x_{jn}^{t+1}, n = 1, 2, \cdots, N,$$

$$z_j \geqq 0, j = 1, 2, \cdots, J.$$

Similarly, the other mixed period problem (9.1.6) that enters into the computation of the input-based Malmquist productivity index is calculated for observation j as the solution to

$$F_i^{t+1}(u^{t,j}, x^{t,j} \mid C, S) = \min_{\lambda, z} \lambda \tag{9.1.12}$$

$$\text{s.t. } u_{jm}^t \leqq \sum_{j=1}^{J} z_j u_{jm}^{t+1}, m = 1, 2, \cdots, M,$$

$$\sum_{j=1}^{J} z_j x_{jn}^{t+1} \leqq \lambda x_{jn}^t, n = 1, 2, \cdots, N,$$

$$z_j \geqq 0, j = 1, 2, \cdots, J.$$

Thus for each observation j, we may now compute the input-based Malmquist productivity index relative to the (C, S) technology as defined in (9.1.3). Next, for each observation j, we can differentiate between changes in efficiency between periods and movements of the frontier, by calculating the following decomposition of (9.1.3)

$$M_i^{t+1}(u^{t+1}, x^{t+1}, u^t, x^t \mid C, S) = \frac{F_i^t(u^t, x^t \mid C, S)}{F_i^{t+1}(u^{t+1}, x^{t+1} \mid C, S)} \quad (9.1.13)$$

$$\cdot \left[\frac{F_i^{t+1}(u^{t+1}, x^{t+1} \mid C, S)}{F_i^t(u^{t+1}, x^{t+1} \mid C, S)} \right.$$

$$\left. \cdot \frac{F_i^{t+1}(u^t, x^t \mid C, S)}{F_i^t(u^t, x^t \mid C, S)} \right]^{\frac{1}{2}}.$$

The two ratios in the square brackets can be thought of as a measure of technical change measured by the ratio of the shifts in the frontier at $t+1$ and t where the two measures of the shift are averaged geometrically. The ratio outside the bracket captures changes in efficiency between the two periods, as measured by the ratio of the two efficiencies.

This decomposition is illustrated in Figure 9.2 for $M_t = M_{t+1} = N_t = N_{t+1} = 1$. In contrast to Figure 9.1, we illustrate relative to the graph rather than the input sets, allowing us to relax the assumption used in the earlier figure that $u^t = u^{t+1}$. Noting that the horizontal distances between points are equal to the distance between the projections of those points onto the x-axis, we can write the decomposition from (9.1.13) for Figure 9.2 as

$$\frac{0e}{0d} \bigg/ \frac{0a}{0b} \left[\frac{0a/0b}{0c/0b} \cdot \frac{0f/0d}{0e/0d} \right]^{\frac{1}{2}} \quad (9.1.14)$$

which simplifies to

$$\frac{0e}{0d} \bigg/ \frac{0a}{0b} \left[\frac{0a}{0c} \cdot \frac{0f}{0e} \right]^{\frac{1}{2}}. \quad (9.1.15)$$

(9.1.16) **Definition**: The (C,S) *Input-Based Technical Change Measure* is

$$TC_i^{t+1}(u^{t+1}, x^{t+1}, u^t, x^t \mid C, S) = \left[\frac{F_i^{t+1}(u^{t+1}, x^{t+1} \mid C, S)}{F_i^t(u^{t+1}, x^{t+1} \mid C, S)} \right.$$

$$\left. \cdot \frac{F_i^{t+1}(u^t, x^t \mid C, S)}{F_i^t(u^t, x^t \mid C, S)} \right]^{\frac{1}{2}}.$$

Now we apply the decomposition (3.1.34) of the (C, S) input-based measure of technical efficiency twice to the Malmquist productivity index (9.1.13). Then it decomposes into

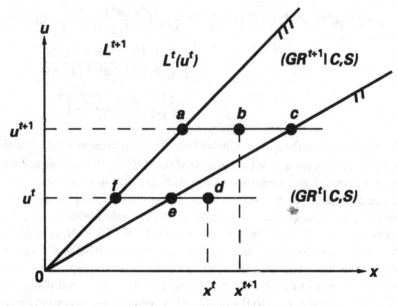

Fig. 9.2. *Decomposition of the (C, S) Malmquist Input-Based Productivity Index*

$$M_i^{t+1}(u^{t+1}, x^{t+1}, u^t, x^t \mid C, S) = \frac{F_i^t(u^t, x^t \mid V, W)}{F_i^{t+1}(u^{t+1}, x^{t+1} \mid V, W)} \quad (9.1.17)$$

$$\cdot \frac{S_i^t(u^t, x^t)}{S_i^{t+1}(u^{t+1}, x^{t+1})}$$

$$\cdot \frac{C_i^t(u^t, x^t)}{C_i^{t+1}(u^{t+1}, x^{t+1})}$$

$$\cdot TC_i^{t+1}(u^{t+1}, x^{t+1}, u^t, x^t \mid C, S).$$

The components of this decomposition are: changes in purely technical efficiency, changes in scale efficiency, changes in congestion and technical change. Improvements in productivity occur when $M_i^{t+1}(u^{t+1}, x^{t+1}, u^t, x^t \mid C, S) < 1$. The four individual components have a similar interpretation: if a ratio is less than unity it is a source of improvement in productivity. It is possible that individual components and productivity may take on values greater than unity. This decomposition highlights the analytical distinction between technical change and productivity change.

9.2   Malmquist Output-Based Productivity Measurement

The second Malmquist productivity index discussed here is output based. It makes use of the output distance function, which is the reciprocal of the output-based technical efficiency measure defined relative to the (C, S) technology, as

$$[D_o^t(x^t, u^t \mid C, S)]^{-1} = F_o^t(x^t, u^t \mid C, S) \tag{9.2.1}$$
$$= \max\{\theta : \theta u^t \in P^t(x^t \mid C, S)\}.$$

We note that as long as $u^t \in P^t(x^t \mid C, S)$, $F_o^t(x^t, u^t \mid C, S) \geqq 1$.

(9.2.2)   **Definition:** The (C,S) *Malmquist Output-Based Productivity Index* is
$$M_o^{t+1}(x^{t+1}, u^{t+1}, x^t, u^t \mid C, S) = \left[\frac{F_o^t(x^t, u^t \mid C, S)}{F_o^t(x^{t+1}, u^{t+1} \mid C, S)} \right.$$
$$\left. \cdot \frac{F_o^{t+1}(x^t, u^t \mid C, S)}{F_o^{t+1}(x^{t+1}, u^{t+1} \mid C, S)} \right]^{\frac{1}{2}}.$$

This index may be decomposed into
$$M_o^{t+1}(x^{t+1}, u^{t+1}, x^t, u^t \mid C, S) = \frac{F_o^t(x^t, u^t \mid C, S)}{F_o^{t+1}(x^{t+1}, u^{t+1} \mid C, S)} \tag{9.2.3}$$
$$\cdot TC_o^{t+1}(x^{t+1}, u^{t+1}, x^t, u^t \mid C, S).$$

(9.2.4)   **Definition:** The (C,S) *Output-Based Measure of Technical Change* is
$$TC_o^{t+1}(x^{t+1}, u^{t+1}, x^t, u^t \mid C, S) = \left[\frac{F_o^{t+1}(x^{t+1}, u^{t+1} \mid C, S)}{F_o^t(x^{t+1}, u^{t+1} \mid C, S)} \right.$$
$$\left. \cdot \frac{F_o^{t+1}(x^t, u^t \mid C, S)}{F_o^t(x^t, u^t \mid C, S)} \right]^{\frac{1}{2}}.$$

The decomposition in (9.2.3) is illustrated in Figure 9.3 for $M_t = M_{t+1} = N_t = N_{t+1} = 1$. Noting that vertical distances between points equal the distances between the projections of those points on the vertical axis, we have that

$$M_o^{t+1}(x^{t+1}, u^{t+1}, x^t, u^t \mid C, S) = \frac{0e/0d}{0a/0b} \left[\frac{0a/0b}{0c/0b} \frac{0f/0d}{0e/0d} \right]^{\frac{1}{2}}, \tag{9.2.5}$$

where the right hand side of (9.2.5) simplifies to $\frac{0e/0d}{0a/0b} \left[\frac{0a}{0c} \cdot \frac{0f}{0e} \right]^{\frac{1}{2}}$.

Of the four components that enter the productivity index (9.2.2), we show how two are computed for observation j.

$$F_o^t(x^{t,j}, u^{t,j} \mid C, S) = \max_{\theta, z} \theta \tag{9.2.6}$$

$$\text{s.t. } \theta u_{jm}^t \leqq \sum_{j=1}^J z_j u_{jm}^t, m = 1, 2, \cdots, M,$$

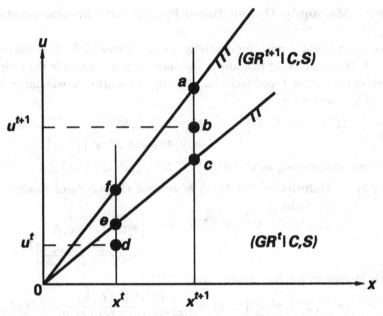

Fig. 9.3. *Decomposition of the (C, S) Malmquist Output-Based Productivity Index*

$$\sum_{j=1}^{J} z_j x_{jn}^t \leqq x_{jn}^t, n = 1, 2, \cdots, N,$$

$$z_j \geqq 0, j = 1, 2, \cdots, J$$

and

$$F_o^t(x^{t+1,j}, u^{t+1,j} \mid C, S) = \max_{\theta, z} \theta \qquad (9.2.7)$$

$$\text{s.t. } \theta u_{jm}^{t+1} \leq \sum_{j=1}^{J} z_j u_{jm}^t, m = 1, 2, \cdots, M,$$

$$\sum_{j=1}^{J} z_j x_{jn}^t \leq x_{jn}^{t+1}, n = 1, 2, \cdots, N,$$

$$z_j \geqq 0, j = 1, 2, \cdots, J.$$

The other two measures in (9.2.2) may be calculated in a similar way. We note that since u^{t+1} need not belong to $P^t(x^{t+1} \mid C, S)$, $F_o^t(x^{t+1}, u^{t+1} \mid C, S)$ may attain a value less than one. This is of course not possible if $u^{t+1} \in P^t(x^{t+1} \mid C, S)$; see Proposition (4.1.10).

A further decomposition of the Malmquist index (9.2.3) is achieved after twice applying (4.1.32), namely

$$M_o^{t+1}(x^{t+1}, u^{t+1}, x^t, u^t \mid C, S) = \frac{F_o^t(x^t, u^t \mid V, W)}{F_o^{t+1}(x^{t+1}, u^{t+1} \mid V, W)} \quad (9.2.8)$$
$$\cdot \frac{S_o^t(x^t, u^t)}{S_o^{t+1}(x^{t+1}, u^{t+1})}$$
$$\cdot \frac{C_o^t(x^t, u^t)}{C_o^{t+1}(x^{t+1}, u^{t+1})}$$
$$\cdot TC_o^{t+1}(x^{t+1}, u^{t+1}, x^t, u^t \mid C, S).$$

The components in this decomposition of the output-based Malmquist productivity index are: changes in purely technical efficiency, changes in scale efficiency, changes in congestion and technical change. All changes are measured as ratios and they are output based, so that improvements are denoted by ratios whose values exceed unity.

In Section 5 of Chapter 4, we proved that the input-based measure of technical efficiency relative to a constant returns to scale technology equals the reciprocal of the output-based measure of technical efficiency relative to the same technology. Thus we may conclude that the input-based and the output-based Malmquist productivity measures (9.1.3) and (9.2.2) assign reciprocal values to changes in productivity and technical change. However, the components of the decompositions (9.1.17) and (9.2.8) will in general not take reciprocal values.

9.3 Revenue Indirect Malmquist Productivity Measurement

Next we turn our interest toward measurement of productivity when technology is revenue constrained and, in particular, we begin by introducing a revenue indirect Malmquist productivity index.

First assume that in addition to observed inputs x^t and outputs u^t, output prices $r^t \in \Re_+^M, r^t \neq 0$ and positive target revenue R^t are known at each period t. The revenue indirect input distance function relative to the (C, S) technology at period t is given by

$$\left[ID_i^t(r^t/R^t, x^t \mid C, S)\right]^{-1} = IF_i^t(r^t/R^t, x^t \mid C, S) \quad (9.3.1)$$
$$= \min\{\lambda : \lambda x^t \in IL^t(r^t/R^t \mid C, S)\}.$$

This distance function is the reciprocal of the (C, S) revenue indirect input measure of technical efficiency defined in equation (5.1.3).

(9.3.2)   **Definition:** The (C,S) *Revenue Indirect Malmquist Input-Based Productivity Index* is

$$IM_i^{t+1}(r^{t+1}/R^{t+1}, x^{t+1}, r^t/R^t, x^t \mid C, S) =$$

$$\left[\frac{IF_i^t(r^t/R^t, x^t \mid C,S)}{IF_i^t(r^{t+1}/R^{t+1}, x^{t+1} \mid C,S)} \cdot \frac{IF_i^{t+1}(r^t/R^t, x^t \mid C,S)}{IF_i^{t+1}(r^{t+1}/R^{t+1}, x^{t+1} \mid C,S)}\right]^{\frac{1}{2}}.$$

This index may be decomposed into

$$IM_i^{t+1}(r^{t+1}/R^{t+1}, x^{t+1}, r^t/R^t, x^t \mid C, S) = \qquad (9.3.3)$$

$$\frac{IF_i^t(r^t/R^t, x^t \mid C, S)}{IF_i^{t+1}(r^{t+1}/R^{t+1}, x^{t+1} \mid C, S)}$$

$$\cdot ITC_i^{t+1}(r^{t+1}/R^{t+1}, x^{t+1}, r^t/R^t, x^t \mid C, S).$$

(9.3.4)   **Definition:** The (C,S) *Input-Based Revenue Indirect Technical Change Measure* is

$$ITC_i^{t+1}(r^{t+1}/R^{t+1}, x^{t+1}, r^t/R^t, x^t \mid C, S) =$$

$$\left[\frac{IF_i^{t+1}(r^{t+1}/R^{t+1}, x^{t+1}|C,S) \cdot IF_i^{t+1}(r^t/R^t, x^t|C,S)}{IF_i^t(r^{t+1}/R^{t+1}, x^{t+1}|C,S) \cdot IF_i^t(r^t/R^t, x^t|C,S)}\right]^{\frac{1}{2}}.$$

Of the four components that enter the input-based revenue indirect productivity index, we show how two are computed for observation j. The other components are computed in a similar fashion.

$$IF_i^t(r^{t,j}/R^{t,j}, x^{t,j} \mid C, S) = \min_{\lambda, z, u} \lambda \qquad (9.3.5)$$

$$\text{s.t. } u_m^t \leqq \sum_{j=1}^{J} z_j u_{jm}^t, m = 1, 2, \cdots, M,$$

$$\sum_{j=1}^{J} z_j x_{jn}^t \leqq \lambda x_{jn}^t, n = 1, 2, \cdots, N,$$

$$\sum_{m=1}^{M} r_{jm}^t u_m^t \geqq R^{t,j},$$

$$z_j \geqq 0, j = 1, 2, \cdots, J,$$

and

$$IF_i^t(r^{t+1,j}/R^{t+1,j}, x^{t+1,j} \mid C, S) = \min_{\lambda, z, u} \lambda \qquad (9.3.6)$$

$$\text{s.t. } u_m^{t+1} \leqq \sum_{j=1}^{J} z_j u_{jm}^t,$$

$$m = 1, 2, \cdots, M,$$

$$\sum_{j=1}^{J} z_j x_{jn}^t \leqq \lambda x_{jn}^{t+1},$$

$$n = 1, 2, \cdots, N,$$

$$\sum_{m=1}^{M} r_{jm}^{t+1} u_m^{t+1} \geqq R^{t+1,j},$$

$$z_j \geqq 0, j = 1, 2, \cdots, J.$$

The two other measures are calculated by substituting $t+1$ for t and t for $t+1$. We note that since x^{t+1} need not belong to $IL^t(r^{t+1}/R^{t+1} \mid C, S)$, then $IF_i^t(r^{t+1}/R^{t+1}, x^{t+1} \mid C, S)$ may exceed one (compare with Proposition (5.1.4)).

If we apply decomposition (5.1.34) to expression (9.3.3) two times, the following grand decomposition holds

$$IM_i^{t+1}(r^{t+1}/R^{t+1}, x^{t+1}, r^t/R^t, x^t \mid C, S) = \qquad (9.3.7)$$

$$\frac{IF_i^t(r^t/R^t, x^t \mid V, W)}{IF_i^{t+1}(r^{t+1}/R^{t+1}, x^{t+1} \mid V, W)} \cdot \frac{IS_i^t(r^t/R^t, x^t)}{IS_i^{t+1}(r^{t+1}/R^{t+1}, x^{t+1})}$$

$$\cdot \frac{IC_i^t(r^t/R^t, x^t)}{IC_i^{t+1}(r^{t+1}/R^{t+1}, x^{t+1})}$$

$$\cdot ITC_i^{t+1}(r^{t+1}/R^{t+1}, x^{t+1}, r^t/R^t, x^t \mid C, S).$$

The components of this decomposition of the (C, S) revenue indirect input-based Malmquist productivity index are: changes in revenue indirect purely technical efficiency, changes in revenue indirect scale efficiency, changes in revenue indirect congestion, and indirect technical change. All changes are measured as ratios and they are input based, so that values less than one denote improvements, and values in excess of one denote the opposite.

9.4 Cost Indirect Malmquist Productivity Measurement

The last productivity measure discussed here is the output-based cost indirect Malmquist productivity index. Assume that in addition to observed inputs x^t and outputs u^t, input prices $p^t \in \Re_+^N, p^t \neq 0$ and positive target cost Q^t are known at each period t. We define the cost indirect output distance function relative to the (C, S) technology at period t as

$$[ID_o^t(p^t/Q^t, u^t \mid C, S)]^{-1} = IF_o^t(p^t/Q^t, u^t \mid C, S) \qquad (9.4.1)$$

$$= \max\{\theta : \theta u^t \in IP^t(p^t/Q^t \mid C, S)\}.$$

The cost indirect output distance function is the reciprocal of the (C, S) cost indirect output measure of technical efficiency defined in (6.1.3).

(9.4.2)　　**Definition**: The (C,S) *Cost Indirect Malmquist Output-Based Productivity Index* is

$$IM_o^{t+1}(p^{t+1}/Q^{t+1}, u^{t+1}, p^t/Q^t, u^t \mid C, S) =$$

$$\left[\frac{IF_o^t(p^t/Q^t, u^t|C,S) \cdot IF_o^{t+1}(p^t/Q^t, u^t|C,S)}{IF_o^t(p^{t+1}/Q^{t+1}, u^{t+1}|C,S) \cdot IF_o^{t+1}(p^{t+1}/Q^{t+1}, u^{t+1}|C,S)} \right]^{\frac{1}{2}}.$$

This index may be decomposed into two components, the first measuring change in technical efficiency and the second measuring technical change, as

$$IM_o^{t+1}(p^{t+1}/Q^{t+1}, u^{t+1}, p^t/Q^t, u^t \mid C, S) = \qquad (9.4.3)$$

$$\frac{IF_o^t(p^t/Q^t, u^t \mid C, S)}{IF_o^{t+1}(p^{t+1}/Q^{t+1}, u^{t+1} \mid C, S)}$$

$$\cdot ITC_o^{t+1}(p^{t+1}/Q^{t+1}, u^{t+1}, p^t/Q^t, u^t \mid C, S).$$

(9.4.4)　　**Definition**: The (C,S) *Output-Based Cost Indirect Technical Change Measure* is

$$ITC_o^{t+1}(p^{t+1}/Q^{t+1}, u^{t+1}, p^t/Q^t, u^t \mid C, S) =$$

$$\left[\frac{IF_o^{t+1}(p^{t+1}/Q^{t+1}, u^{t+1}|C,S) \cdot IF_o^{t+1}(p^t/Q^t, u^t|C,S)}{IF_o^t(p^{t+1}/Q^{t+1}, u^{t+1}|C,S) \cdot IF_o^t(p^t/Q^t, u^t|C,S)} \right]^{\frac{1}{2}}.$$

Of the four components that enter the output-based cost indirect productivity index, we show how one is computed for observation j. The other components are computed in a similar fashion.

$$IF_o^t(p^{t,j}/Q^{t,j}, u^{t,j} \mid C, S) = \max_{\theta, z, x} \theta \qquad (9.4.5)$$

$$\text{s.t. } \theta u_{jm}^t \leqq \sum_{j=1}^{J} z_j u_{jm}^t, m = 1, 2, \cdots, M,$$

$$\sum_{j=1}^{J} z_j x_{jn}^t \leqq x_n^t, n = 1, 2, \cdots, N,$$

$$\sum_{n=1}^{N} p_{jn}^t x_n^t \leqq Q^{t,j},$$

$$z_j \geqq 0, j = 1, 2, \cdots, J.$$

We note that, since u^{t+1} need not belong to $IP^t(p^{t+1}/Q^{t+1} \mid C, S)$, it follows that $IF_o^t(p^{t+1}/Q^{t+1}, u^{t+1} \mid C, S)$ may be less than one.

If we apply decomposition (6.1.34) to expression (9.4.3) two times, the following grand decomposition holds

$$IM_o^{t+1}(p^{t+1}/Q^{t+1}, u^{t+1}, p^t/Q^t, u^t \mid C, S) = \qquad (9.4.6)$$

$$\frac{IF_o^t(p^t/Q^t, u^t \mid V, W)}{IF_o^{t+1}(p^{t+1}/Q^{t+1}, u^{t+1} \mid V, W)} \cdot \frac{IS_o^t(p^t/Q^t, u^t)}{IS_o^{t+1}(p^{t+1}/Q^{t+1}, u^{t+1})}$$

$$\cdot \frac{IC_o^t(p^t/Q^t, u^t)}{IC_o^{t+1}(p^{t+1}/Q^{t+1}, u^{t+1})}$$
$$\cdot ICT_o^{t+1}(p^{t+1}/Q^{t+1}, u^{t+1}, p^t/Q^t, u^t \mid C, S).$$

The components of this decomposition of the (C, S) cost indirect output-based Malmquist productivity index are: changes in cost indirect purely technical efficiency, changes in cost indirect scale efficiency, changes in cost indirect congestion, and cost indirect technical change. All changes are measured as ratios and they are output based. Values greater than one denote improvements between period t and period $t + 1$.

9.5 References to the Literature

The basic models of direct productivity measurement introduced in Sections 9.1 and 9.2 are inspired by the work of Caves, Christensen, and Diewert (1982a, 1982b), who note that the foundations go back to Malmquist (1953), Bergson (1961), Solow (1957), and Moorsteen (1961). Although Malmquist did not analyze productivity change directly, he did develop the requisite price and quantity indexes in terms of distance functions; on this point see Førsund (1991).

Diewert (1980, 1981) and Diewert and Parkan (1983) have proposed a nonparametric approach to productivity measurement. The linear programming approach to the calculation of the Farrell measures that go into the construction of the Malmquist indexes is due to Färe, Grosskopf, Lindgren, and Roos (1989). The decompositions (9.1.17) and (9.2.8) of the Malmquist productivity indexes into changes in purely technical efficiency, changes in scale efficiency, changes in congestion, and technical change, are generalizations of the two-way decomposition of Färe, Grosskopf, Lindgren and Roos (1989) and Färe and Grosskopf (1990b).

The indirect Malmquist productivity indexes and their decompositions (9.3.7) and (9.4.6) extend work of Färe, Grosskopf, and Lovell (1992).

Empirical applications of the nonparametric approach to productivity measurement include Färe, Grosskopf, Lindgren, and Roos (1989) (Swedish hospitals), Färe, Grosskopf, Lindgren, and Roos (1992) (Swedish pharmacies), Berg, Førsund, and Jansen (1992) (Norwegian banking), Färe, Grosskopf, Yaisawarng, Li, and Wang (1990) (Illinois utilities), Førsund (1993) (Norwegian ferries), and Färe, Grosskopf, Norris, and Zhang (1991) (international macro data).

A different nonparametric approach to the measurement of productivity growth and technical change is based on the non-convex "free disposal hull" technology developed by Deprins, Simar, and Tulkens (1984). Empirical applications of this alternative nonparametric approach include Tulkens (1986b) (Belgian post offices), Tulkens, Thiry, and Palm (1988), Nollet, Thiry, and Tulkens (1988), and Thiry and Tulkens (1992) (urban transit in Belgium).

The parametric approach to the decomposition of productivity growth into technical change and efficiency change is illustrated using a translog stochastic cost frontier and data from the U.S. airline industry by Bauer (1990). Nishimizu and Page (1982) employ a parametric linear programming frontier to calculate technical change and change in efficiency for Yugoslavian data. The Nishimizu–Page approach has been generalized and applied to OECD financial services data by Fecher and Pestieau (1993).

10

Topics in Efficiency Measurement

10.0 Introduction

In each of the earlier chapters in this monograph, we have focused on
a single general topic. In contrast, this chapter contains several topics,
all of which allow for customization of the models already introduced in
this manuscript. As we shall see, the programming framework readily
allows such customization – additional constraints may be added in a
straightforward way, and behavioral objectives also may be modified
readily, allowing us to identify the frontier in nontraditional or restricted
cases and to measure easily deviations from those frontiers. These topics
are intended to be suggestive and not exhaustive; they are an invitation
to the reader to extend the models introduced here to suit their area of
interest.

In Section 10.1 we discuss subvector efficiency. By subvector efficiency
we understand that only some inputs or some outputs are exposed to
scaling while the others are fixed. This allows us to consider short-run
efficiency, for example.

Constrained profit maximization is the topic of Section 10.2. In this
section we demonstrate how to formulate profit maximization in a programming framework, and how to modify the basic problem to account
for fixed inputs as well as for constraints which limit expenditure on a
subvector of inputs. An example of this type of constraint is a credit
constraint faced by a producer purchasing variable inputs.

Measures of plant capacity and its utilization are introduced in Section
10.3. Here we investigate capacity in terms of inputs and outputs rather
than in terms of cost, in order to provide an operational measure of

the notion of capacity as defined by Johansen (1968), which seeks maximum achievable output given fixed inputs, but allowing unrestricted application of variable inputs. We specifically allow for multiple output production.

In Section 10.4 we study efficiency gains from diversification, a topic closely related to economies of scope. This approach allows identification of gains from diversification along the cost or production frontier, in contrast to existing approaches which use standard regression techniques. It also generalizes those approaches in allowing diversified and specialized firms to adopt "different" technologies.

10.1   Subvector Efficiency

In earlier chapters, efficiency has been measured with respect to all inputs, as in Chapters 3 and 5, or all outputs, as in Chapters 4 and 6. However, in the short run, some inputs may be fixed or uncontrollable and therefore it may be possible to contract only a subvector of inputs. Alternatively, some outputs may be produced under a fixed contract, for example, while others may be adjustable. In such cases it is natural to measure efficiency relative to a subvector of inputs and outputs rather than relative to the entire vector as in Chapters 3-6. The purpose of this section is to modify our earlier models to measure subvector efficiency. In order not to be overly repetitive, we only discuss (C, S) technologies (constant returns to scale and strong disposability) although less restrictive technologies can be considered as well.

We begin with input-based measures of subvector efficiency, where efficiency is evaluated relative to $L(u \mid C, S)$. We then turn to input subvector measures of efficiency evaluated relative to the indirect technology $IL(r/R \mid C, S)$ in parallel with Chapter 5. We then repeat these exercises with respect to output-based measures of subvector efficiency and evaluate first relative to $P(x \mid C, S)$ as in Chapter 4, and then relative to $IP(p/Q \mid C, S)$ as in Chapter 6.

Suppose the input matrix N and the output matrix M are given, and further suppose that the input matrix is partitioned, so that $N = (N^\alpha, N^{\hat{\alpha}})$, where $\alpha \subseteq \{1, 2, \cdots, N\}$ and $\hat{\alpha} = \{1, 2, \cdots, N\} \backslash \alpha$. Correspondingly write $x = (x_\alpha, x_{\hat{\alpha}})$, where x_α is assumed fixed and $x_{\hat{\alpha}}$ is assumed variable. In the following analysis we assume that all producers have the same subvectors of fixed and variable inputs. This assumption is for notational convenience and can be relaxed.

We may now form a subvector radial efficiency measure relative to the (C, S) technology

$$L(u \mid C, S) = \{(x_\alpha, x_{\hat{\alpha}}) : u \leqq zM, zN^\alpha \leqq x_\alpha, zN^{\hat{\alpha}} \leqq x_{\hat{\alpha}}, z \in \Re_+^J\},$$
(10.1.1)

by means of

(10.1.2)   **Definition:** Assume that $x_{\hat{\alpha}}^j \geq 0$. The function
$$SF_i(u^j, x_\alpha^j, x_{\hat{\alpha}}^j \mid C, S) = \min\{\lambda : (x_\alpha^j, \lambda x_{\hat{\alpha}}^j) \in L(u^j \mid C, S)\},$$
$$j = 1, 2, \cdots, J,$$
is called the (C,S) *Input Subvector Measure of Technical Efficiency.*

The (C, S) input subvector measure $SF_i(u^j, x_\alpha^j, x_{\hat{\alpha}}^j \mid C, S)$ gauges the efficiency of the subvector $x_{\hat{\alpha}}^j$ in the production of u^j when x_α^j is fixed and when technology satisfies constant returns to scale ($L(\theta u \mid C, S) = \theta L(u \mid C, S), \theta > 0$) and strong disposability of inputs ($x \geqq y \in L(u \mid C, S) \implies x \in L(u \mid C, S)$). It does so by computing the ratio of the smallest feasible contraction of $x_{\hat{\alpha}}^j$ to itself, i.e., $SF_i(u^j, x_\alpha^j, x_{\hat{\alpha}}^j \mid C, S) = \| SF_i(u^j, x_\alpha^j, x_{\hat{\alpha}}^j \mid C, S) \cdot x_{\hat{\alpha}}^j \| / \| x_{\hat{\alpha}}^j \|$.

The properties of this measure are summarized in

(10.1.3)   **Proposition:** Given $L(u^j \mid C, S)$, then for each $j = 1, 2, \cdots, J$,

SF$_i$.1 $SF_i(u^j, x_\alpha^j, \delta x_{\hat{\alpha}}^j \mid C, S) = \delta^{-1} SF_i(u^j, x_\alpha^j, x_{\hat{\alpha}}^j \mid C, S),$
$\delta > 0,$

SF$_i$.2 $SF_i(\theta u^j, x_\alpha^j, x_{\hat{\alpha}}^j \mid C, S) = \theta SF_i(u^j, (x_\alpha^j/\theta), x_{\hat{\alpha}}^j \mid C, S), \theta > 0,$

SF$_i$.3 $0 \leqq SF_i(u^j, x_\alpha^j, x_{\hat{\alpha}}^j \mid C, S) \leqq 1,$

SF$_i$.4 $SF_i(u^j, x_\alpha^j, x_{\hat{\alpha}}^j \mid C, S) = 1 \implies (x_\alpha^j, x_{\hat{\alpha}}^j) \in WEff$
$L(u^j \mid C, S)$ or on the boundary of $\Re_+^N$,

SF$_i$.5 $SF_i(u^j, x_\alpha^j, x_{\hat{\alpha}}^j \mid C, S)$ is independent of unit of measurement.

Proof:
(SF$_i$.1)
$$SF_i(u^j, x_\alpha^j, \delta x_{\hat{\alpha}}^j \mid C, S) = \min\{\lambda : (x_\alpha^j, \lambda \delta x_{\hat{\alpha}}^j) \in L(u^j \mid C, S)\}$$
$$= \delta^{-1} \min\{\lambda \delta : (x_\alpha^j, \lambda \delta x_{\hat{\alpha}}^j) \in L(u^j \mid C, S)\}$$
$$= \delta^{-1} SF_i(u^j, x_\alpha^j, x_{\hat{\alpha}}^j \mid C, S).$$

(SF$_i$.2)   Since $L(\theta u^j \mid C, S) = \theta L(u^j \mid C, S), \theta > 0$, it follows that
$$SF_i(\theta u^j, x_\alpha^j, x_{\hat{\alpha}}^j \mid C, S) = \min\{\lambda : (x_\alpha^j, \lambda x_{\hat{\alpha}}^j) \in L(\theta u^j \mid C, S)\}$$
$$= \min\{\lambda : (x_\alpha^j, \lambda x_{\hat{\alpha}}^j) \in \theta L(u^j \mid C, S)\}$$

$$= \min \theta \{\lambda/\theta : (x_\alpha^j/\theta, \lambda x_{\hat{\alpha}}^j/\theta) \in L(u^j \mid C, S)\}$$
$$= \theta SF_i(u^j, (x_\alpha^j/\theta), x_{\hat{\alpha}}^j \mid C, S).$$

(SF$_i$.3)   Follows from the fact that $(x_\alpha^j, x_{\hat{\alpha}}^j) \in L(u^j \mid C, S)$ for each $j = 1, 2, \cdots, J$.

(SF$_i$.4)   Clearly $(x_\alpha^j, \lambda^{*j} x_{\hat{\alpha}}^j) \in L(u^j \mid C, S)$, where the optimum $\lambda^{*j} \leq 1$. If $(x_\alpha^j, \lambda^{*j} x_{\hat{\alpha}}^j)$ is on the boundary of $\Re_+^N$ we are done. Thus if $(x_\alpha^j, \lambda^{*j} x_{\hat{\alpha}}^j)$ does not belong to the $Isoq\, L(u^j \mid C, S)$, then $\exists \delta < 1$ such that $(\delta x_\alpha^j, \delta \lambda^{*j} x_{\hat{\alpha}}^j) \in L(u^j \mid C, S)$. Inputs are strongly disposable, and $\delta < 1$, $(x_\alpha^j, \delta \lambda^{*j} x_{\hat{\alpha}}^j) \in L(u^j \mid C, S)$, thus λ^{*j} is not a minimum. This contradiction shows that $(x_\alpha^j, \lambda^{*j} x_{\hat{\alpha}}^j) \in Isoq\, L(u^j \mid C, S)$. The conclusion now follows from Proposition (2.3.2).

(SF$_i$.5)   Let us consider one input constraint $\sum_{j=1}^J z_j x_{jn} \leq \lambda x_{jn}$, where the nth input is variable, i.e., $n \in \hat{\alpha}$. If the unit of measurement is altered, so that $\hat{x}_{jn} = \gamma x_{jn}, j = 1, 2, \cdots, J$, then clearly λ and z are not affected.

$$Q.E.D.$$

Using the piecewise linear (C, S) technology (10.1.1), the (C, S) input subvector measure of technical efficiency can be calculated for activity j as the solution to the linear programming problem

$$SF_i(u^j, x_\alpha^j, x_{\hat{\alpha}}^j \mid C, S) = \min_{\lambda, z} \lambda \qquad (10.1.4)$$

$$\text{s.t. } u^j \leq zM$$
$$zN^\alpha \leq x_\alpha^j$$
$$zN^{\hat{\alpha}} \leq \lambda x_{\hat{\alpha}}^j$$
$$z \in \Re_+^J$$

or

$$\min_{\lambda, z} \lambda$$

$$\text{s.t. } u_{jm} \leq \sum_{j=1}^J z_j u_{jm}, m = 1, 2, \cdots, M,$$

$$\sum_{j=1}^J z_j x_{jn} \leq x_{jn}, n \in \alpha,$$

$$\sum_{j=1}^J z_j x_{jn} \leq \lambda x_{jn}, n \in \hat{\alpha},$$

$$z_j \geq 0, j = 1, 2, \cdots, J.$$

The (C, S) input subvector efficiency measure is illustrated in Figure 10.1. The minimizing value of λ is denoted by λ^{*j}.

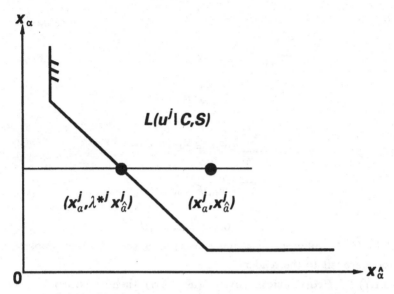

Fig. 10.1. *The (C,S) Input Subvector Measure of Technical Efficiency*

We can also calculate a subvector measure of cost efficiency. Suppose that in addition to the input and output matrices N and M the prices of $x_{\hat{\alpha}}$ are known and that $p_{\hat{\alpha}}^j \in \Re_+^{N^{\hat{\alpha}}}, p_{\hat{\alpha}}^j \neq 0$, for each activity $j = 1, 2, \cdots, J$. Then we can compute for each activity the minimum expenditure on $x_{\hat{\alpha}}$ required to produce u^j at $p_{\hat{\alpha}}^j$ when x_{α}^j is given, i.e., short run variable cost if $x_{\hat{\alpha}}$ denotes variable inputs.

(10.1.5)   **Definition**: The function
$$SQ(u^j, x_{\alpha}^j, p_{\hat{\alpha}}^j \mid C, S) = \min\{p_{\hat{\alpha}}^j x_{\hat{\alpha}} : (x_{\alpha}^j, x_{\hat{\alpha}}) \in L(u^j \mid C, S)\}, j = 1, 2, \cdots, J,$$
is called the (C,S) *Subvector Cost Function.*

This function may be computed as the solution to the linear programming problem

$$SQ(u^j, x_{\alpha}^j, p_{\hat{\alpha}}^j \mid C, S) = \min_{z, x_{\hat{\alpha}}} p_{\hat{\alpha}}^j x_{\hat{\alpha}} \qquad (10.1.6)$$

$$\text{s.t. } u^j \leqq zM$$
$$zN^{\alpha} \leqq x_{\alpha}^j$$
$$zN^{\hat{\alpha}} \leqq x_{\hat{\alpha}}$$
$$z \in \Re_+^J$$

or

$$\min_{z,x_n} \sum_{n=N^\alpha+1}^{N} p_{jn}x_n$$

$$\text{s.t.} \quad u_{jm} \leqq \sum_{j=1}^{J} z_j u_{jm}, m = 1, 2, \cdots, M,$$

$$\sum_{j=1}^{J} z_j x_{jn} \leqq x_{jn}, n \in \alpha,$$

$$\sum_{j=1}^{J} z_j x_{jn} \leqq x_n, n \in \hat{\alpha},$$

$$z_j \geqq 0, j = 1, 2, \cdots, J.$$

The (C, S) subvector cost function satisfies the following properties. Proofs are left to the reader.

(10.1.7)   **Proposition:** Given $L(u^j \mid C, S)$, then for each $j = 1, 2, \cdots, J,$

SQ.1 $SQ(\theta u^j, x^j_\alpha, p^j_{\hat{\alpha}} \mid C, S) = \theta SQ(u^j, (x^j_\alpha/\theta), p^j_{\hat{\alpha}} \mid C, S), \theta > 0,$

SQ.2 $SQ(u^j, x^j_\alpha, \lambda p^j_{\hat{\alpha}} \mid C, S) = \lambda SQ(u^j, x^j_\alpha, p^j_{\hat{\alpha}} \mid C, S), \lambda > 0,$

SQ.3 $SQ(u^j, x^j_\alpha, p^j_{\hat{\alpha}} \mid C, S) \leqq p^j_{\hat{\alpha}} x^j_{\hat{\alpha}},$

SQ.4 $SQ(u^j, x^j_\alpha, p^j_{\hat{\alpha}} \mid C, S) = p^j_{\hat{\alpha}} x^j_{\hat{\alpha}} \Longleftrightarrow x^j_{\hat{\alpha}}$ solves (10.1.5).

We now introduce input subvector efficiency measures for revenue indirect technology, i.e., input efficiency is gauged relative to $IL(r/R \mid C, S)$, along the lines of Chapter 5. In this case, instead of taking outputs as given, the firm faces a revenue target to be achieved at fixed output prices.

Suppose that, in addition to the input matrix N and the output matrix M, output prices $r^j \in \Re^M_+, r^j \neq 0$, and positive target revenue R are given. Moreover, assume that the input matrix is partitioned so that $N = (N^\alpha, N^{\hat{\alpha}})$, where $\alpha \subseteq \{1, 2, \cdots, N\}$ and $\hat{\alpha} = \{1, 2, \cdots, N\} \backslash \alpha$. Also write $x = (x_\alpha, x_{\hat{\alpha}})$ corresponding to the partition of the input matrix, i.e., x_α is fixed and $x_{\hat{\alpha}}$ is variable as before. We form a revenue indirect input subvector technical efficiency measure relative to the (C, S) indirect technology

$$IL(r/R \mid C, S) = \{(x_\alpha, x_{\hat{\alpha}}) : u \leqq zM, zN^\alpha \leqq x_\alpha, zN^{\hat{\alpha}} \leqq x_{\hat{\alpha}},$$
$$ru \geq R, z \in \Re^J_+\}, (r/R) \in \Re^M_+, r/R \neq 0, (10.1.8)$$

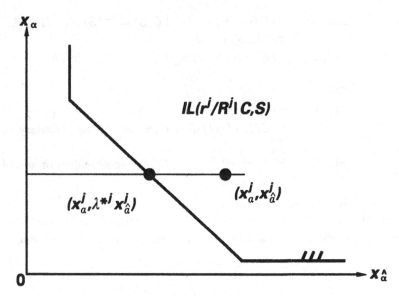

Fig. 10.2. *The (C, S) Revenue Indirect Input Subvector Measure of Technical Efficiency*

by means of

(10.1.9)   **Definition:** Assume that $x_{\hat{\alpha}}^j \geq 0$. The function
$SIF_i(r^j/R^j, x_\alpha^j, x_{\hat{\alpha}}^j \mid C, S) = \min\{\lambda : (x_\alpha^j, \lambda x_{\hat{\alpha}}^j)$
$\in IL(r^j/R^j \mid C, S)\}, j = 1, 2, \cdots, J,$
is called the (C, S) *Revenue Indirect Input Subvector Measure of Technical Efficiency.*

$SIF_i(r^j/R^j, x_\alpha^j, x_{\hat{\alpha}}^j \mid C, S)$ measures the efficiency of an input subvector $x_{\hat{\alpha}}^j$ in the generation of revenue R^j at output prices r^j, when the technology satisfies constant returns to scale and strong disposability of inputs, and when x_α^j is given. It does so by computing the ratio of the smallest feasible radial contraction of $x_{\hat{\alpha}}^j$ in $IL(r^j/R^j \mid C, S)$ to itself, i.e., $SIF_i(r^j/R^j, x_\alpha^j, x_{\hat{\alpha}}^j \mid C, S) = \parallel SIF_i(r^j/R^j, x_\alpha^j, x_{\hat{\alpha}}^j \mid C, S) \cdot x_{\hat{\alpha}}^j \parallel / \parallel x_{\hat{\alpha}}^j \parallel$.

Figure 10.2 illustrates the proportional contraction of the subvector $x_{\hat{\alpha}}^j$, when the observation $(x_\alpha^j, x_{\hat{\alpha}}^j)$ is a member of $IL(r^j/R^j \mid C, S)$. The maximum contraction is λ^{*j}, which equals $SIF_i(r^j/R^j, x_\alpha^j, x_{\hat{\alpha}}^j \mid C, S)$.

We list the properties of $SIF_i(r^j/R^j, x_\alpha^j, x_{\hat{\alpha}}^j \mid C, S)$, and leave the proofs to the reader.

(10.1.10)   **Proposition:** Given $IL(r^j/R^j \mid C, S)$, then for each $j = 1, 2, \cdots, J,$

SIF$_i$.1 $SIF_i(r^j/R^j, x_\alpha^j, \delta x_{\hat{\alpha}}^j \mid C, S) = \delta^{-1} SIF_i(r^j/R^j, x_\alpha^j, x_{\hat{\alpha}}^j \mid C, S), \delta > 0,$

SIF$_i$.2 $SIF_i(r^j/\theta R^j, x_\alpha^j, x_{\hat{\alpha}}^j \mid C, S) = \theta SIF_i(r^j/R^j, (x_\alpha^j/\theta), x_{\hat{\alpha}}^j \mid C, S), \theta > 0,$

SIF$_i$.3 $0 \leq SIF_i(r^j/R^j, x_\alpha^j, x_{\hat{\alpha}}^j \mid C, S) \leq 1,$

SIF$_i$.4 $SIF_i(r^j/R^j, x_\alpha^j, x_{\hat{\alpha}}^j \mid C, S) = 1 \implies (x_\alpha^j, x_{\hat{\alpha}}^j) \in WEff\ IL(r^j/R^j \mid C, S)$ or on the boundary of $\Re_+^N,$

SIF$_i$.5 $SIF_i(r^j/R^j, x_\alpha^j, x_{\hat{\alpha}}^j \mid C, S)$ is independent of unit of measurement.

Employing the piecewise linear technology (10.1.8), the (C, S) revenue indirect input subvector measure of technical efficiency can be calculated for observation j as the solution to the linear programming problem

$$SIF_i(r^j/R^j, x_\alpha^j, x_{\hat{\alpha}}^j \mid C, S) = \min_{\lambda, z, u} \lambda \qquad (10.1.11)$$

$$\text{s.t.} \quad u \leq z\boldsymbol{M}$$
$$z\boldsymbol{N}^\alpha \leq x_\alpha^j$$
$$z\boldsymbol{N}^{\hat{\alpha}} \leq \lambda x_{\hat{\alpha}}^j$$
$$r^j u \geq R^j$$
$$z \in \Re_+^J$$

or

$$\min_{\lambda z, u} \lambda$$

$$\text{s.t.} \quad u_m \leq \sum_{j=1}^{J} z_j u_{jm}, m = 1, 2, \cdots, M,$$

$$\sum_{j=1}^{J} z_j x_{jn} \leq x_{jn}, n \in \alpha,$$

$$\sum_{j=1}^{J} z_j x_{jn} \leq \lambda x_{jn}, n \in \hat{\alpha},$$

$$\sum_{m=1}^{M} r_{jm} u_m \geq R^j,$$

$$z_j \geq 0, j = 1, 2, \cdots, J.$$

We can also calculate a measure of input subvector cost efficiency in the indirect framework. Assume that in addition to the input matrix $\boldsymbol{N}$, the output matrix $\boldsymbol{M}$, the output prices $r \in \Re_+^M$, $r \neq 0$, and a positive desired revenue R, prices of the variable input subvector $x_{\hat{\alpha}}$ are known, with $p_{\hat{\alpha}}^j \in \Re_+^{N^{\hat{\alpha}}}, p_{\hat{\alpha}}^j \neq 0$. Then for each observation j, we can compute the minimum expenditure on $x_{\hat{\alpha}}$ required to generate revenue R^j at output prices r^j when the reference technology is (10.1.8). Let us consider the minimization of subvector cost relative to the revenue indirect input set $IL(r^j/R^j \mid C, S)$. For observation j we seek the minimum expenditure on variable input subvector $x_{\hat{\alpha}}$ required to generate revenue R^j given output prices r^j, input prices $p_{\hat{\alpha}}^j$, and fixed inputs x_{α}^j, which is provided in the following

(10.1.12)   **Definition:** The function
$SIQ(r^j/R^j, x_{\alpha}^j, p_{\hat{\alpha}}^j \mid C, S) = \min\{p_{\hat{\alpha}}^j x_{\hat{\alpha}} : (x_{\alpha}^j, x_{\hat{\alpha}}) \in$
$IL(r^j/R^j \mid C, S)\}, j = 1, 2, \cdots, J,$
is the (C,S) *Revenue Indirect Subvector Cost Function.*

This function is computed as the solution to the linear programming problem

$$SIQ(r^j/R^j, x_{\alpha}^j, p_{\hat{\alpha}}^j \mid C, S) = \min_{z, x_{\hat{\alpha}}, u} p_{\hat{\alpha}}^j x_{\hat{\alpha}} \qquad (10.1.13)$$

$$\text{s.t. } u \leq zM$$
$$zN^{\alpha} \leq x_{\alpha}^j$$
$$zN^{\hat{\alpha}} \leq x_{\hat{\alpha}}$$
$$r^j u \geq R^j$$
$$z \in \Re_+^J$$

or

$$\min_{z, x_{\hat{\alpha}}, u} \sum_{n=N^{\alpha}+1}^{N} p_{jn} x_n$$

$$\text{s.t. } u_m \leq \sum_{j=1}^{J} z_j u_{jm}, m = 1, 2, \cdots, M,$$

$$\sum_{j=1}^{J} z_j x_{jn} \leq x_{jn}, n \in \alpha,$$

$$\sum_{j=1}^{J} z_j x_{jn} \leq x_n, n \in \hat{\alpha},$$

$$\sum_{m=1}^{M} r_{jm} u_m \geq R^j,$$

$$z_j \geq 0, j = 1, 2, \cdots, J.$$

The solution to (10.1.13) measures the minimum expenditure on $x_{\hat{\alpha}}$ needed to yield revenue R^j when output prices r^j, variable input prices $p^j_{\hat{\alpha}}$ and fixed input quantities x^j_{α} are given. Its properties are listed in

(10.1.14)   **Proposition**: Given $IL(r^j/R^j \mid C, S)$, then for each $j = 1, 2, \cdots, J,$

SIQ.1 $SIQ(r^j/\theta R^j, x^j_{\alpha}, p^j_{\hat{\alpha}} \mid C, S) = \theta SIQ(r^j/R^j, (x^j_{\alpha}/\theta),$ $p^j_{\hat{\alpha}} \mid C, S), \theta > 0,$

SIQ.2 $SIQ(r^j/R^j, x^j_{\alpha}, \lambda p^j_{\hat{\alpha}} \mid C, S) = \lambda SIQ(r^j/R^j, x^j_{\alpha},$ $p^j_{\hat{\alpha}} \mid C, S), \lambda > 0,$

SIQ.3 $SIQ(r^j/R^j, x^j_{\alpha}, p^j_{\hat{\alpha}} \mid C, S) \leqq p^j_{\hat{\alpha}} x^j_{\hat{\alpha}},$

SIQ.4 $SIQ(r^j/R^j, x^j_{\alpha}, p^j_{\hat{\alpha}} \mid C, S) = p^j_{\hat{\alpha}} x^j_{\hat{\alpha}} \iff x^j_{\hat{\alpha}}$ solves (10.1.12).

The proof of this proposition is left for the reader.

Thus far we have generalized the (C, S) measures in Chapters 3 and 5 to allow for notions of input subvector efficiency. The undertaking in the next few pages is to similarly generalize the (C, S) measures in Chapters 4 and 6 to measure output subvector efficiencies. Thus suppose that the input matrix N and the output matrix M are known, and further suppose that the output matrix is partitioned so that $M = (M^{\alpha}, M^{\hat{\alpha}})$, where $\alpha \subseteq \{1, 2, \cdots, M\}$ and $\hat{\alpha} = \{1, 2, \cdots, M\} \backslash \alpha$ is its complement. Correspondingly write $u = (u_{\alpha}, u_{\hat{\alpha}})$, where u_{α} is a subvector of fixed outputs and $u_{\hat{\alpha}}$ is a subvector of variable outputs. We may form an output subvector efficiency measure relative to the (C, S) technology

$$P(x \mid C, S) = \{(u_{\alpha}, u_{\hat{\alpha}}) : u_{\alpha} \leqq zM^{\alpha}, u_{\hat{\alpha}} \leqq zM^{\hat{\alpha}}, zN \leqq x, z \in \Re^J_+\},$$
(10.1.15)

by means of

(10.1.16)   **Definition**: Assume that $u^j_{\hat{\alpha}} \geq 0$. The function $SF_o(x^j, u^j_{\alpha}, u^j_{\hat{\alpha}} \mid C, S) = \max\{\theta : (u^j_{\alpha}, \theta u^j_{\hat{\alpha}}) \in P(x^j \mid C, S)\}, j = 1, 2, \cdots, J,$ is called the (C,S) *Output Subvector Measure of Technical Efficiency*.

The (C, S) output subvector measure $SF_o(x^j, u^j_{\alpha}, u^j_{\hat{\alpha}} \mid C, S)$ measures efficiency of the subvector $u^j_{\hat{\alpha}}$ produced from x^j, when u^j_{α} is given and when technology satisfies constant returns to scale ($P(\lambda x \mid C, S) = \lambda P(x \mid C, S), \lambda > 0$) and strong disposability of outputs ($v \leq u \in P(x \mid C, S) \implies v \in P(x \mid C, S)$). The measure computes the ratio of the size of the largest feasible expansion of $u^j_{\hat{\alpha}}$ to the size of $u^j_{\hat{\alpha}}$ itself, i.e., $SF_o(x^j, u^j_{\alpha}, u^j_{\hat{\alpha}} \mid C, S) = \parallel SF_o(x^j, u^j_{\alpha}, u^j_{\hat{\alpha}} \mid C, S) \cdot u^j_{\hat{\alpha}} \parallel / \parallel u^j_{\hat{\alpha}} \parallel$. The properties it satisfies are summarized in

(10.1.17)   **Proposition:** Given $P(x^j \mid C, S)$, then for each $j = 1, 2,$
$\cdots, J,$

$SF_o.1$ $SF_o(x^j, u^j_\alpha, \delta u^j_{\hat{\alpha}} \mid C, S) = \delta^{-1} SF_o(x^j, u^j_\alpha, u^j_{\hat{\alpha}} \mid C, S), \delta > 0,$

$SF_o.2$ $SF_o(\lambda x^j, u^j_\alpha, u^j_{\hat{\alpha}} \mid C, S) = \lambda SF_o(x^j, (u^j_\alpha/\lambda), u^j_{\hat{\alpha}} \mid C, S), \lambda > 0,$

$SF_o.3$ $1 \leqq SF_o(x^j, u^j_\alpha, u^j_{\hat{\alpha}} \mid C, S) < +\infty,$

$SF_o.4$ $SF_o(x^j, u^j_\alpha, u^j_{\hat{\alpha}} \mid C, S) = 1 \Longrightarrow (u^j_\alpha, u^j_{\hat{\alpha}}) \in WEff$
$P(x^j \mid C, S),$

$SF_o.5$ $SF_o(x^j, u^j_\alpha, u^j_{\hat{\alpha}} \mid C, S)$ is independent of unit of measurement.

Proof:
$(SF_o.1)$

$$
\begin{aligned}
SF_o(x^j, u^j_\alpha, \delta u^j_{\hat{\alpha}} \mid C, S) &= \max\{\theta : (u^j_\alpha, \theta \delta u^j_{\hat{\alpha}}) \in P(x^j \mid C, S)\} \\
&= \delta^{-1} \max\{\theta \delta : (u^j_\alpha, \theta \delta u^j_{\hat{\alpha}}) \in P(x^j \mid C, S)\} \\
&= \delta^{-1} SF_o(x^j, u^j_\alpha, u^j_{\hat{\alpha}} \mid C, S).
\end{aligned}
$$

$(SF_o.2)$ Since $P(\lambda x \mid C, S) = \lambda P(x \mid C, S), \lambda > 0$, it follows that

$$
\begin{aligned}
SF_o(\lambda x^j, u^j_\alpha, u^j_{\hat{\alpha}} \mid C, S) &= \max\{\theta : (u^j_\alpha, \theta u^j_{\hat{\alpha}}) \in P(\lambda x^j \mid C, S)\} \\
&= \max\{\theta : (u^j_\alpha, \theta u^j_{\hat{\alpha}}) \in \lambda P(x^j \mid C, S)\} \\
&= \max \lambda \{\theta/\lambda : (u^j_\alpha/\lambda, u^j_{\hat{\alpha}} \theta/\lambda) \\
&\qquad \in P(x^j \mid C, S)\} \\
&= \lambda SF_o(x^j, (u^j_\alpha/\lambda), u^j_{\hat{\alpha}} \mid C, S).
\end{aligned}
$$

$(SF_o.3)$ Follows from the fact that $(u^j_\alpha, u^j_{\hat{\alpha}}) \in P(x^j \mid C, S)$ for each $j = 1, 2, \cdots, J$.

$(SF_o.4)$ Clearly $(u^j_\alpha, \theta^{*j} u^j_{\hat{\alpha}}) \in P(x^j \mid C, S)$, where at its maximum, $\theta^{*j} \geqq 1$. If $(u^j_\alpha, \theta^{*j} u^j_{\hat{\alpha}})$ does not belong to $Isoq\ P(x^j \mid C, S)$, then $\exists \delta > 1$ such that $(\delta u^j_\alpha, \delta \theta^{*j} u^j_{\hat{\alpha}}) \in P(x^j \mid C, S)$. Since outputs are strongly disposable and $\delta > 1$, $(u^j_\alpha, \delta \theta^{*j} u^j_{\hat{\alpha}}) \in P(x^j \mid C, S)$, therefore θ^{*j} is not a maximum: this contradiction implies that $(u^j_\alpha, u^j_{\hat{\alpha}}) \in Isoq\ P(x^j \mid C, S)$. The conclusion now follows from Proposition (2.3.5).

$(SF_o.5)$ Consider just one output constraint: $\theta u_{jm} \leqq \sum_{j=1}^J z_j u_{jm}$ and note that the mth output is variable, i.e., an $m \in \hat{\alpha}$. If the unit of measurement is altered, so that $\hat{u}_{jm} = \nu u_{jm}, j = 1, 2, \cdots, J$, then θ and z are not affected.

Q.E.D.

Invoking the piecewise linear (C, S) technology (10.1.15), the (C, S) output subvector measure of technical efficiency can be computed for activity j as the solution to the linear programming problem

$$SF_o(x^j, u^j_\alpha, u^j_{\hat\alpha} \mid C, S) = \max_{\theta, z} \theta \qquad (10.1.18)$$

$$\text{s.t. } u^j_\alpha \leq z M^\alpha$$

$$\theta u^j_{\hat\alpha} \leq z M^{\hat\alpha}$$

$$z N \leq x^j$$

$$z \in \Re^J_+$$

or

$$\max_{\theta, z} \theta$$

$$\text{s.t. } u_{jm} \leq \sum_{j=1}^J z_j u_{jm}, m \in \alpha,$$

$$\theta u_{jm} \leq \sum_{j=1}^J z_j u_{jm}, m \in \hat\alpha,$$

$$\sum_{j=1}^J z_j x_{jn} \leq x_{jn}, n = 1, 2, \cdots, N,$$

$$z_j \geq 0, j = 1, 2, \cdots, J.$$

The (C, S) output subvector measure of technical efficiency is illustrated in Figure 10.3, where the maximizing value of θ is denoted by θ^{*j}.

To continue the generalization of Chapter 4, suppose that, in addition to the input and output matrices, N and M, the prices of the variable output subvector are known and that $r^j_{\hat\alpha} \in \Re^{M^{\hat\alpha}}_+, r^j_{\hat\alpha} \neq 0$. We can compute the maximum revenue that $u_{\hat\alpha}$ can generate, given the (C, S) technology (10.1.15) together with $r^j_{\hat\alpha}, x^j$ and u^j_α.

(10.1.19)   **Definition:** Assume that $u^j_{\hat\alpha} \geq 0$. The function
$$SR(x^j, u^j_\alpha, r^j_{\hat\alpha} \mid C, S) = \max\{r^j_{\hat\alpha} u_{\hat\alpha} : (u^j_\alpha, u_{\hat\alpha}) \in P(x^j \mid C, S)\}, j = 1, 2, \cdots, J,$$
is called the (C, S) *Output Subvector Revenue Function.*

We note that maximum subvector revenue will never exceed maximum revenue when all outputs are allowed to vary, i.e., $SR(x^j, u^j_\alpha, r^j_{\hat\alpha} \mid C, S) \leq R(x^j, r^j \mid C, S)$. Maximum subvector revenue may be computed as the solution to the linear programming problem

$$SR(x^j, u^j_\alpha, r^j_{\hat\alpha} \mid C, S) = \max_{z, u_{\hat\alpha}} r^j_{\hat\alpha} u_{\hat\alpha} \qquad (10.1.20)$$

$$\text{s.t. } u^j_\alpha \leq z M^\alpha$$

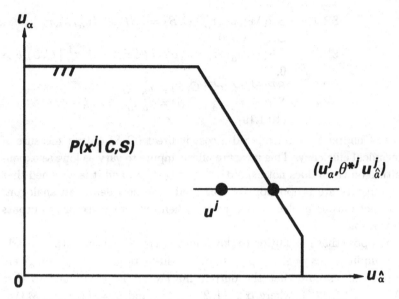

Fig. 10.3. *The (C,S) Output Subvector Measure of Technical Efficiency*

$$u_{\hat{\alpha}} \leqq zM^{\hat{\alpha}}$$
$$zN \leqq x^j$$
$$z \in \Re_+^J$$

or

$$\max_{z,u_m} \sum_{m \in \hat{\alpha}} r_{jm} u_m$$

$$\text{s.t. } u_{jm} \leqq \sum_{j=1}^{J} z_j u_{jm}, m = 1, 2, \cdots, M^{\alpha},$$

$$u_m \leqq \sum_{j=1}^{J} z_j u_{jm}, m = M^{\alpha} + 1, \cdots, M,$$

$$\sum_{j=1}^{J} z_j x_{jn} \leqq x_{jn}, n = 1, 2, \cdots, N,$$

$$z_j \geqq 0, j = 1, 2, \cdots, J.$$

The (C, S) subvector revenue function satisfies the following properties. Proofs are left to the reader.

(10.1.21)   **Proposition**: Given $P(x^j \mid C, S)$, then for each $j = 1, 2, \cdots, J,$

SR.1 $SR(\lambda x^j, u_\alpha^j, r_{\hat{\alpha}}^j \mid C, S) = \lambda SR(x^j, (u_\alpha^j/\lambda), r_{\hat{\alpha}}^j \mid C, S), \lambda > 0,$

SR.2 $SR(x^j, u_\alpha^j, \theta r_{\hat{\alpha}}^j \mid C, S) = \theta SR(x^j, u_\alpha^j, r_{\hat{\alpha}}^j \mid C, S), \theta > 0,$

SR.3 $SR(x^j, u_\alpha^j, r_{\hat{\alpha}}^j \mid C, S) \geqq r_{\hat{\alpha}}^j u_{\hat{\alpha}}^j,$

SR.4 $SR(x^j, u_\alpha^j, r_{\hat{\alpha}}^j \mid C, S) = r_{\hat{\alpha}}^j u_{\hat{\alpha}}^j \iff u_{\hat{\alpha}}^j$ solves (10.1.19).

In Chapter 6 we introduced a cost indirect (C, S) output measure of technical efficiency. This measure allows inputs to vary as long as expenditure on them does not exceed a target cost Q^j, and it is assumed that all outputs are proportionally increased. We now define an analogous indirect output measure appropriate when only a subvector of outputs is variable.

Suppose that in addition to the input matrix N and the output matrix M, input prices $p^j \in \Re_+^N, p^j \neq 0$, and positive target cost Q^j are given. Moreover, assume that the output matrix M is partitioned so that $M = (M^\alpha, M^{\hat{\alpha}})$, where $\alpha \subseteq \{1, 2, \cdots, M\}$ and $\hat{\alpha} = \{1, 2, \cdots, M\}\backslash\alpha$. We correspondingly write $u = (u_\alpha, u_{\hat{\alpha}})$, where u_α is fixed and $u_{\hat{\alpha}}$ is variable. The radial cost indirect output subvector efficiency measure, which is calculated relative to the (C, S) indirect technology

$$IP(p/Q \mid C, S) = \{(u_\alpha, u_{\hat{\alpha}}) : u_\alpha \leqq zM^\alpha, u_{\hat{\alpha}} \leqq zM^{\hat{\alpha}},$$
$$zN \leqq x, px \leqq Q, z \in \Re_+^J\}, \qquad (10.1.22)$$

is defined in

(10.1.23)   **Definition:** The function
$$SIF_o(p^j/Q^j, u_\alpha^j, u_{\hat{\alpha}}^j \mid C, S) = \max\{\theta : (u_\alpha^j, \theta u_{\hat{\alpha}}^j) \in IP(p^j/Q^j \mid C, S)\}, j = 1, 2, \cdots, J,$$
is called the (C, S) *Cost Indirect Output Subvector Measure of Technical Efficiency.*

$SIF_o(p^j/Q^j, u_\alpha^j, u_{\hat{\alpha}}^j \mid C, S)$ measures the efficiency of an output subvector $u_{\hat{\alpha}}^j$ in the presence of a fixed output subvector u_α^j and a budget restriction $p^j x \leqq Q^j$ under constant returns to scale and strong disposability of outputs. It does this by computing the ratio of the size of the largest feasible expansion of $u_{\hat{\alpha}}^j$ in $IP(p^j/Q^j \mid C, S)$ to the size of itself, i.e., $SIF_o(p^j/Q^j, u_\alpha^j, u_{\hat{\alpha}}^j \mid C, S) = \parallel SIF_o(p^j/Q^j, u_\alpha^j, u_{\hat{\alpha}}^j \mid C, S) \cdot u_{\hat{\alpha}}^j \parallel / \parallel u_{\hat{\alpha}}^j \parallel$. Figure 10.4 illustrates.

We list the properties of $SIF_o(p^j/Q^j, u_\alpha^j, u_{\hat{\alpha}}^j \mid C, S)$ below, but leave the proofs to the reader.

(10.1.24)   **Proposition:** Given $IP(p^j/Q^j \mid C, S)$, then for each $j = 1, 2, \cdots, J,$

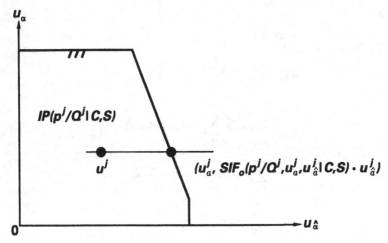

Fig. 10.4. *The (C,S) Cost Indirect Output Subvector Measure of Technical Efficiency*

SIF$_o$.1 $SIF_o(p^j/Q^j, u_\alpha^j, \delta u_{\hat{\alpha}}^j \mid C, S) = \delta^{-1} SIF_o(p^j/Q^j, u_\alpha^j, u_{\hat{\alpha}}^j \mid C, S), \delta > 0,$

SIF$_o$.2 $SIF_o(p^j/\lambda Q^j, u_\alpha^j, u_{\hat{\alpha}}^j \mid C, S) = \lambda SIF_o(p^j/Q^j, (u_\alpha^j/\lambda), u_{\hat{\alpha}}^j \mid C, S), \lambda > 0,$

SIF$_o$.3 $1 \leqq SIF_o(p^j/Q^j, u_\alpha^j, u_{\hat{\alpha}}^j \mid C, S) < +\infty,$

SIF$_o$.4 $SIF_o(p^j/Q^j, u_\alpha^j, u_{\hat{\alpha}}^j \mid C, S) = 1 \implies (u_\alpha^j, u_{\hat{\alpha}}^j) \in WEff\ IP(p^j/Q^j \mid C, S),$

SIF$_o$.5 $SIF_o(p^j/Q^j, u_\alpha^j, u_{\hat{\alpha}}^j \mid C, S)$ is independent of unit of measurement.

Employing the piecewise linear technology (10.1.22), the (C, S) cost indirect output subvector measure of technical efficiency can be computed for each observation j as the solution to the linear programming problem

$$SIF_o(p^j/Q^j, u_\alpha^j, u_{\hat{\alpha}}^j \mid C, S) = \max_{\theta, z, x} \theta \qquad (10.1.25)$$

$$\text{s.t. } u_\alpha \leqq zM^\alpha$$
$$\theta u_{\hat{\alpha}} \leqq zM^{\hat{\alpha}}$$
$$zN \leqq x$$
$$p^j x \leqq Q^j$$
$$z \in \Re_+^J$$

or

$$\max_{\theta, z, x} \theta$$

$$\text{s.t. } u_{jm} \leqq \sum_{j=1}^{J} z_j u_{jm}, m \in \alpha,$$

$$\theta u_{jm} \leqq \sum_{j=1}^{J} z_j u_{jm}, m \in \hat{\alpha},$$

$$\sum_{j=1}^{J} z_j x_{jn} \leqq x_n, n = 1, 2, \cdots, N,$$

$$\sum_{n=1}^{N} p_{jn} x_n \leqq Q^j,$$

$$z_j \geqq 0, j = 1, 2, \cdots, J.$$

Assume that in addition to the input matrix N, the output matrix M, input prices $p \in \Re_+^N, p \neq 0$, and target cost Q, prices of the variable output subvector are known. Then we can compute the maximum revenue that $u_{\hat{\alpha}}$ can generate under the budget constraint $px \leqq Q$, when the technology is (C, S).

(10.1.26)   **Definition:** The function
$SIR(p^j/Q^j, u_\alpha^j, r_{\hat{\alpha}}^j \mid C, S) = \max\{r_{\hat{\alpha}}^j u_{\hat{\alpha}} : (u_\alpha^j, u_{\hat{\alpha}}) \in IP(p^j/Q^j \mid C, S)\}, j = 1, 2, \cdots, J,$
is called the (C, S) *Cost Indirect Subvector Revenue Function.*

This function is computed as the solution to the linear programming problem

$$SIR(p^j/Q^j, u_\alpha^j, r_{\hat{\alpha}}^j \mid C, S) = \max_{z, u_{\hat{\alpha}}, x} r_{\hat{\alpha}}^j u_{\hat{\alpha}} \qquad (10.1.27)$$

$$\text{s.t. } u_\alpha^j \leqq zM^\alpha$$

$$u_{\hat{\alpha}} \leqq zM^{\hat{\alpha}}$$

$$zN \leqq x$$

$$p^j x \leqq Q^j$$

$$z \in \Re_+^J$$

or

$$\max_{z, u_m, x} \sum_{m \in \hat{\alpha}} r_{jm} u_m$$

$$\text{s.t.} \quad u_{jm} \leqq \sum_{j=1}^{J} z_j u_{jm}, m \in \alpha,$$

$$u_m \leqq \sum_{j=1}^{J} z_j u_{jm}, m \in \hat{\alpha},$$

$$\sum_{j=1}^{J} z_j x_{jn} \leqq x_n, n = 1, 2, \cdots, N,$$

$$\sum_{n=1}^{N} p_{jn} x_n \leqq Q^j,$$

$$z_j \geqq 0, j = 1, 2, \cdots, J.$$

The solution to the cost indirect subvector revenue maximization problem yields the maximum revenue obtainable under a budget constraint. Its properties are listed in

(10.1.28)   **Proposition**: Given $IP(p^j/Q^j \mid C, S)$, then for each $j = 1, 2, \cdots, J$,

SIR.1 $SIR(p^j/\lambda Q^j, u_\alpha^j, r_{\hat{\alpha}}^j \mid C, S) = \lambda SIR(p^j/Q^j, (u_\alpha^j/\lambda), r_{\hat{\alpha}}^j \mid C, S), \lambda > 0,$

SIR.2 $SIR(p^j/Q^j, u_\alpha^j, \theta r_{\hat{\alpha}}^j \mid C, S) = \theta SIR(p^j/Q^j, u_\alpha^j, r_{\hat{\alpha}}^j \mid C, S), \theta > 0,$

SIR.3 $SIR(p^j/Q^j, u_\alpha^j, r_{\hat{\alpha}}^j \mid C, S) \geqq r_{\hat{\alpha}}^j u_{\hat{\alpha}}^j,$

SIR.4 $SIR(p^j/Q^j, u_\alpha^j, r_{\hat{\alpha}}^j \mid C, S) = r_{\hat{\alpha}}^j u_{\hat{\alpha}}^j \iff u_{\hat{\alpha}}^j$ solves (10.1.26).

The proof of this proposition is left for the reader.

In this section we have considered only the (C, S) technology. However it is clear that input subvector efficiency may be calculated relative to the other specifications of technology introduced in Chapter 3. The properties of the resulting efficiency measures and cost functions will change in ways which the reader should be able to anticipate.

10.2   Cost- or Revenue-Constrained Profit Efficiency

The theory of cost-constrained profit maximization – or as it is also known, the theory of expenditure-constrained profit maximization – is an extension of the cost indirect model discussed in Chapter 6. In this section we develop a short-run version, in accordance with Section 10.1, and assume that some inputs are fixed while the others are variable, but cost (expenditure) constrained. We develop the model under variable returns to scale. Of course this is not a necessary condition, and constant returns to scale or nonincreasing returns to scale may be imposed, a task which we leave to the reader.

Suppose there are $j = 1, 2, \cdots, J$ observations of inputs x^j and outputs u^j, i.e., the input matrix N and the output matrix M are known. This information can be used to form a nonparametric frontier technology that satisfies variable returns to scale and strong disposability of inputs and outputs, namely

$$(GR \mid V, S) = \left\{ (x, u) : u_m \leq \sum_{j=1}^{J} z_j u_{jm}, \right. \tag{10.2.1}$$

$$m = 1, 2, \cdots, M,$$

$$\sum_{j=1}^{J} z_j x_{jn} \leq x_n, n = 1, 2, \cdots, N,$$

$$\left. z_j \geq 0, j = 1, 2, \cdots, J, \sum_{j=1}^{J} z_j = 1 \right\}.$$

To formalize our short-run cost-constrained profit maximization model, suppose that $x = (x_\alpha, x_{\hat{\alpha}})$, where $\alpha \subseteq \{1, 2, \cdots, N\}$ and $\hat{\alpha} = \{1, 2, \cdots, N\} \backslash \alpha$. The input subvector x_α is the vector of fixed inputs, while $x_{\hat{\alpha}}$ is the vector of variable but constrained inputs.

We begin by showing how to model variable profit maximization when these constraints are not imposed. Then we show how to calculate the impact of the expenditure constraints in terms of lost profit. Thus we first form a benchmark profit level when $x_{\hat{\alpha}}$ is not cost constrained. Suppose that output prices $r^j \in \Re_+^M, r^j \neq 0$, and variable input prices $p_{\hat{\alpha}}^j \in \Re_+^{N_{\hat{\alpha}}}, p_{\hat{\alpha}}^j \neq 0$, are known. We may now calculate variable profit for observation $j = 1, 2, \cdots, J$, as the solution to the linear programming problem

$$\pi(r^j, x_\alpha^j, p_{\hat{\alpha}}^j \mid V, S) = \max_{z, u, x_{\hat{\alpha}}} \left(\sum_{m=1}^{M} r_{jm} u_m - \sum_{n \in \hat{\alpha}} p_{jn} x_n \right) \tag{10.2.2}$$

$$\text{s.t. } u_m \leq \sum_{j=1}^{J} z_j u_{jm}, m = 1, 2, \cdots, M,$$

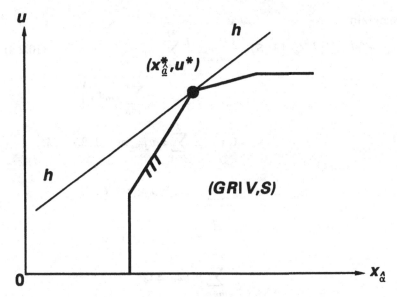

Fig. 10.5. *Variable Profit Maximization*

$$\sum_{j=1}^{J} z_j x_{jn} \leqq x_{jn}, n \in \alpha,$$

$$\sum_{j=1}^{J} z_j x_{jn} \leqq x_n, n \in \hat{\alpha},$$

$$z_j \geqq 0, j = 1, 2, \cdots, J,$$

$$\sum_{j=1}^{J} z_j = 1.$$

We illustrate problem (10.2.2) in Figure 10.5, where output and variable input $x_{\hat{\alpha}}$ are shown. The isoprofit line that maximizes variable profit relative to the technology is denoted by hh, and the maximum is attained at $(x_{\hat{\alpha}}^*, u^*)$.

Now let us assume that the subvector $x_{\hat{\alpha}}$ is expenditure-constrained, i.e.,

$$\sum_{n \in \hat{\alpha}} p_{jn} x_n \leqq Q^j, \tag{10.2.3}$$

where Q^j is allowed cost or expenditure in the variable account. When this constraint is added to the profit maximization problem (10.2.2) we obtain

$$\hat{\pi}(r^j, x_\alpha^j, p_{\hat{\alpha}}^j, Q^j \mid V, S) = \max_{z,u,x_{\hat{\alpha}}} \left(\sum_{m=1}^{M} r_{jm} u_m \right.$$ (10.2.4)

$$\left. - \sum_{n \in \hat{\alpha}} p_{jn} x_n \right)$$

$$\text{s.t. } u_m \leqq \sum_{j=1}^{J} z_j u_{jm}, m = 1, 2, \cdots, M,$$

$$\sum_{j=1}^{J} z_j x_{jn} \leqq x_{jn}, n \in \alpha,$$

$$\sum_{j=1}^{J} z_j x_{jn} \leqq x_n, n \in \hat{\alpha},$$

$$\sum_{n \in \hat{\alpha}} p_{jn} x_n \leqq Q^j,$$

$$z_j \geqq 0, j = 1, 2, \cdots, J,$$

$$\sum_{j=1}^{J} z_j = 1.$$

This problem is illustrated in Figure 10.6. The feature added to Figure 10.5 is the binding expenditure constraint denoted by ee. The constrained variable profit maximization solution is denoted by $(x_{\hat{\alpha}}^{**}, u^{**})$, which differs from $(x_{\hat{\alpha}}^*, u^*)$ due to the constraint ee.

The two profit maximization problems (10.2.2) and (10.2.4) may now be combined to form the following measure of the impact of the cost constraint on maximized profit, namely

$$\hat{\pi}(r^j, x_\alpha^j, p_{\hat{\alpha}}^j, Q^j \mid V, S) - \pi(r^j, x_\alpha^j, p_{\hat{\alpha}}^j \mid V, S) \leqq 0.$$ (10.2.5)

This section illustrates how to model short-run profit maximization with and without expenditure constraints for variable inputs. The reader is invited to generalize or customize: one could model long-run profit maximization or profit maximization restricted to meet revenue targets or minimum expenditure constraints, for example.

10.3   Measures of Productive Capacity and Its Utilization

Leif Johansen (1968; 50,57) posed the question: "Does a measure of capacity exist according to the proposed definition?" and he continued:

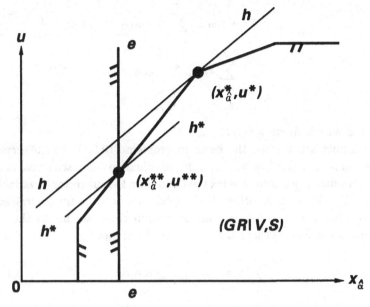

Fig. 10.6. *Cost-Constrained Variable Profit Maximization*

The first, and most natural definition, describes *the capacity of existing plant and equipment*. According to this definition, capacity is the maximum amount that can be produced per unit of time with existing plant and equipment, *provided that the availability of variable factors of production is not restricted.* Let us call this *plant capacity*.

The purpose of this section is to develop a linear programming model to measure plant capacity and plant capacity utilization based on Johansen's definition. We do not, however, restrict ourselves to a single output as Johansen did, but rather allow for the technology to produce multiple outputs from multiple inputs. In particular we alter the output based (C, S) measure of technical efficiency defined in Chapter 4, see (4.1.3), to accommodate our needs.

We assume that there are $j = 1, 2, \cdots, J$ observations on outputs $u^j \in \Re_+^M$ and inputs $x^j \in \Re_+^N$, and we suppose that the input vector x^j consists of two subvectors, the fixed factors x_α^j and the variable factors $x_{\hat\alpha}^j$ so that $x^j = (x_\alpha^j, x_{\hat\alpha}^j)$.

In order to remove possible inefficiency in the measure of productive capacity, we first calculate the (C, S) output-based measure of technical efficiency for observations $j = 1, 2, \cdots, J$.

$$F_o(x^j, u^j \mid C, S) = \max_{\theta, z} \theta \qquad (10.3.1)$$

$$\text{s.t. } \theta u_{jm} \leqq \sum_{j=1}^{J} z_j u_{jm}, m = 1, 2, \cdots, M,$$

$$\sum_{j=1}^{J} z_j x_{jn} \leqq x_{jn}, n = 1, 2, \cdots, N,$$

$$z_j \geqq 0, j = 1, 2, \cdots, J.$$

This measure is discussed in Section 4.1.

All inputs are treated the same in problem (10.3.1), i.e., observed values serve as upper bounds. In order to calculate Johansen's notion of capacity output, we need to relax the bounds on the subvector of variable inputs, $x_{\hat{\alpha}}$. In order to allow the variable inputs to be unconstrained, and to obtain a measure of input utilization rates, we model the $x_{\hat{\alpha}}^j$ constraints as follows (note that $n \in \alpha$ are fixed inputs)

$$\sum_{j=1}^{J} z_j x_{jn} = \lambda_{jn} x_{jn}, n \in \hat{\alpha}, \tag{10.3.2}$$

where $\lambda_{jn} \geqq 0$, for each $n \in \hat{\alpha}$, which allows the bound on $x_{\hat{\alpha}}$ to vary.

Using these modified variable input constraints, we may now compute the maximum proportionate increase in outputs when inputs $x_{\hat{\alpha}}$ are allowed to vary, but bounding x_α by their observed values for each observation j, by calculating

$$\hat{F}_o(x_f^j, u^j \mid C, S) = \max_{\theta, z, \lambda} \theta \tag{10.3.3}$$

$$\text{s.t. } \theta u_{jm} \leqq \sum_{j=1}^{J} z_j u_{jm}, m = 1, 2, \cdots, M,$$

$$\sum_{j=1}^{J} z_j x_{jn} \leqq x_{jn}, n \in \alpha,$$

$$\sum_{j=1}^{J} z_j x_{jn} = \lambda_{jn} x_{jn}, n \in \hat{\alpha},$$

$$z_j \geqq 0, j = 1, 2, \cdots, J,$$

$$\lambda_{jn} \geqq 0, n \in \hat{\alpha}.$$

First, note that if "*" denotes optimum, then $(\theta^{*j} u^j)$ equals the maximum amount of u^j that can be produced when variable inputs are unrestricted, i.e., it provides a multioutput definition of plant capacity as defined by Johansen.

Note also that λ_{jn}^* denotes the capacity utilization rate of the nth variable input for the jth firm, for $x_{jn} > 0$, $n \in \hat{\alpha}$. More formally, we have

(10.3.4) **Definition:** For producer j the variable
$$\lambda_{jn}^* = \frac{\sum_{j=1}^{J} z_j^* x_{jv_i}}{x_{jv_i}}, n \in \hat{\alpha}.$$
is called the *i-th Variable Input Utilization Rate.*

Consequently, λ_{jn}^* measures the ratio of optimal use of input x_{jn} which is equal to $\sum_{j=1}^{J} z_j^* x_{jn}$ to observed use, x_{jn}.

Finally, we arrive at the desired

(10.3.5) **Definition:** For producer j the ratio
$$F_o(x^j, u^j \mid C, S)/\hat{F}_o(x_f^j, u^j \mid C, S), j = 1, \cdots, J,$$
is called the *Plant Capacity Utilization Measure.*

Definition (10.3.5) is the ratio of (10.3.1) and (10.3.3). This measure is consistent with Johansen's notions of capacity, modified to allow for multiproduct technology.

Although the measures of multiproduct productive capacity and utilization were defined for technology satisfying constant returns to scale and strong disposability, one could also define analogs relative to less restrictive reference technologies.

10.4 Efficiency Gains from Combination of Firms and Product Diversification

The thought that it may be efficient to combine two or more activities or firms has a long history in economics. This is distinct from increasing the size by scaling of a firm or an activity, which we refer to as scale properties. In particular, the notions of sub- and superadditivity have been introduced to model gains from combining firms which (may) produce different output bundles. If firms completely specialized in different outputs are combined to form one diversified firm, these super- and sub-additivity notions become the special case of identification of economies or diseconomies of scope.

A wonderful introduction to the economics of diversification is provided by Penrose (1959; Ch. VII), who deplored the inadequate treatment then accorded this topic in traditional economic analysis. In this section we introduce a nonparametric model that can be used to compute gains from combination of firms and diversification of products.

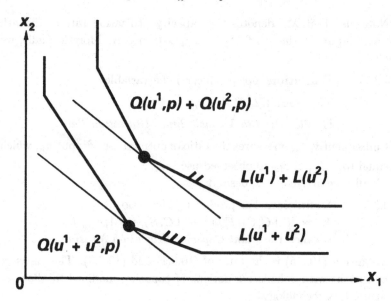

Fig. 10.7. *Superadditivity of Input Sets*

However before presenting the model, we provide an illustrative example.

Suppose there are two firms producing output vectors $u^1, u^2 \in \Re_+^M, u^1, u^2 \neq 0$, respectively, and suppose that they face the same input prices $p \in \Re_+^N, p \neq 0$. If there exists a cost function Q such that

$$Q(u^1 + u^2, p) \leqq Q(u^1, p) + Q(u^2, p), \qquad (10.4.1)$$

we say that the cost function is subadditive (in this particular case the cost function exhibits economies of scope). We note that this definition may be generalized to more than two firms. From duality theory, subadditivity of the cost function for all $p \in \Re_+^N$ is equivalent to superadditivity of the input set, i.e.,

$$L(u^1) + L(u^2) \subseteq L(u^1 + u^2). \qquad (10.4.2)$$

Thus estimating efficiency gains due to combination or diversification can be done by comparing the frontier of $L(u^1 + u^2)$ with the frontier of $L(u^1) + L(u^2)$ or by comparing $Q(u^1 + u^2, p)$ to $Q(u^1, p) + Q(u^2, p)$. Figure 10.7 illustrates these two comparisons. $L(u^1) + L(u^2)$ is contained in the combined or diversified technology $L(u^1 + u^2)$. The cost functions associated with the two technologies are $Q(u^1, p) + Q(u^2, p)$ and $Q(u^1 + u^2, p)$. One measure of the gains is given by $(Q(u^1, p) + Q(u^2, p))/Q(u^1 + u^2, p)$.

In defining subadditivity of the cost function (10.4.1) and superadditivity of the input set (10.4.2), the "specialized" and "diversified" firms are defined relative to the same cost or input correspondence, respectively. Here however, we apply a more general notion which we call diversification, and allow firms of different types to have different cost functions. Thus we compare $Q^D(u^1 + u^2, p)$ and $(Q^1(u^1, p) + Q^2(u^2, p))$, where $Q^D(\bullet)$ represents cost for diversified firms.

Suppose there are two types of firm. The first type produces a proper subset of the outputs while the second type produces all outputs. A typical output vector of type one is then of the form $(u_1, u_2, 0, u_4, \cdots, u_M)$ while the second type has all $u_m > 0, m = 1, \cdots, M$. Denote the observations of type one by $(x^k, u^k), k = 1, \cdots, K$, and observations of type two by $(x^j, u^j), j = 1, \cdots, J$. To determine if there are gains from diversification, we compute for each specialized firm $k = 1, \cdots, K$ the function

$$Q(u^k, p) = \min_{z, x} \sum_{n=1}^{N} p_n x_n \tag{10.4.3}$$

$$\text{s.t. } u_{km} \leqq \sum_{k=1}^{K} z_k u_{km}, m = 1, \cdots, M,$$

$$\sum_{k=1}^{K} z_k x_{kn} \leqq x_n, n = 1, \cdots, N,$$

$$z_k \geqq 0, k = 1, \cdots, K.$$

Thus for each specialized firm we obtain the minimum cost $Q(u^k, p)$ of producing u^k given the input prices p.

Suppose we want to determine the gains from diversification of a subset of the $k = 1, \cdots, K$ specialized firms, say $k = 1, \cdots, L$, where $L \leqq K$. Then we need to compute $Q^D(\sum_{k=1}^{L} u^k, p)$ relative to the *Diversified Technology* given by

$$L^D(u \mid C, S) = \left\{ x : u_m \leqq \sum_{j=1}^{J} z_j u_{jm}, m = 1, \cdots, M, \tag{10.4.4} \right.$$

$$\left. \sum_{j=1}^{J} z_j x_{jn} \leqq x_n, n = 1, \cdots, N, z_j \geqq 0, j = 1, \cdots, J \right\}.$$

This diversified technology is constructed exclusively from observations of type two, i.e., those producing a completely diversified vector of outputs. In contrast, the technology relative to which we calculate $Q(u^k, p)$

for each specialized firm, $k = 1, \cdots, K$, is constructed exclusively from data from the specialized firms.

To calculate possible gains from diversification, we would like to compare the sum of the minimum costs of the specialized firms to the minimum costs of a comparable diversified firm. This is done by solving the (out of sample) linear programming problem

$$Q^D \left(\sum_{k=1}^{L} u^k, p \right) = \min_{z,x} \sum_{n=1}^{N} p_n x_n \tag{10.4.5}$$

$$\text{s.t.} \sum_{k=1}^{L} u_{km} \leqq \sum_{j=1}^{J} z_j u_{jm}, m = 1, \cdots, M,$$

$$\sum_{j=1}^{J} z_j x_{jn} \leqq x_n, n = 1, \cdots, N,$$

$$z_j \geqq 0, j = 1, \cdots, J.$$

This problem gives the minimum cost of a (hypothetical) firm which produces the sum of the outputs of the specialized firms (or some subset of those specialized firms), but faces the same technology as the diversified firms, i.e., $L^D(u \mid C, S)$. To see this, note that the sum of specialized firms' output, $\sum_{k=1}^{L} u_{km}$, is compared to convex combinations of observed diversified firms' output, $\sum_{j=1}^{J} z_j u_{jm}$, for each $m = 1, 2, \cdots, M$. Recall that k indexes specialized firms and j indexes diversified firms.

Given the calculation (10.4.3) and (10.4.5),

(10.4.6)   **Definition**: The ratio
$$\sum_{k=1}^{L} Q(u^k, p) \Big/ Q^D \left(\sum_{k=1}^{L} u^k, p \right)$$
is called the *Measure of Gains from Diversification*.

If (10.4.6) is less than one, we say that there are diseconomies of diversification. If (10.4.6) is greater than one, there are economies of diversification. In the special case when each specialized firm produces only one unique output, our measure of gains from diversification is equivalent to a measure of economies of scope. Note, however, that in contrast to traditional cost function measures, our measure allows specialized and diversified firms to have different cost/production structures. Also since our measure identifies frontier performance, gains from diversification are best interpreted as potential gains.

An alternative approach may also be used to identify gains from diversification in the programming framework. Here we introduce a new type of reference technology which we refer to as the Koopmans technology. If we define this technology for the subset of firms which are "specialized" we have

$$L^S(u \mid K, S) = \{x : u_m \leqq \sum_{k=1}^{K} z_k u_{km}, m = 1, 2, \cdots, M, \quad (10.4.7)$$

$$\sum_{k=1}^{K} z_k x_{kn} \leqq x_n, n = 1, 2, \cdots, N,$$

$$0 \leqq z_k \leqq 1, k = 1, 2, \cdots, K\}.$$

This technology differs from the (C, S) type technology $L^D(u \mid C, S)$ in (10.4.4) in two ways: (1) it constructs technology from data for specialized "k" firms instead of diversified "j" firms, and (2) it imposes the restriction that the elements of the vector of intensity variables be between 0 and 1 rather than merely nonnegative. Constraining those elements to be between 0 and 1 serves to construct a technology which satisfies "additivity" rather than constant returns to scale. Indeed, if we define $L^S(u \mid K, S)$ and $L^D(u \mid C, S)$ with respect to the same set of observations, we have

$$L(u \mid K, S) \subseteq L(u \mid C, S), \quad (10.4.8)$$

or equivalently, $(GR \mid K, S) \subseteq (GR \mid C, S)$, where $(GR \mid K, S)$ is defined as the set of all (x, u) which satisfy the constraints in (10.4.7). This relationship is illustrated in Figure 10.8 for $M = N = 1$.

In this figure, the boundary of the (C, S) technology is a cone, reflecting constant returns to scale, i.e., the ability to multiply or scale any observation of data. The frontier of the (K, S) technology reflects the fact that observations of data may be added, as at point $(a + b)$, where $z = (z_a, z_b) = (1, 1)$, but not scaled or multiplied by factors greater than unity.

Thus $L^S(u^k \mid K, S)$ yields a technology which satisfies additivity. That is, it constructs hypothetical diversified firms which are the sum of specialized firms. If we then compare our "real" diversified firms (or their frontiers) to the frontier of $L^S(u^k \mid K, S)$, we can determine whether the diversified technology is superadditive, see (10.4.2). This is accomplished by solving the following out of sample problem

$$F_i^S(u^k, x^k \mid K, S) = \min\{\lambda : \lambda x^k \in L^S(u^k \mid K, S)\} \quad (10.4.9)$$

calculated for each observation $k = 1, \cdots, K$ of diversified firms as

$$F_i^S(u^k, x^k \mid K, S) = \min \lambda \quad (10.4.10)$$

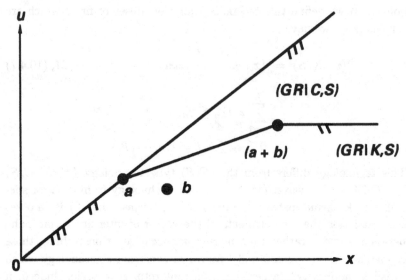

Fig. 10.8. *Comparison of Koopmans' (K, S) and (C, S) Technologies*

$$\text{s.t. } u_{km} \leqq \sum_{j=1}^{J} z_j u_{jm}, m = 1, \cdots, M,$$

$$\sum_{j=1}^{J} z_j x_{jn} \leqq \lambda x_{kn}, n = 1, \cdots, N,$$

$$0 \leqq z_j \leqq 1, j = 1, \cdots, J.$$

If $F_i^S(u^k, x^k \mid K, S) = 1$, for observation k, then at observed output mix at k, diversified technology is additive, i.e., neither sub- nor superadditive. If $F_i^S(u^k, x^k \mid K, S) > 1$, then technology is superadditive at the output mix observed at k. In Figure 10.8, the observation at a would be an example of $F_i^S(u^a, x^a \mid K, S) > 1$, since a is "outside" the additive technology $L(u^1) + L(u^2)$. $F_i^S(u^k, x^k \mid K, S) < 1$ would indicate subadditivity of the input set, i.e., diseconomies of diversification.

Note that the two methods described here both employ out of sample methods, and both yield local measures of diversification. The first method compares a hypothetical diversified firm (constructed as the sum of specialized firms) with the technology constructed from "real" diversified firms. The second method compares "real" diversified firms with an additive technology constructed from specialized firms. Although the first method made comparisons on the basis of cost and the second on the basis of technical efficiency, extensions of the first method to compare on the basis of input-based technical efficiency (or revenue or output-based technical efficiency) are possible and left to the interested reader. Similar extensions are possible using the second method.

10.5 References to the Literature

In the traditional theory of the firm, the short-run problem of efficiently allocating variable inputs in the presence of fixed inputs is well known. A recent collection of studies exploring many variants of this problem is Berndt and Fuss (1986). The empirical efficiency measurement literature contains many studies in which categorical or exogenously fixed variables are treated as being controllable, a notable example being Bessent, Bessent, Kennington, and Reagan (1982). Farrell (1957) recognized the difficulties caused by such variables, which he called "quasifactors." However he dealt inadequately with such variables, as was pointed out by Hall and Winsten in their comments on his paper and in expanded form in Hall and Winsten (1959), in which they explicitly distinguish "target efficiency variables" under the control of management from other variables. Formal measures of subvector efficiency were proposed by Kopp (1981), who called them "single-factor" measures, and by Färe, Lovell, and Zieschang (1983), who extended single-factor measures to what they called "asymmetric" measures. Subsequently Banker and Morey (1986a,b) and Kamakura (1988) have developed linear programming models for subvector efficiency measurement in the case of exogenously fixed and categorical variables. A recent generalization of these models is Adolphson, Cornia, and Walters (1990).

The distinctions among exogenously fixed inputs and outputs, categorical variables, and institutional or environmental variables are not always clear. Consequently two different approaches to the incorporation of such uncontrollable variables have been developed. One, represented by the approach we have used in Section 10.1, and also by the DEA models of Banker and Morey and Kamakura, is to incorporate the uncontrollable variables in the efficiency measurement calculations. This approach corresponds roughly to the inclusion of dummy variables and other control variables in econometric analysis. The second approach deletes the uncontrollable variables from the efficiency measurement stage, usually on the grounds that they are not under the control of management, and employs them in a second stage regression analysis in an effort to explain variation in measured efficiency. Empirical applications of the first approach include Banker and Morey (1986a) (fast food outlets), Banker and Morey (1986b) (branch banks), Deprins (1989) and Deprins and Simar (1989a, 1989b) (European railways), and DeFourny, Lovell, and N'Gbo (1992) and Linvill (1991) (European workers' cooperatives). Applications of the two-stage approach include Byrnes, Färe, Grosskopf, and Lovell (1988) (coal mining), DeFourny (1988) (French workers' cooperatives), Kalirajan and Shand (1988) (Indian agriculture), Sexton et al. (1988) (VA hospitals), Banker and Johnston (1989) (U.S. airlines), Lovell, Walters, and Wood (1989) (secondary education in the U.S.), and Dusansky and Wilson (1989, 1990) (health care). An interesting comparison of the one-stage and two-stage approaches is provided by McCarty and Yaisawarng (1993), who explore the effect of student socioeconomic status on the performance of school districts.

References to the literatures on profit efficiency, and revenue or cost constraints, appear in Chapters 8, 5 and 6, respectively. Models of expenditure-constrained profit maximization have been developed by Lee and Chambers (1986, 1988) and Färe and Sawyer (1988). The treatment in Section 10.2 is closely related to that of Färe, Grosskopf, and Lee (1990). All of these studies contain applications to U.S. agriculture.

The literature on productive capacity and its rate of utilization is voluminous; a representative recent analysis with application to the U.S. automotive industry is Morrison (1985). An interesting attempt to link capacity utilization measurement and efficiency measurement is Hulten (1986). The capacity utilization model developed in Section 10.3 is based on work of Färe (1984a), and Färe, Grosskopf, and Kokkelenberg (1989), who apply the techniques to Illinois electric utilities. Another empirical application, to Michigan hospitals, is Färe, Grosskopf, and Valdmanis (1989).

Most current literature on the benefits of diversification stem from the contestable markets literature spawned by the work of Baumol, Panzar, and Willig (1982) and Sharkey (1982). Our approach is more influenced by the work of McFadden (1978). Section 10.4 extends previous analysis of Färe (1986, 1988b) and Färe and Primont (1988).

A closely related approach which also uses a programming approach and out of sample techniques has been applied to Illinois grain farms (Grosskopf, Hayes, and Yaisawarng (1989)), municipalities (Grosskopf and Yaisawarng (1990)), banks (Ferrier, Grosskopf, Hayes, and Yaisawarng (1990)) and hospitals (Byrnes, Grosskopf, and Valdmanis (1991)).

A

Standard Notations and Mathematical Appendix

Let A and B be two sets, we mean by

$\in$	$a \in A$	a is an element in A;
$\notin$	$a \notin A$	a is not an element in A;
$\subseteq$	$A \subseteq B$	A is a subset of B;
$\emptyset$	$A = \emptyset$	A is an empty set;
$\{a \in A: *\}$		the subset of A formed by the elements satisfying property *;
$\cap$	$A \cap B$	$\{x : x \in A \text{ and } x \in B\}$;
$\cup$	$A \cup B$	$\{x : x \in A \text{ or } x \in B\}$;
$\backslash$	$A \backslash B$	$\{x : x \in A, x \notin B\}$;
$+$	$A + B$	$A + B = \{z : a \in A, b \in B, z = a + b\}$;
$\Re^N$		Euclidean space of dimension N;
$\geqq$		$x, y \in \Re^N, x \geqq y$ if and only if $x_n \geqq y_n$, $n = 1, 2, \cdots, N$;
$\geq$		$x \geq y$ if and only if $x \geqq y$ and $x \neq y$;

$\overset{*}{>}$	$x \overset{*}{>} y$ if and only if $x_n > y_n$ or $x_n = y_n = 0,\ n = 1, 2, \cdots, N$;
$\Re^N_+$	$\Re^N_+ = \{x : x \in \Re^N, x \geqq 0\}$;
$\Re^N_-$	$\Re^N_- = \{x : x \in \Re^N, x \leqq 0\}$;
$2^{\Re^N}$	$2^{\Re^N} = \{A : A \subseteq \Re^N\}$;
$[a, b)$	$[a, b) = \{x : a \leqq x < b\}$;
$[a, b]$	$[a, b] = \{x : a \leqq x \leqq b\}$;
$\sum$	sum sign;
$x^\ell \longrightarrow x^\circ$	the sequence x^ℓ converges to x°;
$\longrightarrow +\infty$	tends to $+\infty$;
$\exists$	there exists;
$\forall$	for all;
A is convex	for all $0 \leqq \lambda \leqq 1, x, y \in A$, $\lambda x + (1 - \lambda)y \in A$;
$\Longrightarrow$	$x \in A \Longrightarrow x \in B$, x belongs to A only if x belongs to B;
$\Longleftrightarrow$	if and only if;
s.t.	subject to;
px	$px = \sum_{n=1}^N p_n x_n, p$ and $x \in \Re^N$, the inner product.

REFERENCES

Adolphson, D.L., G.C. Cornia, and L.C. Walters (1989), "Railroad Property Evaluation Using Data Envelopment Analysis," *Interfaces* 19:3 (May-June), 18-26.

Adolphson, D.L., G.C. Cornia, and L.C. Walters (1990), "A Unified Framework for Classifying DEA Models," *Operational Research 90* (Special edn; H.E. Bradley, ed.), 647-57.

Afriat, S.N. (1967), "The Construction of Utility Functions from Expenditure Data," *International Economic Review* 8:1 (February), 67-77.

Afriat, S.N. (1972) "Efficiency Estimation of Production Functions," *International Economic Review* 13:3 (October), 568-98.

Ahlheim, M. (1988), "A Reconsideration of Debreu's 'Coefficient of Resource Utilization'," in D. Bös et al., eds., *Welfare and Efficiency in Public Economics*. Berlin: Springer-Verlag.

Aigner, D.J. and S.F. Chu (1968), "On Estimating the Industry Production Function," *American Economic Review* 58:4 (September), 826-39.

Aigner, D.J. and P. Schmidt, eds. (1980), "Specification and Estimation of Frontier Production, Profit and Cost Functions," *Journal of Econometrics* (Special Issue) 13:1 (May).

Albriktsen, R.O. and F.R. Førsund (1990), "A Productivity Study of the Norwegian Building and Construction Industry," *Journal of Productivity Analysis* 2:1 (December), 53-66.

Ali, A.I. (1991), "Data Envelopment Analysis: A Unifying Perspective," working paper, Department of Management, University of Massachusetts, Amherst, MA, USA.

Ali, M. and J.C. Flinn (1989), "Profit Efficiency Among Basmati Rice Producers in Pakistan Punjab," *American Journal of Agricultural Economics* 71:2 (May), 303-10.

Atkinson, S. and R. Halvorsen (1980), "A Test of Relative and Absolute Price Efficiency in Regulated Utilities," *Review of Economics and Statistics* 62:1 (February), 81-88.

Atkinson, S. and R. Halvorsen (1984), "Parametric Efficiency Tests, Economies of Scale, and Input Demand in U.S. Electric Power Generation," *International Economic Review* 25:3 (October), 643-62.

Atkinson, S. and R. Halvorsen (1986), "The Relative Efficiency of Public and Private Firms in a Regulated Environment: The Case of U.S. Electric Utilities," *Journal of Public Economics* 29, 281-94.

Banker, R.D. (1984), "Estimating Most Productive Scale Size Using Data Envelopment Analysis," *European Journal of Operational Research* 17:1 (July), 35-44.

Banker, R.D., A. Charnes, and W.W. Cooper (1984), "Some Models for Estimating Technical and Scale Inefficiencies in Data Envelopment Analysis," *Management Science* 30:9 (September), 1078-92.

Banker, R.D., A. Charnes, W.W. Cooper, and A. Maindiratta (1988), "A Comparison of DEA and Translog Estimates of Production Frontiers Using Simulated Observations from a Known Technology," in A. Dogramaci and R. Färe, eds. (1988).

Banker, R.D., A. Charnes, W.W. Cooper, J. Swarts, and D.A. Thomas (1989), "An Introduction to Data Envelopment Analysis with Some of its Models and Their Uses," in *Research in Governmental and Nonprofit Accounting*, Volume 5, Greenwich, CN: JAI Press.

Banker, R.D., R.F. Conrad, and R.P. Strauss (1986) "A Comparative Application of DEA and Translog Methods: An Illustrative Study of Hospital Production," *Management Science* 32:1 (January), 30-44.

Banker, R.D. and H.H. Johnston (1989), "Evaluating the Impacts of Operating Strategies on Efficiency: An Application to the U.S. Airline Industry," in A. Charnes, W.W. Cooper, A.Y. Lewin, and L.M. Seiford, eds. (forthcoming).

Banker, R.D. and A. Maindiratta (1986a), "Piecewise Loglinear Estimation of Efficient Production Surfaces," *Management Science* 32:1 (January), 126-35.

Banker, R.D. and A. Maindiratta (1986b), "Erratum to: 'Piecewise Loglinear Estimation of Efficient Production Surfaces'," *Management Science* 32:3 (March), 385.

Banker, R.D. and A. Maindiratta (1988), "Nonparametric Analysis of Technical and Allocative Efficiencies in Production," *Econometrica* 56:5 (November), 1315-32.

Banker, R.D. and R.C. Morey (1986a), "Efficiency Analysis for Exogenously Fixed Inputs and Outputs," *Operations Research* 34:4 (July-August), 513-21.

Banker, R.D. and R.C. Morey (1986b), "The Use of Categorical Variables in Data Envelopment Analysis," *Management Science* 32:12 (December), 1613-27.

Banker, R.D. and R.M. Thrall (1992), "Estimation of Returns to Scale Using Data Envelopment Analysis," *European Journal of Operational Research* 62:1 (October 9), 74-84.

Barrow, M. and A. Wagstaff (1989), "Efficiency Measurement in the Public Sector: An Appraisal," *Fiscal Studies* 10:1 (February), 72-97.

Bauer, P.W. (1990), "Decomposing TFP Growth in the Presence of Cost Inefficiency, Nonconstant Returns to Scale, and Technological Progress," *Journal of Productivity Analysis* 1:4 (June), 287-300.

Baumol, W.J., J.C. Panzar, and R.D. Willig (1982), *Contestable Markets and the*

Theory of Industry Structure. New York: Harcourt Brace Jovanovich.

Berg, S.A., F.R. Førsund, and E.S. Jansen (1992), "Malmquist Indices of Productivity Growth During the Deregulation of Norwegian Banking 1980-1989," *Scandinavian Journal of Economics*, 94, Supplement, 211-28.

Bergson, A. (1961), *National Income of the Soviet Union Since 1928*. Cambridge, MA: Harvard University Press.

Berndt, E.R. and M.A. Fuss, eds. (1986), "The Econometrics of Temporary Equilibrium," *Journal of Econometrics* (Special Issue) 33:1/2 (October/November).

Bessent, A., W. Bessent, J. Kennington, and B. Reagan (1982), "An Application of Mathematical Programming to Assess Productivity in the Houston Independent School District," *Management Science* 28:12 (December), 1355-67.

Blackorby, C., D. Primont, and R.R. Russell (1978), *Duality, Separability and Functional Structure: Theory and Economic Applications*. New York: North-Holland.

Bol, G. (1986), "On Technical Efficiency Measures: A Remark," *Journal of Economic Theory* 38:2 (April), 380-85.

Bol, G. (1988), "On the Definition of Efficiency Measures: A Note," in W. Eichhorn, ed. (1988).

Boland, I. (1990), "Méthode du bootstrap dans les modèles de frontière," mémoire de maitrise en sciences économiques, Université Catholique de Louvain, Louvain-la-Neuve, Belgium.

Boles, J.N. (1966), "Efficiency Squared-Efficient Computation of Efficiency Indexes," *Proceedings of the Thirty Ninth Annual Meeting of the Western Farm Economics Association*, 137-42.

Borts, G.H. and E.J. Mishan (1962), "Exploring the 'Uneconomic Region' of the Production Function," *Review of Economic Studies* 29, 300-12.

Bowlin, W.F., A. Charnes, W.W. Cooper, and W.D. Sherman (1985), "Data Envelopment Analysis and Regression Approaches to Efficiency Estimation and Evaluation," *Annals of Operations Research* 2, 113-38.

Boyd, G. and R. Färe (1984), "Measuring the Efficiency of Decision Making Units: A Comment," *European Journal of Operational Research* 15 (March), 331-32.

Bressler, R.G. (1966), "The Measurement of Productive Efficiency," *Proceedings of the Thirty Ninth Annual Meeting of the Western Farm Economics Association*, 129-36.

Burgat, P. and C. Jeanrenaud (1990), "Mesure de l'efficacité productive et de l'efficacité-cout: cas des Dechetes Menagers en Suisse," Working Paper No. 9002, Institut de Recherches Economiques et Regionales, Université de Neuchatel, Neuchatel, Switzerland.

Burgess, J.F. and P.W. Wilson (1993), "Technical Efficiency in Veterans Administration Hospitals," in H.O. Fried, C.A.K. Lovell, and S.S. Schmidt, eds. (1993).

Burley, H.T. (1980), "Production Efficiency in U.S. Manufacturing: A Linear Programming Approach," *Review of Economics and Statistics* 62:4 (November) 619-22.

Byrnes, P., R. Färe, and S. Grosskopf (1984), "Measuring Productive Efficiency: An Application to Illinois Strip Mines," *Management Science* 30:6 (June), 671-81.

Byrnes, P., R. Färe, S. Grosskopf, and S. Kraft (1987), "Technical Efficiency and Size: The Case of Illinois Grain Farms," *European Review of Agricultural Economics* 14:4, 367-81.

Byrnes, P., R. Färe, S. Grosskopf, and C.A.K. Lovell (1988), "The Effect of Unions on Productivity: U.S. Surface Mining of Coal," *Management Science* 34:9 (September), 1037-53.

Byrnes, P., S. Grosskopf, and V. Valdmanis (1991), "Economies of Scale and Diversification in Provision of In-patient Services," mimeo.

Byrnes, P. and V. Valdmanis (1989), "DEA and Hospital Management: Analyzing Technical and Allocative Efficiency," in A. Charnes, W.W. Cooper, A.Y. Lewin, and L.M. Seiford, eds. (forthcoming).

Carlson, D.E. (1972), "The Production and Cost Behavior of Higher Education Institutions," unpublished Ph.D. dissertation, GSBA, University of California, Berkeley, CA.

Caves, D.W., L.R. Christensen, and W.E. Diewert (1982a), "Multilateral Comparisons of Output, Input and Productivity Using Superlative Index Numbers," *Economic Journal* 92:365 (March), 73-86.

Caves, D.W., L.R. Christensen, and W.E. Diewert (1982b), "The Economic Theory of Index Numbers of the Measurement of Input, Output and Productivity," *Econometrica* 50:6 (November), 1393-1414.

Chang, K.-P. and Y.-Y. Guh (1989), "Piecewise Loglinear Frontiers and Log Efficiency Measures," working paper, Department of Economics, National Tsing Hua University, Republic of China.

Chang, K.-P. and Y.-Y. Guh (1991), "Linear Production Functions and the Data Envelopment Analysis," *European Journal of Operational Research* 52:2 (May 27), 215-23.

Charnes, A. and W.W. Cooper (1961), *Management Models and Industrial Applications of Linear Programming*. New York: Wiley.

Charnes, A. and W.W. Cooper (1984), "The Non-Archimedean CCR Ratio for Efficiency Analysis: A Rejoinder to Boyd and Färe," *European Journal of Operational Research* 15:3, 333-34.

Charnes, A. and W.W. Cooper (1985), "Preface to Topics in Data Envelopment Analysis," *Annals of Operations Research* 2, 59-94.

Charnes, A., W.W. Cooper, B. Golany, L. Seiford, and J. Stutz (1985), "Foundations of Data Envelopment Analysis for Pareto-Koopmans Efficient Empirical Production Functions," *Journal of Econometrics* 30:1/2 (October/November), 91-107.

Charnes, A., W.W. Cooper, A.Y. Lewin, and L.M. Seiford, eds. (forthcoming), *Data Envelopment Analysis: The Theory, the Method and the Process*. Boston, Dordrecht, London: Kluwer Academic.

Charnes, A., W.W. Cooper, and E. Rhodes (1978), "Measuring the Efficiency of Decision Making Units," *European Journal of Operational Research* 2:6 (November), 429-44.

Charnes, A., W.W. Cooper, L. Seiford, and J. Stutz (1982), "A Multiplicative Model for Efficiency Analysis," *Socio-Economic Planning Sciences* 16:5, 223-24.

Charnes, A., W.W. Cooper, L. Seiford, and J. Stutz (1983), "Invariant Multiplicative Efficiency and Piecewise Cobb–Douglas Envelopments," *Operations Research Letters* 2:3 (August), 101-103.

Charnes, A., W.W Cooper, and T. Sueyoshi (1988), "A Goal Programming/ Constrained Regression Review of the Bell System Breakup," *Management Science* 34:1 (January), 1-26.

Charnes, A., W.W. Cooper, and G.H. Symonds (1958), "Cost Horizons and Certainty Equivalents: An Approach to Stochastic Programming of Heating Oil," *Management Science* 4:3 (April), 235-63.

Chavas, J.-P. and T.L. Cox (1988), "A Nonparametric Analysis of Agricultural Technology," *American Journal of Agricultural Economics* 70:2 (May), 303-10.

Chavas, J.-P. and T.L. Cox (1990), "A Non-Parametric Analysis of Productivity: The Case of U.S. and Japanese Manufacturing," *American Economic Review* 80:3 (June), 450-64.

Collender, R.N., R. Nehring, and A. Somwaru (1991), "Economic Efficiency of Farm Credit System Associations," working paper, Economic Research Service, U.S. Department of Agriculture, Washington, DC.

Cowing, T.G. and R.E. Stevenson, eds. (1981), *Productivity Measurement in Regulated Industries.* New York: Academic Press.

Cyert, R.M. and J.G. March (1963), *A Behavioral Theory of the Firm.* Englewood Cliffs, NJ: Prentice-Hall.

Dantzig, G.B. (1963), *Linear Programming and its Extensions.* Princeton: Princeton University Press.

Debreu, G. (1951), "The Coefficient of Resource Utilization," *Econometrica* 19:3 (July), 273-92.

DeFourny, J. (1988), "Comparative Measures of Technical Efficiency for 500 French Workers' Cooperatives," Working Paper No. 88/07, University of Liège and CIRIEC, Liège, Belgium.

DeFourny, J., C.A.K. Lovell, and A.G.M. N'Gbo (1992), "Variation in Productive Efficiency in French Workers' Cooperatives," *Journal of Productivity Analysis* 3:1/2 (June), 103-17.

Deller, S.C. and C.H. Nelson (1989), "Measures of Technical Efficiency: An Empirical Comparison," working paper, Department of Economics, University of Maine, Orono, ME.

Deller, S.C. and C.H. Nelson (1991), "Measuring the Economic Efficiency of Producing Rural Road Services," *American Journal of Agricultural Economics* 73:1 (February), 194-201.

Deprins, D. (1989), *Estimation de frontières de production et mesures de l'efficacité technique.* Université Catholique de Louvain, Faculté des Sciences Economiques, Sociales et Politiques, nouvelle série No. 186. Louvain-la-Neuve: CIACO.

Deprins, D. and L. Simar (1983), "On Farrell Measures of Technical Efficiency," *Recherches économiques de Louvain,* 49:2 (June), 123-37.

Deprins, D. and L. Simar (1989a), "Estimation de frontières déterministes avec facteurs exogènes d'inefficacité," *Annales d'économie et de statistique* 14, 117-50.

Deprins, D. and L. Simar (1989b), "Estimating Technical Inefficiencies with

Corrections for Environmental Conditions with an Application to Railway Companies," *Annals of Public and Cooperative Economics* 60:1 (January-March), 81-102.

Deprins, D., L. Simar, and H. Tulkens (1984), "Measuring Labor-Efficiency in Post Offices," in M. Marchand, P. Pestieau, and H. Tulkens, eds., *The Performance of Public Enterprises: Concepts and Measurements*. Amsterdam: North-Holland.

Desai, A. and A.P. Schinnar (1987), "Stochastic Data Envelopment Analysis," Working paper WPS 87-23, College of Business, The Ohio State University, Columbus, OH.

Diewert, W.E. (1980), "Capital and the Theory of Productivity Measurement," *American Economic Review* 70:2 (May), 260-67.

Diewert, W.E. (1981), "The Theory of Total Factor Productivity Measurement in Regulated Industries," in T.G. Cowing and R.E. Stevenson, eds. (1981).

Diewert, W.E. (1982), "Duality Approaches to Microeconomic Theory," in K.J. Arrow and M.D. Intriligator, eds., *Handbook of Mathematical Economics*, Volume 2. Amsterdam: North-Holland.

Diewert, W.E. and C. Parkan (1983), "Linear Programming Tests of Regularity Conditions for Production Frontiers," in W. Eichhorn, R. Henn, K. Neumann, and R.W. Shephard, eds. (1983).

Dogramaci, A. and R. Färe, eds. (1988), *Applications of Modern Production Theory: Efficiency and Productivity*. Boston: Kluwer.

Dugger, R.R. III (1974), "An Application of Bounded Nonparametric Estimating Functions to the Analysis of Bank Cost and Production Functions," unpublished Ph.D. dissertation, Department of Economics, University of North Carolina, Chapel Hill, NC.

Dusansky, R. and P.W. Wilson (1989), "On the Relative Efficiency of Alternative Modes of Producing Public Sector Output: The Case of the Developmentally Disabled," *European Journal of Operational Research*, (forthcoming).

Dusansky, R. and P.W. Wilson (1990), "Technical Efficiency in the Decentralized Care of the Developmentally Disabled," *Review of Economics and Statistics*, (forthcoming).

Eakin, B.K. (1993), "Do Physicians Minimize Cost?" in H.O. Fried, C.A.K. Lovell, and S.S. Schmidt, eds. (1993).

Eakin, B.K. (1991), "Allocative Inefficiency in the Production of Hospital Services," *Southern Economic Journal* 58:1 (July), 240-48.

Eakin, B.K. and T. Kniesner (1988), "Estimating a Non-Minimum Cost Function for Hospitals," *Southern Economic Journal* 54:3 (January), 583-92.

Eichhorn, W., ed. (1988), *Measurement in Economics: Theory and Applications of Economic Indices*. Heidelberg: Physica-Verlag.

Eichhorn, W., R. Henn, K. Neumann, and R.W. Shephard, eds. (1983), *Quantitative Studies on Production and Prices*. Würzburg and Vienna: Physica-Verlag.

Epstein, M.K. and J.C. Henderson (1989), "Data Envelopment Analysis for Managerial Control and Diagnosis," *Decision Sciences* 20:1 (Winter), 90-119.

Evans, D.S. and J.J. Heckman (1988), "Natural Monopoly and the Bell System: Response to Charnes, Cooper and Sueyoshi," *Management Science* 34:1 (January), 27-38.

Färe, R. (1975), "Efficiency and the Production Function," *Zeitschrift für Nationalökonomie* 35:3-4, 317-24.

Färe, R. (1984a), "On the Existence of Plant Capacity," *International Economic Review* 25:1 (February), 209-13.

Färe, R. (1984b), "The Dual Measurement of Efficiency," *Zeitschrift für Nationalökonomie* 44, 283-88.

Färe, R. (1986), "Addition and Efficiency," *Quarterly Journal of Economics* 101:4 (November), 861-66.

Färe, R. (1988a), *Fundamentals of Production Theory*. Berlin: Springer-Verlag.

Färe, R. (1988b), "Efficiency Gains from Addition of Technologies: A Nonparametric Approach," in W. Eichhorn, ed. (1988).

Färe, R. and S. Grosskopf (1983a), "Measuring Congestion in Production," *Zeitschrift für Nationalökonomie* 43, 257-71.

Färe, R. and S. Grosskopf (1983b), "Measuring Output Efficiency," *European Journal of Operational Research* 13, 173-79.

Färe, R. and S. Grosskopf (1985), "A Nonparametric Cost Approach to Scale Efficiency," *Scandinavian Journal of Economics* 87:4, 594-604.

Färe, R. and S. Grosskopf (1988), "Measuring Shadow Price Efficiency," in A. Dogramaci and R. Färe, eds. (1988).

Färe, R. and S. Grosskopf (1990a), *Cost and Revenue Constrained Production*, mimeo, Department of Economics, Southern Illinois University, Carbondale, IL.

Färe, R. and S. Grosskopf (1990b), "Theory and Calculation of Productivity Indexes: Revisited," working paper, Department of Economics, Southern Illinois University, Carbondale, IL.

Färe, R. and S. Grosskopf (1990c), "A Distance Function Approach to Price Efficiency," *Journal of Public Economics* 43, 123-26.

Färe, R., S. Grosskopf, and K. Hayes (1990), "A Proposal for Measuring Municipal Government Output," paper presented at the Sixth World Congress of the Econometric Society, Barcelona.

Färe, R., S. Grosskopf, and E. Kokkelenberg (1989), "Measuring Plant Capacity, Utilization and Technical Change: A Nonparametric Approach," *International Economic Review* 30:3 (August), 655-66.

Färe, R., S. Grosskopf, and H. Lee (1990), "A Nonparametric Approach to Expenditure Constrained Profit Maximization," *American Journal of Agricultural Economics* 72:3 (August), 574-81.

Färe, R., S. Grosskopf, B. Lindgren, and P. Roos (1989), "Productivity Developments in Swedish Hospitals: A Malmquist Output Index Approach," in A. Charnes, W.W. Cooper, A.Y. Lewin, and L.M. Seiford, eds. (forthcoming).

Färe, R., S. Grosskopf, B. Lindgren, and P. Roos (1992), "Productivity Changes in Swedish Pharmacies 1980-1989: A Nonparametric Malmquist Approach," *Journal of Productivity Analysis* 3:1/2 (June), 85-101.

Färe, R., S. Grosskopf, and J. Logan (1983), "The Relative Efficiency of Illinois Electric Utilities," *Resources and Energy* 5, 349-67.

Färe, R., S. Grosskopf, and C.A.K. Lovell (1983), "The Structure of Technical Efficiency," *Scandinavian Journal of Economics* 85, 181-90.

Färe, R., S. Grosskopf, and C.A.K. Lovell (1985), *The Measurement of Efficiency of Production*. Boston: Kluwer-Nijhoff.

Färe, R., S. Grosskopf, and C.A.K. Lovell (1986), "Scale Economies and Duality," *Journal of Economics* 46:2, 175-182.

Färe, R., S. Grosskopf, and C.A.K. Lovell (1987a), "Scale Elasticity and Scale Efficiency," *Journal of Institutional and Theoretical Economics* 144:4 (September), 721-29.

Färe, R., S. Grosskopf, and C.A.K. Lovell (1987b), "Nonparametric Disposability Tests," *Zeitschrift für Nationalökonomie* 47:1, 77-85.

Färe, R., S. Grosskopf, and C.A.K. Lovell (1988), "An Indirect Efficiency Approach to the Evaluation of Producer Performance," *Journal of Public Economics* 37:1 (October), 71-89.

Färe, R., S. Grosskopf, and C.A.K. Lovell (1992), "Indirect Productivity Measurement," *Journal of Productivity Analysis* 2:4, 283-98.

Färe, R., S. Grosskopf, C.A.K. Lovell, and C. Pasurka (1989), "Multilateral Productivity Comparisons when Some Outputs are Undesirable: A Nonparametric Approach," *Review of Economics and Statistics* 71:1 (February), 90-98.

Färe, R., S. Grosskopf, C.A.K. Lovell, and S. Yaisawarng (1993), "Derivation of Virtual Prices for Undesirable Outputs: A Distance Function Approach," *Review of Economics and Statistics* 75:2 (May).

Färe, R., S. Grosskopf, and J. Nelson (1990), "On Price Efficiency," *International Economic Review* 31:3 (August), 709-20.

Färe, R., S. Grosskopf, and D. Njinkeu (1988), "On Piecewise Reference Technologies," *Management Science* 34:12 (December), 1507-11.

Färe, R., S. Grosskopf, M. Norris, and Z. Zhang (1991), "Productivity Growth, Technical Progress, and Efficiency Change in Industrialized Countries," working paper, Department of Economics, Southern Illinois University, Carbondale, IL.

Färe, R., S. Grosskopf, and C. Pasurka (1986), "Effects on Relative Efficiency in Electric Power Generation Due to Environmental Controls," *Resources and Energy* 8:2 (June), 167-84.

Färe, R., S. Grosskopf, and C. Pasurka (1989), "The Effect of Environmental Regulations on the Efficiency of Electric Utilities: 1969 versus 1975," *Applied Economics* 21:2 (February), 225-35.

Färe, R., S. Grosskopf, and V. Valdmanis (1989), "Capacity, Competition and Efficiency in Hospitals: A Nonparametric Approach," *Journal of Productivity Analysis* 1:2 (June), 123-38.

Färe, R., S. Grosskopf, and S. Yaisawarng (1989), "Short-Run Price Efficiency: A Nonparametric Approach with Measurement Error," working paper, Department of Economics, Southern Illinois University, Carbondale, IL.

Färe, R., S. Grosskopf, S. Yaisawarng, S. Li, and Z. Wang (1990), "Productivity Growth in Illinois Utilities," *Resources and Energy* 12, 383-98.

Färe, R., S. Grosskopf, and B.J. Yoon (1982), "A Theoretical and Empirical Analysis of the Highway Speed-Volume Relationship," *Journal of Urban Economics* 12, 115-21.

Färe, R. and W. Hunsaker (1986), "Notions of Efficiency and Their Reference

Sets," *Management Science* 32:2 (February), 237-43.

Färe, R. and L. Jansson (1974), "Technological Change and Disposability of Inputs," *Zeitschrift für Nationalökonomie* 34, 283-90.

Färe, R. and L. Jansson (1975), "On VES and WDI Production Functions," *International Economic Review* 16:3 (October), 745-50.

Färe, R. and L. Jansson (1976), "Joint Inputs and the Law of Diminishing Returns," *Zeitschrift für Nationalökonomie* 36, 407-16.

Färe, R. and C.A.K. Lovell (1978), "Measuring the Technical Efficiency of Production," *Journal of Economic Theory* 19:1 (October), 150-62.

Färe, R., C.A.K. Lovell, and K.D. Zeischang (1983), "Measuring the Technical Efficiency of Multiple Output Production Technologies," in W. Eichhorn, R. Henn, K. Neumann, and R.W. Shephard, eds. (1983).

Färe, R. and T. Mitchell (1990), "Multiple Outputs and Homotheticity," *Southern Economic Journal* (forthcoming).

Färe, R. and D. Primont (1988), "Efficiency Measures for Multiplant Firms With Limited Data," in W. Eichhorn, ed. (1988).

Färe, R. and D. Primont (1990), "A Distance Function Approach to Multioutput Technologies," *Southern Economic Journal* 56:4 (April), 879-91.

Färe, R. and C. Sawyer (1988), "Expenditure Constrained Profit Maximization: Comment," *American Journal of Agricultural Economics* 70:4 (November), 953-54.

Färe, R. and L. Svensson (1980), "Congestion of Production Factors," *Econometrica* 48:7 (November), 1745-53.

Farrell, M.J. (1957), "The Measurement of Productive Efficiency," *Journal of the Royal Statistical Society* Series A, General, 120, Part 3, 253-81.

Farrell, M.J. and M. Fieldhouse (1962), "Estimating Efficient Production Functions Under Increasing Returns to Scale," *Journal of the Royal Statistical Society* Series A, General 125, Part 2, 252-67.

Fecher, F. and P. Pestieau (1993), "Efficiency and Competition in Financial Services," in H.O. Fried, C.A.K. Lovell, and S.S. Schmidt, eds. (1993).

Ferrier, G., S. Grosskopf, K. Hayes, and S. Yaisawarng (1990), "Economies of Diversification in the Banking Industry: A Linear Programming Approach," working paper, Department of Economics, Southern Methodist University, Dallas, TX.

Ferrier, G.D. and C.A.K. Lovell (1990), "Measuring Cost Efficiency in Banking: Econometric and Linear Programming Evidence," in A.Y. Lewin and C.A.K. Lovell, eds. (1990).

Ferrier, G.D. and P.K. Porter (1989), "Measuring the Relative Efficiency of Cooperative and Non-Cooperative Forms of Organization: An Application of DEA," in A. Charnes, W.W. Cooper, A.Y. Lewin, and L.M. Seiford, eds. (forthcoming).

Field, K. (1990), "Production Efficiency of British Building Societies," *Applied Economics* 22, 415-25.

Førsund, F.R. (1991), "The Malmquist Productivity Index," working paper, Department of Economics, University of Oslo, Oslo, Norway.

Førsund, F.R. (1992), "A Comparison of Parametric and Nonparametric Efficiency Measures: The Case of Norwegian Ferries," *Journal of Productivity*

Analysis, 3:1/2 (June), 25-43.

Førsund, F.R. (1993), "Productivity Growth in Norwegian Ferries," in H.O. Fried, C.A.K. Lovell, and S.S. Schmidt, eds. (1993).

Førsund, F.R. and E. Hernaes (1990), "Ferry Transport in Norway: An Application of DEA Analysis," in A. Charnes, W.W. Cooper, A.Y. Lewin, and L.M. Seiford, eds. (forthcoming).

Førsund, F.R. and L. Hjalmarsson (1979a), "Generalized Farrell Measures of Efficiency: An Application to Milk Processing in Swedish Dairy Plants," *Economic Journal* 89:354 (June), 294-315.

Førsund, F.R. and L. Hjalmarsson (1979b), "Frontier Production Functions and Technical Progress: A Study of General Milk Processing in Swedish Dairy Plants," *Econometrica* 47:4 (July), 883-900.

Førsund, F.R. and L. Hjalmarsson (1987), *Analyses of Industrial Structure: A Putty-Clay Approach.* Stockholm: Almqvist and Wicksell International.

Førsund, F.R. and E.S. Jansen (1977), "On Estimating Average and Best Practice Homothetic Production Functions via Cost Functions," *International Economic Review* 18:2 (June), 463-76.

Førsund, F.R. and S.A.C. Kittelsen (1992), "Efficiency Analysis of Norwegian District Courts," *Journal of Productivity Analysis* 3:3 (September), 277-306.

Fried, H.O., C.A.K. Lovell, and S.S. Schmidt, eds. (1993), *The Measurement of Productive Efficiency: Techniques and Applications.* New York: Oxford University Press.

Frisch, R. (1965), *Theory of Production.* Chicago: Rand McNally and Company.

Fukuyama, H. (1987), "Alternative Notions and Measures of Returns to Scale: A Multi-Output Duality Approach," unpublished Ph.D. thesis, Southern Illinois University, Carbondale, IL.

Fuss, M. and D. McFadden, eds. (1978), *Production Economics: A Dual Approach to Theory and Applications* (2 Volumes). Amsterdam: North-Holland.

Gong, B.-H. and R.C. Sickles (1992), "Finite Sample Evidence on the Performance of Stochastic Frontiers and Data Envelopment Analysis Using Panel Data," *Journal of Econometrics* 51, 259-84.

Grabowski, R. and C. Pasurka (1988), "The Relative Technical Efficiency of Northern and Southern U.S. Farms in 1860," *Southern Economic Journal* 54:3 (January), 598-614.

Grosskopf, S. (1986), "The Role of the Reference Technology in Measuring Productive Efficiency," *Economic Journal* 96 (June), 499-513.

Grosskopf, S., K. Hayes, and S. Yaisawarng (1989), "Measuring Economies of Scope: Two Frontier Approaches," working paper, Department of Economics, Southern Illinois University, Carbondale, IL.

Grosskopf, S. and S. Yaisawarng (1990), "Economies of Scope in the Provision of Local Public Services," *National Tax Journal* 43:1 (March), 61-74.

Hall, M. and C. Winsten (1959), "The Ambiguous Notion of Efficiency," *Economic Journal* 69:1 (March), 71-86.

Hall, R.E. (1973), "The Specification of Technology with Several Kinds of Output," *Journal of Political Economy* 89:4 (July/August), 878-92.

Hanoch, G. and M. Rothschild (1972), "Testing the Assumptions of Production Theory: A Nonparametric Approach," *Journal of Political Economy* 80:2

(March/April), 256-75.

Härdle, W. (1990), *Applied Nonparametric Regression*. Cambridge: Cambridge University Press.

Hicks, J.R. (1935), "The Theory of Monopoly: A Survey," *Econometrica* 3:1 (January), 1-20.

Hicks, J.R. (1946), *Value and Capital*. Second Edition. Oxford: Clarendon.

Hjalmarsson, L. and A. Veiderpass (1992), "Efficiency and Ownership in Swedish Electricity Retail Distribution," *Journal of Productivity Analysis*, 3:1/2 (June), 3-23.

Hopper, W.D. (1965), "Allocation Efficiency in Traditional Indian Agriculture," *Journal of Farm Economics* 47:3 (August), 611-24.

Hulten, C.R. (1986), "Productivity Change, Capacity Utilization, and the Sources of Efficiency Growth," in E.R. Berndt and M.D. Fuss, eds. (1986).

Inman, R.P. (1978), "A Generalized Congestion Function for Highway Travel," *Journal of Urban Economics* 5, 21-34.

Jamar, M.-A. and H. Tulkens (1990), "Mesure de l'efficacité de l'activité des tribunaux et évaluation de l'arriéré judiciaire," Working Paper No. 90/1, CORE, Université Catholique de Louvain, Louvain-la-Neuve, Belgium.

Johansen, L. (1968), "Production Functions and the Concept of Capacity," in *Recherches recentes sur la fonction de production*. Namur: Centre d'Etudes et de la Recherche Universitaire de Namur.

Johansen, L. (1972), *Production Functions*. Amsterdam: North-Holland.

Junankar, P.N. (1989), "The Response of Peasant Farmers to Price Incentives: The Use and Misuse of Profit Functions," *Journal of Development Studies* 25, 169-82.

Kalirajan, K.P. and R.T. Shand (1988), "Testing Causality Between Technical and Allocative Efficiencies," Working Paper No. 88/6, Research School of Pacific Studies, Australian National University, Canberra.

Kamakura, W.A. (1988), "A Note on 'The Use of Categorical Variables in Data Envelopment Analysis'," *Management Science* 34:10 (October), 1273-76.

Karlin, S. (1959), *Mathematical Methods and Theory in Games, Programming and Economics*. Reading, MA: Addison-Wesley.

Klotz, B., R. Madoo, and R. Hansen (1980), "A Study of High and Low 'Labor Productivity' Establishments in U.S. Manufacturing," in J.W. Kendrick and B.N. Vaccara, eds., *New Developments in Productivity Measurement and Analysis*. National Bureau of Economic Research Conference on Research in Income and Wealth, Studies in Income and Wealth, Volume 44. Chicago: University of Chicago Press, 239-86.

Koopmans, T.C. (1951), "An Analysis of Production as an Efficient Combination of Activities," in T.C. Koopmans, ed., *Activity Analysis of Production and Allocation*, Cowles Commission for Research in Economics, Monograph No. 13. New York: Wiley.

Koopmans, T.C. (1957), *Three Essays on the State of Economic Science*. New York: McGraw Hill.

Kopp, R.J. (1981), "The Measurement of Productive Efficiency: A Reconsideration," *Quarterly Journal of Economics* 96:3 (August), 477-503.

Land, K.C., C.A.K. Lovell, and S. Thore (1988), "Chance-Constrained Efficiency Analysis," working paper, Department of Economics, University of North Carolina, Chapel Hill, NC.

Land, K.C., C.A.K. Lovell, and S. Thore (1990), "Chance-Constrained Data Envelopment Analysis," *Managerial and Decision Economics*, (forthcoming).

Lau, L.J. and P.A. Yotopoulos (1971), "A Test for Relative Efficiency and an Application to Indian Agriculture," *American Economic Review* 61:1 (March), 94-109.

Lee, H. and R.G. Chambers (1986), "Expenditure Constraints and Profit Maximization in U.S. Agriculture," *American Journal of Agricultural Economics* 68, 857-65.

Lee, H. and R.G. Chambers (1988), "Expenditure Constraints and Profit Maximization in U.S. Agriculture: Reply," *American Journal of Agricultural Economics* 70:4 (November), 955-6.

Leibenstein, H. (1966), "Allocative Efficiency vs. 'X-Efficiency'," *American Economic Review* 56:3 (June), 392-415.

Leibenstein, H. (1976), *Beyond Economic Man*. Cambridge, MA: Harvard University Press.

Leibenstein, H. (1978), "X-Inefficiency Xists – Reply to an Xorcist," *American Economic Review* 68:1 (March), 203-11.

Leibenstein, H. (1987), *Inside the Firm*. Cambridge, MA: Harvard University Press.

Leontief, W.W. (1941), *The Structure of the American Economy 1919-1939*. New York: Oxford University Press.

Leontief, W.W. (1953), *Studies in the Structure of the American Economy*. New York: Oxford University Press.

Lewin, A.Y. and C.A.K. Lovell, eds. (1990), *Frontier Analysis: Parametric and Nonparametric Approaches, Journal of Econometrics* 46:1/2 (October/November).

Lewin, A.Y. and J.W. Minton (1986), "Determining Organizational Effectiveness: Another Look, and an Agenda for Research," *Management Science* 32:5 (May), 514-38.

Lewin, A.Y., R.C. Morey, and T.J. Cook (1982), "Evaluating the Administrative Efficiency of Courts," *Omega* 10:4, 401-11.

Linvill, C.B. (1991), "An Empirical Investigation of the Effect of Participation and Ownership on Technical Efficiency and Techncial Change in Italian Producer Cooperatives," working paper, Department of Economics, University of North Carolina, Chapel Hill, NC.

Lloyd, P.J. (1984), "The Theory of Economic Units: Super-Additivity of Functions," Research Paper No. 121, Department of Economics, University of Melbourne, Melbourne.

Lloyd, P.J. (1989), "A Family of 'Agronomic Production Functions' with Economies of Scope," *Australian Journal of Agricultural Economics* 33:2 (August), 108-22.

Lovell, C.A.K. (1991), "Econometric Efficiency Analysis: A Policy-Oriented Review," paper presented at EURO XI meetings, July 16-19, RWTH Aachen.

Lovell, C.A.K. and R.C. Sickles (1983), "Testing Efficiency Hypotheses in Joint Production: A Parametric Approach," *Review of Economics and Statistics* 65:1

(February), 51-58.

Lovell, C.A.K. and R.C. Sickles (1988), "Causes and Consequences of Expert Disagreement: The Methodological Lessons from the *U.S.* v. *AT&T* Debate," in O.A. Davis, ed., *The Methodology of Policy Analysis* (forthcoming).

Lovell, C.A.K., L.C. Walters, and L.L. Wood (1989), "Stratified Models of Education Production using Modified DEA and Regression Analysis," in A. Charnes, W.W. Cooper, A.Y. Lewin and L.M. Seiford, eds. (forthcoming).

Lovell, C.A.K. and L.L. Wood (1992), "Monitoring the Performance of Soviet Cotton Refining Enterprises: Sensitivity of Findings to Estimation Techniques," *Atlantic Economic Journal* 20:1 (March), 25-31.

Maindiratta, A. (1990), "Largest Size Efficient Scale and Size Efficiencies of Decision Making Units in Data Envelopment Analysis," in A.Y. Lewin and C.A.K. Lovell, eds. (1990).

Malmquist, S. (1953), "Index Numbers and Indifference Surfaces," *Trabajos de Estatistica* 4, 209-42.

Maxwell, W.D. (1965), "Short-Run Returns to Scale and the Production of Services," *Southern Economic Journal* 32:1, Part 1 (July), 1-14.

McCarty, T.A. and S. Yaisawarng (1993), "Technical Efficiency in New Jersey School Districts," in H.O. Fried, C.A.K. Lovell, and S.S. Schmidt, eds. (1993).

McFadden, D. (1978), "Cost, Revenue and Profit Functions," in M. Fuss and D. McFadden, eds. (1978).

Moorsteen, R.H. (1961), "On Measuring Productive Potential and Relative Efficiency," *Quarterly Journal of Economics* 75:3 (August), 451-67.

Morrison, C.J. (1985), "Primal and Dual Measures of Economic Capacity Utilization: An Application to Productivity Measurement in the U.S. Automobile Industry," *Journal of Business and Economic Statistics* 3:4, 312-24.

Nerlove, M. (1963), "Returns to Scale in Electricity Supply," in C. Christ, et al., eds., *Measurement in Economics: Studies in Mathematical Economics and Econometrics in Memory of Yehuda Grunfeld.* Stanford, CA: Stanford University Press.

Nerlove, M. (1965), *Estimation and Identification of Cobb–Douglas Production Functions.* Chicago: Rand McNally.

N'Gbo, A.G.M. (1991), "L'Efficacité productive des SCOP francaises: estimation et simulation à partir d'une frontière de production stochastique," mimeo, CORE, Université Catholique de Louvain, Louvain-la-Neuve, Belgium.

Nishimizu, M. and J.M. Page, Jr. (1982), "Total Factor Productivity Growth, Technological Progress and Technical Efficiency Change: Dimensions of Productivity Change in Yugoslavia, 1965-78," *Economic Journal* 92:368 (December), 920-36.

Nollet, C., B. Thiry, and H. Tulkens (1988), "Mesure de l'efficacité productive: applications à la Société de Transports Intercommunaux de Bruxelles," in B. Thiry and H. Tulkens, eds. (1988a).

Nunamaker, T.R. (1985), "Using Data Envelopment Analysis to Measure the Efficiency of Non-profit Organizations: A Critical Evaluation," *Managerial and Decision Economics* 6:1, 50-58.

Panzar, J.C. and R.D. Willig (1977), "Economies of Scale in Multi-Output Production," *Quarterly Journal of Economics* 91:3 (August), 481-94.

Penrose, E.T. (1959), *The Theory of The Growth of the Firm*. Oxford: Basil Blackwell.

Perelman, S. (1986), "Frontières d'Efficacité et Performance Technique des Chemins de Fer," *Annales de l'economie publique, sociale et cooperative* 74:4 (October-December), 445-58.

Pestieau, P. and H. Tulkens (1991), "Assessing the Performance of Public Sector Activities: Some Recent Evidence From the Productive Efficiency Viewpoint," Discussion Paper No. 9060, CORE, Université Catholique de Louvain, Louvain-la-Neuve, Belgium.

Petersen, N.C. (1988), "A Note on the Relationship Between the DEA and the Russell Input Efficiency Index," working paper, Department of Management, Odense University, Odense, Denmark.

Petersen, N.C. (1990), "Data Envelopment Analysis on a Relaxed Set of Assumptions," *Management Science* 36:3 (March), 305-14.

Petersen, N.C. and O.B. Olesen (1989), "Chance Constrained Efficiency Evaluation," working paper, Department of Management, Odense University, Odense, Denmark.

Pfouts, R.W. (1961), "The Theory of Cost and Production in the Multi-Product Firm," *Econometrica* 29:4 (October), 650-58.

Pinkse, C.A.P. (1990), "An Application of Semi-Parametric Methods in the Estimation of Production Frontiers," *Journal of Econometrics*, forthcoming.

Porter, P.K. and G.W. Scully (1987), "Economic Efficiency in Cooperatives," *Journal of Law and Economics* 30:2 (October), 489-512.

Ray, S.C. (1991), "Nonparametric Analysis of Cost-Minimization: A Simple Statistical Test," working paper, Department of Economics, University of Connecticut, Storrs, CT.

Ray, S.C. and D. Bhadra (1991), "Nonparametric Tests of Cost Minimizing Behavior: A Study of Indian Farms," working paper, Department of Economics, University of Connecticut, Storrs, CT.

Respaut, B. (1989), "Mesures de l'efficacité productive des 911 Agencies d'une banque privée belge," in H. Tulkens, ed. (1989a).

Rosenbaum, R.A. (1950), "Sub-Additive Functions," *Duke Mathematical Journal* 17, 227-47.

Russell, R.R. (1985), "Measures of Technical Efficiency," *Journal of Economic Theory* 35:1 (February), 109-26.

Russell, R.R. (1988), "On the Axiomatic Approach to the Measurement of Technical Efficiency," in W. Eichhorn, ed. (1988).

Russell, R.R. (1990), "Continuity of Measures of Technical Efficiency," *Journal of Economic Theory* 51:2 (August), 255-67.

Salter, W.E.G. (1966), *Productivity and Technical Change* (Second Edition, with an addendum by W.B. Reddaway). Cambridge: The University Press.

Samuelson, P.A. (1947), *Foundations of Economic Analysis*. Cambridge, MA: Harvard University Press.

Samuelson, P.A. (1948), "Consumption Theory in Terms of Revealed Preference," *Economica* 15 (November), 243-53.

Sato, K. (1975), *Production Functions and Aggregation.* Amsterdam: North-Holland.

Schmidt, P. (1976), "On the Statistical Estimation of Parametric Frontier Production Functions," *Review of Economics and Statistics* 58:2 (May), 238-39.

Schmidt, P. (1985-86), "Frontier Production Functions," *Econometric Reviews* 4:2, 289-328.

Schultz, T.W. (1964), *Transforming Traditional Agriculture.* New Haven, CT: Yale University Press.

Seaver, B.L. and K.P. Triantis (1989), "The Implications of Using Messy Data to Estimate Production Frontier Based Technical Efficiency Measures," *Journal of Business and Economic Statistics,* 7:1 (January), 49-59.

Seiford, L.M. and R.M. Thrall (1990) "Recent Developments in DEA: The Mathematical Programming Approach to Frontier Analysis," in A.Y. Lewin and C.A.K. Lovell, eds. (1990).

Seitz, W.D. (1966), "Efficiency Measures for Steam-Electric Generating Plants," *Proceedings of the Thirty Ninth Annual Meeting of the Western Farm Economics Association,* 143-51.

Seitz, W.D. (1968), "The Measurement of Productive Efficiency," unpublished Ph.D. dissertation, University of California, Berkeley, CA.

Seitz, W.D. (1970), "The Measurement of Efficiency Relative to a Frontier Production Function," *American Journal of Agricultural Economics* 52:4 (November), 505-11.

Seitz, W.D. (1971), "Productive Efficiency in the Steam-Electric Generating Industry," *Journal of Political Economy* 79:4 (July/August), 878-86.

Sexton, T.R., et al. (1988), "Evaluating Managerial Efficiency of Veterans Administration Medical Centers Using Data Envelopment Analysis," *Medical Care* 27:12 (December), 1175-88.

Shapiro, K.H. (1982), "Efficiency Differentials in Peasant Agriculture and their Implications for Development Policies," *Journal of Development Studies* 19, 179-90.

Sharkey, W.W. (1982), *The Theory of Natural Monopoly.* Cambridge: Cambridge University Press.

Shephard, R.W. (1953), *Cost and Production Functions.* Princeton: Princeton University Press.

Shephard, R.W. (1970), *Theory of Cost and Production Functions.* Princeton: Princeton University Press.

Shephard, R.W. (1974), *Indirect Production Functions.* Mathematical Systems in Economics, No. 10. Meisenheim Am Glan: Verlag Anton Hain.

Shephard, R.W. and R. Färe (1980), *Dynamic Theory of Production Correspondences.* Cambridge, MA: Oelgeschlager, Gunn and Hain.

Sidhu, S.S. (1974), "Relative Efficiency in Wheat Production in The Indian Punjab," *American Economic Review* 64:4 (September), 742-51.

Silkmans, R.H., ed. (1986), *Measuring Efficiency: An Assessment of Data Envelopment Analysis.* New Directions For Program Evaluation, No. 32. San Francisco: Jossey-Bass.

Simar, L. (1992), "Estimating Efficiencies from Frontier Models with Panel Data: A Comparison of Parametric, Non-parametric and Semi-parametric

Methods with Bootstrapping," *Journal of Productivity Analysis* 3:1/2 (June), 171-203.

Simon, H. (1955), "A Behavioral Model of Rational Choice," *Quarterly Journal of Economics* 69:1 (February), 99-118.

Sitorus, B.L. (1966), "Productive Efficiency and Redundant Factors of Production in Traditional Agriculture of Underdeveloped Countries," *Proceedings of the Thirty Ninth Annual Meeting of the Western Farm Economics Association*, 153-58.

Solow, R.M. (1957), "Technical Change and the Aggregate Production Function," *Review of Economics and Statistics* 39:3 (August), 312-20.

Stigler, G.J. (1976), "The Xistence of X-Efficiency," *American Economic Review* 66:1 (March), 213-16.

Sueyoshi, T. (1990), "A Special Algorithm for an Additive Model in Data Envelopment Analysis," *Journal of the Operational Research Society* 41:3, 249-57.

Sueyoshi, T. (1991), "Estimation of Stochastic Frontier Cost Function Using Data Envelopment Analysis: An Application to the AT&T Divestiture," *Journal of the Operational Research Society* 42:6, 463-77.

Sueyoshi, T. and Y.-L. Chang (1989), "Efficient Algorithm for Additive and Multiplicative Models in Data Envelopment Analysis," *Operations Research Letters* 8:4 (August), 205-13.

Summa, T. (1986), *Intra-Industrial Technical Progress and Structural Change*. Helsinki: ETLA.

Tax, S. (1953), *Penny Capitalism*. Chicago: University of Chicago Press.

Thiry, B. and H. Tulkens, eds. (1988), *La Performance économique des sociétés Belges de Transports Urbains*. CIRIEC, Liège.

Thiry, B. and H. Tulkens (1992), "Allowing For Technical Inefficiency in Parametric Estimation of Production Functions for Urban Transit Firms," *Journal of Productivity Analysis* 3:1/2 (June), 45-65.

Thompson, R.G., L.N. Langemeier, E. Lee, and R.M. Thrall (1990), "DEA Sensitivity Analysis of Efficiency Measures with an Application to Kansas Farming," in A. Charnes, W.W. Cooper, A.Y. Lewin, and L.M. Seiford, eds. (forthcoming).

Timmer, C.P. (1971), "Using a Probabilistic Frontier Production Function to Measure Technical Efficiency," *Journal of Political Economy* 79:4 (July/August), 776-94.

Toda, Y. (1976), "Estimation of a Cost Function When Cost is not Minimum: The Case of Soviet Manufacturing Industries, 1958-1971," *Review of Economics and Statistics* 58:3 (August), 259-68.

Törnqvist, L. (1936), "The Bank of Finland's Consumption Price Index," *Bank of Finland Monthly Bulletin* 10, 1-8.

Trosper, R.L. (1978), "American Indian Relative Ranching Efficiency," *American Economic Review* 68:4 (September), 503-16.

Tulkens, H. (1986a), "The Performance Approach in Public Enterprise Economics: An Introduction and an Example," *Annales de l'économie publique, sociale et coopérative* 74:4 (October/December), 429-43.

Tulkens, H. (1986b), "La Performance productive d'un service public. Definitions, méthodes de mesure et application à la régie des postes en Belgique," *L'Actualité économique, revenue d'analyse économique* 62:2 (June), 306-35.

Tulkens, H., ed. (1989a), *Efficacité et management*. Charleroi, Belgium: CIFOP.

Tulkens, H. (1989b), "Mesures de l'efficacité productive à la régie des postes," in H. Tulkens, ed. (1989a).

Tulkens, H. (1990), "Non-Parametric Efficiency Analyses in Four Service Activities: Retail Banking, Municipalities, Courts and Urban Transit," paper prepared for the Third Franco-American Seminar on Productivity Issues in Services at the Micro Level, NBER, Cambridge, MA, July 23-26.

Tulkens, H. (1991), "Economics and the Performance of the Public Sector," lecture prepared for the CIRIEC-Université de Liège Conference on "Public vs. Private Enterprises: in Search of the Real Issues," April 4-5, Liège, Belgium.

Tulkens, H., B. Thiry, and A. Palm (1988), "Mesure de l'efficacité productive: méthodologies et applications aux sociétés de transports intercommunaux de Liège, Charleroi et Verviers," in B. Thiry and H. Tulkens, eds. (1988).

van den Broeck, J., F.R. Førsund, L. Hjalmarsson, and W. Meeusen (1980), "On the Estimation of Deterministic and Stochastic Frontier Production Functions: A Comparison," in D.J. Aigner and P. Schmidt, eds. (1980).

Vanden Eeckaut, P. and H. Tulkens (1989), "Une mesure de l'efficacité-coût de 253 communes francophones," in H. Tulkens, ed. (1989a).

Vanden Eeckaut, P., H. Tulkens, and M.-A. Jamar (1993), "Cost/Efficiency in Belgian 235 Municipalities," in H.O. Fried, C.A.K. Lovell, and S.S. Schmidt, eds. (1993).

Varian, H.R. (1984), "The Nonparametric Approach to Production Analysis," *Econometrica* 52:3 (May), 579-97.

Varian, H.R. (1985), "Nonparametric Analysis of Optimizing Behaviour with Measurement Error," *Journal of Econometrics* 30:1/2 (October-November), 445-58.

Varian, H.R. (1990), "Goodness-of-Fit in Optimizing Models," in A.Y. Lewin and C.A.K. Lovell, eds. (1990).

von Neumann, J. (1938 [1945]), "Über ein ökonomisches gleischungssystem und eine Verallgemeinerung des Brouwerschen Fixpunktsatzes," in K. Menger, ed., *Ergebenisse eines Mathematischen Kolloquiums*; reprinted as "A Model of General Economic Equilibrium," *Review of Economic Studies* 13:1, 1-9.

Wise, J. and P.A. Yotopoulos (1969), "The Empirical Content of Economic Rationality: A Test for a Less Developed Economy," *Journal of Political Economy* 77:6 (November/December), 976-1004.

Yaisawarng, S. (1989), "Measuring Short-Run Price Efficiency: Theory and Application," unpublished Ph.D. dissertation, Southern Illinois University, Carbondale, IL.

Yao, D.D. and S.C. Kim (1987), "Reducing the Congestion in a Class of Job Shops," *Management Science* 33:9 (September), 1165-72.

Yotopoulos, P.A. and L.J. Lau (1973), "A Test for Relative Economic Efficiency: Some Further Results," *American Economic Review* 63:1 (March), 214-23.

Yotopoulos, P.A. and L.J. Lau, eds. (1979), "Resource Use in Agriculture:

Applications of the Profit Function to Selected Countries," *Food Research Studies* (Special Issue) 17:1.

Zhu, J. (1991), "Nonparametric Efficiency Measurement Treating Both Inputs and Outputs Asymmetrically," working paper, Management College, Southeast University, Nanjing, People's Republic of China.

Zieschang, K.D. (1984), "An Extended Farrell Technical Efficiency Measure," *Journal of Economic Theory* 33:2 (August), 387-396.

BIOGRAPHICAL INDEX

INDEX

Text set in *italics* refers to the definition of the concept.